Does the Center Hold?
An Introduction to Western Philosophy
Eighth Edition

Donald Palmer
Professor Emeritus at College of Marin
Former Visiting Assistant Professor,
North Carolina State University

Text and Illustrations
by
Donald Palmer

DOES THE CENTER HOLD?: AN INTRODUCTION TO WESTERN PHILOSOPHY, EIGHTH EDITION

Published by McGraw-Hill Education, 2 Penn Plaza, New York, NY 10121. Copyright © 2021 by McGraw-Hill Education. All rights reserved. Printed in the United States of America. Previous editions © 2017, 2014, and 2011. No part of this publication may be reproduced or distributed in any form or by any means, or stored in a database or retrieval system, without the prior written consent of McGraw-Hill Education, including, but not limited to, in any network or other electronic storage or transmission, or broadcast for distance learning.

Some ancillaries, including electronic and print components, may not be available to customers outside the United States.

This book is printed on acid-free paper.

1 2 3 4 5 6 7 8 9 LCR 24 23 22 21 20

ISBN 978-1-260-25319-1 (bound edition)
MHID 1-260-25319-8 (bound edition)
ISBN 978-1-260-80861-2 (loose-leaf edition)
MHID 1-260-80861-0 (loose-leaf edition)

Product Developer: *Alex Preiss*
Marketing Manager: *Nancy Baudean*
Content Project Manager: *Danielle Clement*
Buyer: *Laura Fuller*
Design: *Beth Blech*
Content Licensing Specialist: *Traci Vaske*
Cover Image: *©Donald Palmer*
Compositor: *SPi Global*

All credits appearing on page or at the end of the book are considered to be an extension of the copyright page.

Library of Congress Cataloging-in-Publication Data

Names: Palmer, Donald, author.
Title: Does the center hold? : an introduction to western philosophy / text
    and illustrations by Donald Palmer, Professor Emeritus at College of
    Marin, Former Visiting Assistant Professor, North Carolina State University.
Description: Eighth edition. | New York, NY : McGraw-Hill Education, 2020.
    | Includes bibliographical references and index. | Audience: Ages 18+
Identifiers: LCCN 2019049971 | ISBN 9781260253191 (hardcover)
Subjects: LCSH: Philosophy—Introductions.
Classification: LCC BD21 .P24 2020 | DDC 190—dc23
LC record available at https://lccn.loc.gov/2019049971

The Internet addresses listed in the text were accurate at the time of publication. The inclusion of a website does not indicate an endorsement by the authors or McGraw-Hill Education, and McGraw-Hill Education does not guarantee the accuracy of the information presented at these sites.

mheducation.com/highered

To Leila

Contents

3 What You See Is What You Get
Empiricist Epistemology   75

4 Who's on First; What's on Second?
Ontology   113

Preface

I've met students whose parents pressured them to major in business or biology or to enroll in pre-law courses, but I can't remember ever meeting students whose parents insisted that they become philosophy majors. Certainly, nobody ever went into this field motivated by greed, unless he or she was laboring under a serious misapprehension. Plato may have gone into philosophy impelled by a frustrated lust for power, but few make that mistake anymore. Most students end up in their first philosophy class with little or no idea of what they are about to engage in. They are there because "philosophy" fulfills a requirement, and it fits conveniently into their schedule—or because they were able to get into it (the class wasn't closed!). Happily, it is not unusual for students to sign up for a philosophy class because of a friend's recommendation and the good reputation of a particular instructor. This is as it should be, because we certainly need good philosophy teachers. To the uninitiated, philosophy is hard. It's also intimidating. It's not clear what the point of philosophy is. Its uses are not easy to detect. Its arguments are often very abstract; it is difficult to see how they relate to "real life." Though its practitioners often seem out of touch with the world (they "have too much time on their hands," as some of my students say), they are obviously very smart, and it seems as though what they claim to be the most important points often depend on the subtlest of distinctions. Students are expected to read whole paragraphs—and sometimes, whole books—written by these philosophers in arcane or highly technical English, often translations. Such reading assignments happen almost nowhere else in one's college career except in literature classes. But at least novelists write for a general audience, because nobody pays them if nobody understands them. For the most part, philosophers seem to write exclusively for each other. (Who pays them?) Worst of all, philosophers are contentious. They each seem to disagree with most other philosophers, so it's hard to know what's really true or whether any progress is ever made.

These barriers are just some of what philosophy teachers are up against. In the face of them, it's amazing that college campuses have as many introductory philosophy classes as they do and that anybody is ever enticed to major in philosophy. Some philosophy teachers are geniuses—or at least magicians. Everything they touch turns to gold. Most of us, however, need some help. I have written this book hoping that it would be such an aid. Besides helping to teach the Western canon—the "great" philosophers and great philosophical ideas, arguments, and debates—I have tried to address the typical queries, puzzlements, and objections introductory students have vis-à-vis philosophy. I have presented these questions both in the Introduction and in medias res. I have tried to leave the impression that philosophy is the legitimate legacy of each student as a citizen of the world. Its history and ideas are there to be appropriated by all. Rather than being an odd and esoteric endeavor, philosophy hovers around all other activities and occasionally bursts through into them.

I want students to recognize that we are all philosophers—that what Sartre says about freedom is true of philosophy—we are condemned to philosophize—and, in conjunction, that what their grandmother told them is true: anything worth doing is worth doing well. I hope students come to feel that the problems of philosophy have an existential import in their lives.

I also hope that students will realize that there is a certain kind of philosophical analysis and form of argumentation whose skills can be learned and applied in other areas of their lives, not just in philosophy classes, and that there are different kinds of payoffs here—even financial ones. (Law schools like philosophy majors.) Also, some students—but not all—will come to realize, once they get the hang of it, that philosophy is fun. As the anthropologist Claude Lévi-Strauss says, just as some food is good to eat, some ideas are good to think. So I hope that this book is a contribution to not only a lively, interesting philosophy class, but also one that is fun. I've tried to write it in an engaging manner without watering down difficult ideas too much and without pandering to simplicity. The vocabulary may sometimes be just a notch beyond the students' familiarity but not so much as to be a turnoff. Students want to be challenged, after all. Do I need to justify using cartoons and jokes in order to make the book more entertaining? I hope not. As I say, philosophy should be fun.

Unlike the authors of many philosophy texts, I've taken personal positions on most of the topics I discuss. This approach probably needs more of a justification than do the cartoons. Well, frankly, a philosophy book that simply lays out the various alternative ideas end to end in a purely antiseptic way is a book I find inherently dull and suspect. You'll no doubt disagree with some of my conclusions, but at least I don't think you'll find them doctrinaire. I'm a hopeless eclectic—or perhaps a Jamesian. (If it works, use it!) Not only that, but according to my experience as student and teacher, part of the dynamics of a good philosophy course, unlike courses in Spanish or biology, consists in slight antagonisms between the text and the class. Think of this antagonism as an opportunity! I'm sure I've given you plenty of fodder.

I hope one of the strengths of this book is found in the connections it makes between philosophy and other fields in which students are interested, especially art, literature, physics, sociology, psychology, and psychoanalysis. Philosophy may no longer be the queen of all disciplines, but she is certainly their consort.

Despite certain appearances to the contrary, the text is fairly conventional in the selection of material. The topics are themes typically taught in introductory philosophy courses on this continent. I think the chapter divisions and subdivisions speak for themselves in this respect. I try to establish continuity throughout the book both by providing a Glossary with a system of cross-references and by keeping certain themes alive from chapter to chapter so that ideas once learned do not simply evaporate. (Here, "use it or lose it.")

The changes in the newer editions are the consequence of numerous communications to me from professors, students, and general readers. I am grateful for the many suggestions proffered, especially for the extensive comments, criticisms, and recommendations made by philosophy teachers who had used the first edition as a college text and who were in a good position to detect the book's strengths and weaknesses. I thank them all. They were acute critics, and the book has been improved because of them.

For this eighth edition I have updated the discussion of materialism in chapter 4 by including new material provided in a recent book by the British philosopher, Galen Strawson. I have rewritten a number of passages throughout in order to clarify complicated ideas. In order to avoid adding substantially to an already long book, I have tried to remove about as much material as I added, choosing for deletion of only segments designated as inessential by a number of readers.

I hope that all these changes and additions have produced an improved version of *Does the Center Hold?*

And now to the acknowledgments. If a long list of names bores you, skip this paragraph because I intend to pay my debts here and thank many of the people who participated in the construction of this book (most without their knowledge or consent). First, the philosophers. . . . Well, that's all the philosophers I've ever studied but particularly Wittgenstein, Kierkegaard, Sartre, Marx, Freud, Nietzsche, Plato, Descartes, Spinoza, Hume, and James; you'll hear from them again. (Some may be rolling over in their graves.) Next, my own teachers, including John Searle, Stanley Cavell, Benson Mates, Stephen Pepper, Jerry Clegg, Juan Rodríguez Rosado, and Leonardo Polo, and (by osmosis) the cartoonists Charles Addams and Virgil "Vip" Partch. Next, thanks to all my students over a thirty-year period at the College of Marin—all six thousand of them. (Well, perhaps not all of them. One student demanded publicly that I be fired after it dawned on him that some of the philosophers he studied in my class contradicted each other. In his letter to the college president he said he only had time to study what was known to be true.) To this list of six thousand I can now add a few hundred more students whom I have since taught at North Carolina State University here in Raleigh. Just as I initially thanked Jim Bull, my editor at Mayfield for the first two editions, I now express my gratitude to the **ansr**source team including Poornima H and Erin Guendelsberger, who handled development editing of the eighth edition, along with other diligent members of the excellent team at McGraw-Hill who coached this edition along: Alex Preiss and Danielle Clement, whose contributions I greatly appreciate.

Also, though it may seem odd, I want to thank the great American desert, where many thoughts were hatched and pages written—the Smoke Creek Desert, the Black Rock Desert, the Mojave, the Organ Pipe National Monument, the Anza-Borrego, and therewith (of course) the late Edward Abbey, wherever you may be. Once again, let me thank my true source of energy, inspiration, and love, the person to whom this book is dedicated, my wife, Leila May. Without her, even philosophy would be worth much less to me.

You're in the driver's seat.

Want to build your own course? No problem. Prefer to use our turnkey, prebuilt course? Easy. Want to make changes throughout the semester? Sure. And you'll save time with Connect's auto-grading too.

65%

Less Time Grading

They'll thank you for it.

Adaptive study resources like SmartBook® 2.0 help your students be better prepared in less time. You can transform your class time from dull definitions to dynamic debates. Find out more about the powerful personalized learning experience available in SmartBook 2.0 at **www.mheducation.com/highered/connect/smartbook**

Laptop: McGraw-Hill; Woman/dog: George Doyle/Getty Images

Make it simple, make it affordable.

Connect makes it easy with seamless integration using any of the major Learning Management Systems—Blackboard®, Canvas, and D2L, among others—to let you organize your course in one convenient location. Give your students access to digital materials at a discount with our inclusive access program. Ask your McGraw-Hill representative for more information.

Padlock: Jobalou/Getty Images

Solutions for your challenges.

A product isn't a solution. Real solutions are affordable, reliable, and come with training and ongoing support when you need it and how you want it. Our Customer Experience Group can also help you troubleshoot tech problems—although Connect's 99% uptime means you might not need to call them. See for yourself at **status.mheducation.com**

Checkmark: Jobalou/Getty Images

SUPPORT AT
every step

FOR STUDENTS

Effective, efficient studying.

Connect helps you be more productive with your study time and get better grades using tools like SmartBook 2.0, which highlights key concepts and creates a personalized study plan. Connect sets you up for success, so you walk into class with confidence and walk out with better grades.

Study anytime, anywhere.

Download the free ReadAnywhere app and access your online eBook or SmartBook 2.0 assignments when it's convenient, even if you're offline. And since the app automatically syncs with your eBook and SmartBook 2.0 assignments in Connect, all of your work is available every time you open it. Find out more at **www.mheducation.com/readanywhere**

> *"I really liked this app—it made it easy to study when you don't have your text-book in front of you."*
>
> - Jordan Cunningham, Eastern Washington University

No surprises.

The Connect Calendar and Reports tools keep you on track with the work you need to get done and your assignment scores. Life gets busy; Connect tools help you keep learning through it all.

Calendar: owattaphotos/Getty Images

Learning for everyone.

McGraw-Hill works directly with Accessibility Services Departments and faculty to meet the learning needs of all students. Please contact your Accessibility Services office and ask them to email accessibility@mheducation.com, or visit **www.mheducation.com/about/accessibility** for more information.

Top: Jenner Images/Getty Images, Left: Hero Images/Getty Images, Right: Hero Images/Getty Images

Introduction

This book is an introduction to philosophy. Such a book should not need much of an introduction, which would be merely an introduction to an introduction. Still, a few preliminary comments are appropriate. First, a word about the style. Everybody's style is both unique and imitative. Consciously or unconsciously, I've imitated the styles of my teachers and of the philosophers I've studied. (I've thanked them in the preface.) This book is written in something of an idiosyncratic style despite all these influences. I hope philosophy teachers, philosophy students, and the general reader will find my style compatible with their own styles of teaching, learning, thinking, and enjoying. My style attempts to be both lighthearted and serious at the same time. It is lighthearted because of my deep conviction that joy and knowledge are not mutually exclusive. (Nietzsche's "joyful wisdom"; Spinoza's "Melancholy is always bad, but there cannot be too much joy.") I hope you'll find at least some of the jokes funny without being distracting. I dare to hope that a few of them might be illuminating. But the book is also serious because it asks serious questions. Several philosophers (e.g., Dewey, Sartre, Heidegger) tell us that to be human is to confront the world with questions. And all of our smaller questions are framed by the bigger questions, such as "What is reality?" "What is knowledge?" "What is value?" "What is it to be human?" These are philosophical questions. They are what philosophy (and life) are about. What annoys some people about philosophy is that these questions never seem to receive a final answer. Each generation appears to answer them; then each new generation rephrases them in such a way as to require new answers. But that's also what is annoying about life (and what's exciting about it as well). We will find one philosopher—Bertrand Russell (p. 34)—saying that our ability to pose these questions is more important than our inability to arrive at completely satisfactory answers.

Another feature of this book to which students should be alerted is its exclusively Western orientation. The philosophers and philosophies studied here are all in the Greco-Roman-European tradition. Rich philosophical veins exist in other cultures, but I do not have the expertise to mine them. Not only are most of the philosophies in this book Western philosophies, but they are systems of thought that have been put forward for the most part by males. This is a weakness in my book for which I am only partly at fault. I agree with feminist philosophers who claim that in the past women have been systematically discouraged from attempting to participate in the history of philosophy and that when women did make such attempts, they were marginalized or even suppressed. I am heartened to note that today the system of barriers that has discouraged women from a philosophical vocation is being dismantled.

Now, what about the title of the book, *Does the Center Hold?* I borrowed the idea from the poet William Butler Yeats, who, in "The Second Coming," says, "Things fall apart; the centre cannot hold." Yet in prereflective thought (life before philosophy), the center certainly *seems* to hold most of the time for most of us. The world we inhabit presents itself to us in a fairly orderly and predictable manner in both its physical and social manifestations. But occasionally, natural or social disasters burst forth (such as tsunamis, earthquakes, terrorism, and wars), the order and reasonableness of things disappear, and there is chaos. Also, at some point in their lives, most individuals suffer bouts of "mini-madness," where the center does not seem to hold. (Such an experience may have inspired Yeats's poem.) Furthermore, as Descartes reminds us, every night we each slip into a dream world that is madder than madness. Then we wake up and minimize the experience of unreason by relegating it to a sphere of unreality.

When I was a child, I liked to go to Playland at the Beach in San Francisco (now covered over with town houses). One of my favorite spots was the Dizzy Dish. You sat at the center of a large disk that slowly began rotating. As it moved faster and faster, only the person sitting at the exact center, marked by an orange circle, was safe (by virtue of centripetal force). All others inevitably began sliding off the disk at first inch by inch; then suddenly, amid much shrieking, they were hurled to the perimeter (centrifugal force). When you first felt yourself slipping, you clawed to reach the middle, but inexorably it seemed to pull away from you. The center did not hold. I suspect that the onset of insanity sometimes provokes similar sensations, but so does the study of philosophy. Under the philosophical scrutiny of thought, knowledge, reality, and values, the commonsensical center and normal orderliness of the world seem to slip away. As Nietzsche said, while philosophizing we sometimes feel as though we have cut our moorings and are floating off into the cold darkness of outer space.

A less picturesque way of posing the central question I am asking is this: When we address the problems about reality, knowledge, and value to which I alluded a moment ago, can we put together solutions that hold? Do these solutions have to last forever, or do time and context require all answers to be partial and relative? Should we, like the medieval and early modern philosophers, demand answers that are *sub species aeternitatus* (from the point of view of eternity)? Is the alternative simply eternal ignorance? Or, to the contrary, can carefully worked out provisional answers still be good answers?

Philosophy, I believe, will prove to be such an always-provisional attempt to achieve a view of "the bigger picture"—to see, as someone has said, "how things hang together," if they do. Returning to the book's title, we can say that *Does the Center Hold?* asks whether a scrutiny of human experience reveals some kind of unity, or it plunges us into chaos. Each of the chapters in this book attempts to be an aid to the reader in answering that overarching question, and each does this by scrutinizing a different feature of experience. Of course, readers must draw their own conclusions. Mine, flavored with what I hope is a healthy skepticism, is that the center does hold but only *roughly.* And some days it seems to hold better than others. The truth is that the history of Western philosophy does not play itself out in terms of a debate between those philosophers who think that the center does hold and those who think that it does not. There are, of course, a few philosophers who think that it does not hold—Friedrich Nietzsche is the most dramatic of these—but the real debate is between those who claim that it holds absolutely and those who claim that it holds relatively well. (Though, ironically, in the absolutists it is sometimes possible to detect an anxiety driving the argument, as if still fearing that the center may not hold despite their protestations to the contrary. One of the absolutists—René Descartes—admitted that his own philosophical questions frightened him.) The debate is already clearly articulated in ancient Greece. Heraclitus (ca. 470 B.C.E.), about whom I will have more to say in Chapter 1, wrote what would prove to be one of the most famous aphorisms in philosophy, "You can't step in the same river twice." No two moments or events are the same. Old things fall apart; new things are born. Everything becomes its own opposite. However, Heraclitus believed he had discovered a hard center in the midst of the apparent chaos in the fact that there is one thing that does not change, namely, change itself. But Heraclitus's philosophy was interpreted historically as a form of deep pessimism, something that had to be refuted. The attempted refutation came in a book by Parmenides (ca. 515–ca. 440 B.C.E.). He defended the astounding thesis that nothing ever changes at all. Everything is eternally still and immutable. Motion and time themselves are illusions whose deception would be swept away by philosophy. The center holds . . . with a vengeance.

Parmenides's theory deeply influenced a philosopher in the next generation who is recognized even by his opponents as one of the two or three most important thinkers in Western history—Plato (427–347 B.C.E.). As you read this book you will see that he, more than any other individual, will represent the paradigm of a philosopher who wants to prove that the center holds—that there is a rational unchanging core at the center of reality and that all apparent chaos is held at bay by its certainty. If you check the index, you will see that Plato's name appears here more often than that of any other philosopher. He will represent a certain standard to which others aspire or from which they slowly drift or hastily retreat. Even anti-Platonists (such as Friedrich Nietzsche) are parasitic on his thought. You will get quite a dose of Plato before you are done studying philosophy.

1

What Are We Doing in This Class?
Is Philosophy Possible?

Very few academic courses devote a big part of the class time to agonizing over what the subject matter of the course is or whether the discipline to be studied even exists. Yet such is the case with philosophy. Philosophy poses a series of questions that it then tries to answer, and one of these questions is "What is philosophy?" This fact itself tells us something about philosophy, because it informs us of philosophy's *self-reflective*

nature. It is part of philosophy's task to think about itself, because philosophy is an activity whose purpose involves questioning the assumptions of every system of thought, including its own. It is this perhaps overly introspective aspect of philosophy that annoys some people and causes them to think of philosophers the way they think of neurotics and psychotics—who also spend a lot of time creating bizarre, convoluted explanations of how they relate to the world and to

Thought Thinking about Itself

themselves. (We shall see that the line between philosophy and madness is sometimes very thin indeed, and more than one philosopher has concluded that what is needed is a cure for philosophical problems, not a solution to them.)

The Origins of Philosophy

One way of trying to understand philosophy is to look at its origins, both linguistic and historical. The word "philosophy" is from the Greek *philosophia*, meaning "the love of wisdom." Plato took this definition very seriously and saw the philosopher as a kind of lover; hence, Plato spent a lot of time trying to determine the meaning of love in order to demonstrate that *true* lovers *always* love wisdom. But the activity we call philosophy went back hundreds of years before Plato. It is generally agreed that the first recorded philosopher in the Western tradition was THALES of Miletus (ca. 580 B.C.E.). Looking briefly at what he had to say may reveal something about the nature of philosophy, though it might also prove to be a bit disappointing because Thales's main theory is so obviously false (his theory:

Everything Is Water

everything is water!) and because his "activity" does not seem so unusual—at least not to us. It is known that, while visiting Egypt, Thales formulated a hypothesis to explain why the Nile, unlike almost every other known river, tended to dry up in the winter and flood in the summer. His hypothesis was that winds were the cause of these phenomena. What's so remarkable about this theory (other than the fact that we now know it to be false)? What catches our attention is that all of Thales's predecessors had tried to explain these facts about the Nile by attributing them to supernatural events. Thales, rather than talking about miracles or the will of the gods, explained the one natural phenomenon (the flooding of the Nile) in terms of other natural phenomena (the desert winds). Even his outrageous claim that everything is water is an attempt to explain natural phenomena in terms of other natural phenomena (and not so outrageous a claim—the leap from "Everything is water" to "Everything is atoms" is smaller than it may seem, and this leap took only a couple of generations; Democritus [ca. 460–ca. 370 B.C.E.] developed the first atomic theory).

The Leap from "Everything Is Water" to "Everything Is Atoms"

From the perspective of our desire to learn something about the nature of philosophy, Thales's erroneous answer is much less significant than his *question* (namely, "What is everything composed of?"), and what is even more interesting than either Thales's question or his answer are the presuppositions behind his question. Like most Greeks, Thales was acutely aware of the dramatic changes that took place in the observable world: day changes to night, then back to day again; summer changes to winter, then to summer again; hot changes to cold and then to hot again. And then the most mysterious of all changes—life to death, which somehow produces life again. Thales's question assumes that *if there is change,* then *there must be something behind change that itself does not change.* Thales also observed that the world was composed of many individual things: rocks, lizards, toothpicks, rainbows, and people. Yet the world was somehow a whole and not just a loose collection of unrelated objects. Thales's question assumes that *if there are "many,"* then somehow there must be a "one"

behind the "many." That is, Thales's question presupposes that the concept of *difference* is logically dependent on the concept of *sameness*, which is more basic, and that difference must somehow be reducible to sameness. Furthermore, Thales's question assumes that the human mind is capable of fathoming that unchanging one behind the many, and having fathomed it, the mind would understand what makes the center hold, would understand the sense in which things hang together. This was Thales's concern twenty-six hundred years ago, and it continues to be the concern of philosophers and scientists today.

Once again, it is important to stress that for Thales, the answer to his question would have to be natural, not supernatural. This is primarily what separates Thales's mode of thinking from the mythic form of thought that preceded him. Myths explain why things are the way they are by tracing these things to their origins. In this respect, **Mythos** (the mythic way of thought) is no different from **Logos** (the philosophic/ scientific way of thought). But myth traces the origins of things to supernatural time, sometimes called "strong time" by mythologists, and

The Center Does Not Hold—Things Fall Apart

to supernatural ancestral beings. Strong time is the period of the early beginnings before "normal" time existed. The magical beings that existed then were unrestricted by the limitations of time and space that constrain people in normal time. The heroic or dastardly actions of those magical beings are the source of our own world. The order of the social and natural worlds is explained by showing how these worlds relate to strong time and to the divine beings that inhabited that time. Myths are usually conservative. They justify the status quo by revealing its relation to strong time ("We do these things because our ancestors did them . . ."). Myths often begin with a formula that refers to the beginning of the world ("Once, a long, long time ago, when the earth was very young . . ."). The recitation of the myth removes both the speaker and the audience from natural time and returns them to strong time. Furthermore, the ritual surrounding the recitation of a myth reconstitutes the social and natural worlds. The mythical mind believes that if these myths were not recited, if these rituals were not performed, the world would fall into chaos, the center would not hold, and things would fall apart. Societies based on myth are traditionally "unhistorical." They do not record history because "history" implies change, and myth-oriented societies deny change. The only change was the fall from strong time into daily time. Since then, nothing has changed. In the Greek world, the two main transmitters of Mythos were the poets Homer (ninth century B.C.E.) and Hesiod (tenth century B.C.E.)—two masterful tellers of heroic tales. Furthermore, many of the theatrical dramas of Greece were based on ancient myths. The depictions by the poets and dramatists of the origins of the world and the activities of the gods on Mount Olympus were the background against which the newly emergent Greek philosophy would come to operate.

The Fall from Strong Time

Like mythical explanations, Thales's "philosophical" theory traces things to their origin—not to their chronological origin but rather to their **ontological** origin, that is, their origin in being. What is the relation of observable objects in the world to ultimate reality itself? What must be the hidden truth behind natural objects for them to exhibit the forms they do exhibit and to undergo the changes they undergo? Thales's hypothesis contains no reference to strong time or supernatural entities (though one curious fragment from his book says, "All things contain gods"). Rather, it involves logical analysis of the discernible facts drawn from observation. The Greeks were aware of the four elements: earth, water, air, and fire. Thales concluded that one of these elements must be more basic than the others and asked himself which of the four was capable of taking on the greatest number of forms. Water seemed the most likely candidate. When heated, water changes to steam, then to air. When frozen, it changes to a solid. It disappears both down into the earth and up into the sky and then bubbles back up from the earth and falls from the sky. Thales saw that rivers deposit deltas at their mouth and (incorrectly) deduced that water was being turned to earth. He saw dew on the ground in the morning and (incorrectly) deduced that earth was being changed to water. He saw the Mediterranean phenomenon called "the sun drawing water" (in which, during certain kinds of storms over the sea, clouds seem to swirl in a vortex around the sun), and he (incorrectly) deduced that the fire in the sun was fed by water.

Then water was the basic element! And not supernatural water—though perhaps very *super* natural water.

The distinction between Mythos and Logos helps determine the nature of philosophy, but it is not without its problems. First, the viability of the distinction itself has been questioned by some. The psychologist C. G. Jung and the anthropologist Claude Lévi-Strauss have both argued that so-called Logos is simply our modern, Western way of mythmaking and is in some respects inferior to other forms of Mythos. For example, they pointed out, the abstractions of Western Logos are too distanced from the actual textures of everyday experience. Scientific theories seem to deny the reality of the sensuous features of the world with which we are in daily contact or mystify them in their attempt to reduce them to invisible enti-

ties like atoms, electrons, and neutrons—**theoretical entities** that take on the status of the magical entities of strong time. To other critics, Western science has become politically contaminated, and its claim to superiority over other forms of Mythos is a version of **ethnocentrism** and cultural colonialism. Although these critics occasionally score some points, they are in a distinct minority among writers on the topic, most of whom defend the view that science represents genuine progress away from Mythos. Still, the separation between Mythos and Logos may not be as clear as we would like.

So far I have been talking as if the Mythos/Logos distinction tries to separate systems of myth from systems of rational thought. But even within the category of Logos we must seek to distinguish between what we today call philosophy and other forms of rational thought such as scientific thinking. (This is not a distinction that the pre-Socratics could have made. Indeed, Thales seems to be the first entry in both the history of Western philosophy and the history of Western science.) Some writers accept this fact and, stressing the speculative nature of philosophy, claim that science is what happens when certain branches of philosophy find a way of becoming **experimental** and empirical. For example, Sir Isaac Newton, whom we consider an exemplary scientist, titled his main work *The Mathematical Principles of Natural Philosophy*. And in truth, much of what was once touched only by philosophers' speculations has bee taken over today by physicists, chemists, sociologists, and psychologists.

However, designating philosophy as merely immature science not only diminishes philosophy but also misses much of what is interesting about it. I suspect (but cannot prove) that many philosophical questions by their very nature *cannot* be made experimental—particularly those having to do with values. (When the first Soviet cosmonauts communicated to earth that they had surveyed the skies and discovered that there was no God to be found up there either, one must think that they were joking or that they badly misconstrued the problem of God's existence.) Furthermore, philosophical questions often arise within science. When physicists claim that certain particles are fundamental, the questions come up: "By what criteria do we determine that something is 'funda-

mental'?" Or, "What criteria shall we use in medicine for determining death?" "What counts as the confirmation of a theory?" These kinds of philosophical queries, which constantly crop up in science, cannot be ignored; and they prove that philosophy is not just unenlightened science.

I think our brief journey to the historical origin of philosophy has been helpful though not definitive. A number of philosophy's features will probably not get addressed by simply returning to the Greek source of philosophy. Another approach, which will get at some of those features, is to list and characterize the various branches of philosophy generally recognized today.

Contemporary Branches of Philosophy

If you pick up the catalogue of a typical four-year college or university in the United States and look under the "philosophy" heading, you will find courses offered in the following areas, among others: epistemology, ontology (or metaphysics), ethics (or moral philosophy), political philosophy, aesthetics, and logic, along with a group of courses whose titles begin with the words "philosophy of ____," for example, philosophy of science, philosophy of religion, philosophy of mind, and philosophy of sport. Let's take a look at what you would study if you signed up for these courses.

Epistemology

Epistemology is theory of knowledge. It concerns questions like these:

> What is knowledge, and how does it differ from opinion? Does knowledge require certainty, or can something be known without being known for certain? Does knowledge in fact exist, or must we be satisfied with mere opinion? If there is knowledge, how do we come by it?

Notice that these questions are conceptual rather than experimental. Only the last of these questions could be made the object of an experiment, strictly speaking, and hence could be claimed to be the dominion of psychology; yet we shall shortly see that even this question is not exclusively, or even mostly, experimental.

Ontology

Ontology is theory of being. (Some writers prefer to call this **metaphysics.**) It concerns the following questions:

> What is it for something to be real? What is the nature of existence? What is the difference between appearance and reality?

Notice that these questions are not experimental, because you would already have to have made some tentative decisions about them before you could begin any experiment. The questions "Do minds exist?" and "Are prime numbers real?" are not like the questions "Do unicorns exist?" and "Are ghosts real?" To answer the latter questions, experiments and explorations can be imagined. But philosophy classes take few field trips because there is no place to go—or, to put it more accurately, no matter where you are, you are already there!

Philosophy Field Trip

The next three branches of philosophy—ethics, political philosophy, and aesthetics—all overlap the rather amorphous concept of **axiology,** the study of value. **Ethics** is moral philosophy and as such is interested in moral value. It deals with concepts like goodness, duty, and right and wrong. **Political philosophy** studies social value and explores the justification of political institutions and political relations. There is some disagreement among philosophers concerning the terms **aesthetics** and **philosophy of art.** Most writers use the terms interchangeably (as will I, except when talking about the so-called aesthetic experience), while others, who concentrate on the emotional effects that art and nature have on humans, think that aesthetics is a broader category, precisely because of nature's ability to move us in the way that art does. As you will see (in Chapter 10), nowadays the philosophy of art involves posing philosophical questions to the "art world," primarily the question, What *is* art? Can art be defined in terms of its own characteristics, or in terms of its effect upon us? Can art be defined *at all*? What is the meaning of art; that is, what implications does it have for history, culture, and the individual?

Ethics

Ethics, or moral philosophy, asks questions like these:

> What is the good life? Are there such things as moral duties and obligations that bind us? That is, is there something we truly <u>ought</u> to do? Are some moral arguments "better" than others, or are all of them equally valid or invalid? Are values absolute, or are they relative to time and place?

Again, notice that these questions are not experimental or empirical. Psychologists may be able to tell us why people hold the moral values they do hold. Sociologists and anthropologists may tell us whether any values are held by all cultures and what the social consequences are of holding certain values. But these questions are not the same ones philosophers ask, though empirical information about values provided by the social sciences may be pertinent to philosophical questions about morality.

Political and Social Philosophy

Political and social philosophy ask questions about the state's legitimate authority over its members and about social values such as justice. Typical questions are these:

> Can the idea of government be rationally justified, or must all governments be irrational? Do humans have any political duties or social obligations? Under what conditions? Are there such things as natural social rights? Can such rights be justifiably overridden as a form of punishment?

Once more, notice that these questions are *related* to questions asked by political scientists and sometimes they overlap them—as in the question "Are some forms of government superior to others?" But generally they are not identical to the questions asked by political scientists, the latter of which are basically empirical.

Aesthetics

Traditionally, aesthetics has been the branch of philosophy that explores the nature of aesthetic objects and of aesthetic judgments. That definition doesn't help much, of course, unless we have some idea what these latter two terms mean. Historically, the main component of the concept of aesthetic objects has been beauty, and the central theme of aesthetic judgments has been judgment about beauty. However, other qualities that are occasionally discussed as objects of aesthetic judgment are the sublime, the ugly, and the comic. Therefore, aesthetics in this traditional sense is wider than the philosophy of art, because many of its objects are associated both with art and with nature. Nevertheless, in terms of both the history of philosophy and the contemporary scene, most discussions within aesthetics relate to art. In the mid-eighteenth century, the German philosopher Alexander Baumgarten coined the term "aesthetics" from a Greek word having to do with sensation. Yet, what we call aesthetics goes back at least as far as Plato in the fourth century B.C.E., and some historians claim that he originated it. Contemporary aestheticians ask, just as Plato did, about the nature of artistic or aesthetic value. They want to know the source of and justification for aesthetic judgment and whether certain necessary features of art or perception exist that make some artwork or perceptions objectively more valuable than others. Aestheticians also want to see how artistic activity fits in conceptually with the rest of human activities.

Since the middle of the twentieth century, the philosophy of art in the English-speaking world has become decidedly analytical in strategy. **Analytic philosophers** who are aestheticians attempt to clarify the key concepts related to discourse about art and especially to clarify the concept of art itself.

Logic

Logic is the most specialized branch of philosophy. It is sometimes defined as the science of valid inference. This science, which was founded by Aristotle in the fourth century B.C.E., is essentially a *formal* study. That is to say, it wants to know what forms of argumentation are valid, and it concerns itself not primarily with the truth status of the argument's conclusion, but rather with the structure of inference in the argument. Look, for example, at this argument:

> All men are mortal.
> Socrates is a man.
> Therefore Socrates is mortal.

This is a *valid* argument. That means that the first two statements (the argument's *premises*) **logically entail** the third statement (the argument's *conclusion*). The argument would still be valid even if it turned out that the first or second premise of the argument was false. Even if we discovered that some men are immortal and that Socrates was actually a fish, the argument would be valid purely because of its *form*, which is the following:

All A is B.
S is A.
Therefore S is B.

Logic, as studied and practiced during the Middle Ages (roughly, 400–1400 C.E.) and the renaissance (roughly 1400–1600 C.E.), was dominated by Aristotelian methods. The first major advance of the

All Men Are Mortal.
Socrates Is a Man.

science beyond Aristotle's insights was made by the German philosopher Gottfried Leibniz (1646–1716), who was the bridge between Aristotle and contemporary symbolic logic. But his work on logical symbolism languished in a drawer until being rediscovered in the nineteenth century. In 1847, the English mathematician George Boole (1815–1864) wrote his *Mathematical Analysis of Logic,* which represents the first working treatment of logic from the standpoint of algebra since that of Leibniz, thereby permanently directing all future developments in logic. The next big leap forward was made in 1879 by the German mathematician Gottlob Frege (1848–1925) with the publication of *Begriffsschrift,* a book whose title means, roughly, "essay on concepts." (The German title was preserved in its English translation.) This work, which was met with incomprehension upon its publication, is now seen as establishing modern symbolic logic. Besides using algebraic methods (taking his cue from Boole), Frege lays out the first extensive discussion of the ideas of existence and generality in logic—the relation between propositions asserting "There exists at least one X where X is Y" (*particularity*) and those stating "All X is Y" (*generality*). This apparently simple notion had been completely missing from Aristotle's logic. In fact, "symbolic logic" is a term hardly seen these days—because now logic pretty much *is* symbolic logic. It has become a very complex body of knowledge that looks more like a form of calculus than like Aristotelian syllogisms.

I now turn from the history of logic to a practical application of some of its fundamentals, because every beginning student of philosophy can benefit from a short lesson on some of the principles of logic and of sound reasoning. My intention here is to provide a table of rules that you can consult as you analyze the arguments presented in this text.

Aristotle listed three fundamental principles of logic (or *"laws of logic,"* as they are sometimes called): the principles of "identity," of "noncontradiction," and of "the excluded middle." Before we look at them, I will make a notational stipulation: the letter A will symbolize any **proposition,** object, or quality, and a tilde ("~"), placed before a proposition, object, or quality, will stand for a negation, "not," as in "it is not the case that *x*."

- *The principle of identity.* This principle can be stated as, "Given anything A, A is equal to itself," or "Everything is the same thing as itself." This may not seem very helpful, but at least it is true. We see instances of this in such simple definitions as "A bachelor is an unmarried adult male," and in arithmetic:

$$(\text{``}1 + 1 = 2,\text{'' or ``}1 + 1 + 6 - [2 \times 3] = 2\text{''}).$$

- *The principle of noncontradiction.* This principle can be stated as, "Nothing can be both A and not-A," symbolized as "~ (A and ~A)." This means (no surprise!) that all cases of contradiction are automatically false. That is, in all possible worlds, a proposition expressing contradiction is false.

- *The principle of the excluded middle.* This principle states, "Either A or not-A." This principle is often symbolized as "A v ~A" (e.g., "At point *p*, either it is raining now or it is not raining now").

Aristotle thought of these "principles" as the *foundation* of logic. There is very little disagreement about the validity of these principles, but these laws, logical truths though they be, are only a tiny number of all possible logical truths. In addition, these days logicians tend not to think in terms of a foundational model (i.e., that logic is like a house built upon a solid foundation).

There are also certain logical "rules of inference," that could also be called principles of logic. Unfortunately, for today's students, many of these rules retain the Latin names they were given during the Middle Ages:

- *Modus ponendo ponens,* usually called *modus ponens,* is the rule governing an inference of the form "If A then B; A; therefore B." (e.g., "If George failed yesterday's test then George will fail the class; George failed yesterday's test; therefore George will fail the class.")

- *Modus tollendo tollens,* usually called *modus tollens,* is the rule governing an inference of the form "If A then B; not B; therefore not A." (e.g., "If George failed yesterday's test then George has failed the class; George has not failed the class; therefore George did not fail yesterday's test.")

Hey, I just proved modus ponens is true. Isn't that worth something?

- *Modus tollendo ponens,* also known as *"disjunctive syllogism,"* is the rule governing an inference of the form "Either A or B; not A; therefore B." (e.g., "Either George failed yesterday's test or George passed yesterday's test; George did not fail yesterday's test; therefore George passed yesterday's test.")

One reason it is good to know logic is to be able to avoid certain fallacies. Fallacies are different from falsehoods. A statement is false if it is untrue, but an argument contains a fallacy if it breaks one of the rules of inference. Some of the standard logical fallacies have been given names by logicians. Perhaps it is not important to memorize the names of the fallacies so much as it is important to avoid committing them.

- *Asserting the consequence.* This fallacy is the result of reversing the logic of *modus ponens.* One commits this fallacy when, instead of asserting, "If A then B; A; therefore B," one asserts, "If A then B; B; therefore A." Here are some contrasting examples:

  > If there is an air raid, then people run for shelter.
  > There is an air raid.
  > Therefore, people are running for shelter.
  > *This is a valid inference.*

  > If there is an air raid, then people run for shelter.
  > People are running for shelter.
  > Therefore, there is an air raid.
  > *This is a fallacy. There might be lots of reasons for seeking shelter other than an air raid.*

- *Negating the antecedent.* This is another perversion of *modus tollens.* One commits this fallacy when, instead of asserting, "If A then B; A; therefore B," one asserts "If A then B; therefore if not A, not B." Here are some contrasting examples:

> If it rains, then the street will be wet.
> It is raining.
> Therefore, the street is wet.
> *This is a valid inference.*

> If it rains, then the street will be wet.
> The street is wet.
> Therefore, it has rained.
> *This is a fallacy. A water truck may have passed by.*

These are two of the most common logical fallacies. There are other kinds of fallacies to be avoided that are more rhetorical than logical:

- *Post hoc ergo propter hoc.* This is the error of claiming that X causes Y just because Y comes after X, as in, "At 5:12 A.M. on April 18, 1906, Herman Bottleheimer of San Francisco, California, sneezed, thereby causing an earthquake of 8.25 on the Richter scale."

- *Petitio principii,* or, more commonly, *begging the question.* To "beg the question" is to engage in a form of circular reasoning. One way of begging the question is to assume in the premises of an argument the very conclusion that the argument is supposed to prove, as in this case: "Theory *t* is valid because it was formulated by Prof. *p,* and we know that Prof. *p*'s opinions are trustworthy because he is the author of theory *t.*" Another form of begging the question is to phrase a statement in such a way as to presuppose in its wording the very thing of which the statement is supposed to be evidence. The sentence, "Killing is wrong," does not beg the question, but neither is it obviously always true. However, the assertion, "Murder is wrong," begs the question because the definition of murder is "wrongful killing." Therefore, the sentence really says, "Wrongful killing is wrong," and is true only because it is a **tautology.** In fact, begging the question often produces *tautologies.*
- *Tautological reasoning.* A tautology is a proposition in which the clause following the word "is" or the word "are" (i.e., what is called in grammar the *copula*) repeats in some form or another all or part of the clause before the copula. Tautologies play an important role in language; for instance, all definitions are generally considered to be tautologies. A sentence is tautological if one side of the equation repeats—often in different terms—all or part of the meaning of the other side (e.g., "A sister is a female sibling," or simply, "A sister is a female"). The sentence "Water is liquid" is a tautology because "liquid" is part of the definition of "water." "Water is H_2O" is not a tautology because the clause after the copula adds new information. (Millions of people knew what the word "water" meant long before anyone knew it is H_2O.)

So, tautologies by themselves are not fallacies (indeed they often are logical truths), but *tautological reasoning* is fallacious because it presents an argument *as if* its conclusion contains new information when in fact the conclusion only repeats its initial premise in a disguised form. For example, "I know that what the Bible says is true because it says in the Bible that it is true."

. . .

As I mentioned earlier, besides the traditional branches of philosophy, you will also find in college catalogue courses called "Philosophy of X," where X is some field or activity that itself is *not* philosophy, such as science, law, sport, religion, or even love and sex.

WHAT IS IT?

I DON'T KNOW. IT SEEMS TO BE SOME COMBINATION OF HYDROGEN AND OXYGEN.

The reason such fields as these are possible is that, especially in analytic philosophy, there is a form of investigation that has been called "second order" level of analysis. Take a look at this attempted definition of philosophy by William Capitan. I think it fails as an exhaustive definition (they all do!), but it has the virtue of revealing the side of philosophy we are discussing now. Capitan says philosophy is "rational inquiry into the structure of any thought system, its presuppositions, concepts, and the status of its claims."[1] This definition shows why it is possible to have the "philosophies of ____" and also shows why a course on Marx or Freud might well be taught in a philosophy department even though neither Marx nor Freud is thought of primarily as a philosopher. Freud, for instance, employs certain key concepts such as "sublimation," "projection," "transference," "displacement," and "reaction formation"; and psychoanalysts look for instantiations of these concepts in human behavior. This is *first order* analysis. Philosophers do not engage in this hands-on approach but take a step back and ask *second order* questions such as "What is the

Philos 110

All right! What are you two doing here?

Marx and Freud Are Discovered in a Philosophy Class

logic of these concepts?" "What presuppositions do these concepts make about the mind, knowledge, and value?" "What would count as establishing a case for or against these claims?" Capitan's definition stresses what we can call the analytical or critical aspect of philosophy, what has already been designated here as its second-order status. A tendency to emphasize this analytical feature of philosophy is also seen in the definition of late Stuart Hampshire, a well-known British philosopher. According to Hampshire, "Philosophy is a free inquiry into the limits of human knowledge and into the most general categories applicable to experience and reality."[2]

This intentionally vague part of his definition calls attention both to the fact that certain key categories are of interest to philosophy (such as time, space, existence, sociality, beauty, love, and death) and also to philosophy's interest in their *general* character. By their general character, Hampshire means something like this: I may ask you what time it is, and in doing so, I am certainly not asking a philosophical question. Or you may tell me that it takes less time to fly from San Francisco to Reno than to fly from Reno to St. Louis, and in doing so, you are not making a philosophical assertion. But if I ask you not "What time is it?" but "What is time?"—then I am asking a general question that is probably a philosophical question (unless, for example, I am simply asking you for the dictionary definition because my English isn't too hot and I'm not familiar with the word "time"). Similarly, if I ask you what it means for something to be located in space, I am asking a philosophical question, but not if I ask, "How many chairs will fit around the dining room table?"

In this book, I call these general questions "the big questions." This is slightly pompous but not quite so pompous as calling them "the most important questions," as some philosophers do. (It should be admitted forthwith that what makes a question "important" are the circumstances in which it is asked.) One could also call these philosophical questions "deep questions," yet they are deep not in some presumptuous sense but in a metaphorically archeological or geological sense. They are deep in that they lie beneath other questions and support them. When I talk about the amount of time it takes to get from point A to point B, then underlying my meaning is some general conception of time, and philosophy critically investigates that underlying general conception.

Let me add yet another attempt to define philosophy. This one is from Professor Craig Channell. According to him, philosophy is the "ongoing critical activity of developing theories to describe, explain, or account for certain aspects of human experience."[3] Though the last part of his definition is so vague as to be practically useless, his reference to philosophy as an "activity of developing theories" emphasizes a feature of philosophy that the other definitions have understressed—philosophy's *constructive* and *creative* side. Some philosophers (especially in the first half of the twentieth century) have thought that philosophy should not develop theories but should be satisfied with engaging exclusively in criticism and analysis; yet, as we shall see, the history of philosophy abounds with grand theoretical schemes trying to show how everything relates to everything else. Most of the individuals studied in the history of philosophy developed such schemes. This feature of philosophy is well captured in Wilfrid Sellars's perhaps slightly facetious definition of philosophy as "an attempt to see how things, in the broadest possible sense of the term, hang together, in the broadest possible sense of the term."[4]

So why are there so many *attempts* to define philosophy? Why not a straightforward, definitive statement made once and for all? After all, we can do that with words like "triangle." "A triangle is a three-sided closed figure." Anything that is a triangle has those features, and anything that has those features is a triangle. Anything that lacks them is not a triangle—*period!* The reason we can give an exhaustive definition of "triangle" but not one of "philosophy" is probably that the former is a *closed* concept and the latter is an open concept. That is, we can state the conditions that are both **necessary** and **sufficient** for something to be a triangle, but such conditions probably do not exist for something to be a piece of philosophy. Philosophy is not the *only* open concept. Some of the best among others are "love" and "art." "Love" doesn't get much treatment in this book, but we will return to the attempt to define "art" in the last chapter.

Most of the questions we will examine are at the center of the concept of philosophy, but a few will be on the periphery. We will discover that we cannot state any one characteristic or any set of characteristics that must necessarily be present to guarantee that we are doing philosophy and that, when absent, guarantee that we are *not* doing philosophy. Rather, philosophical inquiries will have what Ludwig Wittgenstein (much more about him in Chapter 10) called "family resemblances" when he tried to show what an open concept was like. He wrote the following about the open concept "game":

> And we can go through the many, many other groups of games in the same way; can see how similarities crop up and disappear.
> And the result of this examination is: we see a complicated network of similarities overlapping and criss-crossing: sometimes overall similarities, sometimes similarities of detail.

Family Resemblance

I can think of no better expression to characterize these similarities than "family resemblances"; for the various resemblances between members of a family: build, features, colour of eyes, gait, temperament, etc. etc. overlap and criss-cross in the same way.—And I shall say "games" form a family.[5]

The idea of philosophy is probably like the idea of game. The various activities the word "philosophy" designates are not related to each other by virtue of possessing one set of common denominators; rather those activities have "family resemblances" to each other.

Contemporary Styles of Philosophy

It should be emphasized that the activity called philosophy has been and still is practiced differently in different parts of the world. There is a multitude of Asian philosophies, African philosophies, and Native American philosophies, many of which have strong religious components (and may therefore befuddle the Mythos/Logos distinction I drew earlier). *Does the Center Hold?* will not cover those philosophies, though they too ask the question posed by my book's title. But even in so-called Western philosophy there are geographical oppositions, which sometimes get quite contentious. It is worthwhile to address the distinction between what is usually called *Continental philosophy* and *analytical philosophy* (though it must be said that analytical philosophy is sometimes practiced on the European continent and Continental philosophy is sometimes practiced in America and Britain).

Philosophy as taught at most universities in Continental Europe for the last one hundred years seems to have carried on the work of some of the classical philosophers who saw their job as that of constructing overarching, grandiose theories about "big things." The Continental philosophers are not shy of addressing topics such as life, death, love, alienation, culture, war, and chaos. It seems to me to be only a slight exaggeration to say that each school in this tradition has developed its own method and vocabulary. In their manner of addressing the big topics, the Continental philosophers are perhaps more like poets and artists than like the scientists who have inspired much of the analytic tradition, and for this reason, European philosophers seem to have been closer to popular culture and more widely read by the general public—and certainly more publicly controversial—than philosophers have been in, say, the United States. In fact, some schools of Continental philosophy have infiltrated film, fiction, and politics. These schools include **phenomenology, existentialism,** and **deconstruction,** and their vocabulary has penetrated modern culture in ways that the vocabulary of the analytic schools has not aspired to do. Of these Continental schools, only phenomenology and existentialism will make a significant appearance in *Does the Center Hold?*

The term "analytic philosophy" designates roughly the kind of philosophy practiced and taught by most professional philosophers in the North American and British systems of higher education during the last one hundred years. It is called "analytic" because it has viewed the main function of philosophy as being that of *analysis,* primarily the analysis of concepts (general ideas, categories, and classes)—not only concepts used in philosophy but also those employed in science and in everyday discourse. The function of these analyses is basically that of critical clarification. (What are we thinking when we *think* these concepts, and what do we *mean* when we name them in language?) But analytic philosophy also has the goal of solving foundational problems presented to us by the thoughts we think and the language(s) we use. For example, consider the problem called the Cretan liar's paradox: A philosopher from Crete makes the assertion, "Cretans always lie." If this sentence is true, then it is false! Surely, something has gone wrong here. Or, think of one of Bertrand Russell's favorite conundrums, expressed in the sentence, "The golden mountain does not exist." This sentence seems to say, "There is something both golden and mountainous, and it does not exist" (that is, it seems to say there is something that *is not*). Are these kinds of problems just humorous but annoying brain teasers, probably thought up by people with too much time on their hands? Or do they reveal serious problems at the foundational level of thought and language, in the way that the idea of "the set of all sets"—a set that contains itself (and therefore one of its parts is as large as the whole)—has been thought to challenge the very foundation of mathematics?

The Philosophy of Socrates

Let us make one last attempt to understand what philosophy is by trying something different. We will turn to ancient Greece once more and examine the activity of one of the earliest and most famous philosophers, Socrates, and hope thereby to gain some insight into the nature of philosophy itself.

SOCRATES (469–399 B.C.E.), who spent his entire life in Athens, did not give lectures or write treatises. Not only did he not write treatises, but he was also opposed to writing philosophy in any form because he thought that the

Socrates (469–399 B.C.E.)

letter kills the spirit. Philosophy for Socrates was a kind of social activity, a kind of discourse between two or more people who were looking for the truth. Therefore, his philosophizing took place in the streets of Athens and in its shops and parks where Socrates would engage anyone who was interested in conversation about "higher things." Socrates's wife, Xanthippe, sometimes found his habits annoying because she would send him on a simple errand, and he would remain for long stretches of time pursuing his philosophical interests. Sometimes, he would return hours later without the item he'd been sent out to purchase. According to one story, Socrates had been stumped by a question posed to him during one of these conversations, and he remained standing on the spot all night, chin in hand, thinking. According to another (probably **apocryphal**) story, an exasperated Xanthippe hid her husband's robe so he could not go out and philosophize with the boys. But Socrates slipped out nude, so his disciples began bringing along an extra robe in case Socrates arrived naked.

Fortunately, Socrates's brightest disciple, Plato, did not heed his master's advice concerning the written word. Plato wrote down everything he could remember Socrates having said. He transcribed Socrates's words in the same conversational style in which he had heard them, and the result is about twenty famous "Platonic dialogues." If it were not for these, and for the briefer and less philosophical writings of another contemporary, Xenophon, we would know very little of Socrates's teaching. As it is, students of Socrates have certain problems to deal with. How can we be sure that Plato is really giving us the thoughts of Socrates and not his own thoughts? After all, even though Plato's philosophy is an expansion of Socratic thought, we know that Plato developed his own philosophy far beyond Socrates's formulations. There is probably no ultimate solution to this problem, but as a rule of thumb we can say that the earlier the dialogue, the more authentic the record of Socrates's thoughts and the later the dialogue, the more likely that Plato is simply using the figure of Socrates to deliver Plato's own ideas.

Socrates Arriving for a Philosophy Discussion

Each of the main Platonic dialogues emphasizes one philosophical theme—for example, the nature of truth, beauty, justice, virtue, courage, piety, friendship, or the art of governing. Scholars have demonstrated that the typical Platonic dialogue of the early period can be schematically divided into three segments.

In the first segment, Socrates meets a young man who claims to *know* something about one of the aforementioned "big" topics. Socrates flatters the young man and compliments himself on his luck at having found someone who actually knows something that he, Socrates, has been seeking for fifty years—and a young man at that, usually eighteen, nineteen, or twenty years of age. Socrates begs the young man to impart his wisdom to him. When the young man does so, Socrates acts deeply impressed—sometimes awestruck. The young man's head begins to swell.

What we can call the second segment of the dialogue begins when Socrates seems to notice some apparently minor problem with the formulation of the youth's argument. The young man thinks a simple cosmetic job can cover the blemish, but we readers know that Socrates's objection will become the small thread that, when pulled, unravels the garment. By the end of this second segment, the young man is confused and admits

First Segment

ignorance. In some of the dialogues, Socrates's cross-examination is quite gentle; in others, quite harsh. In one dialogue, the protagonist ends up in tears.

What we call the third and final segment of the dialogue begins when both Socrates and his partner have admitted ignorance. The young man does not know what "X" is (virtue, beauty, truth, etc.), and Socrates does not know either. At this point, Socrates will say to his

Second Segment

despairing companion something like this: "Look, here we are, two ignorant men, yet two men who *desire* to know. I am willing to pursue the question seriously if you are willing." And in a certain sense, the real philosophizing begins at this point. It is as if, before any real philosophy can exist, the young man's earlier claim to knowledge had to be shown for what it was—an arrogant, blustering sort of defense mechanism whose function was to disguise the man's ignorance from himself and from others. This is the negative, destructive side of Socrates's method. Then the constructive side comes about in the

Third Segment

third part of the dialogue, where Socrates and the young man try out numerous hypotheses meant to discover the truth. Yet, in almost every case, the truth remains undiscovered. The Socratic dialogues end inconclusively. Why is this? Before we can answer, I will have to say more about "Socratic ignorance."

Socrates Lectures the Jury

Socrates's irreverence offended a number of powerful men in Athens. They managed to have him arrested and tried for impiety, for teaching false doctrines, and for corrupting the youth. During his trial, Socrates told the jury the story of his friend Chaerephon, who had gone to the temple of Apollo at Delphi to worship and had asked the god (through the oracle, the god's spokesperson) who was the wisest man in the world. The oracle answered that Socrates was the wisest. Socrates claimed to be absolutely perplexed by this response because he knew nothing, so how could he be the wisest man in the world? But eventually Socrates came to realize that in some sense, he was wiser than others. Others knew nothing but *thought* they knew something; Socrates *knew* nothing and knew that he knew nothing. Therefore, he knew more than others.

How seriously are we meant to take this story? It is obviously loaded with irony; Socrates is using it to inform his 501 jurors and his accusers that they were not only wrong to charge him with teaching false doctrines (because he knows nothing, he teaches nothing) but also wrong to believe that they were in a position to judge him (because as ignorant people, they were in a position to judge no one). And, indeed, Socrates's discourse is full of irony. It is clearly part of his method of philosophizing to communicate ironically, indirectly, using flattery, insult, humor, overstatement, understatement, misstatement, poetic allusion, and "old wives' tales" ("old husbands' tales"?). Professor Robert Paul Wolff, in his book *About Philosophy*, has a simple but ingenious analysis of "Socratic ignorance" that we will borrow.[6] Wolff says that we can think of

The Three Audiences

the Socratic dialogue as having three audiences. The first is the most naive audience and is usually represented by the young man with whom Socrates discourses. When Socrates says, "I am ignorant," the young man takes this assertion literally and contrasts it with his own supposed state of wisdom. The second audience is more sophisticated and is represented either by characters who appear in the dialogue in some peripheral way or by the readers of the dialogue. This audience thinks, "He is *not* ignorant. His claim of ignorance is purely ironic." And in some sense, this second audience is surely right. Socrates obviously *does* know things and knows more than those to whom he professes ignorance. Yet a third audience exists, the most sophisticated of all, represented, it is hoped, by the most sophisticated readers of the dialogue (namely you and me). This audience says, "He *is* ignorant." That is to say, in terms of the rigorous standards to which Socrates holds himself and others, he truly does not know. There is a *deep* sense of knowledge in which true knowers can give an exhaustive account of what they know and in which they understand how that knowledge relates to all other knowledge. Also, knowers have

TRUTH (trooth):
verity, conformity
with fact. Honesty,
integrity

incorporated that knowledge into their lives in ways that have transformed them. In other words, for Socrates, the person who truly knows justice becomes just, the person who knows truth becomes truthful, and the person who knows beauty becomes beautiful. In certain kinds of knowledge, one understands how all things are linked, and, in this sense, when one knows anything, one knows everything. When one achieves this knowledge, one achieves human excellence—*aretê* in Greek—and one becomes an excellent human being. This is the knowledge Socrates has sought all his life, but it has always eluded him. And in this sense, Socrates does not know. He is *ignorant*. The irony thickens here because both the least sophisticated and the most sophisticated audiences agree that Socrates is indeed ignorant but for very different reasons.

Now we can return to the question of why so many of the Socratic dialogues end inconclusively. They *must* do so. If, at the end of the various dialogues, Plato had made Socrates finally define "X"

All Things Are Linked to All Things

(again, truth, justice, beauty, etc.), this result would have been completely misleading, for it would have implied that knowledge could be purely formal—that we could arrive at a dictionary-type definition and memorize it. Once we had memorized it, we could then say we *knew* it, even though this "knowledge" in no way affected our lives. For Socrates, formulaic definitions by themselves could not count as true knowledge.

Socrates went to his death still pleading ignorance, yet claiming at the same time that "the unexamined life is not worth living." At the end of his trial, he bade farewell to his accusers and the jury with these words: "The hour of departure has arrived, and we go our ways—I to die and you to live. Which is better God only knows." And when asked in his execution room what he would do in the afterlife, if indeed there was an afterlife, he said he would continue doing in death what he had done in life. He would ask the shades in Hades if they had any knowledge. So is this not discouraging that one of the greatest philosophers and deepest thinkers of all time went to his grave

"The Unexamined Life Is Not Worth Living"

never achieving the knowledge he had spent his life seeking, a knowledge whose search is called "philosophy" and that we cannot even define? Is this not especially discouraging to introductory students on their first day?

Perhaps we will be a bit encouraged if we end the chapter with a famous passage from a philosopher who flourished twenty-five hundred

Socrates Quizzing the Shades in Hades

years after Socrates—one of the pioneers of analytic philosophy,
Lord BERTRAND RUSSELL (1872–1970):

> Philosophy is to be studied not for the sake
> of any definite answers to its questions,
> since no definite answers can, as a rule, be
> known to be true, but rather for the sake of
> the questions themselves; because these ques-
> tions enlarge our conception of what is possi-
> ble, enrich our intellectual imagination, and
> diminish the dogmatic assurance which
> closes the mind against speculation;
> but above all because, through the
> greatness of the universe which phi-
> losophy contemplates, the mind is
> also rendered great, and becomes
> capable of that union with the uni-
> verse which constitutes its highest
> good.[7]

Lord Russell (1872–1970)

Conclusion

Plato claimed that philosophy begins in wonder, and Aristotle, a student of
Plato, commenced one of his books with this line: "All men by nature desire
to know." According to this ancient Greek view, we are all philosophers by
nature. We are *Homo philosophicus*. If that optimistic picture is true, then
we have no need to justify an interest in philosophy. If someone sees you
carrying your philosophy book and asks why you are studying philosophy,
all you have to say is, "Because I am a human being."

And there is some truth to this ancient Greek view. One's soul would
have to be very shriveled indeed never to have asked any of "the big questions." Most people do not become professional philosophers, of course.
(And there is something odd about the notion of a "professional philosopher." From the Greek point of view, that would be something like becoming a professional human being. Socrates would have been horrified!) Nor
do many of us spend most of our time philosophizing. Furthermore, some
people are probably more naturally philosophical than others—such a thing
as a philosophical temperament does exist. What provokes us to philosophize? Sometimes hormones. Sensitive adolescents spend much time agonizing over the meaning of life, death, art (i.e., their smartphone), and
sociality; and many people seem to go through a classic midlife crisis in
which the big issues are raised once again. But philosophical questioning
doesn't have to be hormonal. Sometimes a most insignificant occurrence
can plunge us into a philosophical meditation, as can a dramatic or

traumatic event such as the loss of a close relative, a friend, or a lover. These experiences make us feel that, at least momentarily, the center does not hold. But it is not only at moments like these that we philosophize. We will be philosophers all our lives, and I am partial to the Greek/Russellian view that philosophizing magnifies our humanity. I am guilty of holding the opinion that the person who never philosophizes is somehow less of a person.

So if one is necessarily going to philosophize, why not do it well? Why do we think that activities like eating, driving, and earning money should be done well but that thinking about the big questions can be done sloppily with impunity?

Sensitive Adolescent Agonizing over the Meaning of Life while His Father Goes through a Midlife Crisis

Let's have a little *aretê* here too. Therefore, I recommend that you give yourself over to the "professionals," if only for this semester. For many of you, this will be the only philosophy course you take in your lifetime. A bunch of philosophy courses is not everyone's cup of tea, and there are many pressures on one's college planning—even more reason to take this course seriously.

Philosophers and philosophical theories can be read like great novels. The great novelists (Cervantes, Flaubert, the Brontës, Dostoyevsky, Eliot, Proust, Joyce, Mann, etc.) hand you a pair of magical spectacles and invite you to look through them, saying something like "If you look at the world through these glasses, you will see things you have never seen before, and having once seen them, they will be yours to possess forever." So it is with really good philosophy. Philosophical concepts offer themselves as possible interpretations of the world. The world is very complex, and the more interpretations of it that make themselves available to us, the more free and more effective we will be in the world. Philosophical concepts are like tools. The bigger our repertoire of tools, the more effective our work.

In this vein, the twentieth-century Austrian philosopher Ludwig Wittgenstein made great use of a figure now usually referred to as "Wittgenstein's duck/rabbit." Is this a duck or a rabbit? Of course, it can be

The Duck/Rabbit

read either way. The question "What is it *really*?" does not apply here. The suggestion I am making is that the world is much more like Wittgenstein's figure than we first realize. Creative solutions to the problems with which life presents us require the ability to make multifarious interpretations of the world. Philosophy gives us some tools for just such creative interpretation. Often the world is much more varied than to allow even only two interpretations (duck or rabbit?). It is more like this figure, suggested by Virgil Aldrich, who says, "Look at this figure under these five titles: (1) square suspended in a frame, (2) lampshade seen from above, (3) lampshade seen from below, (4) looking into a tunnel, and (5) aerial view of a truncated pyramid."[8]

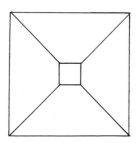

And if, after having inspected some of these philosophical tools, we choose never to use them as viable interpretations of the world, we still come away with an advantage, for they will have served as critical analyses of our ordinary beliefs. If we conclude that our ordinary beliefs withstand philosophical scrutiny, so much the better. To paraphrase Aristotle (taking some liberties in doing so), in terms of getting you a job, philosophy may be the most useless of all studies, but it is nevertheless the best.

Topics for Consideration

1. In what way can the study of the origins of philosophy in the pre-Socratic thinkers illuminate the *nature* of philosophy?
2. Can you find any common denominators underlying the various theories of the pre-Socratic philosophers?
3. Defend one of these views:
   a. Philosophy and science as they are practiced in the West today are part of Logos and radically distinct from Mythos.
   b. Logos is just a kind of Mythos.
4. Defend one of these views:
   a. "Philosophy" can be defined.
   b. "Philosophy" cannot be defined.
5. If Socrates *said* he was ignorant but was in fact knowledgeable, was he simply a liar?
6. At this early stage of your philosophical career, would you say that any *one* of the branches of philosophy listed in this chapter (epistemology, ontology, ethics, political and social philosophy, aesthetics, logic) should have priority over others? Why?

Suggestions for Further Reading: Paperback Editions

Donald Palmer, *Looking at Philosophy: The Unbearable Heaviness of Philosophy Made Lighter,* 6th ed. (San Francisco: McGraw-Hill, 2012). A popularized overview of Western philosophy by a congenial guy. (Buy several copies. They make excellent gifts.)

Robert Pirsig, *Zen and the Art of Motorcycle Maintenance* (New York: Bantam Books, 1975). The modern odyssey of a motorcycle rider on a cross-country journey in pursuit of the answers to the questions posed by the ancient Greek philosophers. Particularly good about the Mythos/Logos question and the nature of *aretê.*

Plato, "Apology," in *Great Dialogues of Plato,* ed. Eric H. Warmington and Philip G. Rouse, trans. W. H. D. Rouse (New York: New American Library, 1956). Plato's account of Socrates' trial.

Merrill Ring, *Beginning with the Pre-Socratics,* 2nd ed. (San Francisco: McGraw-Hill, 2000). Contains extant fragments from the lost works of the earliest philosophers and a commentary filling in the gaps.

Bertrand Russell, *The Problems of Philosophy* (New York: Oxford University Press, 1975). Written in 1912, this insightful book by a brilliant philosopher is somewhat dated but well worth reading.

I. F. Stone, *The Trial of Socrates* (New York: Doubleday Anchor, 1989). A poor grasp of Socratic and Platonic philosophy is counterbalanced by excellent investigative skills and a passion for the defense of free speech by a foremost journalist who learned ancient Greek in his old age just so he could write this book.

Nancy Tuana, *Woman and the History of Philosophy* (New York: Paragon House, 1992). An impressive critique of those features of the history of Western philosophy that have demoted, demeaned, marginalized, or perpetuated the suppression of women.

Notes

1. William H. Capitan, *Philosophy of Religion: An Introduction* (New York: Pegasus, 1972), p. 1.

2. Stuart Hampshire, *The Age of Reason* (New York: New American Library, 1961), p. 12.

3. Craig Channell, "The Advocacy Method: A Reply," *Teaching Philosophy*, Vol. I, No. 1 (Summer, 1975), p. 41.

4. Wilfrid Sellars, quoted in Richard Rorty, "The Fate of Philosophy," *New Republic* (Oct. 18, 1982), p. 28.

5. Ludwig Wittgenstein, *Philosophical Investigations* (New York: Macmillan, 1964), p. 32.

6. Robert Paul Wolff, *About Philosophy*, 4th ed. (Englewood Cliffs, NJ: Prentice-Hall, 1989), p. 14.

7. Bertrand Russell, *The Problems of Philosophy* (New York: Oxford University Press, 1975), p. 161.

8. Virgil C. Aldrich, *Philosophy of Art* (Englewood Cliffs, NJ: Prentice-Hall, 1963), p. 20.

2

Truth Is Beauty;
Beauty Is Truth[1]
Rationalist Epistemology

Epistemology is theory of knowledge. These are the big questions in epistemology: What is knowledge? What is the difference between opinion and knowledge? Does knowledge require certainty? What are the limits of knowledge? Is knowledge in fact possible? (This question is an epistemological version of the question, "Does the center hold?")

The word "knowledge" seems perhaps a bit highfalutin. Still, we are all familiar with it, and we certainly use the verb "to know" many times throughout any day.

- Do you know what time it is?
- I used to know that word in French, but I've forgotten it.
- She knew all the material on the test.
- We didn't know he would arrive today.

In ordinary discourse, what do we mean by "know" when we make such comments? I take it that when we say someone knows what time it is, he or she could state the correct time if asked, and respond in similar practical manner to the other statements. But, justifiably or unjustifiably, philosophers have not been satisfied with this account of the meaning of "knowledge." In fact, this dissatisfaction began early in the history of philosophy. We have already seen that in the fifth century B.C.E., Socrates insisted on a more rigorous notion of knowledge than that provided by common sense.

From the beginning of Western philosophy until now, epistemologists have tended to cluster into one or the other of two opposite camps. The first group, whose theory is now called **rationalism,** sees the primary source of knowledge to be "reason," usually understood as the application of logic, of mathematics, and, in some cases, **innate ideas,** or inborn knowledge. The other group, whose theory is now called **empiricism,** sees the human mind not as a deep well of information but rather as a "blank slate" (as one of its members, John Locke, put it in the eighteenth century). The true source of knowledge for this group is observation, which provides the data that come in through the five senses and are thereby "written" on the "blank slate." The most radical rationalists held that all true knowledge is **a priori**—knowledge that exists independently of sensory input—while the classical empiricists seem to have held that all true knowledge is **a posteriori**—knowledge derived only from sensory input. That is, the radical rationalists held that there is no such thing as a posteriori knowledge, and the radical empiricists held that there is no such thing as a priori knowledge. Neither of these extremes is held by anyone today (except by those few who deny *both* categories), but the debate between the rationalists and the empiricists still plays an important role in the way future philosophers will think. In this chapter, we will discuss rationalism, beginning with one of its foremost proponents, Socrates's student, PLATO (427–347 B.C.E.).

The Philosophy of Plato

Plato's analysis of the concept of knowledge can be set forth in the following manner. Take the sentence "P knows X" (where "P" is any person and "X" is any fact). What must be the case before such a sentence could be true? First, it must be true that "P believes X." You can't claim that you *know* something if you also claim that you don't believe it. (I can think of only one kind of case to the contrary. If someone knocks on your door and you open it to discover a friend with whom you've been out of touch for fifteen years, you may exclaim, "Joe Smith, I don't believe it!" But, of course,

Believing Something Very, Very Strongly

you *do* believe it. Otherwise, you would simply shut the door and go back to watching TV.) Then *belief* is a necessary part of knowledge, but it is certainly not the *whole* of knowledge. (Just because I believe something strongly doesn't mean I know it, . . . not even if I believe it very, very strongly.) Then what more besides belief is needed? Truth is required. X must be the case. No one has ever known that the earth is flat, for the simple reason that the earth is not flat. Even if thousands of people once claimed to know that the earth was flat, we know that all of them were wrong. (C. S. Lewis once

suggested that, before Columbus, people did not think that the earth was flat—not because they thought it was round but because they didn't think about it at all.) So now we have this:

> *P knows X.*
> entails   (a) P believes X,
> and   (b) X is the case.

Here (a) and (b) are necessary parts of knowledge. But are they sufficient? That is, does *true belief* constitute knowledge? Plato denied it, more or less, for the following kind of reason. Suppose you ask me if I know that the earth is round, and I say I do.

Knowing That the Earth Is Flat

Do I believe that it is round? Yes. Is it round? Yes. (I am purposely ignoring here the fact that in truth the earth is slightly pear-shaped—well, you would be pear-shaped, too, if you were spinning at the speed of thousand miles an hour.) So why doesn't this constitute *knowledge*? Suppose you ask me *how* I know that the earth is round, and I say, "Take a look at the bottom of your feet. Do you see how they are arched? Now I ask you, would God give us rounded feet if the earth were flat?"

Being Pear-Shaped while Spinning at 1,000 Miles per Hour

Suddenly, you would realize that I didn't know at all that the earth was round. I had just made a lucky guess!

So if true belief is not sufficient for knowledge, what would be?

Proof That the World Is Round—Direct Method

> *P knows X.*
> (a) P believes X.
> (b) X is true.
> (c) P can give the Logos for X. This is our second encounter with the Greek word "Logos," which is the source of our word "logic" as well as . . . etc.

The Greek word "Logos" is the source of our word "logic" as well as the source of all those terms ending in "-logy" (biology, the theory or study of living things; sociology, the theory or study of society, etc.). So, to give the Logos for X is to be able to give the theory, or the result of a study, that explains X. Logos also means "word" in Greek; one has to be able to say what that theory is. If someone told Plato or Socrates that she or he knew the answer to a question but just couldn't say it, Socrates and Plato would charge that precisely what was proved is that she or he did not know the answer.

For Plato, to give the Logos of X is to justify your belief in X; and, for him, *knowledge is justified belief*. This conclusion seems pretty sound, but the idea of justification is quite technical in Plato, as we have already seen. In fact, it is even more technical than the foregoing analysis revealed, as you will discover when we turn to Plato's famous Simile of the Line, which is the centerpiece of

	EPISTEMOLOGY	ONTOLOGY		
KNOWLEDGE	Pure Reason	the Forms	THE INTELLIGIBLE WORLD	THE GOOD
	Understanding	Scientific Concepts		
OPINION	Belief	Sensible Objects	THE VISIBLE WORLD	THE SUN
	Imaging	Images		

The Simile of the Line[2]

his most important work, the *Republic*. (It is called a simile because in it knowledge and reality are likened to a line that Socrates draws—presumably on the ground with a stick.) What we get here is Plato's whole metaphysical scheme. The right side of the line is his ontology (his theory of being). The left side is his epistemology (his theory of knowledge). There is also implicit here an ethics and an aesthetics. We will concentrate on the left side of the line because it corresponds to the topic of this chapter, but in order to do so, a few words must be said about the ontological side of the line as well.

The *visible world* (i.e., the physical world) can be thought of as representing Heraclitus's world of flux, in which the only thing that does not change is change itself. It is composed of two strata: images and sensible objects. These two levels never remain the same from one moment to the next.

Images

Shadows and reflections are the examples Plato offers us of images. They are dependent on the sensible objects of which they are images. The shadow of a tree is for Plato *less real* than the tree both because the tree lasts longer than the shadow and because the tree can exist without the shadow, but the shadow can't exist without the tree. Now switch to the left side of the line. On this side, we have not *things* (like shadows or trees) but *mental states*—states of awareness. If the object of your state of awareness is an image, you are in a state of imagination. The implication in the *Republic* is that this state is one of deception. The person in this state confuses an image with a thing. (Have you ever been attracted to the photo of someone or yelled, "Go, Niners!" during a televised football game? No? It's never happened to me either—but then, *we* are philosophy students!)

Isolde Mistaking the Shadow of a Tree Trunk for Tristan

Sensible Objects

Sensible objects are the individual things in the physical world: trees, books, cats. They are more real than images, but they are not absolutely real, both because they are not permanent (trees and cats grow old and die; books fall apart or are burned) and because they are dependent. They are dependent first of all on the *sun*. (If the sun were closer, everything would burn up; if it were farther away, everything would freeze; if it did not exist, there would be no trees, books, or cats and no images of them either.) And as we will see shortly, sensible objects are also dependent on the Forms.

Back to the left side of the line, if the object of your awareness is a sensible object, you are in a state of *belief*. Imagine seeing an animal in a field and asking a local farmer what the creature is. He says, "It's a horse." You ask him how he knows it's a horse, and he says (impatiently, no

Trees and Cats Grow Old—Books Fall Apart (The Center Does Not Hold)

doubt), "It's a horse! Take a look. A horse is a horse!" OK. The farmer believes it's a horse (belief); it is a horse (truth); so why does Plato say that the farmer doesn't *know* it's a horse? Because the farmer hasn't given the Logos. What would that be like? Well, perhaps something like this: you ask the farmer:

Cats and Shadows Are Dependent on the Sun

How do you <u>know</u> it's a horse?

A horse is a domesticable quadruped with closed hoofs and 32 pairs of chromosomes; and <u>that</u> creature is such an entity. Ergo, it is a horse!

He knows!

Actually, it's an albino zebra.

This man *knows*. He was able to grasp the objects of individual perception at a higher level—the conceptual level. (There are lots of problems here, of course, including the problem of *elitism*. On this account, of all the millions of people who have dealt with horses, only a select few have actually known what one is—and Plato wasn't one of them! Furthermore, it's hard to see how you could know what a horse is without performing a biopsy and understanding biology and chemistry. Indeed, it's beginning to look as though one would have to know *everything* in order to know *anything*. Some interpreters believe that this dilemma is exactly what Plato had in mind. It would at least make sense of Socrates's claim to be ignorant.)

Concepts

So, we've seen that one moves from belief to understanding (and thereby opinion for knowledge) by grasping the perception at the conceptual level, that is, by subsuming the particular under the general. In doing so, one leaves behind Heraclitus's world of flux and enters into "the intelligible realm," a world of Parmenidean permanence. One elevates objects from the constantly changing physical world and stabilizes them by placing them in the context of Logos, of a *theory* or a *science*. Let's illustrate these levels. Imagine three different episodes: (1) Your pen rolls from the desk and falls to the floor; (2) a meteorite falls into the earth's atmosphere, splashing silver sparks into the night sky; and (3) in the sixth round of a heavyweight boxing match, the champion receives a body-jolting uppercut on the chin and falls to the canvas like a load of bricks. In each of these cases, the imagery would be described very differently (this is the level of perception), but to understand the three events, we would need a *theory*, the very theory later discovered by Sir Isaac Newton: given any two unrestrained masses, these masses mutually attract each other in direct proportion to their mass and in indirect proportion to their distance. This is knowledge. But apparently for Plato, it is not the highest kind of knowledge. There is still pure reason to be dealt with.

Gravity at Work

Forms

According to Plato, the concepts with which we have been dealing here (horse, gravity) are not mere abstractions from concrete cases. These concepts are copies of higher truths, and he called these higher truths the **Forms**. These Forms are the archetypes of everything existing in the visible world. They exist outside time and space. They are not physical, but they aren't mental either. That is, they don't just exist as ideas in people's minds. Because they are not physical, they cannot be grasped by the senses; and even though they are not mental, they can be grasped only by the intellect, which has transcended the senses. These Forms are real in the sense that they are uncreated, indestructible, unchanging, and therefore eternal. Notice that they are not *absolutely* real because they are still dependent—upon something Plato calls "the Good"— in the same way that sensible things are dependent upon the

The Heaven of Forms

sun. The Good seems to be a kind of Super-Form, the Form of all Forms, which is an absolute value that grounds all reality and bestows worth on it, very much the way God would later do in the Judaic and Christian ontology of the medieval period. (Drop one letter, "o," from "Good" [= God], and change the "u" in "Sun" to "o" [= Son], and you have a crude version of medieval Christian Platonism.) It is the Good that is the center of the whole Platonic system. The center holds because the Good holds. It has a kind of Parmenidean permanence. If it did not hold, we would be plunged into a world of Heraclitian flux.

Now how can the mind grasp the Forms? Only by *totally* transcending the senses, which are somehow committed to the world of Becoming, hence naturally hostile to the world of Being. Concepts, though definitely part of the intelligible sphere, are still image-bound and hence, somehow, still *contaminated*. (Notice the anti-materialistic bias that enters into

Transcending the Five Senses

Western philosophy here with Plato including disapproval of the human body. It is very uncharacteristic of the Greeks, whose social practices, art, and even religion showed no signs of disdain for the body.) Earlier, when you were presented with Newton's definition of gravity ("Given any two masses . . ."), you saw two masses in your mind's eye. However, the mind grasps the Form and not merely the concept when it frees itself from that visual imagery. This it does by mathematizing its object. It is as if, for person P, the move from the definition ("Given any two masses . . .") to the formula

Hello, body. This is mind speaking. I hate you!

$$\left(F = \frac{Gm_1m_2}{d^2}\right)$$

liberates the truth from the flux of the world, and to grasp the ultimate intelligible order of the universe is to grasp it purely formally, that is, mathematically. If this interpretation of Plato is correct (and there certainly are other interpretations), then Plato believed that there existed a correct formula not only for horse and gravity, but for love and beauty as well.

Many of us today are prepared to grant the former, but we resist the latter. We point to the notorious relativity in the aesthetic taste of different individuals and cultures to refute Plato. (Parisians and Ubangis do not agree as to what beauty is.) But for Plato, if both the Parisian fashion model and the Ubangi princess are truly beautiful, a common denominator must exist. Perhaps it has to do with a mathematical account of "order" involving grace, balance, and **eros.** Perhaps someday "beauty's" Sir Isaac Newton will come along and finish this equation: "B = . . ."

Finally, concerning Plato, let's ask about the process of learning in his theory. The dialogue that deals with this process is the *Meno*. In it, Socrates and Meno, a young aristocrat, have been discussing "virtue" and whether it can be taught. Socrates has forced Meno to admit that he doesn't know what virtue is, hence that he doesn't know whether it can be taught (i.e., Socrates has brought the dialogue to the end of the "second phase" referred to in Chapter 1). Both Socrates and Meno admit that they are ignorant, and Socrates says that he is willing to pursue the issue seriously if Meno is willing. Here Meno poses a question that has come to be called **Meno's paradox.** Meno asks how it is ever possible to seek knowledge of X, where X stands for anything at all. Such a quest seems impossible, because either one already has knowledge of X, in which case one does not need to seek it, or one does not have knowledge of X, in which case one will not recognize X if one sees it. Socrates seems to take Meno's question as a joke, but in fact, he takes it very seriously.

Meno and Socrates are strolling in a garden, and they come across the gardener, an untutored slave boy. Socrates asks the boy to solve a fairly complicated geometrical problem—that of doubling the square. The boy objects that he hasn't studied mathematics, but Socrates, undeterred,

How Do You Recognize the Truth When You See It?

begins to ask him a series of questions: Should we solve the problem by using arcs or straight lines? (Try straight lines.) Should we put the straight lines inside or outside the square? (First outside, then, when that fails, inside.) After a long series of questions that the boy can answer with a "yes" or a "no," the boy eventually produces the correct answer—a diagram like this:

So, according to Socrates, the unschooled slave boy was able to answer a difficult mathematical question without being given any information he did not already possess. You and I may feel that Socrates's method in this case involved some intellectual sleight of hand. Plato's conclusion, though, is that the slave boy already knew the answer to the question, but he did not *know* that he knew it. The truth, according to Plato, existed in the slave boy's soul. It was a piece of unconscious knowledge, knowledge based on an innate idea, that is, an idea present at birth in the soul of the individual. Plato's view may have been that all true knowledge is an expression of a version of the principle of identity

The Slave Boy Knows More Than He Knows That He Knows

(A = A), and because this principle cannot be learned through observation (i.e., because it is a priori), it must be an innate idea—an idea with which we are all born. However, there is some debate about whether this is the correct interpretation of Plato's view. At any rate, for Plato, all learning is truly remembering, and it answers "Meno's paradox" (how will we recognize something we don't know?) by saying that in fact we do know what we don't know, and recognition is recollection. So, Plato, like Freud and Proust (author of the seven-volume novel, *Remembrance of Things Past*), takes the phenomenon of memory absolutely seriously and makes it a central feature of his theory of knowledge.

Let's review some of the key features of Plato's epistemology. To know is to transcend the ever-changing flux of the physical world and to grasp a permanent rational order behind the flux, an order that will demonstrate the universal in the particular. This "grasping" is an intellectual act of the mind, which, in its purest manifestation, is exclusively formal (i.e., mathematical). Such an intellectual act can only take place if there are certain innate ideas upon which it can be based. Knowing, then, is an act of making the observable world intelligible by showing how it is related to an eternal order of intelligible truths. These features of Plato's epistemology are part of the program of rationalism, one of the two key epistemological poles in Western thought.

Platonic rationalism was immediately countered by the philosophy of Plato's student, Aristotle, which moved toward what would eventually become empiricism (to be discussed in Chapter 3). Yet rationalism managed to dominate later Greek and Roman philosophy and all of the early Middle Ages, only to be countered once again by a revival of Aristotelianism in the work of St. Thomas Aquinas in the thirteenth century.

Updating Plato's Definition of Knowledge

We saw that for Plato, knowledge is justified true belief (i.e., "P knows X" entails [a] "P believes X," [b] "X is true," and [c] "P can justify her belief in

X"). For Plato, justification involved providing the "Logos" for one's belief in terms of a definition or a theory. Most philosophers since Plato's time seem to have accepted his account of knowledge, but today, generally, they would not require that the "Logos" component of the diagram be expressed as a theory or a definition because they disagree with Plato's apparent view that all true knowledge must be theoretical or definitional. Therefore, they say that step (c) of the diagram ("P can justify her belief in X") must be understood as being able to provide good reasons or entitlement for one's belief. This has been the standard view for years, but recently, there have been attempts to fashion "Gettier cases" (named after Edmund Gettier, the philosopher who invented this strategy).[3] These are counter cases in which the thinker has fulfilled all three necessary conditions but proves not to possess knowledge after all. Most of the Gettier cases I have encountered fail, in my view, because they end up involving inferences from false premises by the thinker in each of the examples, which means that the thinker does not after all have "good reasons to believe X, even if she believes it does." There have been numerous **"Gettier cases**." Here's one that has circulated for a few years:

> Sue agrees to help Melissa with her homework. Melissa goes to Sue's room at the agreed-upon time and looks around to see if Sue has remembered her promise. She sees Sue working at her desk. Melissa, relieved, forms the belief: "Ah, Sue is in the room as she promised she would be." In fact, Melissa does not see Sue; she saw an excellent hologram of Sue. Nevertheless, Sue is actually there, in another part of the room hidden from Melissa's view. So, Melissa's belief that Sue is in the room as she promised is true: she can justify her belief ("I see her clearly"), but we can't really say that Melissa *knew* Sue was there at the moment that she formed her belief.

Sue can indeed justify her belief—the hologram was so good that anyone would have made the error of believing that she was seeing Sue. But it *was* an error. So, has Melissa given the "Logos"? We may find a way to refute this Gettier case, but each new Gettier case would have to be defeated on its own, and nobody knows how many there can be.

Many contemporary epistemologists accept Gettier's critique of knowledge as JTB (justified true belief) and have tried to produce better definitions of "knowing"—for example, by adding a causal component (Melissa's belief was *caused* by a true fact), but there seems to be no consensus among these philosophers about an alternative theory. Other epistemologists claim to have found flaws in each of the Gettier cases so far presented. Still, one cannot rule out in advance the possibility that someone will come up with a Gettier case that works, thereby refuting the proffered definition of knowledge in terms of Plato's three necessary conditions.

René Descartes's Rationalism

Rationalism may have achieved its fullest maturity in the seventeenth century in the work of RENÉ DESCARTES (1596–1650). We will inspect his version of rationalism before looking at rationalism's alternatives.

René Descartes (1596–1650)

Theories of knowledge are never created in a vacuum. There are always psychological, economic, social, and political conditions behind them, acting as motives for them. The external circumstances that motivated Plato were very different from those that motivated Descartes. Plato, a man of noble ancestry, lived at a time when the old aristocratic system of governing was collapsing in the face of the emergence of a new commercial class and an incipient democracy. In the two-hundred-year period before Plato's time, social and intellectual conditions had conspired to undermine the moral authority of the old aristocratic values, whose canon was the myths of Homer and Hesiod. As the old values of honor, loyalty, courage, and the natural right of the nobility to govern deteriorated, they were being replaced with what to Plato were plebeian values that thinly disguised greed and the thirst for power. The problems that Plato confronted in the third century B.C.E. were *not* the ones that faced René Descartes in the seventeenth century, C.E.; rather he was confronted by the opposition between religion and science. Descartes lived when new sciences were being born. Copernicus had been dead only forty years when Descartes was born. Descartes was a contemporary of Galileo and Kepler. Newton was eight years old when Descartes died. In fact, Descartes himself had made a major contribution to the history of science while still in his twenties by discovering **analytic geometry.**

I do not know.

Theories of Knowledge Are Never Created in a Vacuum

Now the ever-increasing power of the new science was beginning to challenge the waning authority of the Church, which had dominated for a thousand years but suffered several major setbacks in the two hundred years before Descartes's birth (a series of internal schisms, defeats at the hands of secular rulers, and the emergence of the Protestant Reformation). The Church was fighting to retain not only what political power it still had but also its custody over the

The Contest between Philosophy and Poetry in Plato's Days

human *moral* self-image. It was in this sphere that the new sciences seemed to be most directly challenging religious authority, and the confrontation came to a head in 1632, when the Inquisition arrested Galileo, tried him, and found him guilty of impiety. The specific event that provoked Galileo's arrest was the publication of an essay reporting his discovery that there were four moons orbiting the planet Jupiter. Now, it may not be immediately obvious why the religious authorities would be threatened by such a claim. The traditional view of what was at stake in the

Galileo affair is this[4]: For a thousand years, the concept of human dignity was closely bound to the idea that God had created the Garden of Eden in the very center of the universe and that the rest of the cosmos was formed as a series of concentric circles radiating out of Eden, the belly button of reality. This view meant that the human drama was the *key* drama in the cosmos and that every other being in the universe was simply placed here as a witness to the human drama. This concept had the effect of imbuing every human act with *meaning*. Even if one's life was filled with misery (and there was plenty of misery in the medieval world), at least that misery had significance; hence, there was a certain dignity in even the most miserable human existence.

Now this heroic conception of human life was suddenly threatened by the Copernican theory that the earth was not the center of the universe—that in fact the earth and the other planets actually orbited the sun (i.e., that the

heliocentric and not the geocentric theory was correct). If the earth is just hurtling through space with no more and no less meaning than that of any other body in the universe, what would this finding mean for the concept of human dignity? (Freud once said that human dignity has suffered three mortal blows: first, Copernicus's discovery that the human is not at the center of the universe; second, Darwin's discovery that the human is an animal; and third, Freud's discovery that the animal is sick.) But there was one scientific fact that prevented the Copernican radicals from winning the day. It was the undisputed fact that the earth's moon orbits the earth. If the heliocentric theory were true, why would the moon orbit the earth? Why wouldn't it travel around the sun the same way the earth was supposed to do? Now you can see the significance of Galileo's discovery. If Jupiter's moons orbit Jupiter, that proves moons can orbit planets that are not the center of the

I don't think I can take any more revelations, Doc.

universe, and this proof kicked the last strut out from under the geocentric theory.

Somewhat like Galileo, Descartes found himself in an awkward situation. He was a dedicated Catholic who did not look forward to a confrontation with the ecclesiastical authorities, yet he had just finished a manuscript on physics (*The World*), many sections of which he knew would agree with Galileo. So rather than publishing his manuscript, he decided to write a book of philosophy that would create an intellectual climate of reconciliation between science and religion. He wanted to show that the idea of being a "religious scientist" was not self-contradictory. Indeed, he wanted to show that the possibility of science itself presupposed certain theological assumptions. He called this book *Meditations on First Philosophy* and dedicated it to "the Most Wise and Illustrious Men: The Dean and Doctors of the Sacred Faculty of Theology in Paris."

In his letter of dedication, Descartes fawned and groveled before the theologians at the Sorbonne, but to his friend, Father Mersenne, he wrote in a very different tone, "and I want to say, just between us, that these six *Meditations* contain all the fundamental ideas of my physics. But please keep this quiet, because if they knew it, [the theologians] would be very reluctant to accept my views."[5]

In my own opinion, Descartes was successful in his undertaking. As far as I can determine, Catholicism never again had a head-on confrontation with science. Descartes had demonstrated that such a collision course was not necessary. It seems to me that today most religious opposition to scientific theories comes from certain Protestant camps (e.g., opposition to the teaching of Darwin's theory of evolution). Perhaps the Protestants are still waiting for their Descartes.

The Collision Course between Religion and Science

Well then, let us turn to Descartes's epistemology as he developed it in the *Meditations*. In the first paragraph of that book, Descartes announces his grandiose proposal, "I must once for all seriously undertake to rid myself of all the opinions which I had formerly accepted and commence to build anew from the foundation, if I wanted to establish any firm and permanent structure in the sciences."[6]

Notice a key metaphor in this passage, one taken from carpentry. Knowledge is seen as a building in which all the superstructure is resting on a foundation, and the building is only as strong as the foundation. (You will observe as you proceed that philosophers often develop their ideas around a key metaphor. For instance, think of the role played in Plato's thought by the notions of sunlight and shadows.) Descartes continues:

I shall at last seriously and freely address myself to the general upheaval of all my former opinions.

Now for this object it is not necessary that I should show that all of these are false—I shall perhaps never arrive at this end. But inasmuch as reason already persuades me that I ought no less carefully to withhold my assent from matters which are not entirely certain and indubitable than from those which appear to me manifestly to be false, if I am able to find in each one some reason to doubt, this will suffice to justify my rejecting the whole. (p. 166)

Here we see Descartes's technique, which has come to be known as **methodological doubt.** It has a motto, *De omnibus dubitandum est* (Everything is to be doubted), and it requires Descartes to doubt any proposition whatsoever if he can find the slightest reason to do so. Notice that, unlike courts of law, methodological doubt does not require that the doubt be *reasonable;* rather, any possible doubt will be sufficient to put a proposition out of commission. And the point of all this doubting is to attempt to find something that cannot be doubted, something indubitable, absolutely certain. That absolute certainty, if it exists, will be the foundation of the house of knowledge.

I shall proceed by setting aside all that in which the least doubt could be supposed to exist, just as if I had discovered that it was absolutely false; and I shall ever follow in this road until I have met with something which is certain, or at least, if I can do nothing else, until I have learned for certain that there is nothing in the world that is certain. (p. 170)

Descartes's rule, "Everything is to be doubted," is not recommended by him as a way of life. It is part of a philosophical game, but a serious game. The point of the game is to discover the foundation of knowledge, if there is such a thing to be discovered. And if there is no foundation to discover, then the game will be abandoned, and one will return to real life. But one will return with much more cynicism than one had before the game because one will "know" that there is no such thing as knowledge; only opinions, hearsay, prejudices, and passions exist. In that case, the so-called "house of knowledge" is built only on shifting sands. Descartes's method is his way of seeking a definitive answer to the question, "Does the center hold?"

Let us return to the project of the *Meditations.* Descartes continues:

All that up to the present time I have accepted as most true and certain I have learned either from the senses or through the senses; but it is sometimes proved to me that these senses are deceptive, and it is wiser not to trust entirely to anything by which we have once been deceived. (p. 166)

Here we see that Descartes's dismantling of the rotten timbers from the house of knowledge is done more with a bulldozer than a crowbar. Because the senses are known deceivers, they will be doubted away, which means that all beliefs based on the senses (and that is *most* of them, after all) will be jettisoned. But suddenly, Descartes himself suspects that perhaps his house bashing is moving too fast. He says:

But it may be that although the senses sometimes deceive us concerning things which are hardly perceptible, or very far away, there are yet many others to be met with as to which we cannot reasonably have any doubt, although we recognize them by their means. For example, there is the fact that I am here, seated by the fire, attired in a dressing gown, having this paper in my hands and other similar matters. And how should I deny that these hands and this body are mine, were it not perhaps that I compare myself to certain persons, devoid of sense, whose cerebella are so troubled and clouded by the violent vapours of black bile, that they constantly assure us that they think they are kings when they are really quite poor, or that they are clothed in purple when they are really without covering, or who imagine that they have an earthenware head or are nothing but pumpkins or are made of glass. But they are mad, and I should not be any less insane were I to follow examples so extravagant. (p. 166)

**René Descartes—
Heavy Equipment Operator**

So there is René Descartes, sitting in his pj's alone at his desk in front of his fireplace. (Quite a different stage from that of old Socrates, who philosophized in the streets of Athens, seeing philosophy as essentially a social activity! It is clear that the notion of thinking has undergone a dramatic change since the Greek period.) Descartes stares at his hand and thinks, "This is my hand." How could he possibly be wrong? Only a madman could stare at his hand and wonder if it is his hand. If, after leaving your classroom, you see someone sitting on the campus lawn staring at his hand, and the person says to you, "I'm not sure this is my hand," you won't say to yourself, "A philosopher!" Rather, you'll say, "A lunatic!" Descartes knows this perfectly well; yet, following the strictures of **radical doubt,** he does indeed question whether what he is looking at is his hand. (By the way, did you notice Descartes's marvelous baroque description of madness? ". . . cerebella . . . troubled and clouded by the violent vapours of black bile . . .") Descartes continues:

> At the same time I must remember that . . . I am in the habit of sleeping, and in my dreams representing to myself the same things or sometimes even less probable things than do those who are insane in their waking moments. How often has it happened to me that in the night I dreamt that I found myself in this particular place, that I was dressed and seated near the fire, whilst in reality I was lying undressed in bed! . . . I remind myself that on many occasions I have in sleep been deceived by similar illusions, and in dwelling carefully on this reflection I see so manifestly that there are no certain indications by which we may clearly distinguish wakefulness from sleep that I am lost in astonishment. (pp. 166–167)

Do you get Descartes's point? Can you refute him? Can you *think of a test that will prove you are not dreaming now?* Obviously, pinching yourself (as they do in the comics) won't work because it is quite possible to dream that you are pinching yourself. For the same reason, you can't just ask your neighbor, "Am I dreaming?" It is possible to dream whatever answer she gives. In fact, it seems that Descartes

Philosophy Student Dreaming about Dreams

has us over a barrel because the only way to refute him would be to think of a test that can't be dreamed. But any test you can *think* of, you can *dream.*

Descartes's conclusion is not that one should keep wondering whether one is dreaming but that there is no philosophical proof that at any given moment one is not dreaming. Therefore, the senses and the commonsense picture of the world based on the senses cannot be the foundation of knowledge.

Let's start diagramming some of this:

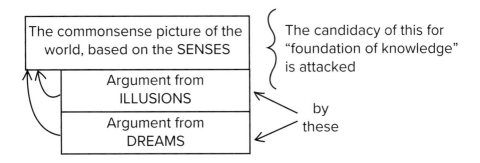

These two arguments disqualify the senses as candidate for the foundation of knowledge. Can there be another candidate for some kind of certain knowledge? What about mathematics? Descartes says, "For whether I am awake or asleep, two and three together always form five, and the square can never have more than four sides, and it does not seem possible that truths so clear and apparent can be suspected of any falsity or uncertainty" (p. 168). Descartes's point here as he states it seems wrong to me. If I can make a mathematical error when I'm awake, I can jolly well make one when I'm dreaming!

But the real point Descartes is trying to make here is worth pausing over. It requires reminding yourself of two technical philosophical terms that you have already learned, "a priori" and "a posteriori." An a priori claim is a claim whose truth or falsity can be known independently of observation. An a posteriori claim is one whose truth or falsity can be known only by appealing to observation. Now Descartes's point can be put this way: the "argument from illusion" and the "argument from dreams" can attack only a posteriori claims. But mathematics is a priori; hence, it should escape both of these skeptical arguments. One does not prove that 2 + 3 = 5 by taking a field trip or doing an experiment. Putting three pieces of chalk next to two pieces of chalk and counting them is no proof that 2 + 3 = 5, any more than finding five white swans is proof that all swans are white. (The way you prove that 2 + 3 = 5 is by demonstrating that that proposition is a version of the proposition A = A and then demonstrating that any denial that A = A leads to a self-contradiction. This kind of proof is not an act of perception but is what Plato would call an act of "pure reason.")

So what Descartes is asking is whether the a priori truths of mathematics might not serve as the absolutely certain foundations of knowledge.

Mathematical Experiment

Descartes was a mathematician, after all, so he would no doubt have loved to answer that question affirmatively, but the rigors of methodological doubt forced him to answer in the negative, as we will see:

> Nevertheless I have long had fixed in my mind the belief that an all-powerful God existed by whom I have been created such as I am. But how do I know that He has not brought it to pass that there is no earth, no heaven, no extended body, no magnitude, no place, and that nevertheless I possess the perceptions of all these things and that they seem to me to exist just exactly as I now see them? And besides, as I sometimes imagine that others deceive themselves in the things which they think they know best, how do I know that I am not deceived every time that I add two and three, or count the sides of a square or judge of things yet simpler, if anything simpler can be imagined? (p. 168)

This text is the introduction to one of the most curious chapters in the history of philosophy: Descartes's "evil genius" hypothesis. Descartes asks himself, How do I know that the universe was not created by a malevolent demon whose only goal is to deceive so that even when I make the most basic mathematical judgments, such as that 2 + 3 = 5, I err; yet I never know that I am erring? Much to Descartes's chagrin, he realizes that he cannot disprove the existence of such a "god" (as Descartes called it in the quoted passage). Therefore, even if it is not very likely that such a demon exists, its existence is **logically possible,** and, using his method of radical doubt, it follows that mathematics is not absolutely certain.

Descartes and the Evil Genius

(Imagine a math teacher who tells her students, "Two plus three is five, . . . unless there is an evil genius, in which case two plus three may not be five." If one has to add that qualification to math, then math is not unqualifiably true, and it cannot be the foundation of knowledge.)

So, Descartes is stuck in the following state (which would surely be taken as the paradigm case of paranoia if methodological doubt were confused with real doubt):

> I shall then suppose, not that God who is supremely good and the fountain of truth, but some evil genius not less powerful than deceitful, has employed his whole energies in deceiving me; I shall consider that the

heavens, the earth, colours, figures, sound, and all other external things are nought but the illusions and dreams of which this genius has availed himself in order to lay traps for my credulity; I shall consider myself as having no hands, no eyes, no flesh, no blood, nor any senses, yet falsely believing myself to possess all these things. (pp. 169–170)

This text is one of the most dramatic descriptions in philosophy of the prospect of the center not holding. As you see, at this point in Descartes's tale, he cannot prove that the center holds, but he does not give up in despair. He looks for a foothold that will allow him to climb out of the abyss into which he has fallen.

Well, then, is there a truth so certain that it can be known indubitably even if the senses deceive Descartes, even if he is dreaming, and even if there is an evil genius?

I myself, am I not at least something? But I already denied that I had senses and body. Yet I hesitate, for what follows from that? Am I so dependent on body and senses that I cannot exist without these? But I was persuaded that there was nothing in all the world, that there was no heaven, no earth, that there were no minds, nor any bodies: was I not then likewise persuaded that I did not exist? Not at all; . . . without doubt I exist also if [the evil genius] deceives me, and let him deceive me as much as he will, he can never cause me to be nothing so long as I think that I am something. So that after having reflected well and carefully examined all things, we must come to the definite conclusion that this proposition: I am, I exist, is necessarily true each time that I pronounce it, or that I mentally conceive it. (p. 171)

This, then, is the absolutely certain foundation of all knowledge. In the *Meditations*, the version is the self-proving proposition "I am." In another work, the *Discourse on Method*, the wording for the foundation of knowledge is, more famously, "I think, therefore I am" (**Cogito** *"ergo sum"*). This truth is certain under any possible conditions. Every time I make the assertion, "I am," I am *right*. Not even an evil genius or madness can falsify this finding.

Now the nature of this "foundation" must be clarified.

I am, I exist, that is certain. But how often? Just when I think; for it might possibly be the case if I ceased entirely to think, that I should likewise cease altogether to exist. I do not now admit anything which is not necessarily true: to speak accurately I am not more than a thing which thinks, that is to say a mind or a soul, or an understanding, or a reason, . . . I am, however, a real thing and really exist; but what thing? I have answered: a thing which thinks. (p. 173)

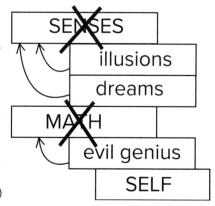

So, selfhood's essence of which Descartes is so certain is thought or consciousness which, as you see, Descartes conveniently equates with "soul." Perhaps his hidden religious agenda is sticking out a bit here.

This discussion is the beginning of Descartes's notorious mind–body dualism. The "self" is defined as mind or soul (a "thing which thinks"), and the body is not an essential part of the self. In order to see Descartes's argument that leads to this strange conclusion (strange because most of us have always assumed that our bodies are rather essential aspects of our selves and not baggage we take along with us when we go out), take a look at a couple of sentences:

1. *"I doubt that I have a body."* Now this is an *odd* doubt, and if you ever heard anyone express it, you would think that person to *be* odd (either odd or a philosopher!). But it is *only* odd. It is not an impossible doubt. So Descartes's method requires consideration of this doubt.
2. *"I doubt that I have a mind."* This is not only an odd doubt; it is an impossible doubt. To *doubt* that one has a mind is to *establish* that one has a mind because doubting is an activity of the mind. To Descartes, this proves that there is a **necessary** relation between self and mind—

and only a **contingent** (i.e., non-necessary) relation between self and body.

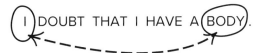

This argument is a difficult one to evaluate, but let's let it slip by just to see what Descartes does with it. "But what then am I? A thing which thinks. What is a thing which thinks? It is a thing which doubts, understands, conceives, affirms, denies, wills, refuses, which also imagines and feels" (p. 174). Here Descartes is defining the mind in terms of its capacity to perform certain mental acts: to doubt, to understand, and so forth. To say that anything has a mind is to say that that thing can perform these acts. For Descartes, this conclusion seems to be a "package deal." If you can do any one of these, you can do them all. If there is any one of them you can't do, then you can't do any of them. It was for this reason that Descartes concluded that animals do not have minds. Dogs do not affirm or deny anything, so (appearances to the contrary notwithstanding) they must not will anything either. (Perhaps there is a religious motive here as well. To admit that dogs have minds is to admit that they have *souls*. Now do we really want dogs barking in heaven? Isn't it enough that they keep us awake and befoul our lawns here on earth?)

I doubt that I have a body.

Well, it's not a very <u>good</u> body . . .

There is another feature of the mind that Descartes wanted to reveal. It comes out in the famous "wax example." Descartes picks up a square piece of hard, cold, white wax that makes a noise when tapped, and he holds it to a candle flame. Suddenly, every one of the observable characteristics of the object changes. It is now formless, soft, hot, and gray, and no sound is emitted when he taps it. Yet, even though every one of its characteristics has changed, Descartes claims to know it is the *same* wax he held before.

This example constitutes another attack on the claim that the senses are the source of real knowledge (the view

I <u>did not</u> steal your chocolate-covered donut!

called "empiricism," which will be inspected in Chapter 3), and Descartes has selected a brilliant example indeed. He goes through the five senses, cataloguing the information about the wax that the senses provide. Then, when

Divine Barking

he holds the wax to the fire, every one of those characteristics changes. Yet we know, he says, that it is the same wax. How can we know this if the senses tell us the opposite? Where do we get the concept of "sameness"? Clearly not from the senses because their data are in constant flux (like Plato's "Becoming"). Descartes's answer is very Platonic. According to him, the concept of "sameness," that is, the concept of identity, must be an *innate idea* because it cannot be derived from observation. We are all born with the (apparently unconscious) knowledge of the "principle of identity," "A = A." This absolutely necessary and a priori truth is presupposed by any other knowledge whatsoever. If we did not know this truth, we could not know any truth.

The wax example also generates the innate idea of **substance** (i.e., of substantiality, of "thingness") and particularly of *material substance* (i.e., the idea of a physical body). According to Descartes, this idea *cannot* be derived from the senses alone. In order to understand Descartes's point, consider it this way. Imagine that we build a computerized robot. We install five sensors in it: one for tactile data, one for visual data, one for olfactory data, one for tastes, and one for sounds; and we teach it a language to name the data of all the sensors. Then we program it to record all the sensory data it receives, and we send it out into the world. Now the robot will send back reports

Blue, cylindrical, hard, cold, here now

like those in the illustration. What the robot could *not* say is, "There is a blue pen on the table," and that's because it would be lacking the two key concepts, "identity" and "thingness." If we preprogrammed these concepts into our robot, they would organize the sensorial data into a coherent picture of the world.

So far, then, much of what we've discussed here is reminiscent of Plato, but Descartes's theory has the advantage of keeping the number of innate ideas down to a manageable handful. (Up to this point, we have only "self," "identity," and "substance.") For Plato, there seemed to be as many innate ideas as there were words, and that view is a bit implausible. But remember, in Descartes's system, before any innate idea can be accepted as true, it will have to be established that it was not placed there by the evil genius.

Now we are going to proceed with the construction of Descartes's house of knowledge, but we are going to speed things up quite a bit. One reason we are going to do so is that this chapter is about the rationalistic conception of knowledge, and we have already discovered its essence in our discussion of Plato's Simile of the Line and of Descartes's quest for the foundation of knowledge. The other reason is that it is generally thought that Descartes's upward building is not as tight as his argument leading down to his foundation.

So, Descartes knows that he is still operating in the shadow of an evil genius and that before he can progress, he must dispose of the demon. There is only one way to do this, according to Descartes, and that is by proving the existence of God, because the concept of God as an all-powerful, all-knowing, all-good creator of the universe is logically incompatible with the concept of an evil genius. Either God or the evil genius could exist but not both. So if Descartes can prove God's existence, he will have disproved the existence of an evil genius. Descartes's proof will have to be strictly a priori because no observation can be trusted. It will have to be absolutely certain and rest firmly on the foundation of the "cogito." Perhaps the simplest version of Descartes's first argument

Operating in the Shadow of the Evil Genius

(he has a number of them) is the one based on the concept of perfection. Rather than quoting it at length, I will formalize it in a series of six steps:

1. A being that doubts is an imperfect being (because a perfect being would have full knowledge, hence no room for doubt).

2. I doubt; therefore, I am an imperfect being.
3. Yet I could know that I am imperfect only by having the concept of perfection; therefore, I do have the concept of perfection.
4. I could not have received the concept of perfection from something imperfect; therefore, my concept was not derived from myself.
5. Therefore, my concept of perfection was derived from something that is in fact perfect.
6. Only God is in fact perfect, so I derived my concept of perfection from him, and therefore he exists.

I have corns, therefore I am imperfect, therefore God exists.

Do you find this argument convincing? (If not, perhaps you would be more convinced by Descartes's second argument, to be discussed in Chapter 5. You may want to jump ahead and look at it.) Here Descartes's "proof" will not be criticized. We will let it stand to see what Descartes does with it.

If Descartes has really proved the existence of God, then he has, by his

Variation on a Cartesian Theme

reckoning, eliminated the evil genius. If he has eliminated the evil genius, then mathematics is valid (because the only argument against math was derived from the possibility of an evil genius). Also Descartes now knows that his innate ideas were not placed in him by an evil genius, so they *may* be true as well. Critics of Descartes point out a form of circular reasoning to which he has resorted to solve his problem. To escape from the evil genius, Descartes must prove the existence of God. To do so, he has constructed an argument employing the principles of logic. But these principles are mathematical in nature, so Descartes has used mathematical principles to justify the validity of mathematical principles. This argument has been dubbed by Descartes's critics as "the Cartesian circle." This is possibly a fatal error on Descartes's part, because if he is disallowed from using logic in his argument, the evil genius might be controlling his every move. However, having pointed this out, I suggest we let him get away with it just to see where his argument means to take us. At this point, Descartes remains in a nearly **solipsistic** universe. That is, with the exception of his knowledge of God, Descartes does not know if anything other

Descartes in His Solipsistic Universe

than his own mind exists. He does not even know if he has a body. So his next task will be to determine whether an external world exists, and his final epistemological task will be to determine what knowledge we can have of such a world.

First, Descartes notes that we have two sources for our idea of material objects. One source is a mathematical idea (i.e., one involving measurable objects). This idea is of something extended in three dimensions, having size, shape, part, and location. These are the objects of geometry. The other source, coming from the senses rather than from the innate ideas of corporeality and math in which geometry is grounded, is perhaps a naive idea of a world populated by physical things such as tables, rocks, and trees (and one's own body). But even if this idea is naive (i.e., not

The Idea That One Has a Body Is a Compelling Idea

philosophically sophisticated), it is nevertheless *compelling*. It can be doubted "methodologically" but not *really*. Now, *could* I be wrong about these ideas? In spite of the compelling nature of my idea of the existence of an external world, is it possible that there is in fact nothing "out there"? No! Because God

> has given me no faculty to recognize that this is the case, but on the other hand, a very great inclination to believe . . . that [my ideas of the corporeal world] are conveyed to me by corporeal objects, [so] I do not see how He could be defended from the accusation of deceit if these ideas were produced by causes other than corporeal objects. Hence we must allow that corporeal things exist. (p. 215)

So we know there is a physical world because if there is not, God is a deceiver, which is impossible. We can now complete the diagram we started on page 59 and continued on pages 61 and 62, and say that Descartes's finished system looks like this:

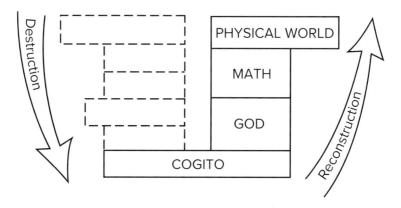

But what is the nature of these corporeal objects that make up the physical world? According to Descartes:

> Corporeal things exist. However, they are perhaps not exactly what we perceive by the senses since this comprehension by the senses is in many instances very obscure and confused, but we must at least admit that all things which I conceive in them clearly and distinctly, that is to say, all things which, speaking generally, are comprehended in the object of pure mathematics, are truly to be recognized as in the objects.
> As to other things, however, . . . for example, [the fact] that the sun is of such and such a figure, etc., or . . . [perceptions of] light, sound, pain and the like, . . . they are very dubious and uncertain . . . and . . . it may easily happen that these judgments contain some error. Take, for example, the opinion . . . that in a body which is warm there is something entirely similar to the idea of heat which is in me; that in a white or green body there is the same whiteness or greenness that I perceive; that in a bitter or sweet

body there is the same taste, and so on in other instances; that the stars, the towers, and all other distant bodies are of the same figure and size as they appear from far off to our eyes, etc. (pp. 215–217)

The upshot of Descartes's conclusion is the following: the physical world that we know as philosopher-scientists is not the world of appearance, the world presented to us by the senses. It is the world as known by mathematical physics. It is, after all, the world as revealed to us by the new sciences— the world of Galileo. The senses continue to be permanent deceivers. They tell us that bodies contain colors, sounds, odors, tastes, and sensations of heat and cold. But in fact, what exists "out there" is whatever math can measure: extension, size, shape, part, location, and moveability—mass in motion, configurations of matter, light waves, and sound waves, but *no* colors, sounds, and tastes. *These* exist only in our sensations as subjective states and not as objective reality.

The Flag's Colors Exist
in Here

The Flag's Molecular Structure
Exists out Here

So, the world we lost is not the world we regained. But at least there is certain knowledge, and the world has been made manageable again. The center, which seemed to wobble, now holds.

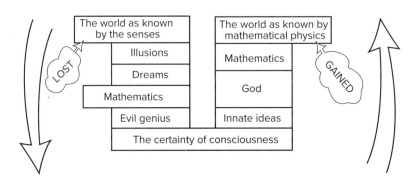

We will speak more about the nature of the Cartesian world in Chapter 4. Here we will take note only of Descartes's success in creating a philosophical–theological compromise. We get both Galileo and God in this system. Not only are Galileo's world and God both *knowable,* but both are also *necessary.* In fact, science rests on a godly foundation. However, the soul (i.e., the self) is not the subject of science because science can know only that which can be measured, and the soul cannot be measured. But it can be known immediately to itself. In truth, the self knows itself before it knows the world. So Descartes leaves our souls to ourselves (perhaps to be shepherded by the Church), and he leaves the physical world (Jupiter's moons included) to the scientists.

The Compatibility of God and Galileo

Despite their historical differences, the epistemologies of Plato and Descartes are similar. Both repudiate the senses as sources of true knowledge. Both find that there is an intelligible order behind the flux of appearance (the center *does* hold). Both conclude that true knowledge must be a priori. Both use mathematics as their model of knowledge. Both derive knowledge of the world from knowledge of a higher reality (the Good for Plato, God for Descartes). Both find the source of all knowledge in innate ideas located in the soul. These points sum up the epistemological program of classical rationalism.

In Chapter 3, you will study rationalism's traditional alternative, empiricism. I will defer until the end of that chapter a brief discussion bringing you up-to-date on what's going on with the rationalist and empiricist schools in the twenty-first century.

Topics for Consideration

1. Pick a general idea (like "gravity" or "justice") and show how it should be analyzed according to Plato's Simile of the Line.
2. Explain Socrates's claim of ignorance (treated in Chapter 1) in terms of Plato's Simile of the Line. If Plato's account of knowledge is right, then are we *all* ignorant?
3. Write a short story in which a young student discovers that Plato was right and discovers that behind the world of apparent change and flux, there is an unchanging world of eternal sameness.
4. State at least three reasons why Descartes thinks that the senses cannot provide certain knowledge. Then, compare Descartes's attitude toward the senses with that of Plato.
5. Descartes asks, "Am I so dependent on body and senses that I cannot exist without them?" Contrast the answer Descartes gives to his question with the answers given by common sense and science.
6. State as clearly as you can what you take to be Descartes's argument proving that there must be "innate ideas."
7. Some of Descartes's critics have argued that if you start with Descartes's foundation (you are certain only of the contents of your own consciousness), you will never escape from solipsism (the view that there can never be knowledge of anything but one's own mind). Show what those critics might mean by this argument.
8. Write an essay called "Descartes's Flirtation with Madness."

Suggestions for Further Reading: Paperback Editions

Susan R. Bordo, *The Flight into Objectivity: Essays on Cartesianism and Culture* (Albany: State University of New York Press, 1987). An exciting feminist critique of Descartes's philosophy and the worldview it supports.

Plato, "Meno," in *Great Dialogues of Plato*, ed. Eric H. Warmington and Philip G. Rouse, trans. W. H. D. Rouse (New York: New American Library, 1956). Plato's discussion of knowledge as recovered memory and an excellent example of a Socratic dialogue.

Plato, "Republic," in *Great Dialogues of Plato*, ed. Eric H. Warmington and Philip G. Rouse, trans. W. H. D. Rouse (New York: New American Library, 1956). Books VI and VII contain Plato's account of the Simile of the Line. Difficult reading but manageable after you've come as far as you have now come.

The Rationalists: Descartes, Spinoza, Leibniz, trans. J. Veitch, R. Elwes, and G. Montgomery (New York: Doubleday, 1974). The basic works of these philosophers in an inexpensive volume.

Bernard Williams, *Descartes: The Project of Pure Enquiry* (Middlesex, England: Pelican Books, 1978). An insightful analysis by an important twentieth-century philosopher.

Notes

1. I borrowed this thought not from Plato but from the last line of a famous poem by John Keats, "Ode on a Grecian Urn": "Beauty is truth, truth beauty,–that is all/Ye know on earth, and all ye need to know." Critics argue as to whether Keats is praising Plato in this poem, or mocking him.

2. There has been much scholarly debate concerning the best English translation of the Greek terms Plato uses in the Simile of the Line. Here is a transcription of the Greek words in question:

   (1) *noesis*   (2) *eide*

   (3) *dianoia*   (4) *hypothemenoi* and *ta mathematica*

   (5) *pistis*   (6) *ta horomeva*

   (7) *eikasia*   (8) *eikones*

   In designating (1) *noesis* as "reason" and (3) *dianoia* as "understanding," I am following the translations of both W. H. D. Rouse and Leo Rauch. But it should be mentioned that *noesis* has also been rendered as "understanding" (by G. M. A. Grube), as "knowledge" (by G. L. Abernathy and T. L. Langford), and as "intellection" (by Allan Bloom). *Dianoia* has been translated as "reasoning" (by Grube), as "thinking" (by Abernathy and Langford), and as "thought" (by Bloom). I have opted for Rouse's and Rauch's translation of *noesis* as "reason" because doing so best reveals the continuity between Plato and the later Western metaphysical tradition through Hegel and Kant. I have chosen to call (4) "scientific concepts." Plato gives us two Greek terms for that slot, *hypothemenoi* and *ta mathematica*. Many choose the second, "mathematical objects," as the key phrase here—and it is true that Socrates uses examples from arithmetic and geometry to explain this concept. I have selected "scientific concepts" because this category includes mathematical ideas but in fact encompasses more. I believe Plato did not mean to restrict *hypothemenoi* (literally "assumptions" or "postulates") to mathematical ideas. M. E. Taylor warns us against being misled by Plato's mathematical language here. He says that Plato "had before him no other examples of systematic and organized knowledge" than "the various branches of mathematics as recognized in the fifth century" (M. E. Taylor, *Plato: The Man and His Work* [New York: Meridian Books, 1960], p. 289). Plato is referring to organized conceptual knowledge, that is, roughly what today we would call scientific concepts. According to Plato, they are inferior to Forms both because they are copies (imitations, "shadows," "reflections") of the Forms and because the individual thinkers still depend on visual imagery when they operate at this level. In this sense, the Forms and not the concepts are mathematical, because Forms are image-free.

3. Edmund Gettier, "Is Justified True Belief Knowledge?" *Analysis*, Vol. 23. No. 6 (Jun., 1963), pp. 121–123. Available at http://www.ditext.com/gettier/gettier.html.

4. One book challenges the traditional interpretation somewhat. See Pietro Redondi, *Galileo Heretic,* trans. Raymond Rosenthal (Princeton, NJ: Princeton University Press, 1988).

5. René Descartes, *Essential Works of Descartes,* trans. Lowell Blair (New York: Bantam Books, 1966), p. x.

6. René Descartes, "Meditations on First Philosophy," in *The Essential Descartes,* ed. Margaret D. Wilson, trans. Elizabeth S. Haldane and G. R. T. Ross (New York: New American Library, 1969), pp. 165–166. Unless otherwise stated, all subsequent quotes from Descartes in this chapter are from this source, and page numbers of future quotations from this book will be included in the text.

3

What You See
Is What You Get
Empiricist Epistemology

The opposite extreme from rationalism is empiricism. According to empiricism, the true foundations of knowledge are found not in "reason" but in observation, that is, in the data provided by the five senses.

We can find a rudimentary version of empiricism in the philosophy of ARISTOTLE (384–322 B.C.E.), a student of Plato. But despite Aristotle's rejection of Plato's disdain for sensory observation and Aristotle's attempt to bring Plato's metaphysics and epistemology back down to earth, Aristotle is still too much under the sway of his teacher to be thought of as a real empiricist. To find this epistemological theory in its true habitat, we must fast-forward to eighteenth-century Britain.

Bringing Plato Back Down to Earth

The Empiricism of John Locke

In the same way that rationalism found its first modern expression in the work of René Descartes, the first modern statement of empiricism appears in the work of the English physician JOHN LOCKE (1632–1704). Locke's main thesis is set forth in the following passage:

75

Let us suppose the mind to be, as we say, a blank slate (**tabula rasa**) of white paper, void of all characters, without any ideas; how comes it to be furnished? Whence comes it by that vast store, which the busy and boundless fancy of man has painted on it with almost endless variety? Whence has it all the materials of reason and knowledge? To this I answer in one word, from **experience**: in that all our knowledge is founded, and from that it ultimately derives itself.[1]

John Locke (1632–1704)

Locke had read Descartes's work, and he knew that in order to establish the theory of the mind as a "blank slate," he would have to refute the rationalists' contention that knowledge is based on innate ideas. About this Locke says:

The way shown how we come by any knowledge, sufficient to prove it not innate.—It is an established opinion among some men that there are in the understanding certain innate principles; some primary notions, . . . characters, as it were, stamped upon the mind of man which the soul receives in its very first being and brings into the world with it. It would be sufficient to convince unprejudiced readers of the falseness of this supposition, if I should only show (as I hope I shall in the following parts of this discourse) how men, barely by the use of their natural faculties, may attain to all the knowledge they have, without the help of any innate impressions, and may arrive at certainty, without any such original notions or principles. (bk. I, chap. II, sec. 1)

Locke is here appealing to a principle that would become dear to empiricism, what is known as **Ockham's razor.** William of Ockham (or Occam), a fourteenth-century Christian philosopher, one with rather radical propensities, set forth as a principle of economy the following thesis, "What can be done with fewer [terms] is done in vain with more." This simple principle sounds like something your English instructor might write in the margin of your essay, but William meant it as more than just a stylistic recommendation. (And indeed, William's principle got him into trouble with the ecclesiastical authorities, who suspected that Ockham was trying to shave off the doctrine of the trinity on the grounds that *one* divine entity is simpler than *three*.) William's point has been restated in modern terms in the

Ockham Wielding Razor

following way, "Do not multiply entities beyond necessity." That is to say, given two theories, both of which are compatible with all the observable data and both of which purport to explain the same phenomena, the *preferable* theory is the one with the fewer theoretical entities.

Let's consider a historical example to explain Ockham's razor. Even before telescopes were first trained on the sky in the seventeenth century, it was noticed that certain heavenly bodies seemed not simply to be traveling in a consistent orbit but to stop suddenly, back up, and then lurch forward. This discovery was startling—even embarrassing—because people were used to thinking of the movements of the heavenly bodies as exemplars of God's geometrical genius. Some scientific account was needed to "save the appearances." It came about in the theory of epicycles. According to this hypothesis, some heavenly bodies moved around the earth like this: In this case, from the perspective of the earth, these bodies would *appear* to be stopping, moving backward, then moving ahead. So, indeed, the appearances had been saved along with God's geometrical genius. (Now Heaven's architect was still a mathematical wizard—even though his tastes did run a bit to the baroque.) But then, as telescopes got better, a new embarrassment came to light. Not only did these epicycling bodies seem to stop, move backward, then start forward again, but they also appeared to stop, *wiggle* backward, then *wiggle* forward again. This problem was solved by putting epicycles on the epicycles. Now the Great Architect had become positively rococo. Appearances had been saved but at what cost? This whole structure had now become so top-heavy that, obviously, it would soon come crashing down. The explanation was crying out for Ockham's razor to come along and shave off the extra weight.

The razor appeared in the form of the theory of planetary motion created by Johannes Kepler (1571–1630), who modified the heliocentric theory of Copernicus (1473–1543) by suggesting that the earth does indeed travel around the sun but not in a circle, rather in an ellipse and in such a way that "equal areas are swept in equal times." Then, the *apparent* retrograde motion of some heavenly bodies would be explained by the speeding up and slowing down of the earth in its elliptical orbit. And what if the little wiggly movements are the result of the aberration caused by looking back through our own atmosphere? So much for the epicycles and epicycles on the epicycles. Kepler's theory is simpler. It has fewer entities. It represents a triumph of Ockham's razor.

The System of Epicycles Comes Crashing Down

Now perhaps you can see what Locke hoped to accomplish. He hoped to do to "innate ideas" what Kepler had done to epicycles. He also wanted to do the same to Platonic Forms. A theory in which *only particulars exist* would be simpler than one in which there existed particulars *and* abstractions. Locke believed that with the simple image of the "blank slate," he could account for all possible knowledge. He began with several sets of distinctions, one between simple and complex ideas, another between particular and general ideas, and a third between primary and secondary qualities.

Simple and Complex Ideas

Simple ideas are those that cannot be further analyzed into simpler components, for example, the idea of "solidity" (if someone doesn't understand this idea, you take him by the wrist and press his hand against a wall) or the idea of "yellow" (the person who doesn't understand this idea must be shown a ripe banana or a canary). These ideas usually come in through one sense, though some of them, such as the idea of "motion," can be derived from either the sense of touch or the sense of sight.

Complex ideas are (1) compounds of simple ideas (e.g., "beauty," "gratitude," "a man," "an army," "the universe"), (2) ideas of relations (larger than, smaller than) created by setting two ideas next to each other and comparing or contrasting them, or (3) abstractions, wherein the mind separates out a feature of an idea and generalizes it (e.g., blueness). Abstractions are formed when we recognize a certain characteristic that a group of objects has in common. That characteristic is assigned a name, which is a symbol for that characteristic. This theory has traditionally been called **conceptualism.** Locke's view is that the rationalists had confused these "abstract

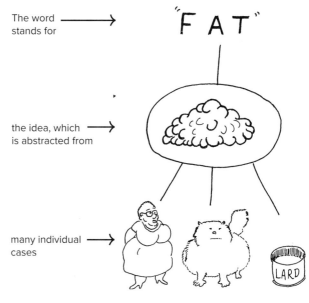

The word ——→ stands for

"FAT"

the idea, which ——→ is abstracted from

many individual ——→ cases

Locke's Conceptualism

general ideas" with actual existing entities (Platonic Forms) or with innate ideas. (For their part, the rationalists were quick to charge Locke with presupposing the truth of the very thing he thought he was refuting. They asked how the mind can *recognize* a characteristic that a number of objects have in common unless the mind already has the concept of "sameness.")

Primary and Secondary Qualities

Locke's distinction between primary and secondary qualities had been popularized by both Descartes and Galileo. **Primary qualities** were said by Locke to be characteristics that necessarily inhered in material bodies. They comprised "solidity, extension, figure, motion or rest, and number." **Secondary qualities** were defined as "such qualities, which in truth are nothing in the objects themselves but powers to produce various sensations in us by their primary qualities, that is, by the bulk, figure, texture, and motion of their insensible parts, as colours, sounds, tastes, etc." (bk. II, chap. VIII, sec. 10).

Now, our *ideas* of primary qualities are, according to Locke, *correct* ideas. That is, these ideas are caused in our minds by those qualities, and these ideas correctly represent those qualities. On the other hand, the ideas we have of secondary qualities do not correctly represent the world. Locke says, "The ideas of primary qualities of bodies are resemblances of them, and their patterns do really exist in the bodies themselves; but the ideas produced in us by these secondary qualities have no resemblance of them at all. There is nothing like our ideas existing in the bodies

SECONDARY QUALITIES
(colors, sounds, tastes, odors,
tactile sensations)
EXIST IN HERE

PRIMARY QUALITIES
(extension, size, shape,
location, motion/rest)
EXIST OUT THERE.

themselves." (bk. II, chap. VIII, sec. 15). This epistemological view is now known as **representative realism.** It is a version of *realism* because it holds that there really is a real world "out there." It is *representative* realism because, according to this view, the mind does not give us direct access to reality; rather, it represents reality much in the way that a photograph does. And just as some characteristics of a photo correctly represent the world (e.g., number, shape, relative size, etc.), so do some features of the mind correctly represent the world (these are our ideas of primary qualities). And just as some characteristics of a photo are purely features of the photo (e.g., its black and white presentation, its two-dimensionality, its glossiness and portableness, and the like), so do some features of the mind pertain only to the mind and not to the world (these are our ideas of secondary qualities).

This is a picture of you!

But I'm not flat, glossy, black and white, three inches tall with a white border around my head!!

Substance

Now, with these tools in hand, Locke believed he had refuted Descartes because he thought he had given a complete account of knowledge using a theory simpler than that of Descartes. But perhaps things aren't that simple, as we see when we turn to Locke's account of the key philosophical category, substance (borrowed, at a distance, from Descartes, who borrowed from Aristotle).

Our Obscure Idea of Substance in General. So that if anyone will examine himself concerning his notion of pure substance in general, he will find he has no other idea of it at all, but only a supposition of he knows not what support of such qualities that are capable of producing simple ideas in us. . . . If anyone should be asked, "What is the subject wherein colour or weight inheres?" he would have nothing to say but, "The solid extended parts." And if he were demanded, "What is it that solidity and extension inhere in?" he would not be in much better case than the Indian . . . , who, saying that the world was supported by a great elephant, was asked what the elephant rested on? to which his answer was, "A great tortoise"; but being again pressed to know what gave support to the broad-backed tortoise, replied—something he knew not what. (bk. II, chap. XXIII, sec. 2)

Locke's rather cavalier account of substance is devastating to his own project, though he didn't seem to realize it. Once you buy into the metaphysics of substance, as both he and Descartes had done (i.e., once you accept the view that, given anything in the world, it is either a substance or a characteristic of a substance), then you'd better be prepared to render a coherent account of *substance*. Remember in the wax example it was precisely Descartes's inability to come up with an *empirical* account of "substance" and "identity" that allowed him to posit innate ideas. Now Locke has claimed he can get rid of innate ideas by using Ockham's razor; yet when he turns to that key ontological category, substance, he says it is a "something I know not what." Locke's confusion could be the beginning of the end either of empiricism or of the metaphysics of substance. We shall soon see that it is the latter.

The Beginning of the End of Substance

Berkeley's Correction of Locke

Locke's empiricist successor, GEORGE BERKELEY (1685–1753), a Northern Irishman who became a bishop in the Church of England, saw Locke's errors clearly and thought they could be corrected simply by a more vigorous application of Ockham's razor—

George Berkeley (1685–1753)

this time, to the notion of material substance itself. Locke had written, "Since the mind, in all its thoughts and reasonings, hath no other immediate object but its own ideas, which it alone does or can contemplate, it is evident that our knowledge is only conversant about them." (bk. IV, chap. I, sec. 1). Berkeley immediately realized that if this statement was literally true, then it is impossible to know something that is not an idea. But Locke, perhaps contradicting himself, had claimed that we *know* that many of these ideas are caused by real things in the physical world (material substances) and particularly by their primary qualities, which have powers to produce the ideas of both primary and secondary qualities in our minds.

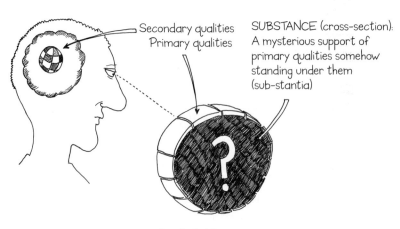

Secondary qualities
Primary qualities

SUBSTANCE (cross-section):
A mysterious support of primary qualities somehow standing under them (sub-stantia)

Locke's View

Sense Data

One of Berkeley's first tasks would be to demonstrate Locke's self-contradiction by undoing the primary–secondary quality distinction. Berkeley argued that primary qualities and secondary qualities really are the same thing. For instance, Locke supposed "size" and "shape" to be primary qualities. How does one establish the size and shape of a table except by looking at it or feeling it? The first act produces the secondary qualities of color, and the second act produces the secondary qualities of tactile sensation (hard, smooth, etc.). I know the size and shape of the brown table by contrasting the brown of the table against the white of the wall and the green of the rug or by running my hand along its surface and noting where the sensations of smoothness and resistance end. In other words, our ideas of primary qualities are really nothing but interpretations of secondary qualities. In fact, for Berkeley, all of our ideas (except for our idea of "self,"

The Collapsing of the Primary-Secondary Quality Distinction

which is known in a Cartesian manner and, as we shall see, our idea of "God") are nothing but our ideas of secondary qualities or interpretations of them. In *A Treatise Concerning the Principles of Human Knowledge,* Berkeley wrote:

> It is evident to anyone who takes a survey of the *objects of human knowledge,* that they are either *ideas* actually imprinted on the senses, or else such as are perceived by attending to the passions and operations of the mind; or lastly, *ideas* formed by help of memory and imagination, either compounding, dividing, or barely representing those originally perceived in the aforesaid ways. By sight I have the ideas of light and colours with their several degrees and variations. By touch I perceive hard and soft, heat and cold, motion and resistance . . . , smelling furnishes me with odours; the palate with tastes; and hearing conveys sounds to the mind in all their variety of tone and composition. And as several of these are observed to accompany each other, they come to be marked by one name, and so to be reputed as one *thing.* Thus, for example, a certain colour, taste, smell, figure, and consistence having been observed to go together are accounted one distinct thing, signified by the name "apple"; other collections of ideas constitute a stone,

a tree, a book, and the Like sensible things; which, as they are pleasing or disagreeable, excite the passions of love, hatred, joy, grief, and so forth.[2]

Almost the whole of Berkeley's theory is encapsulated in this remarkable passage. Let's summarize that theory: Like Descartes, Berkeley wants to start with what is *certain,* with what we can call "the given," and for him, "the given" is what earlier philosophers designated as "ideas of secondary qualities" and what he simply calls "ideas" or "sensations." (We will call them **sense data** from now on.) Babies come into the world, and they are "given" sense data: colors, sounds, tastes, odors, and "feelies" (tactile sensations). These data do not constitute a world for the baby; rather, they comprise a chaos of fluctuating sensations. (Actually, they constitute *five* chaotic worlds.) But slowly the child

The Newborn Infant Confronts "the Given"

learns to "read" these data, very much the way we learn to read script as children. The baby does this by beginning to notice patterns in the appearance of these data (the rationalist, of course, asks how the baby *recognizes* these patterns without knowing the principle of identity) and by having parents teach the child a language (". . . a certain colour, taste, smell, figure, and consistence having been observed to go together, are accounted one distinct thing, signified by the name 'apple' . . ."). Now, to see how very radical Berkeley's theory is, we have to understand that (1) any given "physical object" in the world is just the *totality of its sense data* and (2) sense data are exclusively mental—they exist only in *minds.* In other words, all so-called physical objects exist only as possible or actual perceptions in consciousness. Berkeley's Latinized motto is "esse is

See Jane, run. Run Jane, run.

Amazing! How does she do it? She must be an absolute genius.

DICK AND JANE HAVE FUN

percipi"—"to be is to be perceived." His philosophy is a version of **idealism,** the prioritizing of the mental world over the physical world, or in his more radical version, the view that *only* the mental world exists. There is no physical world, if that term is meant to denote some unperceived matter that exists independently of consciousness. It is important to recognize, however, that Berkeley is not denying that things like tables, cherries, and mountains exist. Rather, he is trying to prove that the correct analysis of such notions as "the table in the next room" or "the cherry on the tree" or "the mountain beyond the horizon" is carried out exclusively in terms of the memory, the perception, or the prediction of sense data. Do you get it?

Dr. Johnson Refutes
Bishop Berkeley

If you *do* get it, then at this point you may feel that Berkeley's view, reducing everything to mental states (sense data), is far out of touch with common sense. Indeed, you may begin to feel that in this theory, the center of the world does not hold. Certainly, Berkeley's contemporary, Dr. Samuel Johnson, thought so when he tried to refute Berkeley by simply kicking a stone. But this act of Johnson shows a failure to understand Berkeley's theory. He never denied the truth of the sentence, "Kicking rocks hurts." His argument was that the sentence could be analyzed totally in terms of sense data.

Notice that there are two features here in Berkeley's account of how we interpret our sense data, transforming them into a picture of a *world*. First, there is the objective fact that sense data appear in recognizable *patterns* (". . . having been observed to go together . . ."). This is *nature's* role in making interpretation possible because these are *natural* patterns— bright red, yellow, and orange flamelike sense data are associated with heat and pain. Second, there is the fact that language is used to unify these ideas in our minds (". . . signified by the name 'apple' . . ."). This is *convention's* role in making interpretation possible.

What makes Berkeley's theory so modern is the large part he assigns to language in his epistemology. Doing so allows him to account for a fact that modernity had discovered and traditional rationalism could not explain, namely that different people cut up the world so differently (all those stories that you've learned in your anthropology classes). If human conventions—primarily linguistic conventions—can determine which ideas are associated with each other, then this finding can explain quite nicely why Inuits have no word for "snow" in their language but have a number of nouns designating different substances, all of which look like "snow" to us and to the Caucasian Yukon neighbors of the Inuits; and why Spanish speakers think that there are two kinds of "being" (*ser* and *estar*), although English speakers find only one kind.[3] If Descartes's theories of substance and innate ideas were true, we should all see the world identically. Keep in mind, however, that Berkeley's theory is not primarily one about language; it is one about sense data. *Esse* is *percipi;* there are only sense data and interpretations of sense data. Some interpretations are "natural," that is, there is pretty much universal agreement on them (like "pain" and "water"), and some are conventional (perhaps like color words—"purple" and "chartreuse"). Different languages will express these conventional differences differently.

But language does play a big role in Berkeley's epistemology as a bridge of intersubjectivity. This role can be seen in the following consideration: No two people have exactly the same sense data because no two people can share exactly the same geometrical perspective on any object. If thirty people in a room look at a book on a table, each has a slightly different datum in consciousness. In fact, it is logically possible that no two people have the same experience when they use such basic terms as the word "red." But none of this matters practically because even if I see what you call "green" when I look at something "red," we both describe it as being red because we were taught to associate that particular noise

No Two People See Exactly the Same Thing

("rĕd") with that particular experience. So the upshot is that each of us dwells in his or her little solipsistic world of sensorial consciousness, but language allows us to build bridges between those solitary islands.

Language Forms the Bridge of Intersubjectivity

Also, there is a kind of "democratic" element in Berkeley's theory. Our picture of the world (i.e., our interpretation of sense data) is built up not only conventionally but also partly by consensus. All sense data are in some ways qualitatively identical. The sense data that lead the delirious person to say, "There's a pink elephant in this room," are as real as mine are when mine lead me to say, "No, the room is empty." The visual sense data involved in claiming to see a pink elephant should allow us to predict certain tactile sense data from them. The sentence, "There's a pink elephant in the room," entails the prediction, "If you walk twelve steps in that direction, you will be blocked by something whose skin feels hard and rough." Of course, the delirious person may say that she feels that she is blocked by something hard and rough. Or if not, she may reinterpret her sense data, saying, "There's an *intangible* pink elephant in the room." In either of those cases, we call in other perceivers at this point. If thirty-nine people look into the room and all say that the room is empty, and if the fortieth person says that there's a pink elephant there, then the majority wins. Even though all sense data are individually equally existent, what we mean by "*reality*" are those sense data from which we can consensually predict with success the greatest number of other sense data. If there were only one person in the world, then her sense data would be "reality." It turns out, however, that there are more than one. This analysis constitutes Berkeley's solution to the famous problem of the distinction between reality and appearance.

The Source of Sense Data

Now, a typical objection to Berkeley's theory at this point will be this: If there exist only sense data (ideas, sensations), where do these sense data come from? Normally (or at least in the Cartesian–Lockean picture of normality), we would say that they come from material things "out there." But Berkeley has eliminated those "things" with Ockham's razor, so where *do* these sense data come from? Before we make Berkeley answer that

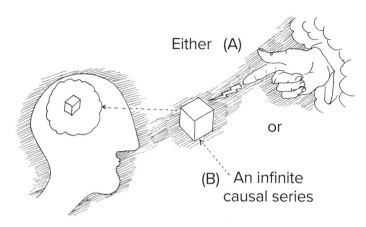

Either **(A)**

or

(B) An infinite causal series

Locke's Version of Causality

question, let's ask Descartes and Locke where *material substances* come from. Sense data are caused by substance, they would say, but what causes substance? Both Descartes and Locke answer, "They come from God." (In fact, the only other obvious answer would seem to be that it comes "from an infinite series of causes"—the table comes from atoms, and the atoms come from the "atomic bake" that took place in the "Big Bang." But where does the stuff that was baked into atoms by the Big Bang come from? Presumably from something yet earlier and so on to infinity.) Now back to Berkeley, by eliminating material substance from this chain of events, he has simply eliminated "the middle person" (formerly "the middleman"). Consequently, he can give exactly the same answer to the question, "Where do sense data come from?" that everybody else gives to the question of where matter comes from: either from God or from an infinite causal series.

Berkeley preferred the first alternative, of course. He was a bishop, after all. In fact, God plays a key role in Berkeley's theory, just as it did in

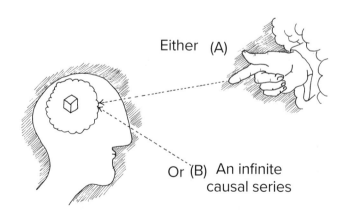

Either **(A)**

Or **(B)** An infinite causal series

Berkeley's Version of Causality

that of Descartes. Without God, the center would not hold. The center *does* hold; therefore, God exists. God is the guarantor of the orderliness of the universe (i.e., the orderliness of sense data). He is the "eternal perceiver" who guarantees by his perpetual vigilance that the room we are in does not flash out of existence when we all leave it. (And if it did flash out of existence, who knows if it would flash back on?) Ronald Knox wrote a lovely limerick to express this point:

There was a young man who said, "God
Must think it exceedingly odd,
If he finds that this tree
Continues to be
When there's no one about
      in the Quad."

Dear Sir:
Your astonishment's odd.
I am always about in the
      Quad.
And that's why the tree
Will continue to be
Since observed by me,
      Yours faithfully,
      GOD

There does seem to be a big problem here, however. How can God exist in a system whose main claim is that *esse* is *percipi* (*to be* is *to be perceived*)? In such a system, it would seem that either God can be perceived (which he can't) or he doesn't exist. Berkeley was obviously troubled by this dilemma and hoped he could escape it by calling our thought of God a "notion" rather than an "idea." But very few critics have accepted Berkeley's semantic solution. Indeed, Berkeley has the same problem with the idea of selfhood that he has with the idea of God. He writes:

But, besides all that endless variety of ideas or objects of knowledge, there is likewise something which knows or perceives them; and exercises diverse operations, as willing, imagining, remembering about them. This perceiving, active being is what I call mind, spirit, soul, or myself.[4]

He admits that this "something" cannot be perceived. He does this in the same paragraph in which he states, "The existence of an idea consists in being perceived." It's as if Berkeley's (and Descartes's) two favorite terms, "God" and "self," designate nonexisting categories. As you will see momentarily, the next empiricist, David Hume, will carry Berkeley's admission to its logical conclusion.

Hume's Radicalization of Berkeley's Empiricism

The third of the three classical empiricists was DAVID HUME (1711–1776), who became a librarian at the University of Edinburgh in his native Scotland but who, despite his early brilliance, was never offered the professorial chair for which he hoped. (He was one of those annoying teenagers who had figured out many of his best ideas by the time he was nineteen years old.)

Hume was committed to the general tenets of empiricism ("blank slate" theory, adoption of Ockham's razor, denial of innate ideas, and the view that all knowledge derives from sense data), but he thought that neither Locke nor Berkeley had been consistent in applying them.

Perhaps the best way of scrutinizing Hume's view is to begin with his distinction between two kinds of sentences: those that express "relations of ideas" and those that express "matters of fact." (Later philosophers have preferred the terminology invented in the next century by Immanuel Kant and called these two categories "analytic" and "synthetic," respectively. We will follow that custom here.)

David Hume (1711–1776)

Analytic propositions ("relations of ideas") have the following characteristics:

A. Their negation leads to a self-contradiction.
B. They are a priori.

C. They are true by definition.

D. They are necessarily true.

Take, for example, the sentence, "All triangles have three angles."

A. If you deny it ("*Not* all triangles have three angles"), you say something not merely *false* but something *self-contradictory,* because any figure that does not have three angles is *not* a triangle.

B. The sentence is a priori. You don't discover its truth by looking anywhere or by counting angles. You understand its truth by contemplating its meaning.

C. The sentence is true by definition. That is, given the definition of a triangle as "a three-sided closed figure," it follows that a triangle *must* have three (and only three) angles. (Another way of saying that a sentence is true by definition is to say that it expresses a **conceptual truth,** because the concept of triangularity logically entails the idea of three angles.)

D. The sentence is *necessarily* true. It *can't* be false given the current conventions of the English language.

So far, all these characteristics sound like a rationalist's delight. *But* Hume adds another characteristic of analytic sentences:

E. *They are all tautologies.* That is, they are redundant and repetitious. The predicate (e.g., "has three angles") only repeats what was already in the subject (e.g., "A triangle").

So even though there is a priori knowledge, it is never about anything but itself. A priori truths can never tell us about reality, so the rationalistic dream of a deductive system of knowledge composed of purely a priori truths is a phantom. (Basically, analytic truths comprise definitions, parts of definitions, mathematics, and logic. They are all true but only show how we can relate ideas to each other: "A = A," "2 + 3 = 5," "brothers are males.")

Synthetic propositions ("matters of fact") are the opposites of analytic propositions on all counts. They must be derived from sense data (Locke's "secondary qualities," Berkeley's "ideas" and "sensations"). To find out whether a sentence like "Jill has a brown dog" is meaningful, we have to ask ourselves whether the key ideas could be traced back to simple perceptions. In fact, our sentence *can* be traced back to sense perceptions. At least we know what it would be like to do so. (It may turn out that Jill's dog is green or that she has no dog at all [one of the features of synthetic propositions is that they are not necessarily true], but we know what it would be like to find out.)

A Priori Thought Misplaced

Now, according to Hume, analytic and synthetic propositions are the only possible kinds of meaning in a truly empiricist program. Any sentence that is neither analytic (not a tautology) nor synthetic (its ideas can't be traced to sense perceptions) is nonsense—period!

So much for Berkeley's God! The sentence "God exists" when negated ("God does not exist") does not produce a self-contradiction. (See Chapter 5 for St. Anselm's view to the contrary.) And the *idea* of God cannot be traced back to sense data. It is literally *nonsense*. Ockham's razor slashes again!

But Berkeley had argued that without the idea (or "notion") of God, we could not explain what makes the center hold—how could there be any consistency in reality (i.e., in the appearance of sense data)? Well, Hume had to admit that on purely empirical grounds it would be hard to answer that question. This difficulty is because Hume assumed that it is not God but universal causality that holds things together, and there is no sense datum to which we can trace the idea of a cause. That is, no perceptual difference exists between causality and repeated seriality. (The sentences "X causes Y" and "First X happens, then Y happens" are confirmed by exactly the same sense data, yet they seem to have very

Finding Out the Hard Way That Jill Has a Dog (A Posteriori Proof)

different meanings.) Hume does not seem to have seriously doubted that there are causal relations among objects in the world (i.e., using Hume's terminology, that there are "necessary connections" between events in the world), but he admits that he is unable to provide a rational justification of his commonsense belief in causality. Even this much of a concession is bad news for his empiricism. There are hints of a suspicion that, after all, the center does not hold or at least that the belief that it *does* hold is irrational. (Søren Kierkegaard, the founder of existentialism, was a close reader of Hume, and it has been said that Friedrich Nietzsche, another early existentialist, was the first to feel in his bones what Hume only experienced intellectually. We will run into Kierkegaard and Nietzsche later.)

What about Descartes's absolutely certain idea of the self—an idea that neither Locke nor Berkeley felt the need to criticize? Hume was as skeptical of that idea as he was of the ideas of "innate knowledge" and of "God" and "causality." In his *Treatise of Human Nature* (1738), he wrote:

> There are some philosophers who imagine we are every moment intimately conscious of what we call our *self*; that we feel its existence and

its continuance in existence; and are certain, beyond the evidence of a demonstration, both of its perfect identity and simplicity. . . . For my part, when I enter most intimately into what I call *myself*, I always stumble on some particular perception or other, of heat or cold, light or shade, love or hatred, pain or pleasure. I never can catch *myself* at any time without a perception, and never can observe anything but the perception. . . . But setting aside some metaphysicians of this kind, I may venture to affirm of the rest of mankind that they are nothing but a bundle or collection of different perceptions, which succeed each other with an inconceivable rapidity and are in a perpetual flux and movement. Our eyes cannot turn in their sockets without varying our perceptions. Our thought is still more variable than our sight; and all our other senses and faculties contribute to this change; nor is there any single power of the soul which remains unalterably the same, perhaps for one moment.[5]

Nooo. Not the self! Don't take that too!

Hume Discovers the
Self—Such As It Is

This is an amazing passage. The self—the foundation of certainty and the centerpiece of Cartesian rationalism—is an empty idea (". . . consequently, there is no such idea" [p. 252]). There is no experiential continuity of selfhood. In fact, there is no experience of selfhood at all. According to Hume, this discovery is so repugnant to us mortals that "we feign [its] continued existence . . . and run into the notion of a *soul*, and *self*, and *substance*, to disguise the variation" (p. 254). This discovery cuts to the heart not only of the philosophy of rationalism, but also of Western religion and of common sense itself.

So Hume's radical empiricism could find no justification for the concepts of "God," "causality," or "selfhood." In fact, his view led to a **skepticism** so deep that it seemed to be untenable. Upon reading Hume, it is as if we feel the ground begins to slide beneath our feet. The center begins to give. Yet, in the twentieth century, a group of influential philosophers adopted his views with only minor modifications. Their ideas came to be known as **logical empiricism** or **logical positivism.**

Logical Positivism: The Further Radicalization of Empiricism

The logical positivists—some of whom preferred the name of logical empiricists—were a bunch of hard-nosed, scientific-minded philosophers who formulated their original position at the University of Vienna in the early 1920s. There, a small group of philosophers calling themselves "the Vienna Circle" was led by Professor Moritz Schlick. The positivists agreed with Hume that math and logic are tautological but appreciated the analytic power of math and logic more deeply than did Hume, and in fact, most of their work was in the logical analysis of the propositions of science and so-called common sense. They agreed roughly with Hume about causality but solved his problem by redefining the idea. "Causality" no longer named some mysterious necessary connection between events; instead, they suggested "X causes Y" simply predicts the occurrence of Y after the occurrence of X. That is, they decided that "causality" is after all nothing but "repeated seriality." They solved Locke's problem of "substance" ("thingness") in a similar way. To say "There is a table in room 506" is a way of making predictions about future sense data. It means, "*If* you went into room 506, *then* you would have the following sense data: brown, rectangular, resistant, etc., etc." By claiming that the meaning of a declarative sentence can be correctly analyzed by translating it into an if-then hypothesis—where the *if* clause contains an action ("If you went into room 506, . . .") and the *then* clause contains a prediction of sense data ("then you would have the following sense data . . .")—the positivists totally bypass the problem of the table that flashes on and off. A table just is, to use the phrase of John Stuart Mill, "a permanent possibility of sensation."

Hume Hanging Out in a Pool Hall
Studying Causality

The positivists had great difficulty with the *idealistic* implications of Berkeley's and Hume's versions of empiricism. (Idealism is the view that the only things we can know to exist are *ideas*.) Because both Berkeley and Hume thought that only sense data can be known and believed that sense data were mental, they seemed to be idealists. The logical positivists believed that idealism was both too metaphysical and not scientific enough. Their solution was to adopt a version of *neutral* **monism,** the view that reality (in this case, sense data) is neither mental nor physical; rather, it is some third kind of unanalyzable, neutral "stuff." According to the positivists, the categories "mental" and "physical" are simply **logical constructs** that are interpretations of sense data from different perspectives. We call "material" those sense data that we can categorize in terms of concepts like dimensionality, size, and shape; and we call "mental" those that somehow escape those categories. If the empirical facts about sense data were slightly different, perhaps we would draw the boundaries of these categories differently. For example, if every time people entered room 506 they immediately got a headache, we might talk about headaches differently, warning folks to avoid that room because it contained a headache. We would thereby be placing headaches in the category of the physical instead of the mental. So headaches, tables, mountains, rainbows, sandstorms, and acts of revenge are "logical constructs"; that is, they are conceptual organizations of sense data in ways that allow for objective analysis of them and communication about them. This view is not so far from that of Berkeley, after all, but it robs him of both his idealism and his theism.

The positivists were impressed by Hume's empiricist critique of the concept of selfhood, and they took the heroic step of declaring that other people are also merely "logical constructs." In other words, you are my sense data (sounds like the title of a positivistic country and Western song, though perhaps not a very romantic one). Or, at least, you are constructed out of my sense data. The technique of reducing selfhood to categories of observable data bypasses the need for any theory of consciousness and, indeed, for any psychology at all. In other words, the positivists became

radical **behaviorists** about everyone but themselves, and they
even attempted a behavioristic
account of themselves, that is, of
the self in the first person. (We
will return to the idea of behaviorism shortly.)

Finally, the logical empiricists introduced a category called
theoretical entities. This notion
was meant to account for such
items as atoms and electrons,
whose esse is clearly not *percipi*
because they can't be perceived
at all. Theoretical entities are
entities that are neither sense
data nor logical constructs composed of sense data. Rather, they
exist solely as entities in *theories,*
and these entities are included in
theories in order to facilitate

Sung to the Tune of "You Are My Sunshine"

more precise predictions of sense data. For example, consider the notion of
"the average American housewife." Obviously, it would be a big mistake to
suppose that she actually exists, and it would be ludicrous to imagine trying
to find her (perhaps in Akron, Ohio?) in order to interview her. The mistake
becomes obvious once we remember that she has 1.78 children!

Nevertheless, the notion of the average American
housewife can be very useful in fields such as
economics and sociology because it allows us
to articulate information about consumer habits and demography in America and make
accurate predictions concerning them.

So, logical positivism is yet
another radical application of
Ockham's notorious razor. One
begins to get the feeling that it is
perhaps an *abuse* of that razor,
and one is reminded of Einstein's
felicitous version of that principle,
"Say everything as simply as possible but not more so."

**The Average American Housewife
Has 1.78 Children**

Attacks on Logical Positivism's Notion of Sense Data

Despite the flourish of interest in radical empiricism among philosophers from Britain, America, and Austria in the 1930s and 1940s, it has fallen on hard times more recently. Logical positivism (and, with it, most of classical empiricism) stands or falls with **psychological atomism**—the view that our knowledge of the world is built up from discrete sensorial impressions such as "yellow," "sharp," and "hot." According to this hypothesis, we construct the whole from the assemblage of parts. But recent developments in philosophical theory and psychological investigation have brought this hypothesis into doubt. The **gestalt psychologists,** for example, claim that we move in the other direction, from whole to part, and that what creates the "whole" is not the bricks of ineffable, absolutely certain sensation (raw feels, sense data) but a complicated and probably inextricably fused combination of neurological and social facts about perception. The neurological facts—expressed psychologically—have to do with the discovery that perception always takes place in a *field* where a foreground is contrasted with a background. A sensation becomes a perception in a field of meaning, in which that sensation is given a specific *meaning* by being distinguished from its background. The background, in turn, also has a meaning, though perhaps a vaguer, more inarticulate one than the "something" that upstages it in the foreground. The social fact (i.e., conventional fact) here is the fact that what bestows meaning on the field is a combination of knowledge and expectation that can be traced ultimately to a specific social structure.

The concept of sense data as a serious epistemological category may have taken its last gasp because of the impact of J. L. Austin's *Sense and Sensibilia* (1962), according to which there really are no such things as sense data. According to Austin, the notion of sense data had been generated out of a mishandling of kinds of unusual but philosophically uninteresting features of perception—such as optical illusions, the odd shape of a stick placed in water, or the double vision of someone who presses a finger against one of her own eyes. But, according to Austin, these curiosities are perfectly well-understood aspects of perceptual reality, and the theory of knowledge does not need to be accommodated to them.

Attacks on Logical Positivism's Language

Yet another major flaw occurs in the empiricist program, according to contemporary wisdom. It has to do with the role of language in empiricism. Because of his Lockean suspicion about innate ideas, Berkeley ingeniously

Skinnerian Linguistics

displaced the role of innate ideas (particularly the role of generating our concepts of "identity" and "thingness") onto language. For that move to work, however, it would have to be demonstrated that a consistent empiricistic theory of language is possible, one compatible with the "blank slate" hypothesis. This task was taken up in the mid-twentieth century by the behaviorist psychologist (or "behavioral engineer," as he preferred to be called) B. F. SKINNER (1904–1990). In his book, characteristically named *Verbal Behavior,* he used his notion of **operant conditioning** (involving the repetition of noises, reinforced or discouraged by a system of rewards and punishments) to show how we learn the language we speak. His idea has a certain natural plausibility. We've all watched the linguistic exchange when a parent teaches a small child the "color words" or the parts of the body. But Skinner's book was soundly trounced in a review of it by NOAM CHOMSKY (b. 1928), then a relatively unknown young linguist, now perhaps the best-known living linguist in the world. Chomsky demonstrated that if all that were involved in language learning were the "blank slate" and operant conditioning, no one would ever learn a language. Among other things, Chomsky pointed out that Skinner's theory could not account for the linguistic novelty of which any competent native speaker is capable. Any such speaker can produce a completely new sentence that every other competent speaker can understand even though none of them has heard it before. In fact, I shall produce such a sentence now, "It is not a good idea to freeze small woolly mammoths into tinted ice cubes that will be served in the dry martini of Uncle Elmo (whose grandmother fought in the Crimean War)." I am reasonably certain that no one has ever uttered just that sentence before I wrote it (and for good reason!). Yet, according to Chomsky, Skinner cannot account for the fact that all of us understand it perfectly well.

Furthermore, Chomsky reminded us of the kinds of grammatical mistakes children make. The little boy comes crying to his mother, saying, "Johnny hitted me!" This sentence is, of course, incorrect; yet, it is incorrect in an interesting way. What the little boy had to "know" in order to make that error is that the way to form the past tense in English is to add "ed" to the infinitive. It's not *his* fault that this particular verb is irregular. Where did he learn to say "hitted"? Not from imitating his parents or even from other kids, according to Chomsky, but from his *native* ability to generate rules. This ability, which Chomsky calls the capacity for "deep grammar," results from the structuring of the human

Noam Chomsky (b. 1928)

brain. It is something we bring to the phonetic system we learn and not something we derive from it. All this sounds suspiciously like the function of Descartes's *innate ideas,* and, indeed, Chomsky has no qualms about making the connection between himself and the classical rationalists. He went as far as to title one of his books *Cartesian Linguistics,* and he has this to say:

Uncle Elmo's Martini

> On the basis of the best information now available, it seems reasonable to suppose that a child cannot help constructing a particular kind of **transformational grammar** to account for the data presented to him, any more than he can control his perception of solid objects or his attention to line and angle. Thus it may well be that the general features of language structure reflect, not so much the course of one's experience, but rather the general character of one's capacity to acquire knowledge—in the traditional sense, one's innate ideas and innate principles.[6]

Kant's Compromise

I swimmed in the river!

Swam, stupid! Make that mistake again and I'll belt ya one!

Chomskyan Linguistics
(Followed by a Skinnerian Attempt
at Negative Conditioning)

So we have seen problems with each of the two traditional Western epistemologies, rationalism and empiricism. (Briefly, one ignores Ockham's razor and the other takes it too far.) Is it possible to construct any compromise that salvages the best of each view while eliminating the worst? The first serious attempt came from IMMANUEL KANT (1724–1804), whose *Critique of Pure Reason* was written as a direct response to David Hume's radical empiricism. Kant rejected the empiricists' "blank slate" hypothesis on the grounds that the mind was not simply a passive receptacle of neutral sense data. However, Kant also rejected the rationalistic notion of "innate ideas" on the grounds that claiming babies are born with ideas is just too far-fetched. He replaced these innate ideas with innate *structures,* which he called "categories of the understanding." These structures were formal and active features of the mind that imposed a kind of order on the raw data of the senses. Kant detected as innate structures of the mind a spatial–temporal perceptual gridwork (space and time) and twelve categories of the understanding, including the following:

unity
plurality
totality
relations and characteristics of substance
relations of cause and effect
and relations of reciprocity.

Je pense, donc je suis.

CARTESIAN LINGUISTICS
noam chomsky

It is important to understand that these innate categories are not the same as innate idea; they aren't ideas at all, according to Kant, they are structures that generate and organize ideas. To desigate the hybrid nature of these categories Kant identifies them as **synthetic a priori.**

Again, these categories are not derived passively by the mind from sensorial data but rather are actively brought by the mind to the world and imposed upon the raw data. But raw data themselves are never perceived; we perceive only data that have already been "processed" by the categories of the understanding and the spatial–temporal gridwork. This explains the meaning of Kant's famous dictum, "Thoughts without content are empty, intuitions without concepts are blind." This conclusion grants to the empiricists that there can be no knowledge in the absence of sensorial contribution and grants to the rationalists that sense data alone cannot provide knowledge. It also squares with the gestaltist insight about the relation between part and whole in our understanding of the world.

Immanuel Kant (1724–1804)

Kant's view, though definitely a compromise between rationalism and empiricism, sides more with the former than with the latter. As such, it still suffers from a few of the old Cartesian problems. Like Descartes's doctrine of innate ideas, Kant's theory is still incapable of explaining why some cultures conceive differently than others such categories as space, time, unity, plurality, thingness, and causality. To bring Kant up-to-date, we might make Berkeley's move of supposing that these categories are more related to conventionality than Kant realized, particularly to language. But then we could preserve some rationalism by asserting Chomsky's thesis that these categories may be culturally relative because they are partially bound to "surface grammar." Then, in turn, this surface grammar itself is bound to "deep grammar," which is derived from innate neurological facts.

Conclusion: Getting Up-to-Date

I think it is safe to say that the empiricist program in the twentieth century did not work out. Philosophers no longer tend to take the idea of sense data very seriously, and therefore, the attempt to reduce all empirical knowledge to sense data seems over. One hears very little of psychological atomism these days. It is fair to say that the failure of logical positivism took the wind out of the sails of the empiricist project. This does not at all mean that nothing was learned from that project, but very few living philosophers think of their main job as that of contributing to empiricism. Still, there have been certain developments out of the history of empiricism that are very much alive, and I will end the discussion of empiricism by giving you a glimpse of one of the most important of these developments.

Quine's Contribution

One of the most influential philosophers in the last half of the twentieth century was WILLARD VAN ORMAN QUINE (1908–2000). Although he rarely called himself an empiricist, many writers who discuss his philosophy do not hesitate to do so. As a young man, Quine became fascinated with logical positivism and went to Europe, where he engaged in conversation with several leading members of the movement, leaving a strong impression of his philosophical skills. Though his most famous essay, "Two Dogmas of Empiricism" (1951),[7] seems to be an attack on empiricism in general, and thereby on logical positivism, Quine actually meant to present an advance in the tradition by liberating it from some dead weight.

W.V.O. Quine (1908-2000)

The first "dogma of empiricism" Quine took on is reductionism. This procedure was part of the empiricists' search for certainty by locating the most basic kinds of sentences that described sensorial experience. This involved reducing synthetic sentences to their simplest forms, such as so-called confirmation sentences (e.g., "Red here now"), and finally to "ostensive definitions" (simply pointing at something red and grunting [!]).

Not surprisingly, almost all philosophers today agree with Quine's critique and do so for his reasons—namely, that earlier empiricists were misguided in believing that knowledge had to have a "foundation" and that such a foundation would have to be discovered in some indubitable synthetic sentence referring to sensorial experience. The second "dogma of empiricism" that Quine attacked is the distinction between analytic and synthetic propositions. This attack seems to go to the very heart of both empiricism and rationalism, having been made central to the former by Hume and to the latter by Leibniz.[8]

Quine does not deny that there are analytic sentences but accepts as successful only the most useless, such as "All bachelors are bachelors." His reason for denying the possibility of other candidates, such as "All bachelors are unmarried males," is that their success depends on replacing words in one part of the sentence with

Logical Positivists Arguing

perfect synonyms in the other part of the sentence, and the thrust of his argument is to show that all existing theories of synonymy are either circular or ultimately unintelligible. Nor, according to him, is there any reason to think that anyone will ever come up with a successful theory of **synonymy.**[9]

If the idea of analyticity has been derived from a failed theory of synonymy, then we should expect arbitrariness in the way the distinction is currently drawn, and, according to Quine, we do find such arbitrariness. Take this sentence, "Owls hoot." Is it synthetic or analytic? It *ought* to be synthetic because its negation does not lead to a self-contradiction. Yet, our *certainty* of the sentence "Owls hoot" seems greater than that of the sentence, "Owls are members of the order Strigiformes," which is supposed to be analytic. Similarly, sentences like "Strawberries are red when ripe" or "Heavy objects fall when unsupported"—which are apparently synthetic—seem to have at least as much certainty as "Tomatoes are fruits, not vegetables"—which is apparently an analytic truth.

Quine's theory, if accurate, definitely does more damage to rationalism than to empiricism. As Christopher Peacocke, a contemporary rationalist philosopher, says, "The Quinean challenge [in 'Two Dogmas of Empiricism'] leaves little room for the notion of an a priori proposition, or more generally for any experience-independent justification of belief. Both of these are central to any rationalist conception. . . ."[10] We will hear more from Peacocke shortly.

Quine and other philosophers such as Richard Rorty have forced philosophers to make other adjustments as well. We may have to consider abandoning the search, shared by both rationalists and empiricists, for the *foundations* of knowledge. Descartes and all his epistemological followers as well as his detractors latched onto the architectural metaphor of "a house of knowledge," believing that knowledge could exist only if it were based on something absolutely foundational. For the rationalists, this certainty was to be found in the a priori truths derived from innate ideas. For the empiricists, it was derived from the privileged experience of sense data. But it is beginning to look as though there is something wrong with the metaphor. Perhaps (as Quine and Rorty suggest) rather than being like a house, knowledge is more like a net or spiderweb. If some segments prove weak or worn out, we repair them while hanging on to the relatively stable parts, which still offer support.

Besides objecting to the knowledge-house metaphor, Rorty suspects that the main error in epistemology was that of accepting Plato's simile that *knowing* is like a kind of *mental seeing,* in which case knowledge is always a relationship between a belief and its object. In Rorty's influential book *Philosophy and the Mirror of Nature,* he accepts the Platonic view that knowledge is justified belief, but he tries to show that "justification" is constituted by establishing a relation not between a belief and an object of belief but between a belief and *arguments.* He says, "If . . . we think of 'rational certainty' as a matter of victory in argument rather than of relation to an object known, . . . we shall be looking for an airtight case rather than an unshakeable foundation."[11] We will then realize that there is no

Is Our System of Knowledge More Like a Spiderweb Than a House?

natural end to justification. Rather, the defense *could* go on forever. Perhaps, as in a court of law, the defense is usually terminated somewhat arbitrarily. Certainly, no claim to knowledge is ever immune to revision. Furthermore, according to Rorty, we have to realize that justification

is a *social*—hence a historical—phenomenon. It cannot be defined in terms of necessary or sufficient condition.

Rationalism in the Twenty-First Century

A large number of twentieth-century philosophers thought that rationalism had been mortally wounded in attacks upon it, first by the logical positivists in the early part of the century, then by Quine in the later part. But it is important to note that rationalism appears to be making a strong comeback these days. We will take a quick look at some of the works of British philosopher CHRISTOPHER PEACOCKE (b. 1950) and let that represent contemporary rationalism for us. His books present the most thoroughly developed version of contemporary rationalism. But Peacocke's theory did not appear **ex nihilo.** The bridge between classical rationalists such as Descartes and Leibniz, on the one side, and today's intellectual world, on the other side, was constructed in the beginning of the twentieth century by the philosophically inclined mathematicians, Gottlob Frege and Kurt Gödel, from whose ideas Peacocke draws support, even though he thinks his rationalism has solved some of the problems inherent in theirs.

In his recent book, *The Realm of Reason*, Peacocke presents his "Three Principles of Rationalism," which, he believes, establish a strong modern defense of that epistemology. These principles are complicated and require more study than I have space for here, but I hope that a glance at them and a brief commentary will give you a sense of why, under his influence and that of a few other contemporary philosophers,[12] rationalism is regaining ground. These are Peacocke's principles:

Principle I: The Special Truth-Conduciveness Thesis.

A fundamental and irreducible part of what makes an inference one to which a thinker is entitled is that the inference tends to lead to true judgements.

Principle II: The Rationalist Dependence Thesis.

The rational truth-conduciveness of any given inference to which a thinker is entitled is to be philosophically explained in terms of the nature of the intentional contents and states involved in the inference (p. 52).

Principle III: The Generalized Rationalist Thesis.

All instances of the entitlement relation, both absolute and relative, are fundamentally a priori (p. 148).

In a crude paraphrase, these principles say:

1. A theory of knowledge does not create truth; it explains how we arrive at truth.
2. The way we arrive at truth must be explained in terms of the working of the mind (logic, reference, recognition, mental experiments, etc.).
3. All components of the inference described in II are a priori (i.e., they are derived not from observable facts in the world, rather from the working of rational processes).

According to Peacocke, Principle 3 follows from 2, and 2 follows from 1. Traditional rationalists, such as Plato, Descartes, and Leibniz, derived the idea of truth from the idea of rationalism; that is, the system of rationalism generates the correct definition of truth. Notice, however, that the distinctive feature of Peacocke's first principle is that truth is prior to and independent of any theory (such as the theory of rationalism). In fact, rationalism's strength is that it shows what ways lead to truth and is itself characterized in terms of its ability to do so. That is, rationalism *leads* to truth rather than *produces* truth. The notion of truth has been downplayed in many contemporary epistemological theories because it seems to present so many problems, but this concept is very important in Peacocke's philosophy. Theories should be judged by their "truth-conduciveness," and rationalism shows that the structure of truth-conduciveness is a priori. That is, the justifiable "transitions" (inferences, deductions, and other logical connectors) from "contents" (thoughts and perceptual data) to judgments of truth or falsity will prove to be independent of observation.

One of the first claims presented by Peacocke in his defense of his three principles is that "[t]hinkers are entitled, prima facie [i.e., in the absence of evidence to the contrary], to take the content of their perceptual experiences at face value" (pp. 12–13). This is a somewhat surprising claim to be coming from a rationalist, because we might expect such an assertion to come from empiricists, who have spent a lot of time trying to show that the content of perceptual experience is the foundation of truth about the world. But Peacocke does indeed defend this view as a rationalist. However, before trying to prove this claim as a principle of rationalism, he first clarifies that he rejects the old rationalist dream of absolute certainty. Notice the emphasis here on "entitlement" rather than "certainty." Webster's dictionary defines "entitlement" in its primary sense as "to give a person a right or a claim to something: to furnish with grounds for laying a claim." Peacocke abandons the search for certainty and replaces it with "entitlement," which is the epistemological function of recognizing beliefs as reasonable rather than certain. The move between a conscious state that is unexamined to a conscious state that has been examined and judged is what Peacocke calls "a transition." He insists that this transition is itself a priori. It is a movement of reason, not a movement forced by observation, and not an induction that is forced upon us by the observable facts themselves. (Oddly, it sounds to me that Peacock is close to that radical empiricist, Hume, here. Remember the illustration earlier in this chapter of Hume watching one billiard ball (A) hitting another billiard ball (B), that then moves. Hume said that we cannot know from with certainty based on previous observations that (A) caused (B) to move, and that it will do so in the future. Peacocke seems to agree but holds that we are entitled to this judgment nevertheless, and the judgment itself is not empirical but a priori. Peacocke writes:

> Absolutely **indefeasible** [i.e., absolutely certain] entitlement is simply not to be had. There can always be some evidence that would rationally make us think we had made a mistake in believing something to be a proof. To have indefeasible grounds we would have to be infallible, and indeed to have conclusive grounds that we are. (p. 29)

Now, having said this, Peacocke claims there are some perceptual states that, in the absence of evidence to the contrary, entitle one to judge that their content is true. Peacocke gives as examples "proprioception of limb position." Imagine that you take notice of the fact that you have extended your arm. According to Peacocke, it is highly likely that "an awareness of one's arm being straight is caused by one's arm being straight" (p. 69). But, as we've seen, philosophers have designed arguments to make us doubt even beliefs such as this one. The kind of skeptical arguments against such deductions, and also against *all* perceptual judgments, is typically some claim about the possibility of a Cartesian evil demon, or of an evil scientist who has placed your brain in a vat and connected your brain to electrodes that give you false sensations that you are wandering freely about the world, or that random physical events have caused hallucination. (In other words, says the skeptic, in the same way that the coloring of a moth's wings has evolved to give it survival value rather than "truth," perhaps the human brain has also evolved providing survival value, but not truth.) According to Peacocke, the refutations of such skepticism are the indirect "transitions" that allow one to judge rationally that one is not being deceived in normal circumstances. These antiskeptical arguments are always a priori. So are the

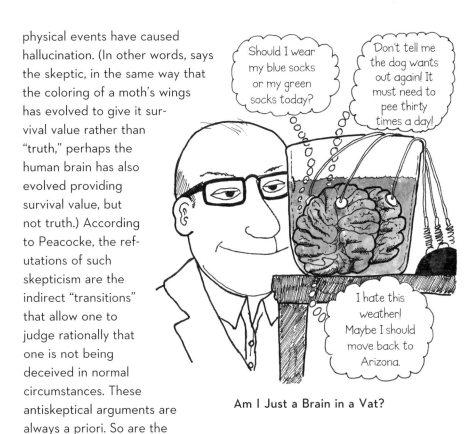

Am I Just a Brain in a Vat?

arguments of probability that directly support such judgments. For example, this is what Peacocke calls the "Complexity Reduction Principle":

> Other things equal, good explanations of complex phenomena explain the more complex in terms of the less complex; they reduce complexity. (p. 83)

This, I take it, is Peacocke's version of Ockham's razor; so if he is right, one of the primary tools proudly touted by the empiricists is justified only on a priori grounds. If an empiricist responds by saying that sensorial experience teaches us the likelihood of the truth of Ockham's razor, Peacocke can point out that the theory of probability to which the empiricist is appealing is itself a priori. It can justify experience, but experience cannot justify it. (In other words, the truth of the proposition "The future [in general] will behave like the past [in general]" is not one learned through observation, if only because—as Hume reminded us—there never is an observation of the future as such. And yet, we are entitled to accept this proposition as true and to make it the basis of our theories of probability.)

Employing the Complexity Reduction Principle, Peacocke is able to conclude that there is the likelihood of the truth of some theory of natural selection as the theory that best reduces the complexity of the organic world to a system of simple elements and that "perceptual states generated by a system produced and sustained by natural selection[13] can be expected to be in large part correct in their representational contents" (p. 89). There is more survival value provided by a brain that gives you correct information about the external world than by one that would give you hallucinations. From the combination of these a priori principles, Peacocke is able to deduce a refutation of skepticism, "The easiest way for a perceptual experience to occur is one in which it is unlikely to be a hallucination" (p. 92). This claim, then, is a priori. You don't find it out by looking at something or touching something.

According to Peacocke, if one were to reject these a priori principles, "then it would not be clear how one could become entitled to believe anything about the observable world at all" (p. 91). In other words, if empiricism is true, then no knowledge of the world is possible (again, a view that David Hume seemed at moments to have suspected).

It's as if Peacocke is claiming that there really are no empiricists; all philosophers are crypto-rationalists despite themselves.

It's difficult to evaluate Peacocke's theories thoroughly based only on the rather simplistic paraphrases of his very complicated ideas I have presented. Still, *prima facie,* they look pretty good, don't they? They must at least have convinced you that rationalism is alive and well in the twenty-first century.

Topics for Consideration

1. Write a short essay stating how you think Plato would analyze an idea like "justice" or "mammal" (see Chapter 2), and compare it with the way you suppose Locke or Berkeley would treat the same topic.
2. Why does Locke think that his "blank slate" theory of the mind is superior to Descartes's theory of the mind based on "innate ideas" (see Chapter 2)? How does Locke go about establishing his proof? Why, according to the presentation of Locke's theory in this chapter, does his argument falter?
3. Locke says, "Since the mind . . . hath no other immediate object but its own ideas, which it alone can contemplate, it is evident that our knowledge is only conversant about them." Show how this view, taken very literally, "deconstructs" Locke's own general theory and leads directly to Berkeley's theory that *esse* is *percipi.*
4. State the main principles of empiricism, then show how Hume applies them more consistently than either Locke or Berkeley and how his radical empiricism leads to skepticism.
5. Take these three propositions and show how the logical positivists would analyze them:
   a. No unicorn has more than one horn.
   b. Removing support from weighted objects causes them to fall.
   c. God is love.

6. Try to clarify the difference between Descartes's theory of "innate ideas" (Chapter 2) and Kant's theory of "innate structures."

7. Berkeley thought he could apply Ockham's razor to the rationalists' notion of "innate ideas" by showing that we learn the concepts of "sameness" (= identity) and "thingness" (= substance) when, as children, we acquire a language. Show how Chomsky's critique of this empiricistic view takes us right back to the rationalists.

8. Take a look at the way Quine treats sentences such as "Owls hoot" and "Owls are members of the order Strigiformes." Try to come up with a similar pair of sentences that Quine could have used in place of this pair to illustrate his point about the synthetic/analytic distinction.

9. What features of classical rationalism (e.g., Plato and Descartes) has Peacocke's rationalism abandoned, and what features of empiricism has he adopted?

Suggestions for Further Reading: Paperback Editions

Alfred Jules Ayer, *Language, Truth, and Logic* (New York: Dover, n.d.). A short, well-written presentation of the main tenets of logical positivism by one of its most able practitioners.

George Berkeley, *Three Dialogues between Hylas and Philonous* (New York: Bobbs-Merrill Library of the Liberal Arts, 1954; also in *The Empiricists*). Berkeley's theory presented for the general reader in the form of a humorous Platonic dialogue. "Hylas" is John Locke, and "Philonous" is Berkeley himself.

John Lyons, *Noam Chomsky* (New York: Viking Press, 1970). A short, comprehensive overview of Chomsky's main arguments. In the "Modern Masters" series.

Christopher Peacocke, *The Realm of Reason* (Oxford, England and New York: Oxford University Press, 2005). This book, like that of Quine, is not addressed to introductory philosophy students, but it is available in paperback.

Steven Pinker, *The Language Instinct: How the Mind Creates Language* (New York: Harper Perennial, 1995). A readable, spirited defense of a Chomsyan picture of language, written by a very bright, annoyingly opinionated guy.

W. V. O. Quine, *From a Logical Point of View* (Cambridge, MA: Harvard University Press, 1960). Like Peacocke's book, this would be very tough going for a beginner, but if you choose philosophy as your major, it's likely that at some point you will be asked to read essays from this famous book.

Richard Rorty, *Philosophy and the Mirror of Nature* (Princeton, NJ: Princeton University Press, 1980). Quite exciting.

Roger Scruton, *Kant* (Oxford, England: Oxford University Press, 1982). A nice overview of the work of a very difficult philosopher. In the "Past Masters" series.

Notes

1. John Locke, *An Essay Concerning Human Understanding,* ed. A. C. Fraser (Oxford, England: Clarendon Press, 1894), bk. II, chap. I, sec. 2. Unless otherwise stated, all subsequent quotes from Locke in this chapter are from this source.

2. George Berkeley, *A Treatise Concerning the Principles of Human Knowledge*, ed. G. J. Warnock (Cleveland: World Publishing, 1963), part I, sec. 1.

3. The theory of Inuit semiology here is based on the account of this language found in the notebooks of anthropologist Franz Boas (1858–1942), interpreted by his student Edward Sapir (1884–1939) in *Selected Writings of Edward Sapir in Language*, ed. David G. Mandelbaum (Berkeley: University of California Press, 1983). The theory was further developed by Sapir's student, Benjamin Lee Whorf (1897–1941) in *Language, Thought, and Reality: Selected Writings of Benjamin Lee Whorf*, ed. John B. Carroll (Boston: MIT Press, 1956). The theory is now called the "Sapir—Whorf hypothesis." It has been challenged by several linguists and anthropologists, most boisterously by linguist Geoffrey Pullum in *The Great Eskimo Vocabulary Hoax and Other Irreverent Essays* (Chicago: Chicago University Press, 1991), 3–17. A moderate version of the Sapir—Whorf hypothesis has been defended by linguists Igor Krupnik and Ludger Müller-Wille in "Franz Boas and the Inuktitut Terminology for Ice and Snow: From the Emergence of the Field to the 'Great Eskimo Vocabulary Hoax,'" in *SIKU (Sea Ice Knowledge and Use): Knowing Our Ice*, eds. Krupnik et al. (Berlin: Springer Verlag, 2010), 390–395. The authors conclude that Pullum's article "is based on a misunderstanding of Boas' legacy. . . . [It] has little to contribute to the study of Inuit knowledge of snow and ice, except that it subjects this knowledge to misunderstanding and condescending boasting" (p. 395).

4. Berkeley, *A Treatise Concerning the Principles of Human Knowledge*, part I, sec. 1.

5. David Hume, *A Treatise of Human Nature*, ed. L. A. Selby-Bigge (Oxford, England: Clarendon Press, 1941), bk. 1, part IV, sec. 6, pp. 251–253. All subsequent quotes from Hume in this chapter are from this source.

6. Noam Chomsky, *Aspects of the Theory of Syntax* (Cambridge, MA: MIT Press, 1965), p. 59.

7. Reprinted in *From a Logical Point of View* (Cambridge, MA: Harvard University Press, 1960).

8. Gottfried Leibniz (1646–1716), who has not been discussed in this book, was a close reader of Descartes's philosophy. He and Baruch Spinoza (1634–1677) were the best-known rationalists in the generation after Descartes. Leibniz discovered infinitesimal calculus simultaneously with Isaac Newton. He is the first philosopher to have systematically developed what Immanuel Kant would later name the analytic/synthetic distinction (Leibniz called them simply "necessary" and "contingent" judgments). His radical rationalism can be detected in his claim that, ultimately, all judgments are necessary (analytic) *sub specie aeternitatis* (roughly, from the point of view of God).

9. Not all analytic philosophers agree that Quine has dismantled the synthetic/analytic distinction. See especially H. P. Grice and P. F. Strawson, "In Defense of a Dogma," *Philosophical Review*, Vol. 65 (1956), pp. 141–158.

10. Christopher Peacocke, *The Realm of Reason* (Oxford, England and New York: Oxford University Press, 2005), p. 24. Page numbers of future quotations from this book will be included in the text.

11. Richard Rorty, *Philosophy and the Mirror of Nature* (Princeton, NJ: Princeton University Press, 1980), pp. 156–157.

12. Such as philosophers George Bealer of Yale University, who wrote *Quality and Concept* (1982), and Laurence BonJour of the University of Washington, who wrote *In Defense of Pure Reason* (1998).

13. I say *some* theory of natural selection because Peacocke writes, "What has been important for the argument is not the empirical truth of Darwinian hypotheses but the special, complexity-reducing status of explanations by some natural-selection mechanism" (p. 108). See the Glossary for *the* theory of natural selection.

4
Who's on First; What's on Second?
Ontology

Ontology is theory of reality or theory of being. As I mentioned earlier, many contemporary philosophers prefer the term "metaphysics" over "ontology" to designate the issues covered in this chapter; but, as you will see by consulting the Glossary, I see metaphysics as a broader category covering topics that go beyond the problem of reality. The big questions in ontology are these:

- What is real and what is merely appearance?
- Can there be a theory that draws the distinction between reality and appearance and accounts for everything that exists, or must these distinctions always remain contextual, ad hoc, and informal?

The historical framework for ontological discussions has been in terms of the following categories:

What Is Real and What Is Merely Appearance

Monism: the view that there is only one reality or only one kind of thing that is real.

Dualism: the view that there are two forms of reality or two kinds of real things and that neither is reducible to the other.

113

Pluralism: the view that, despite scientific attempts to reduce all components of reality to ever more basic elements, common sense is correct to tell us that reality is composed of many different kinds of real things.

Nihilism: the view that nothing is real (or sometimes, as a *moral* doctrine, that nothing *deserves* to exist).

We have inadvertently witnessed quite a bit of ontological discussion in Chapters 1 through 3 because most of the traditional epistemologists defined knowledge in terms of its *object,* which was always some real entity (e.g., forms for Plato and sense data for Berkeley). We have seen that Plato, Descartes, and Locke should all be categorized as dualists. Berkeley's idealism is a form of monism.

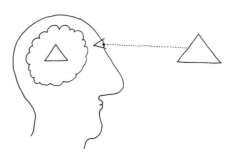

Knowledge Defined in Terms of Its Object—Which Is Some Real Thing

If we look at this list of ontological categories from the point of view of the famous "person-in-the-street," it seems that the least plausible candidate of the three is nihilism. If everyday experience tells us anything, it is that *something* exists. You will be pleased to hear that all philosophers agree with the person-in-the-street on this subject (with the possible exception of the ancient Greek philosopher, Anaximander, who may have held a view that could be called *moral* nihilism: not that nothing exists, but that nothing *deserves* to exist, because existence itself is an offense, perhaps against the idea of a perfect void).

The person-in-the-street remembers that her high school physics teacher claimed that everything is made of atoms. Is this monism? But the person-in-the-street is more likely to hold a view like pluralism, because she knows there are all sorts of

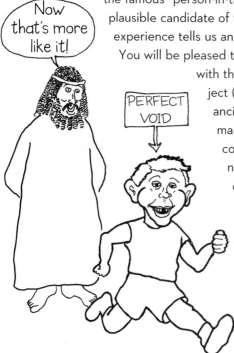

Anaximander Finds Happiness

things in existence: dogs, dreams, loopholes, lies, magpies, memories, wars, warts, warblers, zits, and zoos, among others. But what if all these could be reduced to a combination of mental things or physical things (imaginary dogs are *something* like real dogs, but not *very much* like them after all). In that case, dualism would be true. Let us start our discussion of ontology with dualism, and there is no better place to begin it than with our seventeenth-century acquaintance, René Descartes, who defends as the centerpiece of his ontological theory a dramatic version of dualism, a theory that smacks up against the boulder-sized problems strewn on the philosophical landscape of his dualism.

Dualism

Descartes's version is the most radical form of dualism, and even though it is an extreme version, its very exaggeration throws light on the problems of dualism in general. We saw in Chapter 2 that Descartes circumscribed two distinct spheres of being: the mental (mind, or as Descartes some-times calls it, "spiritual substance") and the physical (body, or "material substance"). The subtitle of Descartes's *Meditations on First Philosophy* includes this line, "in which . . . the Distinction between Mind and Body [Is] Demonstrated." (In fact, in his first draft, the subtitle had been "in which the Immortality of the Soul Is Demonstrated," but when a critic pointed out that Descartes had nowhere even *mentioned* the immortality of the soul, much less proved its existence, Descartes changed the subtitle word-ing to refer to the absolute distinction between mind and body, which to

	MIND	BODY
Substance	MIND	BODY
Essence	Thought	Extension
Modes	affirmation denial doubt volition hope . . .	size shape location part mobility
	. . .	

Descartes's Ontology of Finite Things

Descartes's way of thinking at least made *possible* the immortality of the soul.) According to Descartes, a body is "an extended thing" ("*res extensa*") whose characteristics are these: extension, size, shape, location, divisibility, motion, and rest. At the other extreme is mind (or soul or self), which is "a thing which thinks" ("*res cogitans*"). Descartes asks, "What is a thing which thinks? It is a thing which doubts, understands, conceives,

"I Am Absolutely Distinct from My Body and Can Exist without It"

affirms, denies, wills, refuses, which also imagines and feels."[1] These two "things" (*res extensa* and *res cogitans*) are completely different from each other and can exist independently of each other.

Descartes says:

> I rightly conclude that my essence consists solely in the fact that I am a thinking thing (or a substance whose whole essence or nature is to think). And although possibly (or rather certainly, as I shall say in a moment) I possess a body with which I am very intimately conjoined, yet because, on the one side, I have a clear and distinct idea of myself in as much as I am only a thinking and unextended thing, and as, on the other, I possess a distinct idea of body, inasmuch as it is only an extended and unthinking thing, it is certain that this I (that is to say, my soul by which I am what I am), is entirely and absolutely distinct from my body, and can exist without it. ("Meditation IV," pp. 213–214)

The Ghost in the Machine

Well and good! Descartes has established that, given his definitions of mind and body, they can exist without each other. But the real question is how they can exist *with* each other. How can a nonextended spiritual substance located *nowhere* have any effect on something so different from itself as inert matter? How can the human being be some strange combination of mind and body? (This issue is what the British philosopher Gilbert Ryle called the problem of "the ghost in the machine.") Now, we know that there is interaction between mind and body. (If I stomp on your foot, you will be conscious of a sensation of pain [body influencing mind], and if you remember that you left your car lights on, you will rush to the parking lot to extinguish them [mind influencing body].) The question is, on Descartes's account, how is this possible? Descartes addressed the issue in the following way:

> I am not only lodged in my body as a pilot in a vessel, but . . . I am very closely united to it, and so to speak so intermingled with it that I seem to compose with it one whole. For if that were not the case, when my body is hurt, I, who am merely a thinking thing, should not feel pain, for I should perceive this wound by understanding only, just as the sailor perceives by sight when something is damaged in his vessel. ("Meditation VI," p. 216)

This is good! Imagine a ship's pilot on his bridge trying to maneuver his vessel between two rocky promontories. It is a narrow passageway, but he thinks he can make it. He keeps looking from left to right. As he is looking port side, suddenly there is a sickening "cruuunch" on his right. He looks starboard and sees that he has scraped a rock, and a yawning tear is gouged in the ship's hull. "Oh criminey," he thinks,

The Smell of Burned Flesh

"now I'm in trouble!" What if our relation to our body were like that of the captain to his ship? You are standing in the kitchen talking to a friend, resting your hand on the stove. After a while you smell the odor of burning flesh. You look to the stove and see your skin smoking. You pull your burning hand from the stove and say, "Oh criminey, *now* I'm in trouble!" Or what if you were walking along, heard a sharp "snap," felt a loss of support, looked down, and *noticed* that you'd broken your leg. Descartes is right. This is *not* the relation that exists between our mind and our body. We do not observe that our

Copy of a Seventeenth-Century Wood Engraving Demonstrating Descartes's Theory of the Pineal Gland

body is damaged, then deduce that we are in pain. As Descartes says, our consciousness and our body are "so intermingled" as to "compose . . . one whole." Yet, once again, on his account, how is this possible? Here is what Descartes has to say about this problem when he addresses it specifically:

> I had clearly ascertained that the part of the body in which the soul exercises its functions immediately is in nowise the heart, nor the whole of the brain, but merely the most inward of all its parts, to wit, a certain very small gland which is situated in the middle of its substance and so suspended above the duct whereby the animal spirits in its anterior cavities have communication with those in the posterior, that the slightest movements which take place in it may alter very greatly the course of these spirits; and reciprocally that the smallest changes which occur in the course of the spirits may do much to change the movements of this gland.[2]

Herr Professor Doktor Freud and Monsieur Descartes

Descartes has selected what is now called the *pineal gland* as the locus of interaction between body and soul. Perhaps his logic was this: that gland doesn't seem to do anything else—probably it serves this function. Using this logic, he could as easily have decided in favor of the tonsils or the appendix. (Besides, although some debate continues about the pineal gland's function, apparently it has something to do with controlling the size of the gonads. If so, his conclusion makes Descartes much more of a Freudian than he'd like to be.)

But the real problem with selecting the pineal gland as the place where mind and body meet is that in doing so, Descartes has *located* mind, and as you will recall, "location" is a characteristic of *body*, not of mind. If Descartes locates the mind *anywhere*, he thereby transforms it into body, and then he becomes a materialist. This conclusion, of course, would be exactly the opposite of the one Descartes set out to prove, and his whole ontology seems to unravel right here. At this point, Descartes conveniently died of the common cold and left the paradox to be sorted out by later generations.

Materialistic Monism

Materialism

Descartes had made the relation between mind and body so mysterious that it is no surprise to find later philosophers turning away from his dualism to monism. We have seen how Berkeley tries to apply Ockham's razor to dualism by eliminating the whole material side of it. But idealism has never been very popular in the West. Berkeley and G. W. F. Hegel (the other famous European idealist) each had followers, but even these disciples tried to rewrite their mentors' works to avoid their idealistic conclusions. A much more popular form of monism in the West is **materialism,** particularly in current times, because many people, both philosophers and nonphilosophers, feel that the authority of modern science is on the side of materialism. We will look at several versions of this doctrine: behaviorism, the **mind–brain identity theory, eliminative materialism,** and **functionalism.**

Behaviorism

Though this doctrine is primarily promulgated by psychologists, it has philosophical import and philosophical disciples. It is the creature of the American psychologist JOHN WATSON (1878–1958), and its most energetic spokesman was B. F. SKINNER (1904–1990), whom we have already encountered. One reason that this doctrine is a bit difficult to get ahold of is that several variations exist, and sometimes its defenders slide from one version to another (perhaps so as not to get cornered). I will try to reduce these variations to a manageable handful, namely, to what I will call **hard behaviorism, soft behaviorism,** and **logical behaviorism.**

You see? What'd I tell you? No mind.

Hard behaviorism is the view that there are no such things as minds or mental events, mental states, or mental processes. There are only bodies in motion (and these motions are "behaviors"). This radical theory is open to a number of fairly obvious criticisms. From a commonsense point of view, it is difficult to accept the claim that the sentence "Mary is in pain" is either always false or always meaningless or that the word "pain" merely designates a grouping of various behaviors (grimacing, groaning, grasping the "painful" limb, etc.). One objection to this view is that we can feign pain or sometimes suppress the behavior associated with pain. Another objection points out that some mental activities have no particular outward behavior associated with them (e.g., wondering).

Soft behaviorism avoids some of the problems faced by hard behaviorism. It is the view that there *may* be minds and mental events, states, and processes but that *methodologically*, scientists can provide adequate explanations and predictions of activity in general, human or otherwise, without ever referring to anything mental. This second view is not really a philosophical (i.e., ontological) one, and it is much less controversial than the first—though not without difficulties of its own. The problem is that behaviorists who seem to be asserting the "hard" version sometimes slip into the "soft" version when cornered. But when left alone again, they return to the "hard" position.

What both versions of behaviorism assert is something like this: all statements about human activity, including statements about people's so-called mental life, can be translated into statements about observable "behaviors" or, if not, can be shown to be either false or nonsense. So if I say, "Mary thinks it's going to rain," I should be able to show that making this statement is really shorthand for a whole bunch of other assertions, like:

> "Mary utters the sentence, 'I think it's going to rain.'"
> "Mary has worn her raincoat and taken her umbrella."
> "Mary is wearing her boots, not her sandals."
> "Mary canceled her reservation at the outdoor restaurant."

And if I say, "Bill is angry at Sam," I should be able to show that some or all of the following assertions are true:

> "Bill utters the sentence, 'I am angry at Sam.'"
> "Bill raises his voice and he says rude things whenever Sam's name is mentioned."
> "Bill's face is red; his knuckles are white."

I know it doesn't seem like it, but they are absolutely furious with each other.

Behaviorism has some plausibility. In a certain sense, we *are* all behaviorists vis-à-vis other people. Whatever you know about anybody, including your best friends, you know by observing their *behavior* (which includes listening to what they have to say, of course). None of us has an antenna to pick up thoughts of others. The only access to other people's mind is in fact through observation of these people's activity, which I suppose is in some sense observation of their body. Furthermore, behaviorism becomes philosophically plausible because we were led to it through certain problems with dualism. It was, after all, Descartes who unwittingly opened the floodgates for behaviorism: first, by failing to show how mind–body interaction was possible, and second, by never dealing satisfactorily with "the problem of other minds." (How do I know that anyone besides myself has a mind?) Descartes addressed this problem, writing:

> When looking from a window and saying I see men who pass in the street, I really do not see them but infer that what I see is men. . . . And yet what do I see from the window but hats and coats which may cover

automatic machines? Yet I judge these to be men. And similarly, solely by the faculty of judgment, which rests in my mind, I comprehend that which I believed I saw with my eyes. ("Meditation II," p. 177)

Most critics find this conclusion very unsatisfactory. Descartes may have proved that *he* has a mind (or, as he says, that he *is* a mind), but he certainly hasn't proved that anyone else does. The observable data are quite compatible with the view that "everyone else" is really just a complicated robot (perhaps a *meaty* robot, but a robot just the same). Furthermore, the mind that Descartes proved to exist—that is, his *own* mind—is *not located*; it is nowhere. The behaviorist asks how much better is a mind that's nowhere than no mind at all?

Hats, Coats, and Automatic Machines

All these problems with dualism support the behaviorist's claims. Nevertheless, problems exist for the behaviorist, and some are quite Cartesian in nature. For example, it may well be that I know that *you* have a stomachache because I see you grimace, hold your tummy, go to the medicine cabinet, and prepare yourself a "fizzy." But that is certainly not the way that I discover that *I* have a stomachache. I find out that I have a stomachache just the way Descartes says I do—I am immediately *conscious* of my pain. The soft behaviorist (but not the hard behaviorist) can retort that the scientist doesn't study herself; rather, she is studying others. Even so, a theory that is true for everyone but oneself is an odd one. (What if Newton had claimed that bodies on the earth's surface fall at thirty-two feet per second squared . . . except for his own body, which was exempt from that law!)

I am popping aspirin; therefore, I am in pain.

The view called logical behaviorism is an important philosophical theory. In one sense, however, perhaps a treatment of it doesn't belong precisely at this

Sir Isaac Newton Discovers the Law of Gravity, Which Applies to Everything but Himself

point of our discussion, because logical behaviorists are not necessarily materialists—some are and some aren't. We will inspect the version of logical behaviorism set forth by GILBERT RYLE (1900–1976), the British **ordinary language philosopher,** who in fact considered himself not a materialist but a pluralist. Indeed, Ryle never even used the term "logical behaviorism" to describe his own view. But because Ryle's theory came to be the most widely discussed version of logical behaviorism, I will include it here, even if it fits a little awkwardly.

Ryle's influential book of 1949, *The Concept of Mind,* constitutes a sustained attack on Cartesian dualism (though it also provides a critique of Skinner's hard behaviorism, to be discussed shortly). In the first chapter of his book, Ryle wrote:

> The official doctrine, which hails chiefly from Descartes, is something like this. With the doubtful exceptions of idiots and infants in arms, every human being has both a body and a mind. Some would prefer to say that every human being is both a body and a mind. His body and his mind are ordinarily harnessed together, but after the death of the body, his mind may continue to exist and function.
>
> Human bodies are in space and are subject to the mechanical laws which govern all other bodies in space. Bodily processes and states can be inspected by external observers. So a man's bodily life is as much a public affair as are the lives of animals and reptiles and even as the careers of trees, crystals, and planets.
>
> But minds are not in space, nor are their operations subject to mechanical laws. The workings of one mind are not witnessable by other observers; its career is private. Only I can take direct cognizance of the states and processes of my own mind. A person therefore lives through two collateral histories, one consisting of what happens in and to his body, the other consisting of what happens in and to his mind. The first is public, the second private. The events in the first history are events in the physical world, those in the second are events in the mental world.
>
> . . . .

Such in outline is the official theory. I shall often speak of it, with deliberate abusiveness, as "the dogma of the Ghost in the Machine." I hope to prove that it is entirely false and false not in detail but in principle. It is not merely an assemblage of particular mistakes. It is one big mistake and a mistake of a particular kind. It is, namely, a category-mistake. It represents the facts of mental life as if they belonged to one logical type or category (or range of types or categories) when they actually belong to another.[3]

A **category-mistake** is the mistake of taking a term or phrase that belongs in one logical or grammatical category and erroneously placing it in another category and then drawing absurd conclusions from that miscategorization.

In fact, the whole of Lewis Carroll's books, *Alice's Adventures in Wonderland* and *Through the Looking Glass,* are great repositories of category-mistakes. Consider the discussion between Alice and the White King. The King is concerned about two messengers he is awaiting and says to Alice:

"Just look along the road, and tell me if you can see either of them."

"I see nobody on the road," said Alice.

"I only wish *I* had such eyes," the King remarked in a fretful tone. "To be able to see Nobody! And at that distance too! Why, it's as much as *I* can do to see real people, by this light!"[4]

(After Sir John Tenniel)

The source of the joke here is obvious. The sentences "I see somebody" and "I see nobody" *look* similar. Grammatically, they each have a subject, a verb, and an object. But the category-mistake is that of believing that the terms "somebody" and "nobody" are both names of existing entities.

One of Ryle's examples of a category-mistake involves a foreigner visiting his first cricket game. Having been shown all the features of the playing field and hearing all the functions of the players, he says, "But no one is left on the field to contribute to the famous element of team spirit. I see who does the bowling, the batting, and the wicket-keeping, but I do not see whose role it is to exercise *esprit de corps.*"

This second example is especially instructive. Let's change the sport in the example from cricket to baseball because, if you're like me, you *are* a foreigner at a cricket game. Imagine that you are attending a baseball game with an interested but ignorant visitor from another culture who, after seeing you point out the bats, mitts, pitcher's mound, bleachers,

pitchers, infielders, outfielders, base runners, and umpire and after hearing you explain base hits, home runs, and balls, asks, "Where is the team spirit?" Obviously, you are not going to respond by saying, "Oh, terribly sorry to have left it out. It's right there between second and third base." It's not a *thing* you could point out at all.

TEAM SPIRIT

When Team Spirit Departs

Now, what Ryle would say about "team spirit" (which he thinks is what you and I would say about it in our "nonphilosophical" moments, and this is why he is called an ordinary language philosopher) is approximately what he says about other mentalistic terms like "intelligent," "stupid," "hopeful," and "intentional." He would say that these terms are *not* names of ghostly events that may or may not exist; rather, they are references to ways people do things.

To clarify this view, imagine the following scenario: I am your philosophy teacher. I am lecturing to you about Descartes. Suddenly, the classroom door flies open and in strides a young man with a particularly intense look on his face. Before I can prevent it, he reaches into his pocket, pulls out a bottle of ink, uncaps it, and pours it on my head.

With a malicious grin on his face, he turns to you and says, "Palmer flunked me last semester." Then he strides out. I yell, "He did that on purpose!" Naturally, I sue! You are my witnesses at the trial. In the state of California, in order to find a person guilty of a criminal act in the first degree, it must be established that he had *mens rea*, criminal intent. Suppose the young

An Intentional Act

man's lawyer is Descartes. He addresses the jury, saying, "My client is accused of intentionally injuring Professor Palmer, but in fact no one can know anyone's intention except his own because intentions are purely private phenomena. Therefore, in the absence of a confession by my client, there can be no evidence whatsoever that he had such an intention. Therefore, he must be found 'not guilty'."

This defense would not stand up in court for a minute. In order to establish that the act was done intentionally, all the prosecuting attorney would have to do is call you as witnesses and you would describe the *manner* in which the young man performed his act. According to Ryle, when we say that someone did something intentionally, all we mean is that the person did it in a certain manner. *What* manner? What is the function of saying that someone did something intentionally? It is to distinguish that action from something done *accidentally*. There is a big difference between running down the stairs to get the

Just Going Downstairs to Check the Mail

mail (intentionally) and falling down the stairs because you stepped on your son's skateboard (accidentally). Skinner's attempt to get rid of intentions has the consequence of abolishing that important distinction. Would the loss of this distinction really be a scientific advance? It's difficult to think so.

The upshot of this discussion is that Ryle falls somewhere between Descartes and Skinner. He is in agreement with Descartes that it not only makes sense to use mentalistic terminology to describe human activity but is absolutely necessary. But, despite his agreement with Descartes that mental terms are appropriate for describing features of human activity, Ryle is still closer to Skinner's behaviorism than to Descartes's dualism because Ryle thinks that the meaning of mental terms must ultimately be linked to observable behavior. To say that the young man intentionally poured ink on Professor Palmer is to describe *a way of doing something*; it is not to describe a ghostly event. This distinction is why

A Ghostly Event

Ryle is called a "logical behaviorist." The logic of a term like "intentional" must link that term up with some observable behavior.

I think it would be fair to say that Ryle has gone a long way toward dispelling the myth of the ghost in the machine. Yet, problems remain. Ryle thinks that mental terms generally refer to *dispositions to behave* in certain ways. In the same way that we can talk about a pane of glass being

Either some one-eyed, striped, paranoid cannibal anteaters are diaphanous, or they are not. . . .

Not All Thoughts Can Be Acted Upon

disposed to break if struck by a stone, or sugar being disposed to dissolve if placed in liquid, so, according to Ryle, we can discuss human characteristics: "Jill is courageous."—She is disposed to stand her ground. "John knows long division."—He is disposed to be able to solve certain kinds of problems. "Jane is thoughtful."—She is disposed to pause in efficacious ways and not act precipitously. So far, so good. But it is certainly possible to be generally courageous yet uncharacteristically do a cowardly thing. And it is certainly possible to think deeply about long division without being disposed to do anything. Despite Ryle's efforts, the ghost in the machine has not been completely exorcised. It still haunts us in philosophy.

The Mind–Brain Identity Theory

The version of materialism referred to as the mind–brain identity theory does not deny the existence of mental events (as does hard behaviorism) or claim that mental terminology is really a reference to ways of doing things (as does logical behaviorism). Rather, as the name indicates, it claims that mental terms do name real entities but what they name are in fact neurological events. This theory has the advantage over most forms of behaviorism of not needing to deny the Cartesian and commonsensical claim that mental states exist that are experienced as essentially private. (Only I can experience my thought, my headache.) Yet, it avoids all the pitfalls of dualism and seems to have the authority of science behind it.

It goes back more than sixty years (as does behaviorism), when the Australian philosopher J. J. C. SMART wrote, "everything should be explicable in terms of physics," including "sensations and states of consciousness."[5]

Smart's thesis was simply that "sensations are nothing over and above brain processes." He admitted that his thesis could not be *proven* to be true in his day, but he expected that someday it would be proven, and he tried to pave the way for the development. Smart thought that the forthcoming discovery that mental states and processes are just brain states and processes would be very much like the earlier discoveries such as:

- Lightning is an electrical discharge from cloud to cloud or cloud to surface.
- Water is H_2O.
- The morning star is the evening star.

It is important to see that Smart is not claiming that the terms on the left side of the verb "is" *mean* the same things as the terms on the right side. People used the words "lightning" and "water" long before the physical composition of lightning and water were discovered. So, Smart's equation is not just a linguistic one but a scientific one. It can be proved not by looking at words but by looking at facts.

Early on, a number of philosophers (including Jerome Shaffer, Norman Malcolm, and Richard Taylor) registered objections to the identity theory's claim to be scientific by asking exactly *what* facts would have to be discovered to prove the **identity theory** true.[6] Keep in mind the nature of a *strict identity* of the type that holds between the morning star and the evening star (and between mental events and brain events, according to Smart). In terms of spatial and temporal features, everything that is true of the one side of the equation must be true of the other. If the morning star is the evening star, and if the morning star is X miles from the sun at time T^1, then the evening star must also be X miles from the sun at time T^1. If the evening star has a mass of Y, then the morning star must have a mass of Y. If there is any difference in these characteristics, then the morning star is not the evening star. What about thoughts and brain events? Do they have the same spatial and temporal features? But here's the rub. Does it make any sense at all to attribute spatial features to thoughts? Shaffer says:

> However, so far as thoughts are concerned, it makes no sense to talk about a thought's being located in some place or places in the body. If I report having suddenly thought something, the question where in my body that thought occurred would be utterly senseless. It would be as absurd to wonder whether that thought might have been cubical or a micron in diameter.[7]

Shaffer's point is not that it is impossible to prove that thoughts have location, nor that the view that they are located may turn out to be false, but that that view is *absurd*. You can say all sorts of things about the physical properties of neurons—you can talk about their size, shape, color, and weight. But what sense would there be in asking whether the realization that you left your lunch at home was a triangular or tubular realization, a yellow or a gray one, a light or a heavy one? According to Shaffer, if there are things that make perfect sense to say about brain states but are nonsense when said about mental states, then mental states are not brain states, and the identity theory is false (in the same way that if there were things that made perfect sense when said about the morning star but were nonsense when said about the evening star, then the morning

We seem to have a rapidly fading, erratic, incoherent, possibly psychotic neuron firing here.

That's the morning star. It guides sailors across the wine-dark sea.

That's the evening star. Its slithy toves do gyre and gimble in the wabe.

Talking Nonsense about the Evening Star

star could not be the evening star). In other words, Shaffer is accusing Smart of committing a category-mistake.

It is difficult to evaluate Shaffer's view. Is it really impossible that someday linguistic conventions will develop that will allow the association of mental phenomena with physical models? Probably it would have once seemed absurd to associate the experience of warmth or cold with a numerical value, but after the invention of the thermometer, we find that association perfectly normal. Who's to say that a future scientific discovery or invention won't result in the normalization of sentences like "My C-fibers, section M12-0332, just fired at intensity n" instead of "I just realized I left my lunch at home"? Of course, Shaffer would ask how C-fibers firing could be *false* or *misleading* in the way that thoughts and sensations can be. But if enough neurological studies get popularized, who knows?

Another argument arises against the identity theory that is easier to understand and evaluate. This criticism intends not to show the identity theory to be nonsense but to demonstrate it as nonempirical, as not scientific. Suppose that neurophysiology advances so far that someday a kind of brain scanner will exist capable of showing that every time any conscious activity takes place (thoughts, sensations, and emotions), certain neurological activities are identified with exactitude. Every time, for example, María reports that she realizes she left her lunch at home, the scanner demonstrates that her C-fibers, section M12-0332, fired at intensity n and vice versa. Would this demonstration prove that mental states *are* brain states? No. The most it would prove is that mental states are *correlated* with brain states; that is, that every time one happens, the other happens simultaneously. But correlation—even strict correlation—is not identity. Even with the most advanced technological equipment, it would be impossible to establish that just because thoughts are always correlated with events in the brain, they are identical with those events. Therefore, even if the mind–brain identity theory were true, it could never be *known* to be true. It could not, as the philosophers of science say, be "falsified." That is, no evidence could possibly exist that would tend to establish its truth or falsity. This fact certainly detracts from the identity theory's claim to be scientific.

Eliminative Materialism

More recently, some materialists have come to the conclusion that these arguments against the identity theory are cogent, so they have modified the theory to what is called eliminative materialism, or **eliminativism.** According to this version, the identity "Mental events are brain events" should be thought of no longer as being like "The morning star is the evening star" but as being like the following:

> "'Zeus's thunderbolts' are discharges of static electricity."
> "'Demonical possession' is a form of hallucinatory psychosis."
> "The 'quantity of caloric fluid' is the mean kinetic energy of molecules."
> "'Unicorn horns' are narwhals' tusks."[8]

In other words, the correct formula is no longer "X = Y." Rather, it is, "What people used to call X is now known to be Y." Richard Rorty suggests that future scientific discoveries may so upstage our currently ordinary way of talking about "mental-phenomena" that we may someday say, "My C-fibers are stimulated," instead of, "I am in pain." Rorty is not actually claiming that a sentence like "I am in pain" is *false* but that there might someday prove to be a better way of making this report. (By "better," he means better in terms of explanation and predictability.) In fact, Rorty seems loath to say that even sentences like "Zeus's thunderbolts are lighting up the evening sky" or "Dora is possessed by demons" are false. (This reluctance is because he apparently thinks that terms get their meaning and their truth value from being part of a theoretical or quasi-theoretical system and not from some permanent and ahistorical thing called "meaning.") It is just that we have now eliminated these language games for "better" ones.

Nevertheless, Rorty admits that the claim that there might turn out to be no such things as sensations of pain (in the way that there turned out to be no such things as demons) seems scandalous, but he thinks that the scandal alone does not constitute a refutation of his theory.

Not surprisingly, a goodly number of philosophers do think that the scandal is enough to refute eliminative materialism. However, even though eliminative materialism is no longer the most popular theory among materialistically inclined **philosophers of mind,** eliminativism still has some distinguished defenders today, most notably PATRICIA and PAUL CHURCHLAND, philosophers at the University of California at San Diego. For the Churchlands, mentalistic talk is simply part of "folk psychology"—the common, prescientific way of speaking about feelings, motivation, and conscious phenomena. For them, folk psychology has approximately the same status as folk physics, a quasi-theoretical system we still use

Ben Is about to Learn Something Important

when we say things like "The sun is setting in the west," even though we now know better. According to the Churchlands, some of the components of folk psychology will eventually be shown to be reducible to components of neurobiology, and the rest will be shown to refer to nothing at all (like the "it" in "it is raining") and therefore will prove to be expendable. In this latter category, we may find such items as mental images, beliefs, feelings, and desires.

Another important example of eliminative materialism is that of DANIEL DENNETT in his book of 1991, *Consciousness Explained.* This is an ironic title, because it could have been called *Consciousness Eliminated* or, at least,

> Doc, I'm in terrible pain!

> Not really.

Consciousness Redefined. Dennett apparently believes that scientific discourse can take place only in the objective third person, and (if his critic JOHN SEARLE is right) the only objects that really exist in the world are those that can be the object of scientific scrutiny. Given those two presuppositions, the concept of consciousness can only be treated behavioristically. (In his youth, Dennett was a student of GILBERT RYLE (1900–1976) at Oxford.) Therefore, for Dennett, to be scientifically respectable, the word "consciousness" must have a different meaning than the one we derive from our own first-person experiences. The common "folk meaning" is null and void. In a book attacking Dennett's position, Searle asks his reader to perform a small experiment: to reach to your left arm with your right hand and pinch with some force the skin of that arm. Then he asks you to describe exactly what happened when you did this. Then Searle points out that the content of whatever you report (e.g., "it hurts") is, according to Dennett, an appearance and not a reality. Does that mean it *doesn't* really hurt? If not that, what does it mean?[9]

Since the mind is not what we thought it was, what is it, according to Dennett? The eliminative position Dennett defends is called Strong Artificial Intelligence (Strong AI), according to which the brain is a digital computer and the so-called mind is a computer program. (Weak AI holds that the computer model is only a metaphor to help understand the mind's function.) To refute AI, strong or weak, Searle has constructed a thought experiment called "The Chinese Room Argument." It is a mental experiment involving carrying out the steps in a program for answering questions in a language you do not understand.

> I imagine that I am locked in a room with a lot of boxes of Chinese symbols (the database), I get small bunches of Chinese symbols passed to me (questions in Chinese), and I look up in a rule book (the program) what I am supposed to do. I perform certain operations on the symbols in accordance with the rules (that is, I carry out the steps in the program) and give back small bunches of symbols (answers to the questions) to those outside the room. I am the computer implementing a program for answering questions in Chinese, but all the same, I do not understand a word of Chinese. And this is the point: *if I do not understand Chinese solely on the basis of implementing a computer program for understanding Chinese, then neither does any other digital computer solely on that basis, because no digital computer has anything I do not have.* (p. 11)

The moral of the story is this:

1. (Computer) programs are entirely syntactical (i.e., rule-following procedures).
2. Minds have a semantics (i.e., produce and deal with meanings).

3. Syntax is not the same as, nor by itself sufficient for, semantics.
4. Therefore, (computer) "programs are not minds" (p. 12). End of argument.

Searle believes that this simple demonstration refutes Strong AI and shows Weak AI to be misleading. He believes he has eliminated the most recent version of eliminative materialism.

Functionalism and Its Discontents

Despite the problems that have plagued behaviorism and the mind–brain identity theory and eliminativism, most philosophers of mind seem to agree that *some* form of materialism (or "physicalism," as it is also sometimes called) must be true. More recently, the theory that has had the most appeal is functionalism. A great number of philosophers subscribe to it, but it is associated primarily with Jerry Fodor and Hilary Putnam, who are the pioneers, along with David Armstrong, David Lewis, and William Lycan. It emerged from the concerns expressed by **cognitive science,** a synthesis of philosophy, computer science, and neurology. Functionalism attempts, therefore, to develop a theory of mind that takes advantage of the insights of all three fields of study. According to functionalism, the mind must be thought of not as a *thing* (such as a Cartesian substance or a brain) but as a *system*. A system is an ensemble of related components with a function. This function can be described as the job that the system accomplishes—what it gets done. Or, to put it differently, it is the way that the collection of components interacts with the environment. In defining functions it is as if we were giving job descriptions. Think of a nurse or a welder. To qualify for either position you must possess certain knowledge and skills and you must be able to perform certain actions. Such requirements are also true of artifacts like knives and engines. But two different knives or two different engines can be composed of very different materials. They remain knives or engines just so long as they are able to perform their functions—to cut and to produce power, respectively.

Now, what function do minds perform? According to the functionalist model, minds primarily carry out computations. The process of computation can be characterized as the manipulation of symbols in accordance with formal rules. So far, it sounds as if the functionalists are defining minds as computers (and in that sense, are in Dennett's camp), and, indeed, most of them do not hesitate to say that computers think. But it is not only humans and computers that have minds, according to functionalism. Lower animals such as jellyfish or aliens such as Martians have minds if they can carry out computations. Functionalists want to avoid what they call "human chauvinism"—the error of defining minds so that, a priori, they could be attributed *only* to humans.

Functionalists like to say that mental phenomena are "multiply realiz-

able." The same function, or "job description," might be realized in physical systems that are very different from each other. In fact, if it could be demonstrated that a row of tin cans, or a row of tin cans and jellyfish, could produce computations, then the functionalists would assert that that "system" had a mind. And if it could be empirically established that there exist angels or gods that can engage in computation, then the functionalist would be committed to agreeing that they too had minds.

This last example shows that functionalism is not *necessarily* a form of materialism. However, it will tend to remain materialistic until empirical evidence of the existence of computational angels or gods becomes overwhelming. Then in what sense can we call functionalism a form of materialism? Well, for example, in human beings, thoughts and intentions are caused by events in the brain. Events in the brain are material events, but thoughts and intentions are not material events. The brain relates to its products (mental events) in the same way that a computer relates to its computations. The solution to a mathematical problem—say, the square root of nine—whether reached by a human or a computer, is not itself a material state or event. Mental events are realized in parts of brains but are not themselves identical to parts of brains. If we speak of minds or mental capacities, we are abstracting from the brains that realize them and speaking about a higher level—the actions that the brains realize. These mental events enter into causal networks. A decision or an intention can produce something in the world, so decisions and intentions have causal power. We do not have to choose between the language of the programmer and the language of the engineer who builds the computer. They are both right; they are talking about different levels of reality. Similarly, we do not have to choose between the language of the neurologist and the language of common sense. Ordinary language is right. There *are* mental events (I *do* intend to go to the movies tonight), and they are real (my intention will produce some action). Materialism is also correct. All mental events are realized in material systems (as far as we know). As philosopher of mind JOHN HEIL says:

> Functionalism is staunchly anti-reductionist, firmly committed to a conception of the world as containing distinct and irreducible levels of properties. Although higher levels are thought to be "autonomous" with respect to lower levels—higher levels are not reducible to, identifiable with, or collapsible into lower levels—higher levels are typically said to "supervene" on (to "depend on" and/or be "determined by") lower levels.[10]

Well, then, is functionalism the definitive answer to the mind–body problem? I am sure that you will not be surprised when I tell you that, despite its general popularity among professional philosophers, it has suffered some criticism. We have already seen that Professor Searle has argued against the adequacy of any computer-based model of the mind. According to Searle, no successful concept of mind can be generated that lacks a *semantics,* and no system involving merely the manipulation of uninterpreted symbols can produce such a theory; it can only produce a *syntax*—a set of formal rules for maneuvering meaningless cyphers. As Searle says, "A computer has a syntax, but no semantics."[11] To repeat, a set of purely formal rules (*syntax*) cannot produce meaning (semantics). If I teach a parrot to utter the sounds "finthangks" whenever it hears the sounds "hou är yōō?" I will not have bestowed a mind on it. Furthermore, according to Searle, functionalists place far too much emphasis on the idea that computer programs follow rules. Following rules, too, requires a semantics. He says, "In order that a rule be followed, the meaning of the rule has to play some causal role in the behavior. . . . *In the sense in which human beings follow rules . . . , in that sense computers don't follow rules at all. They only act in accord with certain formal procedures*" (p. 47). He calls this point a metaphorical sense of rule following and claims that functionalism trades on the confusion between the literal and metaphorical senses of the term.

Another kind of argument against functionalism has to do not with the semantic components of mental experience but rather with its *qualitative* features, an area that functionalism almost totally ignores. You will recall that in his *Meditations,* Descartes asked how it was possible to be certain that the people who surrounded him were not in fact merely well-functioning "automatic machines" that duplicated human behavior and language (see pages 121–122). Although these machines could manipulate symbols and carry out calculations, they would have no thoughts and no feelings. They could simulate smiles and frowns and produce the sounds equivalent to saying that they had forgotten their umbrellas, but they would feel no pain, no joy, no dread, no excitement, could taste no sweetness, nor feel any breeze caress their "skin." They could distinguish between a fine burgundy and a cheap jug wine (perhaps by molecular analysis), but they could not taste the difference. The sensations that these machines lack have come to be known in the literature as **qualia,** from the Latin word for "qualities." Descartes's automatic machines would experience no qualia. They would be, for all intents and purposes, zombies. Now, the question we must ask is, how do you know that your functionalist philosophy professor is not a zombie? Functionalism seems perfectly compatible with the possibility that no minds experience qualia. So, the next question is, how do you know that *you* experience qualia? And if you think that you *do* experience them (and you probably do think so), how do you know that they are real? Is the last question I posed absurd, as some of the critics of functionalism believe? If so, we seem to be plunged right back into Descartes's world, and it appears that not much progress has been made since his time.

Because of considerations like these, a number of philosophers have once again turned their attention to the problem of the *experience* of mental states. As one of them has recently written, "Consciousness is back. [Despite] becoming a taboo topic for much of the last fifty years, consciousness currently enjoys the status of a 'hot' topic in both psychology and the philosophy of mind."[12] The contemporary version of the problem of consciousness was first dramatically raised by Thomas Nagel in his influential article of 1974, "What Is It Like to Be a Bat?" Nagel points out that "anyone who has spent some time in an enclosed space with an excited bat knows what it is to encounter a fundamentally *alien* form of life."[13] This is because bats

> perceive the external world primarily by sonar, or echolocation, detecting the reflections, from objects within range, of their own rapid, subtly modulated, high-frequency shrieks. Their brains are designed to correlate the outgoing impulses with the subsequent echoes, and the information thus acquired enables bats to make precise discriminations of distance, size, shape, motion and texture comparable to those we make by vision.

Now, as scientists we might someday learn everything there is to know about how the brains and nervous systems of bats work, but we still would have no idea what it is like to be a bat—what "bat experience" is like. Nagel reminds us that he is not asking what it would be like if you were a bat (eating insects, hanging from the rafters by your feet, etc.). Rather, he is asking what's it like for a *bat* to be a bat. Nagel and his followers conclude from this failed thought experiment that exhaustive studies of the human brain and nervous system may be able to explain what causes human mental experience but not what that experience is. The only way to answer the question, "What is it like to *be* a human being (to have human experiences)?" is to be a human being. Luckily, we are human beings, so we know what it is like, but we still have no idea how to give any scientific or philosophical account of mental experience.

We will look at three responses to this new concern about the problem of consciousness. Keep in mind (no pun intended) that each of these responses is well known among contemporary philosophers, but each is a minority report. It seems that most philosophers of mind have opted to stick with one version or another of functionalism.

John Searle, whom we have already met, believes that the mind–body problem is easy to solve. Conscious states are perfectly real *and* they are material in nature. That is, they are biological states of the brain. He writes:

> Mental phenomena, all mental phenomena whether conscious or unconscious, visual or auditory, pains, tickles, itches, thoughts, indeed, all of our mental life, are caused by processes going on in the brain. (p. 18)

But mental phenomena are not just caused by brain processes. They *"just are features of the brain (and perhaps the rest of the central nervous system)"* (p. 19). In the same way that microproperties in physics (such as molecules, atoms, and subatomic particles) can be said to produce or constitute macroproperties (such as liquidity or hardness), so the microproperties of the human brain (neurons) produce macroproperties of consciousness (thoughts, emotions, etc.). In the same way that no individual molecules are wet or hard, no individual neurons are subjective or exhibit **intentionality** (i.e., neurons are not *about* other things; they do not refer to other things). But in certain dynamic combinations, oxygen and hydrogen molecules manifest liquidity and the lattice structure occupied by the molecules of which the table is composed manifests solidity. Similarly, the firing of neurons at the microlevel produces consciousness at the macrolevel. Such neurological activity manifests itself as the desires that make me *want* liquid or tables. That is, some biological states are intentional. This is simply a scientific fact, according to Searle. Furthermore, the reason that mental events can be the cause of physical events is that mental events *are* physical events. (Remember, Descartes declared the mind to be an independent substance because mental states seemed to him to be so completely different from physical states; but because of these gross differences, he could not explain how mental events could cause physical events. This was the modern beginning of the mind–body problem.)

According to Searle, the reason many philosophers reject his simple solution to the mind–body problem is that they fail to see how the same micro–macro relationship that applies in physics also applies in neurology. Furthermore, they misguidedly assume that the scientific world-picture entails that every fact must be an objective fact, that is, every fact can be described from a third-person point of view. But according to Searle, it is

> a mistake to suppose that the definition of reality should exclude subjectivity. If "science" is the name of the collection of objective and systematic truths we can state about the world, then the existence of subjectivity is an objective scientific fact like any other. . . . [I]t is just a plain fact about biological evolution that it has produced certain sorts of biological systems, namely human and certain animal brains, that have subjective features. (p. 25)

Well-known analytic philosopher, Galen Strawson, whom we will meet again in chapter 6, begins a recent essay with this question:

"What is the silliest claim that has ever been made? The competition is fierce, but I think the answer is easy. Some people have denied the existence of consciousness: conscious experience, the subjective character of experience, the what-is-it-like of experience."[14]

Strawson calls this "the Great Silliness" (130). He includes Daniel Dennett and the early Richard Rorty in this group of "Deniers" (132), and makes them

sound something like
Holocaust deniers. Then, is
Strawson a Cartesian dualist? No, he claims to be a
naturalist (viz., "there are
no supernatural or unnatural events in the universe
[nor out of it].") (154). In
fact, "naturalism is the
same thing as physicalism"
(154), which is the same
thing as materialism. So
how can a materialist think
that consciousness is real
and knowable? In fact,
according to him, con-
sciousness cannot be
explained by traditional
physics, which is still an
incomplete science: "we

WHAT IS THE SILLIEST CLAIM THAT HAS
EVER BEEN MADE?

are in many ways profoundly ignorant of the fundamental nature of things"
(139). He points out that physicists still argue about quantum mechanics,
"dark energy . . . and even gravity" (139). Strawson concludes with one
word, "*Ignoramus.*" (Latin for "We do not know.")

Another, more radical response to the question of the relation between
the mind and the world comes from DAVID CHALMERS. It too is a minority
report, but his 1996 book, *The Conscious Mind: In Search of a Fundamental
Theory,* published by the Oxford University Press, made a big splash. Chalmers
doesn't deny that functionalism does a pretty good job of dealing with certain
cognitive computational skills, such as cataloguing similarities, discriminating
among stimuli, and responding to challenges, but he chides the materialistic
philosophers of mind for avoiding the "hard" questions about consciousness.
They never did give a theory of consciousness; rather, they gave theories of
everything else. What is missing for Chalmers is exactly what was missing for
Nagel, namely, an account of the fact that there is something like being conscious, (as in Nagel's question, "What is it like to be a bat?"), that there is
something called *conscious experience* that is rich, deep, and undeniable.

According to Chalmers, a successful theory must deal with consciousness as a fundamental property in the way that physicists deal with fundamental properties in their own fields. Similarly, just as physicists show that
these properties behave in accord with basic laws that relate them to other

fundamental properties, so must the philosophy of mind face up to the fact that there must be basic laws that relate conscious life to the rest of reality. Chalmers is committed, therefore, to a blatant form of dualism, though it should be called **property dualism** rather than **substance dualism,** as in Descartes's ontology. Mental properties, for example, intentionality, are real features of the world, just as are physical properties such as three-dimensionality. But the fact that these properties are real does not entail that there are real substances (such as "minds") to which these properties belong. It is enough that these are real properties of the real world. According to Chalmers, once we have stated those laws, there will be no mysterious gaps between the physical and the mental features of the world. This dualistic picture will become part of the scientific understanding of reality.

Though Chalmers has impressed many of his opponents with his refutations of some of the standard arguments of functionalism and has gained sympathizers with his demonstration that functionalism as it now exists can never produce a real theory of consciousness, what appear to be the weakest links in his own theory are the psychophysical bridging laws that his theory requires. Critics say that these laws have yet to be clearly conceived.

The last of the antifunctionalists we will look at is COLIN MCGINN, who is not only a minority voice in the discussion of the mind–brain problem but is more like a voice crying in the wilderness. But like Saint John the Baptist—the first such voice—McGinn is heard by many and has baptized a few converts. His several books on the topic are well known, and his articles appear in many anthologies of the philosophy of mind.

In his book of 1999, *The Mysterious Flame: Conscious Minds in a Material World,* McGinn starts with a very Cartesian idea:

We are aware of consciousness inwardly, while we are aware of the brain

Colin McGinn: A Voice in the Wilderness

outwardly. . . . You can look into your mind until you burst, and you will not discover neurons and synapses and all the rest; and you can stare at someone's brain from dawn to dusk and you will not perceive the consciousness that is so apparent to the person whose brain you are so rudely eyeballing.[15]

Yet there *must* be a unity, McGinn argues. (He is, after all, a materialist.) He agrees with Searle, whom he does not mention in his book, that consciousness must arise from neural states in accordance with a "principle of emergence," the way ice emerges from the properties of liquid. But unlike Searle, McGinn does not believe that anyone—philosopher or neurologist—has come anywhere near explaining what those neurological properties are or "how the brain contrives to generate consciousness to begin with" (p. 69). Furthermore, we "have no idea what an explanation of consciousness would even *look like*" (p. 61). Because our ignorance is so abysmal, McGinn concludes that the sciences of physics and neurophysiology are radically incomplete—given their current formulations, they *cannot* solve the problem—and he begins to suspect that they are incompletable.

We have stumbled onto such an intractable problem that it shows that science cannot answer all questions about material reality. This barrier does not stop McGinn from speculating that perhaps what we have failed to grasp is something about space itself, because, as Descartes pointed out, it is impossible to understand mental states spatially. Yet, says McGinn, being physical events, they must in some sense be spatial. McGinn wonders "whether the cognitive abilities with which evolution has equipped us are adequate to developing the radically new conception of space that [may be] required for understanding consciousness" (p. 130).

After briefly surveying the history of evolution and the kinds of tools for survival that it has provided us, McGinn pessimistically concludes that there is no good reason to suppose that Mother Nature installed in us the necessary conceptual apparatus. He says, "We are facing a problem that points to an enormous hole in our conceptual resources, a theoretical blindspot of epic proportions. This is why I refer to the problem as a *mystery*" (p. 62). He seems to delight in the fact that his enemies have called him a "hard-core mysterian" (p. 134), and he thinks that the mystery is not completely a bad thing. Perhaps it will humble us humans a bit and return us to the awe with which the original Greek philosophers faced in wonder the mystery that anything exists at all.

So, the purple haze descends,[16] the mysterious flame burns, and the ghost still haunts the machine.

Pluralism

So far we have looked at dualism and materialistic monism. Another alternative exists, and that is pluralism. Ontological pluralism is the view that there is a plurality of real things and that this plurality cannot be reduced either to a duality or to a oneness.

A version of this view emerged during the twenty-year period after World War II at the hands of a group of British philosophers to whom we have already referred as ordinary language philosophers. Under the influence of Cambridge philosopher G. E. Moore's (1873–1958) influential paper "A Defense of Common Sense" and the philosophy of Ludwig Wittgenstein (see more about him in Chapter 10), these philosophers defended a version of **naive realism** according to which reality is pretty much what it seems to be. Neither the categories of dualism or monism nor Kant's "categories of the understanding" but the categories of ordinary

The Argument between the Monist and the Dualist

language correctly account for the real world. Members of this school, such as Gilbert Ryle (whose logical behaviorism we just inspected), ask why we should accept the dualists' claim that everything in the world must fit in either of two boxes (mind or matter) or the materialists' view that everything must fit in *one* box. There are *hundreds* of boxes. There are humans, rocks, clouds, newts, prime numbers, plans, leopards, carrots, square roots, political parties, corporations, marriages, and birthday parties (just for starters). There are also symphonies. Take Beethoven's Fifth. Is it physical, is it mental, or is it a combination

Maybe this one will be mental and the Ninth physical ...

Ludwig van Beethoven Contemplating the Fifth Symphony, Trying to Decide Whether It Is a Mental or a Physical Thing

of a physical thing and a mental thing? Nobody (but a philosopher) would ever ask such a question. Very little of interest can be said about Beethoven's Fifth in terms of these categories, and people who do have interesting things to say about it hardly ever deliver that information in terms of its being a physical thing or a mental thing.

Well, that's it! Now nothing is illegal.

What's true of Beethoven's Fifth is true of the U.S. Constitution. Is it a physical thing? No. Even if the parchment in Washington, D.C., burned, we would still have a constitution. Nor does it make much sense to say that it is a mental thing (in which case, if for a moment everyone stopped thinking about it, would it cease to exist?). If it is a thing at all, it is a *social* thing, which is not at all the same as being a physical and a mental thing.

Ryle and the ordinary language philosophers did not deny that some things that exist in reality could be analyzed in terms of physics and chemistry. But they insisted that those things cannot be *reduced* to the categories of physics and chemistry. There is a fallacy involved in saying that because a table can be analyzed in terms of its molecular structure, therefore, the table itself is unreal (or even less real than the molecules). A colleague of mine, a physics professor, tells his students that tables are not really solid. Then he explains that this is so because there is more space taken up by the distance between the atoms in the table than by the atoms themselves. Ryle would say that this argument is absurd (another category-mistake). Here the scientist is wrong and ordinary language is right. Tables are solid (or at least good tables are solid) even though the space between the atoms is greater than the space taken up by the atoms. As Ryle points out, the so-called world of science is not a more *real* world than the world of tables and chairs, any more than "the poultry world" (the name of a magazine for chicken farmers) is a more real world than the everyday world.

The Table Is Not Solid

Conclusion

What conclusion should we draw from the various ontological alternatives presented and the welter of arguments for and against them? First, it seems to me that there is no good reason to believe radical dualism and lots of reasons to disbelieve it. In my opinion, the claim that there are two kinds of substances, a physical one and a spiritual one, has very little, if any, scientific evidence to back it up; and the philosophical problems generated by this view are so great as to overshadow any advantage the theory may have.

What about materialism? My own view is that in *some* sense, materialism must be true. That is, it must be true that our small corner of the universe is composed of the same "stuff" that the rest of the universe is composed of, and at this point in the history of science, this truth means that the universe is apparently composed of subatomic parti-cles that are themselves composed of bundles or quanta of energy. But the sense in which materialism is true may turn out to be fairly trivial because I don't think there's much reason to expect that the accounts of human activity given by anthropologists, sociolo-

Dualism, If True, Does Have One Distinct Advantage

gists, psychologists, and by ourselves as ordinary individuals describing our own and other people's thoughts, actions, hopes, fears, and suspicions will ever be given in a more accurate form in terms of molecules, atoms, elec-trons, and quanta of energy. As the important American philosopher Saul Kripke puts it:

> Materialism, I think, must hold that a physical description of the world is a *complete* description of it, that any mental facts are "ontologically depen-dent" on physical facts in the straightforward sense of following from them by necessity. No identity theorist seems to me to have made a con-vincing argument against the intuitive view that this is not the case.[17]

It isn't just with "mental facts" that materialism seems inadequate but perhaps even more so with "institutional facts." Consider three examples.

The first one is, "Bill sees Mary." Is it possible that someday there may exist a purely physical description—a description in terms of the laws and entities of physics and chemistry—that logically entails this statement? I'm not sure what that description would look like, but I think it is plausibly the case, so we'll concede victory to the materialist here.

The second example is, "Bill loves Mary." Is it possible that someday there may exist a purely physical description—a description in terms of the laws and entities of physics and chemistry—that logically entails the second statement? Can we imagine some kind of brain scanner, biopsy, or blood test that would definitely answer the question, "Does Bill love Mary?" I don't think this scenario is likely, but, because of a newspaper article about a neurological study I recently read, I'll grant this possibility to the materialist too. In the study, researchers found that one particular spot in the MRI images, in the caudate nucleus, was especially active in people who had scored high on a questionnaire measuring passionate love.[18]

The third example is, "Bill is married to Mary." Can we anticipate a purely physical description that replaces this statement? I think not. There will be no brain scanner, biopsy, or blood test that can determine that this third statement is true or false for the simple reason that being married is not a *physical* state at all, nor is it merely an emotional or mental state. It is a *legal* state, a social state. If Bill is an unmarried, eligible male, and he stands before an ordained clergyman alongside Mary, who is an unmarried, eligible female, and if they both respond to certain questions the clergyman poses to them by saying, "I do," then they are married, and no brain scanner, biopsy, blood or urine test will be pertinent to determine or refute that fact. Of course, it must be true that in *some* sense

Fraggely daggely doop?

Then I pronounce you frizzly dap and lazltap.

I do.

I do.

all of Bill's and Mary's molecules had to be in a certain condition for this marriage to take place, but this is the trivial sense in which materialism is true. Sociology and anthropology are the sciences of human conventions, and there is no reason to expect that their descriptions of those conventions, along with our ordinary discourse about them, will someday be replaced by descriptions of molecules. The error of materialism is that of accepting J. J. C. Smart's claim, "everything should be explicable in terms of physics." Why *should* everything be explicable in terms of physics? Why, for example, should a description of the historical significance of Velázquez's painting *The Surrender of Breda* and of its aesthetic qualities be "explicable in terms of physics"? There are, as Ludwig Wittgenstein said, *many* forms of life, and it is a philosophical error to assume that there must be one model to account for all of them.

In rejecting dualism and in rejecting materialism in any but a trivial sense, I seem to be making a pitch for a Rylean kind of pluralism, and in some ways, I am. I find some loose combination of the categories of discourse of ordinary language, philosophy, literature, and the physical and social sciences to be adequate, or at least very helpful, in trying to make my way about in the world. But what about myself as an *ontologist?* Remember the big questions we asked at the beginning of this chapter: What is real and what is

Look it up in the chapter on Spanish art.

BASIC PHYSICS

merely appearance? Can there be a *theory* that draws the distinction between reality and appearance and accounts for everything that exists, or must these distinctions always remain contextual, ad hoc, and informal? I think at this point in our intellectual development the latter option seems to be the correct one. But what does this option mean for ontology? Can there not be a *theory of reality*? Maybe not. J. L. Austin, who was trashing the idea of sense data last time we saw him, has this to say about the word "real":

[the word "real" is] highly exceptional; exceptional in this respect that, unlike "yellow" or "horse" or "walk," it does not have one single, specifiable, always-the-same meaning. (Even Aristotle saw through this idea.) *Nor* does it have a large number of different meanings. . . .

"A real duck" differs from the simple "a duck" only in that it is used to exclude various ways of being not a real duck—but a dummy, a toy, a picture, a decoy, etc.; and moreover I don't know *just* how to take the assertion that

it's a real duck unless I know just what, on that particular occasion, the speaker has it in mind to exclude.

. . . .

It should be quite clear, that there are no criteria to be laid down *in general* for distinguishing the real from the not real. How this is to be done must depend on *what* it is with respect to which the problem arises in particular cases.[19]

What if Austin is right, and there is no such *thing* as "reality," hence no such study as "the study of reality"? Does that mean that the center does not hold and that our only function as ontologists is to communicate that dizzying truth? No. We can still philosophically scrutinize the various "forms of life" (political, religious, artistic, moral, and scientific) and try to see how they hang together, if in fact they do hang together. And we must be vigilant for new breakthroughs in some of these areas—for new **paradigm shifts,** as they are now called—because a major shift in science, art, or politics may well call for a shift both in our "ordinary" way of looking at the world and in the content of our philosophy. So the ontological task, like most philosophical tasks, is ongoing.

Topics for Consideration

1. Take the following sentences from ordinary English and relate them to Descartes's mind–body problem:
   She has a good mind.
   He has a good body.
   She almost lost her mind.
   Unfortunately, he is senile. He is no longer the uncle I once knew.
2. Descartes believed that we dream all night and that even when we have been knocked "unconscious," we must still have thoughts moving through our minds. Explain why he is committed to this view.
3. Discuss "the problem of other minds." How do *you* know that the person sitting next to you in class is not just a (very well made and perhaps attractively constructed) robot?
4. Descartes says that to have a mind is to be able "to affirm, to deny, to conceive, to know, to hope, to expect, to will," and so forth. He denies that animals have this capacity. Do you think *your* dog can perform all or some of these mental acts? On what evidence do you base your conclusion? Are you convinced that the evidence really supports your conclusion? (In other words, do we really need psychological categories to explain animal behavior? What about plant behavior?)
5. In reference to question 4, Skinner says that if we don't need psychological categories for plants and animals, we don't need them for humans either. Explain that view and criticize or defend it.
6. State the difference between the mind–brain identity theory set forth by J. J. C. Smart and the theory of eliminative materialism as defended by Richard Rorty.

7. What exactly do you see as Galen Strawson's stance concerning the role of *consciousness* in philosophical and scientific theories?
8. John Searle claims to have solved the mind–body problem; Colin McGinn believes it still remains a mystery. Which of these assertions seems most accurate to you and why?
9. What exactly is J. L. Austin saying about the word "reality"? Is Austin calling for the end of ontological theory?

Suggestions for Further Reading: Paperback Editions

Brian Cooney, ed., *The Place of Mind* (Belmont, CA: Wadsworth, 2000). An excellent anthology that includes selections from almost all the philosophers mentioned in this chapter: Descartes, Ryle, Smart, the Churchlands, Kripke, Rorty, Fodor, Putnam, Searle, Nagel, and McGinn.

Daniel Dennett, *Consciousness Explained* (Boston, MA: Little, Brown, 1991). Dennett is a forceful thinker and a good writer. He seems to have a small chip on his shoulder.

René Descartes, *Meditations on First Philosophy*. You should read Descartes firsthand. His short book is quite manageable. For Descartes's ontology, concentrate on Meditations I, II, and VI.

Colin McGinn, *The Mysterious Flame: Conscious Minds in a Material World* (New York: *Basic* Books, 1999). A statement of McGinn's reasons for believing that the mind–body problem may never be solved. Written in a spirited fashion for a general audience.

Thomas Nagel, *The View from Nowhere* (New York: Oxford University Press, 1986). A book by an important American philosopher showing, among other things, why we are probably not in a position to solve the mind–body problem.

Thomas Nagel, "What Is It Like to Be a Bat?" *Philosophical Review*, Vol. 83, No. 4 (October 1974), pp. 435–450. Also available in a number of philosophical anthologies including the Cooney text listed here. A strong, readable argument explaining why consciousness cannot be eliminated in the way the hard-core materialist wants to do.

Gilbert Ryle, *The Concept of Mind* (Chicago, IL: University of Chicago Press, 1984). A classic of linguistic philosophy. Concentrate particularly on Chapter 1, "Descartes's Myth."

John Searle, *Minds, Brains, and Science* (Cambridge, MA: Harvard University Press, 1984). One of America's most interesting philosophers tackles the mind–body problem and claims to solve it.

John Searle, *The Rediscovery of the Mind* (Cambridge, MA: MIT Press, 1992). Another readable book by Professor Searle, showing why the mind has not been eliminated yet from philosophy and why it's not likely to be.

B. F. Skinner, *Beyond Freedom and Dignity* (New York: Bantam Books, 1972). A readable firsthand account of behaviorism by its most famous architect.

Notes

1. René Descartes, *Meditations on First Philosophy, in The Essential Descartes,* ed. Margaret D. Wilson, trans. Elizabeth S. Haldane and G. R. T. Ross (New York: New American Library, 1969), "Meditation II," p. 174. Unless otherwise stated, all subsequent quotes from Descartes in this chapter are from this source.

2. René Descartes, *The Passions of the Soul, in The Essential Descartes,* ed. Margaret D. Wilson, trans. Elizabeth S. Haldane and G. R. T. Ross (New York: New American Library, 1969), p. 362.

3. Gilbert Ryle, *The Concept of Mind* (Chicago, IL: University of Chicago Press, 1984), pp. 11–13, 15–16.

4. Lewis Carroll, *Alice's Adventures in Wonderland* and *Through the Looking Glass* (New York: New American Library, 1960), p. 194.

5. Smart, J. J. C., "Sensations and Brain Processes," *Philosophical Review,* Vol. 68 (1959), pp. 141–156.

6. See Norman Malcolm, *Problems of Mind: Descartes to Wittgenstein* (New York: Harper and Row, 1971); Jerome Shaffer, "Recent Work on the Mind-Body Problem," *American Philosophical Quarterly,* Vol. 2, No. 2 (1965), pp. 81–104; Richard Taylor, *Metaphysics,* 2nd ed. (Englewood Cliffs, NJ: Prentice-Hall, 1974), pp. 11–37.

7. Jerome A. Shaffer, "Recent Work on the Mind-Body Problem," p. 97.

8. All these examples are from Richard Rorty, "Mind-Body Identity, Privacy and Categories," *Review of Metaphysics,* Vol. 19, No. 1 (September 1965), pp. 24–54.

9. John Searle, *The Mystery of Consciousness* (New York: A New York Review Book, 1997), p. 97. Further quotations from this book will be included in the text.

10. John Heil, *Philosophy of Mind: A Contemporary Introduction* (London and New York: Routledge, 1998), p. 99.

11. John Searle, *Minds, Brains, and Science* (Cambridge, MA: Harvard University Press, 1984), p. 33. Subsequent quotes from Searle are from this source.

12. Henry Jackman, "Review of The Nature of Consciousness," eds. Ned Block, Owen Flanagan, and Güven Güzeldere (Cambridge, MA: MIT Press, 1997), in *Teaching Philosophy,* Vol. 23, No. 1 (March 2000), p. 100.

13. Thomas Nagel, "What Is It Like to Be a Bat?" *Philosophical Review,* Vol. 83 (October, 1974), pp. 435–450. Reprinted in *The Place of Mind,* ed. Brian Cooney (Belmont, CA: Wadsworth, 2000), pp. 321–330. Reference is to page 324 of Cooney. All subsequent quotes from Nagel are from this source.

14. Galen Strawson, *Things that Bother Me: Death, Freedom, the Self, Etc.* (New York: New York Review Books, 2018), p. 130.

15. Colin McGinn, *The Mysterious Flame: Conscious Minds in a Material World* (New York: Basic Books, 1999), p. 47. Subsequent quotes from McGinn are from this source.

16. A readable book on the philosophy of mind is Joseph Levine's *Purple Haze: The Puzzle of Consciousness* (New York and Oxford, England: Oxford University Press, 2001).

17. Saul Kripke, quoted in the *New York Times Magazine* (August 14, 1977), sec. 6, p. 14.

18. The article, by Benedict Cary in *The International Herald Tribune,* May 31, 2005, was titled "A Crazy Thing Called Love." The study was conducted by Helen Fisher, Lucy Brown, and Arthur Aron.

19. John L. Austin, *Sense and Sensibilia,* ed. G. J. Warnock (New York: Oxford University Press, 1964), pp. 64–76.

5

Mount Olympus, Mount Moriah, and Other Godly Places
Philosophy of Religion

The big questions here are: Are there any good reasons for believing in God's existence or nonexistence? What kind of God exists or does not exist? What are the implications of God's existence or nonexistence for humans?

It looks as though every culture that has ever flourished has had some concept of divinity. Of course, it doesn't follow from that fact that therefore there *is* a divinity (any more than the fact that every culture believes itself to be superior to its neighbors means that every culture *is* superior to its neighbors). Still, the mere cultural universality of religious belief is an impressive fact. The answer to the question "Why do so many people believe in gods?" is a very complicated one because it entangles us in a

What Are the Implications of God's Existence . . . or Nonexistence?

thicket of psychological, sociological, anthropological, and philosophical—not to mention purely religious—issues. In this chapter, we shall be primarily interested in the philosophical issues, which means that we will attend to the kinds of *arguments* to consider when asking whether there are any good reasons to believe or disbelieve in the existence of god(s).

Every Culture Has Had a Conception of Divinity

Presenting the discussion this way, however, may make us sound unduly rational, as if on issues like religion we all start with Locke's famous "blank slate," then fill it with different arguments for different positions, and then choose the most reasonable one and discard the others. But such an approach is not likely. On the issue of religious belief, very few of us are this antiseptically objective. Bertrand Russell was perhaps an exception. In his autobiography, he tells us that he became an **atheist** at eighteen when he decided that the "first cause" argument was invalid. But he became a theist again in his fourth year at Cambridge when he concluded that an alternative proof of God's existence was valid. Russell wrote:

> I had gone out to buy a tin of tobacco and was going back with it along Trinity Lane when suddenly I threw it up in the air and exclaimed: "Great God in boots!—the ontological argument is sound!"[1]

Later, however, he discovered what he took to be a flaw in the argument and reverted to atheism.

I suspect that most of us have views on God's existence that are less obviously determined by the mere validity of arguments than Russell claimed to be the case for himself. (Keep in mind, however, that this is the man who wrote about his sixteenth year, "There was a footpath leading across the fields to New Southgate, and I used to go there alone to watch the sunset and contemplate suicide. I did not, however, commit suicide because I wished to know more of mathematics.")[2] Then perhaps those of us who are not as dispassionate about religion are merely rationalizing when we give our "reasons" for believing or disbelieving in God (rationalizing in the pejorative sense, the sense of using reason and logic illegitimately

to support biases and opinions that we dearly *want* to
believe). Not necessarily.
Probably, no such thing as
the pure and blind pursuit of
reason exists. Russell himself
once said that the way the
mind works on such things is
like this: First you decide
where you want to go. (At
this point, will, passion, bias,
and wishful thinking are a
legitimate part of the process
of rationality.) Then you must
ask yourself, "What arguments will
I need to get me from A to X?"

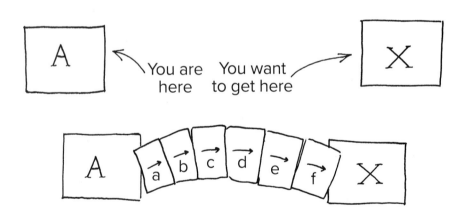

Next you need to ask, "Can such arguments be constructed, and are
these *good* arguments?" (At this point, we need to be most vigilant against
rationalization, wishful thinking, and other forms of self-deception.) If the
arguments withstand criticism and link up well with each other, then you
have good reason to hold belief X. If not, then you should abandon X.

Theism

Well, what kinds of arguments have been set forth to get us to X, where
X is a belief in the existence of God or gods? That is, what kinds of

arguments have been generated to justify **theism?** The best ones in the Western tradition stem from the late medieval period, a time that has been called "God-intoxicated." This period was one in which, astonishingly, there does not seem to have been any atheism (though there was much heresy). If this is true, then it isn't quite accurate to say that the "proofs" of the Middle Ages provided reasons for believing in God because apparently no alternative existed. Rather, it's as if the medievals were giving an account to themselves of the rational status of their belief—or their knowledge—of God.

God-Intoxicated

The Ontological Argument

Such an attitude is reflected in the curious introduction to one of the most famous medieval arguments and in the fact that this argument proving God's existence is addressed not to the atheist but to God himself! It's hard to believe that God needed proof of his own existence, but its author, ANSELM of Canterbury (1033–1109), was probably offering his meditation as a form of worship or a gift that could not possibly add anything to God's store (nothing could!) but that nevertheless would be pleasing in God's sight. Here is Anselm's introduction: "I do not seek to understand that I may believe, but I believe in order to understand. For this also I believe, that unless I believed, I should not understand." Anselm goes on to refer to the "fool" of Psalms 53:1, who "says in his heart, 'There is no God.'" Even this fool

I will now prove that I exist.

is convinced that something exists in the understanding, at least, than which nothing greater can be conceived. For when he hears of this he understands it. And whatever is understood exists in the understanding. And assuredly that than which nothing greater can be conceived, cannot exist in the understanding alone. For suppose it exists in the understanding alone: then it can be conceived to exist in reality, which is greater.

Psalm 53:1

Therefore, if that than which nothing greater can be conceived exists in the understanding alone, the very being than which nothing greater can be conceived, is one than which a greater can be conceived. But obviously this is impossible. Hence, there is no doubt that there exists a being than which nothing greater can be conceived, and it exists both in the understanding and in reality.

And it assuredly exists so truly that it cannot be conceived not to exist. For it is possible to conceive of a being which cannot be conceived not to exist. Hence, if that than which nothing greater can be conceived, can be conceived not to exist, it is not that than which nothing greater can be conceived. But this is an irreconcilable contradiction. There is, then, so truly a being than which nothing greater can be conceived to exist, that it cannot even be conceived not to exist; and this being thou art, O Lord our God.[3]

This argument looks suspicious. It appears as though it should be pretty easy to knock over, but it is a slippery argument and more resistant to criticism than you might think. Maybe we can get a little clearer about the structure of the argument if we paraphrase a simpler version of it, one

One that exists only here is less perfect than one . . . that exists out there.

expounded by René Descartes some five hundred years after Anselm's version. It goes something like this:

1. God, by definition, is that being that is absolutely perfect.
2. It is more perfect to exist than not to exist.
3. Therefore, to conceive of God (i.e., to conceive of a being that is absolutely perfect) is necessarily to conceive of him as existing (because to conceive of God as not existing is self-canceling).
4. Therefore, to say "God does not exist" is to contradict oneself.
5. Therefore, the sentence "God exists" is necessarily true.

It Is More Perfect to Exist Than Not to Exist (A Hamburger That Is Perfect in Every Respect except That It Does Not Exist)

The Cartesian definition of God as the absolutely perfect being is consistent with the official Roman Catholic understanding of God in René Descartes's day: God is the transcendent (outside the world, not in it), omniscient (all-knowing), omnipotent (all-powerful), omnibenevolent (all-good), and omnipresent (all-present) creator of the universe. Could any being be more perfect than this?

Still, if Descartes's or Anselm's version of this argument (which has come to be known as the **ontological argument**) bothers you, it is probably because you think there is some illegitimate move in it from a mere *definition* (an a priori claim) to a statement of *fact* (an a posteriori claim). In that case, you might want to challenge Descartes's version of the argument, perhaps at step 2, by saying that the assertion "It is more perfect to exist than not to exist" is a debatable value judgment, not a necessary truth of logic. But Descartes could retort that if it is a value judgment, it is one *you* obviously accept because if you had thought that nonexistence was better than existence, you would have shot yourself this morning. The fact that you are here proves that you accept the value of existence. So you can only reject step 2 hypocritically. Furthermore, Descartes might offer an example like this: Suppose you ordered a truckload of bricks from the local brickyard, and the truck driver came to deliver your order, saying, "These are excellent bricks in most respects, but they have one little flaw, namely, they don't exist." If he tried to charge you for these nonexistent bricks, you would certainly refuse to pay—or perhaps you would pay with an equally "flawed" hundred-dollar bill (one that doesn't exist). "All this shows that you agree with me," Descartes might say, "that existence is more perfect (i.e., better) than nonexistence."

(You might ask Descartes what if, instead of bricks, the driver were delivering an unsolicited load of horse manure. Then [because you don't want any manure], nonexistent manure is *better* than existent manure. But wouldn't Descartes be right to say that in terms of *manure*, real manure is better than unreal manure?)

It's very good horse manure.

But I don't want any manure!

In spite of this defense, one may well feel that some sleight of hand is involved in the ontological argument. Indeed, even Thomas Aquinas, the most religious of philosophers, thought the argument was invalid. One of the most famous critiques of the proof was written by David Hume. The following passage is taken from his posthumously published *Dialogues Concerning Natural Religion:*

> There is an evident absurdity in pretending to demonstrate a matter of fact, or to prove it by any arguments a priori. Nothing is demonstrable unless the contrary implies a contradiction. Nothing that is distinctly conceivable implies a contradiction. Whatever we conceive as existent, we can also conceive as non-existent. There is no being, therefore, whose non-existence implies a contradiction. Consequently there is no being whose existence is demonstrable. I propose this argument as entirely decisive and am willing to rest the whole controversy upon it.[4]

Hume's point boils down to this: it is always illegitimate to move from a pure definition to a statement of fact about reality. Definitions are only about the relation between meanings and as such are purely representations of logic and of linguistic conventions. Statements of fact about reality are always based on observation. Because Anselm's proof moves from the purely ideational sphere to the factual sphere without any reference to observation, its argument must be invalid.

Hume is certainly correct in thinking that if there is a problem with the proof, it has to do with the transition from the realm of pure ideas to the realm of factual reality. But is Hume correct in saying that we can never move from the realm of definition to statements about existence? Consider the definition of a

The Hunt for the Elusive Square Circle

"square circle" (four-sided equilateral figure any point of which is equidistant from its center). From the definition, we can deduce the following: "no square circles exist."[5] If even once we can go from a definition to a statement of fact about reality, then Hume's argument loses much of its force.

Hume's criticism implied that there must be something wrong with the *logic* of Anselm's argument. Another well-known and more modern criticism is that there is something wrong with its *grammar*. Look at this famous passage from the *Critique of Pure Reason* by Immanuel Kant:

> Being is evidently not a real predicate, or a concept of something that can be added to the concept of a thing. It is merely the admission of a thing and of certain determinations in it. Logically, it is merely the copula of a judgment. The proposition, *God is almighty,* contains two concepts, each having its object, namely, God and almightiness. The small word *is*, is not an additional predicate, but only serves to put the predicate *in relation* to the subject. If, then, I take the subject (God) with all its predicates (including that of almightiness) and say, *God is,* or there is a God, I do not ascribe a new predicate to the concept of God, but I only posit the subject by itself, with all its predicates, in relation to my concept, as its object. Both must contain exactly the same kind of thing, and nothing can have been added to the concept, which expresses possibility only, by my thinking its object as simply given and saying, it is. And thus the real does not contain more than the possible. A hundred real dollars do not contain a penny more than a hundred possible dollars.[6]

The central points of Kant's criticism are contained in the first line and the last line of the passage: "Being [existence] is evidently not a real predicate" and "A hundred real dollars do not contain a penny more than a hundred possible dollars."

These points can be clarified by returning to Descartes's version of the argument. Descartes saw "perfection" as a predicate of God in exactly the same way that he saw "three-sidedness" as a predicate (or attribute or characteristic) of any triangle. Then he saw "existence" as following from perfection, so "existence" becomes a predicate of God. Now, Kant's claim that existence is not a predicate *at all*, hence not a predicate of God, might be demonstrated by imagining the following game called "Guess the Predicate." Suppose I take something from my pocket and hide it in my hand behind my back and allow you to ask questions concerning its characteristics to which I will answer either yes or no. You may ask, "Is it green?" "Is it round?" "Is it heavy?" But could the question "Does it exist?" be a move in *this* game? The rules of the game already presuppose the existence of the object. If the object does not exist (i.e., if I have nothing in my hand), then I am not playing the game at all. I am simply deceiving you. Or try another game. This one is called "Imagine the Rose." First imagine a rose. Now imagine a *yellow* rose. Now imagine a yellow *rose with thorns*. Now imagine a yellow rose with thorns and *dew on the petals*. Now imagine a yellow, thorned rose with dew on the petals *that exists*. Notice the point. Nothing was added to the concept in the last instance. To imagine a rose and to imagine a rose that exists is to imagine the same thing. In the cases of the yellow color, the thorns, and the dew, we added something to the concept, so those were examples of real predicates. But in the case of existence, nothing was added, so existence "is not a real predicate."

Kant's criticism certainly does seem to have identified a linguistic weakness, if not a logical error, in the ontological proof. Is that the end of the story? Probably not. I mentioned earlier that Anselm's argument has proved to be tremendously versatile and elastic, able to bounce back from apparently deadly assaults. For example, the twentieth-century American philosopher Norman Malcolm has claimed to have discovered in Anselm's

See if you can guess what I have behind my back.

The Predicate Game

writings a version of the ontological proof that is immune to
Kant's criticism. The argument,
paraphrased, runs something
like this:

1. If God does not exist, his
   existence is logically impossible (because by definition
   God is eternal and independent so he cannot come into
   being or be caused to come
   into being).
2. If God does exist, his existence is logically necessary
   (because he cannot have
   come into existence [for the
   reasons given above] or cease to exist,
   for if he did, he would be limited, and
   by definition God is unlimited).
3. Hence, either God's existence is logically impossible or it is logically
   necessary.
4. If God's existence is logically impossible, then the concept of God is
   self-contradictory.
5. The concept of God is not self-contradictory.
6. Therefore, God's existence is logically necessary.
7. Therefore, God exists.[7]

Here we will not try to analyze Malcolm's argument (though it has
attracted a number of critics).[8] Rather, we will attend to the somewhat
amazing conclusion that Malcolm draws from this argument:

> What is the relation of Anselm's ontological argument to religious belief?
> This is a difficult question. I can imagine an atheist going through the
> argument, becoming convinced of its validity, acutely defending it against
> objections, yet remaining an atheist. The only effect it could have on the
> fool of the Psalm would be that he stopped saying in his heart "There is
> no God" because he would now realize that this is something he cannot
> meaningfully say or think. It is hardly to be expected that a demonstrative
> argument should, in addition, produce in him a living faith. Surely there is
> a level at which one can view the argument as a piece of logic, following
> the deductive moves but not being touched religiously? I think so. But
> even at this level the argument may not be without religious value, for it
> may help to remove some philosophical scruples that stand in the way of

faith. . . . It would be unreasonable to require that the recognition of Anselm's demonstration as valid must produce a conversion.[9]

It was Immanuel Kant who gave the name "ontological proof" to the kind of argument invented by St. Anselm. As we've seen, "ontological" means "having to do with the study of being," and Kant noticed that Anselm's argument was derived purely from the logical analysis of the concept of a "most real being" or a "most perfect being," hence the name "the ontological argument." Notice that, unlike the argument we shall now examine, Anselm's argument is a very Platonic one. It is derived from "pure reason." In it, "most perfect" and "most real" turn out to be identical (as on the top of Plato's Line). And it is an exclusively a priori argument. Nowhere did Anselm or Descartes ask you to *look* anyplace or *touch* anything or perform any physical experiments. All they asked you to do was to *think*. Anselm derived God's existence from pure thought. (That fact is probably what, in the final analysis, is wrong with the ontological proof, if something *is* wrong with it, but one must also admit that the genius of the argument is its purely a priori nature.)

The Cosmological Argument

There is another kind of argument for God's existence, which Kant called **cosmological.** It's called cosmological because the first premise of such an argument makes reference to some observable fact in the universe ("cosmos") and is therefore an argument with an a posteriori first premise. Surely, the most famous versions of cosmological arguments were formulated by THOMAS AQUINAS (1225–1274), whose thought has inspired most Catholic philosophy ever since his time.

Take a look at one of the arguments from Thomas Aquinas's *Summa Theologica,* a book that, like the great Gothic cathedrals of the same period, is a testament to the genius of the medieval mind:

> In the world of sense we find there is an order of efficient causes. There is no case known (neither is it, indeed, possible) in which a thing is found to be the efficient cause of itself; for so it would be prior to itself, which is impossible. Now in efficient causes it is not possible to go on to infinity, because in all efficient causes following in order, the first is the cause of the intermediate cause, and the intermediate cause is the cause of the ultimate cause, whether the intermediate cause be several or one only. Now, to take away the cause is to take away the effect. Therefore, if there be no first cause among efficient causes, there will be no ultimate, nor any intermediate cause. But if in efficient causes it is possible to go to infinity, there will be no first efficient cause, neither will there be an ultimate effect, nor any intermediate efficient causes; all of which is plainly false. Therefore it is necessary to admit a first efficient cause to which everyone gives the name of God.[10]

Thomas Aquinas (1225–1274)

The term **efficient cause** is one St. Thomas borrowed from Aristotle, and it is roughly equivalent to what we mean today by the word "cause." Therefore, Thomas's argument seems to boil down to this:

1. Every event in the observable world is caused by some event prior to it.
2. Either (a) the series of causes is infinite, or (b) the series of causes goes back to a first cause, which is itself uncaused.
3. But an infinite series of causes is impossible.
4. Therefore, a first cause exists outside the observable world; this first cause is God.

Recently, new attention has been paid to versions of the cosmological proof by cognitive science of religion (CSR). CSR has been defined nicely by the authors of a new book, *A Natural Theology and Philosophy of Religion*, who state that the aim of their book is to "[use] evidence and theories from the cognitive science of religion [CSR] and cognate disciplines—such as evolutionary ethics, evolutionary aesthetics, and the cognitive science of testimony. . . . [W]e aim to show that natural theological arguments and inferences rely to an important extent on intuitions that arise spontaneously and early in [childhood] development and that are a stable part of human cognition."[11]

THE BUCK STOPS HERE

That is, they try to show that a belief in supernatural beings (God, ghosts, angels) is natural and not simply culturally induced. "Religious beliefs and practices result from normally functioning human cognitive processes. From a cognitive point of view there is nothing exceptional about religion" (p. 15). Infants and children worldwide early on develop neurological functions that give them the concepts of "other minds," "causality," and "substantiality" (thingness) and the ability to attribute essential characteristics to substances (cats scratch and say "Meow," things fall down). They also attribute teleology to animate objects or at least as a cause of these animate objects. Many CSR theorists hold that these capacities were "chosen" by natural selection. That is, the possession of these beliefs has survival value. Children who have a belief in the force of gravity get along better than they would without such a belief. They do not need to understand gravity. Even though they don't understand it without instruction, their beliefs are true. According to most of these CSR theorists, it is a small jump from these "common sense" intuitions to a belief in divine causality. Many evolutionary psychologists seem to agree that holding religious beliefs has survival value. For example, "Belief in punishing deities increases cooperation between members of a group. Members of groups who believe in punishing deities [i.e., deities that punish disobedience] are thus more successful than members of groups who do not, regardless of whether or not punishing deities exist" (p. 185).

As we see, many of the universal natural intuitions of children and adults produce beliefs that are true, as in the case of gravity, causality, and in other minds. (Kant would be OK with this because he held that these concepts are a priori structures of the human mind, but not Hume, who believed he had demonstrated that these concepts could not be rationally justified. [Hume must be rolling in his grave.])

Should we be tempted to suspect that religious beliefs are therefore also likely true? If natural selection has given us brain functions that do "track truth" (p. 189) in the case of these natural intuitions, do religious intuitions

David Hume Rolling in His Grave

also track truth? Well, we certainly cannot deduce that claim logically from the doctrine of natural selection, which may have given us a natural propensity toward racism and xenophobia. It may also have given us the "above average trait" (pp. 188–189), "Most people [believe that they] are better than average drivers and [that] they are kinder and smarter than others" (p. 189).

Also, there may be some intellectual objections to these beliefs that have nothing to do with natural selection. We will look at a few such objections now.

Hume's Criticism of the Cosmological Proof

Philosophers such as Hume and Kant, who rejected this argument, attacked the first and third premises and also questioned the conclusion. Hume is probably most famous for his critical analysis of the concept of "causality." We looked at a bit of Hume's controversial analysis in Chapter 3 but not in enough detail to evaluate its application to Thomas's argument. Suffice it to say that Hume asserts that no good reason at all exists to claim to know the first premise because it cannot be proven a priori that every event is caused, and no set of observations can establish it a posteriori either. Also, Hume thought that the third premise was false. Why is an infinite series of causes impossible? Unlike Thomas, Hume believed that nothing in the concept of a series of causes required that there be a beginning other than the need arbitrarily imposed by the human mind. Hume thought that no matter what event you imagine, you can always imagine an earlier event preceding it, regardless of how far back into time the imagination goes, just as an infinite series of numbers is possible in mathematics. Therefore, there is no *logical contradiction* in the notion of an "infinite series of causes." And because there are no observable data with which to prove the third premise, Hume concluded that we must remain at least skeptical concerning its claim.

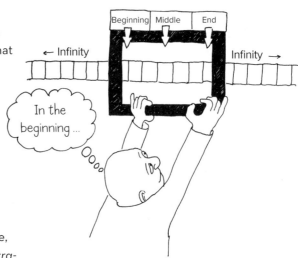

The Need of the Human Mind to Impose a "Beginning" on Things

Finally, even if the argument were valid from steps 1 through 3, would it prove the existence of the Christian God in whom St. Thomas believed? Aristotle himself, from whom Thomas borrowed elements of his cosmological proof, believed in a narcissistic God who was so "into himself" that he did not even know that human beings existed. Surely, Thomas would not have wanted to prove the existence of *that* God.

Lest we think that Hume has soundly refuted the cosmological argument once and for all, I should mention that recent Thomistic scholars have warned that Thomas's argument is more complicated than it appears, involving both a horizontal system of causes (in which an infinite series of causes cannot be ruled out) and a hierarchical system of dependencies (which, according to Thomas, cannot admit of an infinite regress).[12] This version of the argument, with its "hierarchy of dependencies," is much more Platonic than the earlier one, reminding us as it does of Plato's Simile of the Line. A refutation of this interpretation of the proof would involve a rejection of Platonic metaphysics.

Narcissus

HIERARCHICAL SYSTEM

Absolute terminus here

Infinity this way (maybe)

HORIZONTAL SYSTEM

The Teleological Argument

A third kind of argument for God's existence goes by several names, the **"teleological argument,"** the "argument from design," and the "argument from analogy." Though this proof was particularly popular in the eighteenth century, we find a thirteenth-century version once again in the *Summa Theologica* of Thomas Aquinas:

> The fifth way is taken from the governance of the world. We see that things which lack intelligence, such as natural bodies, act for an end, and this is evident from their acting always, or nearly always, in the same way, so as to obtain the best result. Hence it is plain that not fortuitously, but designedly, do they achieve their end. Now whatever lacks intelligence cannot move toward an end, unless it be directed by some being endowed with knowledge and intelligence; as the arrow is shot to its mark by the archer. Therefore some intelligent being exists by whom all natural things are directed to their end; and this being we call God.[13]

A **teleological** explanation is one that operates in terms of goals, purposes, and intentions (from the Greek *telos*, "goal" or "end"). We are familiar with teleological explanations because we use them every day to explain our own actions and those of people surrounding us: "Why did John go to the other room?" "In order to phone Jill." This explanation of John's behavior in terms of his purposes and goals makes his behavior intelligible to us.

Notice how different this teleological explanation of John's behavior is from a strictly causal explanation of the type we often employ to make intelligible to us the behavior of natural nonhuman objects: "Why did the tree fall?" "The roots were shallow and could not support the tree's weight in last night's windstorm."

We also use causal, nonteleological accounts in the case of *accidental* human events: "What's John doing on the floor?" "He tripped on his shoelace." Notice that here there were no references to goals, intentions, or purposes, so these explanations were not teleological. Now it might seem that the use of the two distinct forms of explanation is very clear; we use teleological accounts for certain kinds of human behavior (i.e., purposeful as opposed to accidental) and causal explanations for natural phenomena. But consider such exchanges as these:

> "Why do ospreys have
>   such good eyesight?"
> "In order to see fish from
>   high in the air."

> "Why does that moth have
>   brown spots on its wings?"
> "In order to blend in with its environment to protect itself from natural enemies."

> "Why do we faint when not enough blood gets to the brain?"
> "So that the heart can pump blood horizontally."

Each of these explanations is teleological. They explain in terms of goals and purposes. It may turn out that something is wrong with these accounts, as Darwin would claim, but it can't be denied that people (usually parents talking to their children) say things like this all the time. To many people, these kinds of explanations seem perfectly natural. Now it is precisely the "naturalness" of these accounts from which the teleological proof gets its mileage. This proof says that natural phenomena are such that they demand a teleological explanation or at least that the totality of natural phenomena taken as a system demands such an explanation; no other

Myopic Osprey

kind proves satisfactory. This type of claim has strongly resurfaced in the last few years in the movement called **creationism,** whose participants are putting political pressure on school boards of public high schools and boards of trustees of colleges and universities, trying to force them to include versions of the argument from design in the science curriculum of U.S. schools or at least to offer the argument as a scientific alternative to the theory of evolution.

A common version of the argument runs like this: if you found a watch on a mountain path, you would deduce from the functioning of the watch that it was designed to serve a purpose and that there had to be an intelligent watchmaker who created the artifact. It would be unreasonable to explain the watch in terms of natural accidents and coincidences. But nature is even more marvelous in the intricacies of its workings than a watch is. The human heart pumps blood at exactly the right pressure to sustain human life; the planets move in their orbits with absolute mathematical precision; each plant is in nearly perfect harmony with its environment. In summary, the universe is such an intricate system of balanced mechanisms that it can be explained only in terms of the purposes and intentions of an intelligent creator, as in the case of the watch. In the case of the universe, that intelligent creator is God.

The Not-So-Intelligent Watchmaker

Darwin's and Hume's Criticisms of the Teleological Proof

The most famous critics of the teleological argument are Charles Darwin and (once again) David Hume. Darwin's criticism, stated simply, runs like this: a difference occurs between the concept of "design" and the concept of "order." It is true that whatever has been designed must have been designed by *somebody* but not everything that exhibits order was designed. Take the example of a gravel beach. There we find a distinct order. The smallest grains of sand compose the top layers of the beach, the grains of the second layer are a bit larger, and the largest compose the bottom layer. But no "designer" is needed to explain this order; much less is there any mystery. It is perfectly obvious why the larger pebbles are on the bottom. They are the heaviest, hence were deposited by the surf first. The smallest are the lightest and were deposited last.

Similarly, the order throughout nature, though often more complex than the gravel beach example, can be explained in the same kind of **naturalistic** terms. The perfect harmony between the heart and the body is explained by the fact that the heart could sustain only a body that could survive with exactly as much blood pressure as that size heart could produce. All other bodies would not survive (and indeed did not survive). The coincidental combination of that particular heart size and this particularly structured body produced the organism that would survive (and did survive). The heart does not pump five quarts of blood per minute *in order to* sustain the body; rather, the body flourishes because the heart does pump five quarts of blood per minute. Similarly, ospreys do not have excellent vision in order to spy fish; rather, they spy fish because they have excellent vision. The moth does not have spots in order to avoid its enemies; it avoids its enemies because it has spots—and so it goes on and on. If Darwin's argument is successful, it shows that the teleological terminology ("in order to") can be replaced with purely causal terminology, thereby destroying the force of the teleological proof.

David Hume, in his *Dialogues Concerning Natural Religion*, had at least a pair of arguments against the teleological proof. First, he challenged the validity of the analogy, "Watch is to watchmaker as world is to world creator." Hume claimed that the relation between the watch and the watchmaker that allows us to infer the existence of the latter

Smog breathing, styrofoam eating, radiation powered

Evolutionary Future of the Human

when we find the former is an *empirical* relation. We are able to infer the existence of the watchmaker from the existence of the watch because we have *seen* watchmakers make watches. Any successful analogy based on the relationship between a watch and a watchmaker will also have to contain the empirical element of that relationship. But because the purported relation between the world and the world creator is not and *cannot* be empirical, the analogy fails. Besides, says Hume, the aspect of the world that excites the need for a theological explanation is very often the *organic* aspect of the world. The organic world is more like a plant than a watch. Because we know (empirically) where plants come from, Hume states rather mischievously that the argument from analogy should lead us to conclude that the world creator is more like a kind of super turnip than like a watchmaker!

Super Turnip

Another of Hume's criticisms of the argument from design can be stated in terms of these diagrams. Notice how orderly the three dots are in fig. 5.1. They form a perfect triangle. Fig. 5.2 contains even more order. The addition of only three dots created four triangles within the triangle, and an even more complex system of order appears in figs. 5.3 and 5.4. Then we get to fig. 5.5, and we realize what we are actually looking at is a pile of pebbles, hardly what we think of as an orderly system, rather, a purely random kind of haphazardness. Hume is suggesting that order is in the eye of the beholder. The human mind imposes order on the chaos of nature, then infers a divine orderer to account for it. Notice that Hume's point is much more radical than that of Darwin. Darwin questioned the notion of "design in nature" but never doubted whether there was "order" in nature. Hume questions the very notion of order.

Fig. 5.1

Fig. 5.2

Fig. 5.3

Fig. 5.4

Fig. 5.5

Certainly, this section has not been a complete catalogue of the philosophical attempts to *prove* God's existence, and it does not even pretend to have exhausted the richness or variations of the three arguments we've inspected. But it is a fair sampling of this kind of attempt to demonstrate that there are rational arguments that give us good reasons to believe that God exists.

There is a sandpile; therefore, God exists.

It should be added, however, that not all attempts to justify the rationality of a belief in God are attempts to *prove* God's existence. For instance, the contemporary American philosopher of religion, John Hick, concludes that none of the traditional proofs of God's existence is satisfactory, but he holds that drawing a connection between one's moral views and one's religious views is neither merely arbitrary, nor only the result of blindly following tradition. Hick writes:

> To recognize moral claims as taking precedence over all other interests is, in effect, to believe in a reality, other than the natural world, that is superior to oneself and entitled to one's obedience. This is at least a move in the direction of belief in God.[14]

Hick argues that a person's moral beliefs might provoke her to see the world in a different light, and he evokes the "duck/rabbit" figure that you encountered on page 36 to suggest that religious beliefs are related to the phenomenon that Wittgenstein called "seeing as" or, as Hick prefers to put it, "experiencing as" (p. 70). Just as one can see the same drawing as either a duck or a rabbit, God's presence or his absence can be experienced in the world that we know. Hick quotes with approval a passage from the French mathematician and philosopher BLAISE PASCAL (1623–1662) concerning the *deus absconditus*—the hidden God:

> He has willed to make Himself quite recognizable by those [who sincerely seek him]; and thus, willing to appear openly to those who seek Him with all their heart, and to be hidden from those who flee from Him with all their heart. He so regulates the knowledge of Himself that he has given signs of Himself, visible to those who seek Him, and not to those who seek him not. (p. 71)

Hick associates this phenomenon of experiencing God's presence with what religious individuals refer to as "revelation" (p. 73). Whether these "revelations" establish a "correct" perspective on reality cannot be established by scientific investigation.

As we have already seen, often there seems to be irresolvable tension between science and religion. However, in the modern world, not all scientists are opposed to religion and not all religious scholars are opposed to science. This accommodation was recently made evident in the awarding of the 2008 Templeton Prize to the Polish Roman Catholic priest and scientist, the Reverend Michael Heller, a philosophy professor at the Pontifical Academy of Theology in Krakow, Poland. This prize, worth almost two million dollars, is bestowed upon the author of the best work of the year exploring the overlap between science and religion. Heller's scientific work deals with the origins of the universe, but—perhaps surprisingly—Heller rejects creationist and intelligent design theories and all other religious views that try to explain features of the world that are rightfully dealt with scientifically. He has argued for years that the religious objection to teaching evolution "is one of the greatest misunderstandings," because it "introduces a contradiction or opposition between God and chance." According to Heller, "Science gives us knowledge, and religion gives us meaning. Both are prerequisites of a decent existence."[15]

Perhaps it should be added that the attempted proofs of God's existence that we inspected earlier are not merely historical fossils. Although I have attributed their origins to certain historical periods, especially in the Middle Ages, these arguments are still actively defended today by serious contenders, just as these arguments are still actively opposed. Hardly a year goes by but some newly constructed defense or revision of the old arguments appears in journals or books, followed by new articles or books attempting to refute them. Just because chess is governed by strict rules, that doesn't mean that every possible chess game has already been played. The same goes for human argumentation—only more so.

Atheism

We have seen that each of the arguments for God's existence is problematic but perhaps no more than the arguments attempting to prove that God does *not* exist. Such proofs are arguments for atheism. Here we will catalogue a few such arguments, but we will not delay long to inspect them. These kinds of discussions could go on forever. (Indeed, after several hundred years of debate during the medieval period, it began to seem as if they *would* go on forever.) Notice that some of these arguments will be kinds of reverse ontological proofs, trying to show that the very concept of

God, as Western culture has conceived it, is self-contradictory. Other arguments here will be kinds of reverse cosmological proofs, trying to show that certain facts in the world are incompatible with the concept of God. Here are the truncated versions of a few.

1. God's omniscience is incompatible with the freedom he gave his creatures. (If God is omniscient, he knows the future. If God knows what humans will do in the future, then they *must* do what God knows they will do [or else God is wrong]. If God does not know what they will do, then he is not omniscient.)

2. God is defined as omnipotent, but nothing can be defined as omnipotent because the concept of omnipotence is incoherent. (Can God create a rock that is too large for him to move? If he cannot, then he is not all-powerful. If he can, then he is not all-powerful.)

3. God's omnibenevolence is incompatible with his creation of the devil and of eternal punishment. (If God is all-good, how can he let loose such a potent evil force as Satan to tempt weak creatures as humans are and then punish with eternal damnation those poor souls who succumb, even momentarily, to the devil's superior wiles?)

4. God's omnipotence, omniscience, omnibenevolence, and omnicreativity are not compatible with the presence of evil in the world. (There is evil in the world—natural disasters, disease, crime, starvation, phlegm. If God did not create them, then he is not the creator of the universe. If he could not prevent them in his creation, then he is not all-powerful. If he didn't foresee them, he is not all-knowing. On the other hand, if he did willfully create them, then he is not all-good.)

Most of these arguments had already appeared in the medieval world, not as real attempts to raise doubts about God's existence—atheism was never a serious threat in the Middle Ages—but as a pretext for theologians to flex their philosophical muscles while clarifying to themselves their understanding of God's nature. Yet, it is obvious that one of these problems—the problem of evil—is more powerful than the others. I have framed that problem here in its logical form, but to common believers it is not at all like a mere logical puzzle because the evidence supporting it is discovered not primarily through philosophizing but in one's daily journey through life, and unfortunately that evidence is sometimes experienced personally and painfully, by both theologians and nontheologians. The medieval world was so full of sufferings at all levels that the argument from evil daily crossed the minds of many of the faithful. We know about this preoccupation from the great number of sermons and theological tracts whose goal was to counteract the thoughts and emotions caused by the suffering, either by explaining away the appearance of evil, or by showing why evil was compatible with God's grace, or even by demonstrating it as a necessary part of God's grace.

The Bible itself seems to address the problem of evil in the book of Job. There, in a discussion with Satan and other angels, God points out his servant Job, complimenting him before the devil as being a perfect, upright man. Satan retorts that Job is perfect only because God has protected him and blessed him. However, should God allow evil to befall Job, Satan wagers that Job would curse God. In order to prove the devil wrong, God delivers Job to Satan, giving him a free rein to torment Job, though the devil may not kill Job. ("Behold, he is in thine hand; but save his life" [Job 2:6].) The first day of the torment begins with a slave running to tell him that all his oxen and asses have been stolen and all his herdsmen murdered. Before the first slave is done relating his story, a second comes to inform Job that a fire has fallen from heaven and burned all his sheep and shepherds. Before this servant finishes his tale, a third runs up and

BEHOLD MY SERVANT, JOB.

Oh, Oh.

announces that the Chaldeans have stolen all of Job's camels and killed the camel keepers. While Job is reeling from this news, yet another slave approaches, telling Job that a great wind has toppled the home of his eldest son, killing all ten of Job's children. Job rends his robe, shaves his head, and mourns, only to awaken on the second day of the torment to find himself smitten with painful boils from the soles of his feet to the crown of his head. Job's wife, seeing Job sitting among the ashes with his shaven head, his running sores, and his misery, says to Job, "Curse God and die" (Job 2:9). Though Job does not curse God, he does curse the day he was born, and he talks bitterly of the impossibility of fathoming God's ways. He says to God, "Show me wherefore thou contendest with me"; "Thou knowest that I am not wicked." (This version of the question "Why me?" seems like a perfectly reasonable question under the circumstances.) When God, speaking from the whirlwind, does answer Job, he asks a series of intimidating questions: "Who is this that darkeneth counsel by words without knowl-

edge?" (It's only Job.) "Where wast thou when I laid the foundations of the earth?" (Job doesn't know.) "Hast thou an arm like God?" (Job doesn't.) "Canst thou thunder with a voice like him?" (Job can't.) Finally Job understands. One does not question the ways of God. In God's case, might is right. When Job understands, he recovers all that was lost and more—new livestock, new lands, new slaves, and new children.

And if I am all these things, then you are nothing! (And don't you ever forget it!)

Apparently, one must be resigned to the misery inflicted upon one, never questioning the system that perpetrated it and never fighting it.[16]

Indeed, in the Middle Ages, even at the intellectual level, the arguments for God's existence may have been trying to hold in abeyance the unthinkable, that is, that the world was as it appeared—chaos and horror. During great periods of the Middle Ages, famine and plague were interrupted only by violence and death at the hands of marauding troops undisciplined by any rules or rulers. It must have seemed like the visions of the Four Horsemen of the Apocalypse (pestilence, war, famine, and death) depicted in the Book of Revelation, except that in the Bible, the chaos and horror were part of God's plan. That is, for many, the great suffering was seen not as evidence against God's existence but as evidence for it. Yet, there must have been moments when the question crept across the minds of suffering individuals and of observers of such suffering: What if this is all there is? What if there is no God? What if the center does not hold? Part of medieval piety involved the silent acceptance of an idea that had been articulated by the ancient Greek playwright Aristophanes, "When Zeus is toppled, chaos succeeds him, and whirlwind rules"—an idea that would later be expressed by Ivan Karamazov, a character in a novel by Fyodor Dostoyevsky, "If there is no God, everything is permitted."

The Four Horsemen of the Apocalypse (After Albrecht Dürer)

After a thousand years, the medieval period did come to an end, and when it did, the totalizing obsession with God ended. There are many reasons for this loosening of the viselike grip religion had on the Western mind during the medieval period, and most of these reasons are historical and sociological rather than purely philosophical (e.g., the great schisms in Christianity that detracted from the appearance of uniformity and universality of religious persuasion; the revelations of corruption within certain religious institutions, which detracted from the moral authority of religion; and the advent of scientific discoveries that seemed to contradict biblical explanations of the world). Since the eighteenth century, most philosophical arguments for atheism have not taken the form of proofs attesting to the incoherence of the concept of God or demonstrating the incompatibility between that concept and the empirical facts. Rather, these arguments have had as their goal the undermining of religious faith by claiming to reveal that our motives for religious belief are fallacious and illusory, including the fear that the center does not hold.

Karl Marx: Religion as Opium

One of the most famous atheists of the nineteenth century was KARL MARX (1818–1883), whose political theory you will encounter in Chapter 9. Unlike certain twenty-first-century atheists whom we shall meet shortly, Marx did not believe that the idea of God was individually or socially destructive; rather, he thought that the idea was itself the by-product of a genuinely destructive social phenomenon—the domination of the wealth of a society by a privileged ruling class that kept the working classes in a state of subjugation. Economic facts are the foundation of all social and cultural facts, the latter being mere "phantoms" and "sublimates" of the economic facts. These "phantoms" include all "legal, political, religious, aesthetic, or philosophical" forms of thought. Marx calls these forms **ideology** and implies that all of these cultural forms are the product of "**false consciousness.**"[17]

So, for Marx, it is a waste of time to attack the idea of God, or religion itself, because these ideological forms of thought and behavior will evaporate once social oppression has been eliminated. In fact, Marx's writing on religion is actually surprisingly sympathetic:

> Religious distress is at the same time the expression of real distress and the protest against real distress. Religion is the sigh of the oppressed creature, the heart of a heartless world, just as it is the spirit of an unspiritual situation. It is the opium of the people.
>
> . . . .
>
> Thus the criticism of heaven turns into the criticism of the earth, . . . and the criticisms of *theology* into the criticism of politics.[18]

Notice that one of the ironies in Marx's theory is that there is a significant sense in which religion contains the truth—a spiritual truth that should become a social truth. Usually the reference to opium is quoted in isolation from its context, in which case one thinks of opium as a soporific that lulls one into a grinning, drooling, undignified stupor. But Marx had in mind opium's medicinal powers. It kills the pain. And for Marx, the pain is real so that at least religion is addressing the correct issue—human misery. This view has been understood very well by the twentieth-century Marxian philosopher Herbert Marcuse, who wrote in his book *Eros and Civilization*:

> Where religion still preserves the uncompromised aspirations for peace and happiness, its "illusions" still have a higher truth value than science which works for their elimination. The repressed and transfigured content of religion cannot be liberated by surrendering it to the scientific attitude.[19]

Marcuse was not against science by any means, but in 1955, he believed that American scientists kowtowed to their paymasters, the military-industrial complex.

Sigmund Freud:
The Psychoanalysis of Religion

In spite of his belief in the hidden truth value of religion, Marx was an atheist who thought religion was ultimately an illusion. One of the most famous atheists of the twentieth century was SIGMUND FREUD (1856–1939). He too

Memory of yesterday's breakfast (fading) }
Fallacious and innocuous memories from childhood, screening off more painful and traumatic memories } CONSCIOUS MEMORIES

Memories of traumatic events and unresolved conflicts in childhood
Memories of infantile desires
Memories of the origins of civilization
Memories of the origin of organic matter } UNCONSCIOUS MEMORIES

The Human Mind Preserves All of Its Earlier Stages

thought religious belief was a kind of illusion, and he and Marx shared the same ontological explanation of religion's status—that of being a "sublimate." His book on religion is called *The Future of an Illusion*. His view of religion is deeply entwined with the rest of his **psychoanalytic** theory of the mind; however, thankfully, we have to recount not the whole of Freud's psychology but only a few of its essentials in order to get at the heart of his claim about religion. According to Freud, the human mind preserves all of its earlier stages alongside its final form. This retention is true both ontogenetically and phylogenetically (i.e., true of the history of the individual and also of the history of the human race). Unlike in a city, where some parts must be destroyed for newer parts to be constructed, in the mind, the earliest stages and the latest are contemporaneous.

However, the earlier ones are to a great extent submerged or even repressed into the unconscious. Therefore, from the point of view of consciousness, the structures and content of the earlier stages seem to have been forgotten forever, but in fact, they are present and in some ways active as motives for behavior, as are our conscious thoughts. Now, concerning religion, Freud says:

The Bulk of the Mind Is Submerged

The derivation of religious needs from the infant's helplessness and the longing for the father aroused by it seems to me incontrovertible, especially since the feeling is not simply prolonged from childhood days but is permanently sustained by a fear of the superior power of Fate. I cannot think of any need in childhood as strong as the need for the father's protection.[20]

The infant comes into the world in some way believing itself to be omnipotent. The smallest and greatest of its needs are attended to upon simple registering of a complaint. It does not take long, however, for the horrible realization to dawn on the infant that she is not only not all-powerful and in command of reality but also completely vulnerable and

The Infant Comes into the World Thinking It Is Omnipotent

dependent. This discovery (from which she will never recover) produces both fear and resentment. The infant reluctantly recognizes her utter need of a protector to shelter her from the many sources of pain and unhappiness in the world. She comes to see this protector in the guise of the father.

This fearful discovery of her vulnerability and dependence on the father, and the emotional luggage that accompanies this discovery—fear, need, love, resentment—remains an active force in the unconscious of the adult. As adults,

> each one of us behaves in some one respect like a paranoic, corrects some aspect of the world which is unbearable to him by the construction of a wish and introduces this delusion into reality. A special importance attaches to the case in which this attempt to procure a certainty of happiness and protection against suffering through a delusional remoulding of reality is made by a considerable number of people in common. The religions of mankind must be classed among the mass-delusions of this kind. No one, needless to say, who shares a delusion ever recognizes it as such. . . . [Religion's] technique consists in depressing the value of life and distorting the picture of the real world in a delusional manner—which presupposes an intimidation of the intelligence. At this price, by forcibly fixing them in a state of psychical infantilism and by drawing them into a mass-delusion, religion succeeds in sparing many people an individual neurosis. (pp. 30–31, 34)

Although Freud does realize that religion can spare people a neurosis, he nevertheless seems to have contempt for it. He says, "The whole thing is so patently infantile, so foreign to reality, that to anyone with a friendly attitude to humanity it is painful to think that the great majority of mortals will never be able to rise above this view of life" (p. 49).

So according to Freud, religion is for weaklings, for people who need delusions to accompany them into the harshness of the world. In *Civilization and Its Discontents*, Freud deals with alcohol and drugs in the same paragraph in which he deals with religion. For him, too, religion is truly "the opium of the people." Religion can be escaped only by those who can develop the courage to face the harshness of life without delusions and replace them with scientific truth or by those who can create a different kind of paranoid-like illusion in the production of art. (See Chapter 10 for a development of this idea.)

God and the Theory of Evolution

Very few twenty-first-century writers who defend atheism derive their antireligious arguments from either Marx or Freud. Marx's theory of religion, once it is understood, might seem too cozy with religion. Indeed, the "liberation theology" practiced in the name of the poor by certain Catholic priests in South America sometimes employs Marxian ideas. For others, it is bad enough to be called "Godless" by one's opponents (a category something like being "toothless," only worse), but to have to defend oneself against the accusation of being a "Godless Communist" is too much of a distraction. Similarly with Freud: the popularity of psychoanalytic arguments has taken a big dip in recent years—partially because of the demythologizing work of Professor Frederick Crews and others.[21]

But there are a number of atheists writing who derive a large part of their arguments from the theory of evolution by **natural selection** developed by CHARLES DARWIN (1809–1882). In some ways, this is surprising, because Darwin distanced himself from atheism. Writing to a friend, he said, "I have never been an atheist in the sense of denying the existence of a god"; however, he added that he was more willing to accept the name "agnostic." He was reticent all his adult life to discuss his religious views, though he admitted in a letter to another friend, "I may have been unduly biased by the pain which it would give some members of my family, if I aided in any way direct attacks on religion."[22] Darwin is surely referring to the sensibilities of his very religious wife, Emma Wedgwood Darwin.

However, Darwin's theory as interpreted by many biologists today seems to leave very little need for God. Darwin's most recent biographers write, "His God was an absentee landlord, and nature self-sufficient."[23] It seems inevitable that such a theory would soon attract a swipe by Ockham's razor. Indeed, the two most prominent Darwinian members of the contemporary group called "the New Atheists" wield precisely that tool. They are Daniel Dennett, a philosopher of science whom you have already met in this chapter, and the noted evolutionary biologist, Richard Dawkins. Dennett is the author of *Breaking the Spell: Religion as a Natural Phenomenon*—his book promoting atheism—and of *Darwin's Dangerous Idea*, his book on the significance of the theory of natural selection. Dawkins's book defending atheism is *The God Delusion*. Along with Sam Harris (*The End of Faith: Religion, Terror, and the Future of Reason* [2004]) and the late Christopher Hitchens (*God Is Not Great: How Religion Poisons Everything* [2007]), they are known as "The Four Horsemen of Atheism," after the angels of destruction in the biblical Book of Revelation.

Many of Dennett's and Dawkins's arguments against religion can be stated independently of Darwin's theory of evolution, and I will briefly summarize those aspects of their program before bringing the theory of natural selection into the picture. Both Dennett and Dawkins see religious belief as a clear form of irrationality. All traditional Western religions justify belief in the content of their "holy" documents by consulting those documents themselves (the Old Testament, the New Testament, and the Quran). This is a form of the logical fallacy called "begging the question" (see the Glossary). Yet when Jews or Muslims read the New Testament, or when Christians read the Quran, they do not see it as obviously holy, and certainly when members of any of the groups read L. Ron Hubbard's *Dianetics* (the founding document of Scientology) or *The Book of Mormon* (the founding document of the Latter-day Saints), they often think they are ridiculous. Readers see absurdities and contradictions in the sacred documents of other religions but not in those of their own religion. Dawkins asks:

> Shouldn't a literalist worry about the fact that Matthew traces Joseph's descent from King David via twenty-eight intermediate generations, while Luke has forty-one generations? Worse, there is almost no overlap in the

names on the two lists! In any case, if Jesus really was born of a virgin, Joseph's ancestry is irrelevant and cannot be used to fulfill, on Jesus' behalf, the Old Testament prophecy that the Messiah should be descended from David.[24]

Both Dennett and Dawkins are outraged that, in the West at least, the patent irrationality of belief in the absurd holy documents is exempted from rational scrutiny. According to Dennett, religion sequesters "a special subset of cultural items behind a veil of *systematic* invulnerability to disproof."[25]

Then there is a second veil, *"These are mysteries beyond all comprehension! Don't even try to understand them!"* And as often as not, a third veil is provided, "It is *forbidden* to ask too many questions about all these mysteries" (p. 165). Dawkins adds, "Faith is an evil precisely because it requires no justification and brooks no argument" (p. 347).

Apparently, many people, both religious and nonreligious, justify belief in God, saying that without such a belief, morality is unenforceable. (Recall that in his novel, *The Brothers Karamazov,* Dostoyevsky's Ivan Karamazov says, infamously, without God, "everything is permitted.")

Is it true that without religion, people would not behave morally? Dawkins cites a sociological study comparing the making of moral decisions between religious and nonreligious individuals that concludes that "There is no statistically significant difference between atheists and religious believers in making [moral] judgements. . . . We do not need God in order to be good—or evil" (p. 258). Dawkins compares Christian and non-Christian responses to Hurricane Katrina and to the 2004 tsunami; he also examines Pat Robertson's comment on these natural disasters. The Reverend Mr. Robertson called them God's punishment for sin. Dawkins goes through the Old Testament; he discusses Noah's Ark along with such stories as Lot and the Sodomites, the Levite who hands over to the rabble his concubine to be gang-raped and murdered (Judges 19:25–26), Abraham and Isaac, Jephthah's sacrifice of his daughter to God, and Moses's slaying of the Midianite men and boy children, making slaves of the women and girls, and burning all the cities. In the Battle of Jericho, Joshua didn't rest until his warriors "utterly destroyed all that was in the city, both men and women, young and old, and ox, and sheep, and ass, with the edge of the sword" (Joshua 6:21). This is how the Jews entered "the promised land." They also had to drive out of their land the Amorites, Canaanites, Hittites, Perizzites, Hivites, and Jebusites. Dawkins concludes that "the God character" of the Old Testament had no scruples about the massacres and genocides that accompanied the seizing of the Promised Land, and he invites his reader to test this claim by reading Deuteronomy 20 (Dawkins 280). Apparently intent on angering his Jewish and Christian readers, Dawkins calls Yahweh "an evil monster" (Dawkins p. 282). Clearly, for Dawkins, our morality, whether we are religious or not, does not derive from the Old Testament. If it did,

> we would strictly observe the sabbath and think it just and proper to execute anybody who chose not to. We would stone to death any new bride who couldn't prove she was a virgin, if her husband pronounced himself unsatisfied with her. We would execute disobedient children. (p. 283)

Compared with the Old Testament, the New Testament is relatively admirable, according to Dawkins, with the exception of the doctrine of the atonement for original sin—the central doctrine of Christianity—which Dawkins calls "vicious, sadomasochistic and repellent" (p. 287). In an assertion that is surely more likely to enrage his opponents than to win them over, Dawkins states that "the God of the Old Testament," who is supposed to be a role model for Jews and Christians,

> is arguably the most unpleasant character in all fiction: jealous and proud of it; a petty, unjust unforgiving control-freak; a vindictive, bloodthirsty ethnic cleanser; a misogynistic, homophobic, racist, infanticidal, genocidal, filicidal, pestilential, megalomaniacal, sadomasochistic, capriciously malevolent bully. (Dawkins p. 51)

Finally, Daniel Dennett asserts that extremism and even terrorism are the logical extension of the irrationalism and the absolutism of religious

Charles Darwin (1809—1882)

beliefs. Dawkins goes even further, rejecting the phrase "religious extremism," believing as he does that religious thought itself is a form of extremism. Speaking of terrorists who operate in the name of religion, Dawkins writes, "The take-home message is that we should blame religion itself, not religious *extremism*—as though that were some kind of terrible perversion of real, decent religion" (p. 345).

These are powerful claims, and they do provoke thought, as Dennett and Dawkins hoped they would. But one might wonder if they do not sometimes border on extremism themselves. Is it really insightful to suggest that Francis of Assisi, Mahatma Gandhi, Martin Luther King, Jr., and the terrorists who flew the planes into the Twin Towers on September 11, 2001 were all motivated by the same ideals?

Let us now turn to those aspects of the atheistic arguments of Dennett and Dawkins that are derived from Darwin's theory of evolution.

Dawkins defines what he calls "the God hypothesis": *"There exists a superhuman supernatural intelligence who deliberately designed and created the universe and everything in it, including us"* (p. 54, emphasis in the original). Evolutionary thinkers are *naturalists who*, by definition, reject any explanatory argument that involves the supernatural. Religious thinkers who try to explain the universe and everything in it believe that reason forces us to posit a supernatural creator, primarily because without such a creator the design that we find in the universe cannot be explained—that is, they appeal to the argument from design. Richard Dawkins, as a biologist, asserts, *"Any creative intelligence, of sufficient complexity to design anything, comes into existence only as the end product of an extended process of gradual evolution. Creative intelligences, being evolved, arrive late in the universe, and therefore cannot be responsible for designing it"* (p. 54, emphasis in the original). This is clearly an appeal to Ockham's razor. Humans look at the nature that surrounds them. They see natural systems that are so intricate that they appear to have been intentionally designed. However, this appearance of design is an illusion. What appears to be designed is the result of natural selection, which has no goals, purposes, or intentions.

How is it possible that brute force, the laws of nature, and chance could produce all that is beautiful and complex in nature? If there is an infinite amount of space and time, almost all possible combinations will occur at some point. If a simple form of organic life appears at a certain moment in time, those combinations of living elements that survive and can replicate themselves will remain while the others will not. This same process will result in further modifications of the surviving combinations, which will evolve through time in ways that advance adaptability. This theory of natural selection is a *simpler* theory than one that involves a supernatural designer—God—because the question, "Who or what designed the designer?" cannot be answered, or, if there is an answer, it is much more complicated than the theory of natural selection. Therefore, of the two options, the God hypothesis and natural selection, Ockham's razor demands the latter.

OK, but Ockham's razor works only if the simpler theory can explain everything that the more complicated theory can explain. Then, if the naturalistic theory of evolution is true, and if religion is as bad for us as the "Four Horsemen" argue, why has religion survived so long? Does religion offer survival value to individuals and groups that accept its belief systems? (Obviously, the "God hypothesis" *can* answer this question: There *is* a God, and he deserves praise for his amazing designs; he offers rewards to those who praise him.) Dennett and Dawkins realize that they must address this question, and a major part of their books deals with it. To make matters worse for them, in 2004, neurobiologist and geneticist Dean Hamer published a book he called *The God Gene* in which he claimed to have discovered a gene that would be conducive to religious thought and behavior. This book must have produced glee in the religious camps and dismay in the naturalist camps, especially when the popular press got ahold of Hamer's discovery. *Time* magazine published an article titled, "Is God in our Genes?" in which its readers were told, "Humans who developed a spiritual sense thrived and bequeathed that trait to their offspring. Those who didn't risked dying out in chaos and killing. The evolutionary equation is a simple but powerful one."[26] Dennett says that in this article people are being told that religion "is good for you because it was endorsed by evolution" (p. 316). He calls this idea "simple-minded Darwinism" (p. 317), and he claims that Hamer's hypothesis "is marked by more enthusiasm than subtlety" (p. 139), but he is willing to keep an open mind. Below, I will return to this idea of a "God center" in the brain, to see specifically how Dennett responds to this suggestion.

If religion has survived as long as it seems to have done, it was transmitted either culturally or biologically. If its development is purely cultural (in terms of "**memes**" rather than genes, as both Dennett and Dawkins say),[27] then it would be more easy to eradicate, but Dawkins and Dennett seem to suspect that the origin of religion is somehow genetic, as is borne out by how much space in their books each gives to testing biological possibilities. Dennett divides them into three categories: *mutualist,* a genetic transmission that is directly beneficial to an organism ("enhancing human fitness or even making life possible"); *commensals,* "neither good nor bad for us, but along for the ride"; *parasites,* deleterious but connected to something else that is mutualist (p. 84). Both Dennett and Dawkins suspect that religion is in the third category—a by-product of a useful genetic endowment, as moths fly into candle flames because their normally useful compass system based on light and darkness betrays them. This is a deadly misfiring of something useful.

One possible source of religious beliefs could be an unhealthy extension of **animism.** Children and isolated tribes read agency into whatever frightens them. This erroneous "intentional stance" (as Dennett calls it, a "stance" that could have a biological base) produces strategies that have survival value. It can "speed up decision making in dangerous circumstances," according to Dawkins (p. 212). It is a form of HADD, a "hyperactive detection device." We hyperactively detect agency where there is only nature. This form of dualistic thinking can lead to religious beliefs.

Another possibility is that religious beliefs could have had the early beneficial result of *group selection,* fostering the idea of group loyalty and in-group altruism, helping religious groups in competition with other groups. Journalist Ezra Klein paraphrases the view of the psychologist Jonathan Haidt, saying, "We are descended from ancestors who would not have survived if they hadn't been very good at belonging to groups." If religion's main function is creating groups of like-minded believers, the beliefs of these members would be "memes" that have survival value, no matter how absurd those beliefs are.[28] This answer to the question of the origin of religion seems convincing to a number of theorists, but it is not attractive to either Dawkins or Dennett, who are loath to credit group selection with any serious role in evolution. Darwin himself believed in group selection, where nature "selects" certain groups whose organizing principles and behavior give them survival advantage over competing groups. Following Darwin, the noted evolutionary biologist David Sloan Wilson also is committed to the idea of group selection and its role in the history of evolution, which he develops in his book of 2002, *Darwin's Cathedral: Evolution, Religion, and the Nature of Society.* But Dawkins, much of whose public fame is based on his book *The Selfish Gene* (1976), apparently sticks with the gene (something of which Darwin was unaware) as the real object of natural selection and therefore is suspicious of group selection.

Religion might also be an extension of a genetic tendency for human children to obey their elders. According to Dawkins, there would be a selective advantage to a rule of thumb followed by the brains of children, "Believe without question whatever adults tell you." Dawkins writes, "It doesn't matter what particular style of nonsense infects the child's brain. Once infected the child will grow up and infect the next generation with the same nonsense, whatever it happens to be" (pp. 218–219). (This theory might explain the transmission of religious belief but not the origin of religion. And how do adolescents fit in here?)

Returning once more to the idea of a "God center" in the brain, Dennett thinks that the gene that Dean Hamer discovered (called WMNA$_2$) may well be a "hypnotizability-enabler," and, in a world in which shamanism and witchcraft were the only sources of medicine, the placebo effect and the ability to be easily hypnotized would have survival value. Such a gene, according to Dennett, "might have provided major health benefits in earlier times, and would be one way of taking Hamer's 'God gene' seriously" (p. 317). Dennett connects the religious mentality with the placebo effect and the hypnotic state.

Neither Dennett nor Dawkins *knows* that any or all of these suggestions about the genetic origins of religion are correct, but they apparently think they are plausible and that eventually either these explanations or something like them will prove to be true. In the meantime, they urge us to keep the (Darwinian) faith.

What about the origin of life itself? According to Dawkins, the theory of natural selection can account for the evolution of life once it has started, but he concedes that the theory of evolution cannot explain life's origins. He admits that the chemical origin of life, considered by itself, is an improbable event, but he reminds us that this lucky chance only needed to happen one time. He appeals to theory of probability, saying, "Even a near-impossible chemical event must come to pass given enough planet years to play with" (p. 419). Dawkins is convinced that science will eventually be able to replicate this "near-impossible event." Theologians jump on this gap, calling it a fatal flaw in the theory of evolution, but Dawkins thinks that inventing an inexplicable deity to fill this gap is worse than admitting that we do not yet know how the first living cell emerged, because conjuring up a God to whom we can attribute that event is a "dreadful exhibition of self-indulgent, thought-denying skyhookery" (p. 185).

What's "new" about the New Atheism? First, it is more in-your-face than earlier generations of atheism (e.g., the atheist Bertrand Russell does not hurl insults at those who disagree with him in his "Why I Am Not a Christian" [1925]), and the New Atheism is more out-of-the-closet. (In America, no politician who is a self-declared atheist could be elected to office.) Beyond that, the New Atheism's novelty is its grounding in evolutionary theory. Yet, this grounding seems tentative. Dennett and Dawkins are convinced that there are evolutionary reasons showing how such a deleterious organism as religion could be born and survive, but they are not sure what those reasons are. If one does not find their evolutionary hypotheses sufficiently compelling to move toward atheism, one might prefer the theory of an opponent of Dawkins and Dennett, the late Stephen Jay Gould, a noted evolutionary biologist and science writer. Gould argues in his book of 1999, *The Rock of Ages,* that science and religion are two "non-overlapping *magisteria*" that are not in competition with each other. Science deals with factual truth and religion deals with values and the meaning of life. In addition, Gould writes, "Science cannot (by its legitimate methods) adjudicate the issue of God's possible superintendence of nature. We neither affirm nor deny it; we simply cannot comment on it."[29] Dawkins challenges this assertion, claiming that the God hypothesis is a scientific claim (because a universe with a "superintendent of nature" would be a very different universe from one without such a superintendent) but almost surely a *false* scientific claim, refutable on probabilistic grounds. (Chapter 4 of Dawkins's book is titled "Why There Almost Certainly Is No God.")

Plantinga's Proof That Evolutionary Theory Cannot Eliminate Supernaturalism

We will end this discussion with a rather ironic twist. Alvin Plantinga, a well-known American philosopher of religion, claims to have constructed a proof that evolutionary theory leaves open the question of divine intervention in the universe. Plantinga tries to show that if the theory of evolution (call this theory E) is true, then naturalism (only natural objects, properties, and events are real [call this theory N]), or materialism (only material objects, properties, processes, or events are real [call this theory M]), or atheism (no supernatural objects, properties, processes, or events are real [call this theory A]) cannot be known to be true, and, worse, it is irrational to believe in the theory of evolution and to be at the same time a naturalist (or a materialist, or an atheist). Here's how his argument works.

To have arrived at the belief that any or all of these views ([E], [N], [M], or [A]) are correct is to presuppose that human cognitive faculties are reliable (i.e., human memory, perception, and reasoning are reliable). However, if one believes in evolution, then one believes that human cognitive faculties have *evolved* in such a way as to be reliable. However, according to Plantinga, if the brain has *evolved* in such a way as to give humans adaptability and survival benefits, there is no guarantee that it has also evolved in such a way as to tend to produce *true* beliefs. That is, sets of beliefs could be false but adaptive. If we cannot show that it is impossible for belief systems to be both adaptive and false, then there is no good reason to believe in any of the views above ([E], [N], [M], or [A]). Then Plantinga lists a number of imagined cases in which sets of false belief could be adaptive: Imagine a prehistoric hominid, Paul, who believes that tigers are divine beings and that you offend them if you let them see you. The behavior produced by this false belief would be adaptive—as adaptive as the behavior produced by a true belief. Assume that *most* of Paul's beliefs were similarly false but adaptive. Plantinga asks, "Could Paul's beliefs really be mainly false, but still lead to adaptive action? Yes indeed."[30] Plantinga concludes that if evolutionary theory is true, then the probability that we have reliable cognitive faculties is either "low, or inscrutable" (i.e., unknowable). Plantinga asserts, "If I can't rationally believe that the faculties that produce [a specific] belief are reliable, I have a reason for rejecting the belief" (p. 12).

Plantinga first published his argument in 1991. In none of the versions I have read does he point out two paradoxes he has created. First, if his argument is valid, then not only theories [E], [N], [M], and [A] all have a low probability or are inscrutable, but so is the case with Plantinga's own theory (call it [P]), for exactly the same reasons that [E], [N], [M], and [A] have low probability or are inscrutable. The second paradox is that, according to his argument, if the theory of evolution [E] is true, it has low probability of being true or it is inscrutable. It almost seems that Plantinga's argument is meant as a philosophical joke—both because of the paradoxes it creates and because it makes belief in virtually any theory, including atheism and Darwinism, a leap of faith, that is, it puts them in the same category as religious beliefs. But serious philosophers have taken Plantinga's argument seriously. Most of the articles in James Beilby's anthology, *Naturalism Defeated?* are critical of Plantinga. Many of them challenge his move from the *possibility* of the evolved brain's producing false but adaptable beliefs to the *probability* of that dilemma. Others argue that it is much more likely that true beliefs rather than false beliefs would be adaptable. These two problems do seem to be likely points of attack, but I think that Plantinga might profit, ironically, from the books by Dennett and Dawkins that we have been discussing. Both Dennett the philosopher and Dawkins the biologist hold religious beliefs to be false from top to bottom, yet they both see them either as having survival value of their own or as commensal with genetic material that does have genetic survival value. This would be a real case of a false belief system that has adaptability rather than just the imaginary ones that Plantinga invented as examples. If Plantinga—and David Hume—are right, then all beliefs are acts of faith, hence in the same category as religious beliefs.

Do All Beliefs Have the Same Status?

Volitional Justifications of Religious Belief

Earlier we looked at a number of arguments claiming to demonstrate the rationality of a belief in God's existence. These arguments stressed reason and evidence. There have been other kinds of arguments for God's existence, appealing not so much to the rational and intellectual side of our nature as to its passional side. (There have also been passional arguments *against* God's existence. Nietzsche's argument probably takes the cake, "If there were gods, how could I stand not being one? Therefore there are no gods.") One of the most famous of such heartfelt arguments for God's existence is that of the American pragmatist, WILLIAM JAMES (1842–1910).

First, a bit about **pragmatism.** The term was coined by another American philosopher, CHARLES PEIRCE (1839–1914), and for him, it was essentially the name of a *method* whose goal was to clarify our thought processes by tracing out the practical consequences of beliefs in various ideas.

Friedrich Nietzsche Makes an Important Discovery

You mean I'm not God? I can't stand it!

You win. Here's the cake.

James's version of pragmatism (which so repelled Peirce that he changed the name of his own view from "pragmatism" to "pragmaticism"—a name he said was "ugly enough to be safe from kidnappers") ultimately became a justification of a certain kind of religious belief. Before developing that justification, we must distinguish between the pragmatic theory of *meaning* and its theory of *truth*. Concerning the former, James wrote:

> Is the world one or many?—fated or free?—material or spiritual?—here are notions either of which

Ugly Enough to Be Safe from Kidnappers

may or may not hold good of the world; and disputes over such notions are unending. The pragmatic method in such cases is to try to interpret each notion by tracing its respective practical consequences. What difference would it practically make to any one if this notion rather than that notion were true? If no practical difference whatever can be traced, then the alternatives mean practically the same thing, and all dispute is idle.[31]

In other words, a sentence is *meaningful* only if believing it would make a practical difference in your life as opposed to believing some alternative to it. For example, take the sentence, "There is a table in the middle of this room." If you wanted to travel from one end of the room to the other, then believing that sentence to be true (as opposed to believing its opposite) would make a practical differ-

ence because your
path across the room
would be different in
one case as opposed
to the other. Now
consider a slightly more
complicated case: "Jupiter has

four moons." Whether you believe that sentence or an alternative (such as "Jupiter has no moons"), it probably won't make much difference in your life either way unless you are an astronomer or an astronaut. But if you *were* an astronomer or an astronaut, we could certainly imagine conditions in which believing the one alternative as opposed to the other would have definite practical consequences. (You won't try to land a space shuttle on Jupiter's fourth moon unless you believed that Jupiter *has* a fourth moon.)

So, the examples about tables and moons that we have considered are meaningful because believing any of them could make a difference. Contrast those examples with this:

"There are many diaphanous, unknowable, invisible, intangible beings hovering over such items as daisies and hamburgers." Believing this sentence or believing its opposite will produce exactly the

There's just something about this hamburger...

Hey Dad, check out this flower!

Yes, but _was_ it brilling? .... And _do_ the slithy toves gyre and gimble in the wabe? I mean do they _truly?_

Only Meaningful Sentences Can Be True or False

same practice; hence, each belief is _practically_ identical.

Now what about _truth?_ First of all, notice that only meaningful sentences can be either true or false. (From this, it seems to follow rather curiously that my last example about diaphanous beings is neither true nor false.)

Having said that, let me create a more general context for a philosophical discussion of truth by contrasting James's **pragmatic theory of truth** with the other two theories of truth that have competed with each other throughout the history of Western philosophy: the **correspondence theory** and the **coherence theory.** The correspondence theory has been the dominant one and has been especially favored by empiricists. It simply says that a proposition is true if it corresponds with the facts. The sentence "The cat is on the mat" is true if and only if the cat is in fact on the mat. The main attractions of this theory are its simplicity and its appeal to common sense. The main weaknesses are (1) the difficulties in explaining how linguistic entities (words, sentences) can _correspond_ to things that are nothing like language; (2) the difficulty in providing a noncircular explanation of exactly _what_ it is that sentences are supposed to correspond to (facts? What is a "fact" if not that which a true sentence asserts?); and (3) a particular awkwardness in its application to mathematics (What is it to which the proposition "$5 + 2 = 7$" corresponds?). The coherence theory of truth asserts that a proposition is true if it coheres with all the other propositions taken to be true. This theory has been preferred by many rationalists. Its greatest strength is that it makes sense out of the idea of mathematical truth ("$5 + 2 = 7$" is true because it is entailed by "$7 = 7$," and by "$1 + 6 = 7$," and by "$21 \div 3 = (2 \times 3) + 1$," etc.). Its greatest weakness is its vicious circularity. Proposition A is true by virtue of its coherence with propositions B, C, and D. Proposition C is true by virtue of its coherence with propositions A, B, and D, and so forth. (Think of the belief system of a paranoid. All his beliefs cohere perfectly with one another. Everything that happens to him is evidence that everybody is out to get him.)

Now, the pragmatist says that the test of correspondence and the test of coherence are not competing theories but simply different tools to be applied to beliefs to see if those beliefs "work." James had this to say about truth, "Ideas (which themselves are but parts of our experience) become true just insofar as they help us to get into satisfactory relations with other parts of our experience, . . . truth in our ideas means their power to 'work'" (p. 49). So the key notion here is that of an idea "working," which James defines as "help[ing] us to get into satisfactory relations with other parts of our experience." James also calls this notion the "cash value" of ideas. Now, if believing that there is a table in the middle of the room prevents you from bruising your legs and making a fool out of yourself, then that belief *works*. That is, it is true.

Let us, finally, turn to the pragmatists' thoughts about believing in God. James's discussion of this topic was a response to the scientific view that we have no right to hold any beliefs for which we do not have adequate evidence. This view (held by Hume in the eighteenth century and Bertrand Russell in the twentieth) was popularized in James's own time by the British mathematician W. K. CLIFFORD (1845–1879), who said, "Belief is desecrated when given to unproved and unquestioned statements for the solace and private pleasure of the believer. . . . It is wrong always, everywhere, and for everyone, to believe anything upon insufficient evidence."[32] To this, James responded:

> Our passional nature not only lawfully may, but must, decide an option between propositions, whenever it is a genuine option that cannot by its nature be decided on intellectual grounds; for to say, under such circumstances, "Do not decide, but leave the question open," is itself a passional decision—just like deciding yes or no—and it is attended with the same risk of losing the truth.[33]

Now, for James, the issue of God's existence is one that the intellect by itself definitely cannot resolve. So if it is a "genuine option" (i.e., a meaningful belief), it may be entertained on purely volitional grounds. Is the proposition "God exists" prag-matically meaningful? Does believing it make a practical difference in one's life? These questions are problematical. I take it that for some people it does, but for some others it doesn't. Some people would behave exactly the same whether they believed in God's existence or not. But others would behave very differently if they believed in the existence of the God of the Judeo-Christian tradition from the way they would behave if they did *not* believe in him. (If they believe, perhaps they will be nicer to their neighbor than if they do not believe.)

But not everybody for whom a belief in God makes a difference would behave in exactly the same way. Some might become monks or nuns; in the case of others, the only difference their belief makes is that on Sundays they dress up and go to church. This point shows the *subjective* side of James's theory of meaning because the meaning of a proposition is just the difference in behavior, resulting from belief in the proposition. So for some, there is no *practical* difference between the sentences "God exists" and "God does not exist." For others, belief, as opposed to nonbelief, would make a radical difference. For yet others, belief would result in very minor differences (e.g., putting on a dark suit on Sundays).

Now, what about the *truth* of the claim "God exists"? According to James, a proposition is true if believing *it works*—that is, if the belief puts the believer in a more satisfactory relationship with the rest of his or her experience. Concerning this, James says:

On pragmatic principles, if the hypothesis of God works satisfactorily in the widest sense of the word, it is true. Now whatever its residual difficulties may be, experience shows that it certainly does work, and that the problem is to build it out and determine it so that it will combine satisfactorily with all the other working truths. (p. 192)

A Pragmatic Proof of God's Existence

So we see that for James, both meaning and truth are relative. To some people, the sentence "God exists" is true; for others, it is false. Most philosophers rejected James's solution to the problem of religious belief because they balked at his relativism concerning meaning and truth. Others felt that James left untouched the real question, which they took to be this: regardless of the personal satisfaction or lack of it found in a belief in God's existence, does God really exist?

Religious Mysticism

Religious belief is sometimes grounded in certain kinds of extraordinary personal experiences. These experiences can be felt as events lasting only seconds ("We shall all be changed, in a moment, in the twinkling of an eye" [1 Corinthians 15:52]), or they can be experienced as lasting minutes, hours, days, or even weeks. They can be experienced as spontaneous implosions upon the mind. (As apparently was that most famous of conversions—the one that transformed Saul of Tarsus, persecutor of Christians, into Saint Paul, author of most of the books of the New Testament. On the road to Damascus, he suddenly saw a blinding light that knocked him from his horse, and he heard the voice of Jesus saying, "Saul, Saul, why persecuteth

Mysticism: Long-Range Plan

thou me?" Another example is the experience of the Roman emperor Constantine, who, riding through the Alps with his army, looked into the sky and saw the clouds swirling into the sign of the cross and spelling out, "In this sign conquer." [Maybe there's some connection between horseback riding and religious experience?]) Or

How Saul Became Paul

such experiences can be intentionally brought about by engaging in a series of physical and mental preparations of the type outlined by St. Ignatius of Loyola in his book *Spiritual Exercises*. Because these experiences are extrarational—that is, they seem to transcend logical explanation—they are often called **mystical** experiences. What they all seem to have in common is that during them, and sometimes after them, everything is seen in a new light—"all things are transformed." Whole conceptions of religion are based on mystical experiences, especially in certain Asian philosophies. In this text, we are restricting ourselves to the Western philosophy of religion, where mysticism has never been mainstream, yet there has always been a strong undercurrent of mystical thought in Judaism (the Cabbalistic tradition), in Islam (the Sufi tradition), and in both the Catholic and Protestant variations of Christianity. We can trace each of these Western mystical traditions not only to their own holy texts but also, ironically, to certain Neo-Platonic interpretations of Plato's Simile of the Line. In an almost unintelligible passage of the *Republic,* Plato has Socrates say:

The good isn't being but is still beyond being, exceeding it in dignity and power!

Huh???

Using this assertion as one of their bases, some of the more mystically oriented Neo-Platonists interpreted Plato's Line in the following manner:

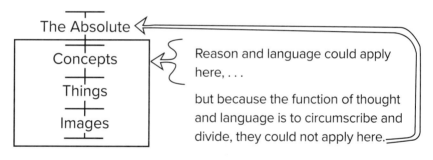

The Absolute

Concepts

Things

Images

Reason and language could apply here, . . .

but because the function of thought and language is to circumscribe and divide, they could not apply here.

Avila, España

The Absolute (ultimate reality, God) is one and indivisible; therefore, it is "accessed" not by a rational analysis and understanding (as the traditional Platonists thought) but through an extrarational mystical experience.

We will use as our example of Western mysticism the stellar case of TERESA of Avila (1515–1582)—later *Saint* Teresa of Avila. She was born in the ancient and austere walled city of Avila on the stark, arid plateau of Castile in northwestern Spain. As a child, she read the novels of romance and chivalry, popular at that time (the same ones satirized a century later by Cervantes in *Don Quixote*), and biographies of the saints. Motivated by these stories of adventures, when she was seven years old she and her brother ran away from home heading for "the land of the Moors," hoping to be beheaded there and become saintly martyrs. Luckily, their uncle ran across them a few blocks from home and brought them back to their worried mother.

As a young woman, Teresa attracted much attention for her beauty, but she was not interested in the few pleasures that the society of Avila could offer her. She entered the order of the Carmelites when she was twenty. She was always frail and, for much of her first year as a nun, ill. She heard strange noises in her head and fell into a four-day trance that was so deep the sisters thought she was dead. This trance may have been a precursor to her later mystical

visions. She took on as her life's work the reformation of the Carmelite order, which had its roots in twelfth-century Palestine but had lost its original spark and zeal, according to Teresa. She traveled the length and breadth of Spain, living entirely on alms, and established thirty-two convents of the Reform. Her practical acumen in the everyday world contrasts remarkably with the "otherworldliness" of her religious experiences. William James, in his masterful book *The Varieties of Religious Experience*, says of Teresa that she was

> one of the ablest women, in many respects, of whose life we have the record. She had a powerful intellect of the practical order. She wrote admirable descriptive psychology, possessed a will equal to any emergency, great talent for politics and business, a buoyant disposition, and a first-rate literary style.[34]

Teresa was beatified (made eligible for sainthood) only thirty-two years after her death and was canonized (officially declared "saintly") in 1622, along with her Basque counterpart, Ignatius of Loyola. She has always been one of Spanish Catholicism's favorite figures.

We cannot call Teresa a philosopher in any strict sense; nevertheless, she is associated with the Platonic tradition through her reading of Augustine's *Confessions* and her conversations and correspondence with contemporary figures in the movement. She lived at a time when the Inquisition suppressed many books—especially for women! This restriction saddened her, but in one of her visions Christ himself said to her, "Be not troubled. I will give thee a living book." That book was nature, and to nature she paid the closest attention and from nature she drew the images for her mystical philosophy. Even in this respect, she was participating unwittingly in the Platonic tradition, for the Neo-Platonic medieval Christian world had left as a legacy the view that everything in nature is a symbol of some higher truth and therefore each natural object gives analogical—though not literal—knowledge of God. Ironically, this view means that "images" are more highly valued in the Neo-Platonic tradition than they were by Plato himself. As we turn to Teresa's mystical thinking,

Saint Teresa of Avila (1515–1582)
(After the Sixteenth-Century Statue
by Gregorio Fernández)

Out, damnable weed!

we will see how she uses these images from the natural and human world to describe and perhaps to achieve a mystical state of religious knowledge.

Teresa wrote about her mystical experiences in a number of works, most prominent of which are her autobiography, *Book of Her Life*, and *Mansions*, or *Inner*

Castles as it was subtitled. In the latter book she discusses religiosity in terms of the imagery of householding, while in the first book she uses the imagery of gardening. There, she identifies four stages of religious life, each of which she calls "water." In the final stage, "the Prayer of Quiet," the soul is permitted to irrigate the garden with the aid of water running from a stream or a spring. Where before she had to struggle to bring water to the garden, it is as if God himself is doing the gardening now, and the soul is able to benefit from the delicious fragrances of the flourishing plants.

Teresa calls this pleasure a "celestial frenzy," a "glorious folly." Now the soul is as if in a state of sleep or in a "swoon." It does not know if it speaks or is silent, if it is "laughing or weeping." The ears hear, but what they hear is "a torrent of holy nonsense." Eating is torturous; sleeping produces anguish. In this third "water," it is as if a spark has been ignited that God will now nurture and lead to the next stage of progress. This fourth "water" is like a heavenly shower that saturates the whole garden. Then, reverting to the ignition simile, she says the fire has burst into full flame, and

A Torrent of Holy Nonsense

the flame rises high above the fire. Teresa calls this, in *Mansions,* the "Prayer of Union." Here God completely possesses the soul. Mad words escape the soul, but they are really meaningless though meant as praise and exclamations of almost unendurable joy. Teresa also uses imagery from that most erotic of all biblical books, *The Song of Songs.* The soul is "wounded with love for her spouse." It experiences the "kiss of the mouth" from the Bridegroom. The fire in the soul causes pain but also warmth and pleasure. In the final moment, the "self truly appears not to exist." One wishes for nothing, neither life nor death. It is as if, Teresa says, two candles have been brought together and now produce a single flame as their wax melts together.

Associated with Teresa's mystical "raptures" are always visions. Her most famous vision, the one captured in the statue by Bernini, is called the "Vision of the Transverberation of the Heart." She saw a small angel with a beautiful face holding "a long golden spear," tipped with "a little fire," which he thrust into her heart so that, she says,

> it penetrated into my entrails. When he drew out the spear he seemed to be drawing them out with it, leaving me all on fire with a wonderous love for God. The pain was so great that it caused me to utter several moans; and yet so exceedingly sweet is this greatest of pains that it is impossible to desire to be rid of it, or for the soul to be content with less than God.[35]

Teresa was given this vision many times. It must have been difficult to come down off a "high" like this—very difficult, as she says, to do dishes after you've seen the face of God. Yet, she adds, we must also find God *entre los pucheros*—among the pots and pans.

The scarcely suppressed sexual imagery of Teresa's vision might suggest a pathology to some. In William James's study of Teresa, he says, "To the medical mind, these ecstasies signify . . . hypnoid states, on an intellectual basis of superstition, and a corporeal one of degeneration and hysteria" (p. 450). But, sticking with his pragmatic principles, James goes on to say, "To pass a spiritual judgment upon these states, we must not content ourselves with superficial medical talk but inquire into their fruits for life." (James is here applying the principle that he elsewhere calls "the genetic fallacy"—that of thinking one has refuted the truth of an idea by tracing the idea back to its psychological roots, a charge that could certainly be brought against Marx, Nietzsche, and Freud.) And James clearly thinks that Teresa's visions indeed produced good "fruits for life," because they motivated her to great activity and a high degree of practical success and happiness.

Teresa admitted that some of her confessors had problems with her descriptions of her visions. Indeed, the brothers of the Inquisition kept a close eye on her. Why? Perhaps

Saint Teresa in Ecstasy (After Gianlorenzo Bernini, 1652)

Trying to Do Dishes after Having Seen the Face of God

The Brothers of the Inquisition and Sister Teresa Discussing Her Night Out

because, in the West, religious beliefs have become institutionalized and hence structures of authority and power.

But mystical ecstasies are subversive of established power and so are worrisome to the authorities. It is as if the inquisitors would have liked to ask her, "Sister Teresa, if *you* have seen the face of God, why hasn't the *Pope* seen it?" Teresa probably would have answered humbly that she did not know.

Religious Existentialism

One of the most interesting antirationalistic religious stances (I am loath to call it a *theory*) is that of the nineteenth-century Dane SØREN

KIERKEGAARD (1813–1855).
Kierkegaard—whom I would call a radical
Christian, but who never dared in his writings to call himself a Christian (he was
busy attempting to *become* a Christian)—
loathed all attempts to prove God's existence. Indeed, Kierkegaard took such
attempts as a personal affront. ("Woe unto
all those unfaithful stewards who sat down
and wrote false proofs.") Kierkegaard felt
that for something to be a truly religious
belief, it had to be just that—*a belief*,
something that is not knowledge. Indeed,
a religious belief would have to be something not only that *is not* knowledge but

Søren Kierkegaard (1813–1855)

that *cannot be* knowledge. Rather, it could be accounted for only in terms
of what Kierkegaard called "the category of the absurd"—a category he felt
Kant had left out of his twelve "categories of the understanding." (This is
reminiscent of the view of the early Christian theologian TERTULLIAN
[169–220], whose motto was "I believe that which is absurd.") According to
Kierkegaard, knowledge must be something *objective*—in the case of mathematics (e.g., $3 \times 3 = 9$), science (e.g., $f = ma$), history (e.g., Caesar crossed
the Rubicon in 49 B.C.E.), or common sense (e.g., the cat is on the mat),
there are objective criteria for establishing their truth value. But in the case
of religious claims (e.g., God is love, whosoever believeth in him shall inherit
everlasting life), there are only subjective criteria, which is to say, *personal*
criteria. Arriving at a religious perspective requires a "leap of faith."

Perhaps this notion can be best addressed by taking a look at
Kierkegaard's perplexing account
of the biblical story of Abraham
and Isaac as it is related in his
book *Fear and Trembling*
(1843), for it is there
that we find his most sustained, if convoluted,
discussion of religious
belief. Our problem is
confounded by the fact
that Kierkegaard wrote
the book under one of
his many pseudonyms,

Credo Quia Absurdum

that of "Johannes de Silentio" (an intentional irony worthy of Kierkegaard's hero, Socrates—John the Silent speaks!), and later claimed that he took no responsibility for any views held by his pseudonyms. The curious relation between Kierkegaard and the volumes he wrote under fictitious names has been the topic of more than one book, but here we will ignore Kierkegaard's disclaimer and attribute the views in *Fear and Trembling* to Kierkegaard himself.

Let us begin by reviewing the pertinent aspects of the biblical text as related in Genesis, Chapters 11 through 22. Abraham was a hereditary tribal leader of the Hebrews. Late in life he married his half sister, Sarah, who was barren. When Abraham was seventy-five years old, God made a covenant with Abraham and promised him that Sarah would become the mother of a son who would be the father of a great nation. The years passed and Sarah did not conceive. Then when Abraham was ninety-nine and Sarah ninety ("and it ceased to be with Sarah after the manner of women" [Genesis 18:11]), God appeared to Abraham again and renewed the promise. Sarah conceived and gave birth to Isaac. The circumcision and weaning of the child were celebrated with great joy by Abraham, who loved his son. Then came that terrible night described in Genesis 22:1–2.

> And it came to pass . . . that God did tempt Abraham, and said unto him, Abraham: and he said, Behold, here I am. And he said, take now thy son, Isaac, whom thou lovest, and get thee into the land of Moriah; and offer him there for a burnt offering upon one of the mountains which I will tell thee of.

Without hesitation and telling no one, Abraham took Isaac, traveled with him three days through that lonely desert, placed him on the appointed altar, lifted the sacrificial knife and was prepared to make the fatal thrust when the Angel of the Lord stopped him, saying that Abraham had passed the test, and allowed him to sacrifice in Isaac's stead a ram that was conveniently caught in a nearby thicket. So Abraham got Isaac back, returned to his people, and lived in blessedness the rest of his days.

Now, this story provokes a state of deep perplexity in

Johannes de Silentio, the pseudonymous author of *Fear and Trembling*. First of all, Johannes is perplexed because he cannot understand the story; second, he is perplexed because everyone else seems to understand the story perfectly well. (Why else would all the others replace the Bible on the shelf after reading the account, comment, "What a wonderful story of faith!" and then go along on their merry way without being the least bit affected by the story? Yet the story leaves Johannes sleepless in the night and inspires in him the fear and trembling of the book's title.) Johannes cannot understand the story because he cannot understand Abraham himself. He asks:

Johannes de Silentio Reads before Retiring

> Who gave strength to Abraham's arm? Who held his right hand up so that it did not fall limp at his side? He who gazes at this becomes paralyzed. Who gave strength to Abraham's soul, so that his eyes did not grow dim, so that he saw neither Isaac nor the ram? He who gazes at this becomes blind.[36]

Johannes tries to conceive of Abraham as a real human being of flesh and blood, not as a fantastic personality from mythological literature. As an existing human, Abraham is incomprehensible. How could he be so resolute in the face of the horror of his task? "And if . . . the individual was mistaken— what can save him? . . . and if the individual had misunderstood the deity— what can save him? . . . if this man is disordered in his mind, if he had made a mistake!" (pp. 71–72)

Furthermore, Johannes cannot be certain what it is that makes Abraham "the father of faith" and hence the father of us all. Many say that Abraham is great because he was willing to sacrifice to God the best thing he had. Johannes demonstrates the falsity of this view by way of an illustration. He imagines a clerical orator who eloquently presents his flock with such a misleading interpretation of the story of Abraham. One of his parishioners, taken by the sermon, returns home and kills his son. When the preacher hears of this, he goes to the sinner and thunders down on him in righteous indignation, "O abominable man, offscouring of society, what devil possessed thee to want to murder thy son?" The point, of course, is that this attitude is precisely the one the preacher should have had toward Abraham. Johannes de Silentio asks:

> How is one to explain the contradiction illustrated by that orator? Is it because Abraham had a prescriptive right to be a great man, so that what he did is great, and when another does the same it is sin, a heinous sin? In that case I do not wish to participate in such thoughtless eulogy. If faith does not make it a holy act to be willing to murder one's son, then let the same condemnation be pronounced upon Abraham as upon every other man. (p. 41)

Johannes's conclusion is that "either Abraham was every minute a murderer, or we are here confronted by a paradox which is higher than all mediation." This thought horrifies Johannes, who says, "Abraham enjoys honor and glory as the father of faith, whereas he ought to be prosecuted and convicted of murder." But if Abraham is not to be condemned as a potential murderer (surely *that* cannot make him the father of faith), then he must be condemned as insane. "Humanly speaking, he is crazy and cannot make himself intelligible to anyone. And yet it is the mildest expression to say that he is crazy" (p. 86).

One of the most striking ideas to emerge from Kierkegaard's account of Abraham's madness (and one that is meant to provoke the fear and trembling of the book's title) is that granting the theological premise changes nothing. Abraham is mad whether or not God really did speak to him. If a law-abiding moral man "hears the voice of God" and becomes so inspired as to become socially irresponsible, if he sacrifices his son without criminal intent in order to obey a secret order that God has communicated to him alone, then certainly from the medical-social point of view (i.e., "humanly speaking"), that man is mad.

Jean-Paul Sartre was particularly impressed with this aspect of Kierkegaard's analysis of the plight of Abraham, and he referred to it in order to elucidate his own theory of anguish. Sartre wrote:

> You know the story: an angel[37] has ordered Abraham to sacrifice his son; if it really were an angel who has come and said, "You are Abraham, you shall sacrifice your son," everything would be all right. But everyone must first wonder, "Is it really an angel and am I really Abraham? What proof do I have?"
>
> If an angel comes to me, what proof is there that it's an angel? And if I hear voices, what proof is there that they come from heaven and not from hell, or from the subconscious, or a pathological condition? What proves that they are addressed to me?[38]

Abraham is mad not only in the sense referred to earlier (unable to communicate, and prepared to perform an act that goes against his own moral standards and will horrify all) but in the following sense as well: He not only believes his son will die but, at the same moment, he believes his son will *not* die. (Abraham still has faith that God will keep the old covenant.) Abraham believed with certainty two mutually exclusive theses, and he acted on each of them in a single project. (It is as if Columbus believed both that the world was flat and that it was round, and he set out to prove both points by embarking on a single voyage.)

So either Abraham is a murderer or he is mad, or the story of Abraham is rationally unintelligible. It will probably come as no surprise to you to discover that Kierkegaard (or, at least, Johannes de Silentio) draws the latter conclusion. Faith, he says, is "a paradox which is capable of transforming a murder into a holy act well-pleasing to God." Abraham acted "by virtue of the absurd," and "by virtue of the absurd" he became the father of faith. "Abraham was greater than all, great by reason of his power whose strength is impotence, great by reason of his wisdom whose secret is foolishness, great by reason of the love which is hatred of oneself" (p. 31). Adopting a term from Plato, Kierkegaard calls Abraham's condition "divine madness." For Kierkegaard, of course, the question was not whether Abraham was mad but whether his madness was divinely or demonically inspired. Still, "humanly speaking," it does not matter. In either case, society has an asylum for such heroes.

Earlier I mentioned that, for Kierkegaard, there could be no objective but only subjective, or personal, justification for religious belief. This idea can be clarified if one considers certain features of Kierkegaard's account of Abraham's story. Notice that Abraham's act is not authorized or justified by God's command; rather, God's command is authorized by Abraham's decision to obey it. When Abraham was awakened on that horrible night by a voice commanding him to kill his child, he could have responded in a number of ways. He might have said, "This is the voice not of God but of the devil. Only the devil tempts men to do evil deeds. Get thee hence, O Satan!" Or he might have said (especially if he had read Freud), "This is not the voice of God but the voice of my own madness. I shall kill myself rather than perform this insane act!" Or he might have said,

Abraham Reads Freud

"This is the voice of God, who is testing me to see if I am willing to perform an immoral act for no good reason. I shall pass the test by refusing to perform the act!" Or he might have said, "If this is the voice of God, then he is not the God I thought he was; rather, he is an evil and cruel monster whose bidding I shall not do!"

Or, . . . he might have said any number of other things. Instead Abraham chose to accept the assignment, and in so choosing, he bestowed his *own* authority on God's command. Kierkegaard is suggesting that ultimately the individual is the source of all authority and is totally responsible for all his or her decisions and actions. (This belief is the beginning of the school of thought known in the twentieth century as existentialism, which puts the existence of the individual human being at the center of the philosophical stage. [See Chapter 10 for a more thorough discussion of existentialism.] Kierkegaard's views greatly influenced such members of that school as Jean-Paul Sartre, Simone de Beauvoir, Martin Heidegger, Karl Jaspers, Albert Camus, Miguel de Unamuno, and Gabriel Marcel.)

Kierkegaard's complex demonstration of the irreducibility of faith to intellectual categories (which is even more complex than has been presented here) is indeed profound. Both the traditional proofs of God's existence *and* the traditional atheistic criticism of the irrationality of religious belief seem lifeless and shallow in the face of Kierkegaard's account. Especially weak vis-à-vis Kierkegaard's explosive treatment of faith are those rationalistic arguments like that of Freud, which see religion as a crutch for the frail. Kierkegaard's religious discourse is meant to strengthen, not weaken, the soul. It is not "lemonade-twaddle" for the fainthearted (as he calls most sermonizing); rather, it is only for those who can stand the drama of striving with God and with oneself.

Kierkegaard Driving People from Religion

Yet, it must be obvious that this account raises tremendous philosophical problems, not the least of which is the problem of fanaticism (and our poor world has been plagued with plenty of *that* since Kierkegaard's day). Also, we may ask, *must* we accept Kierkegaard's implication that a truly religious conception of life is ultimately incompatible with a social conception of life? Must one become "divinely mad" to be considered authentically religious? Well, Kierkegaard could at least point to plenty of biblical evidence for his thesis, but it isn't surprising that, as one scholar says, Kierkegaard's harshness has driven at least as many from religion as it has into religion's embrace.[39]

Conclusion

What conclusion do we draw from these discussions of religion? I must be very careful here, for in talking about religion, everything is controversial. No matter where you walk,

Stepping on Toes

you tread on someone's toes. Still, walk we must. Let it be a relatively gentle path!

Concerning the various arguments meant to prove God's existence, it seems to me that no one of them is powerful enough to force rational assent. (The same is true concerning the arguments for atheism.) Yet, taken altogether, it is possible to imagine the *combination* as powerful enough to remove certain philosophical scruples one had against belief. And what is wrong with taking them altogether? Usually people have more than *one* reason for believing what they believe. Our systems of belief and justification are usually multilayered. If I asked you why you enrolled specifically in this class, you would probably answer with a number of reasons: "I needed three units of humanities credit." "This is a good hour for me—it frees my time up for work." "I heard the professor was good." "I noticed that the course attracts bright people, and I would like to be considered in that category." "There are a number of attractive members of the opposite sex in this class." "My parents said they would cut off my finances if I didn't take some philosophy." Maybe no *one* of these reasons is a sufficient explanation, but the group together is compelling.

As I said, I can imagine someone finding all the arguments for God's existence similarly compelling as a group. Frankly, I do not find them to be so. (Nor do I find compelling all the arguments for atheism together.) Perhaps more subtle versions of the arguments than I have presented would do the trick, but in their absence, I have to think that there are too many obvious problems with each of them as they stand. So I have to conclude with a negative answer to the question "Is there any good reason for believing in God's existence?"—if by "reason" we mean "logical argument" or "a compelling piece of evidence." However, I have learned enough from Kierkegaard, James, and the mystical poets to know that such a definition of "reason" is too confining and that there are, as Pascal said, "reasons of the heart." These reasons are perplexing and, as are so many things of the heart, very personal and difficult to evaluate, but one scoffs at them at one's risk. Such a "reason" just may sneak up on one fine day as a "thought that wounds from behind" (Kierkegaard's phrase).

Thoughts That Wound from Behind

If one had to make a decision based only on the material presented in this chapter, perhaps one would arrive at a kind of impressionable **agnosticism,** asserting a negative answer based on the "evidence" presented so far but open to new evidence or new interpretations of old evidence. I state this opinion knowing full well the disdain with which Kierkegaard would greet my response. He would be quick to point out that the word "agnostic" translates into Latin as *ignoramus.* He was not surprised that there *were* lots of igno-ramuses. He was only surprised that they touted their ignorance as an important philosophical position—usually at cocktail parties.

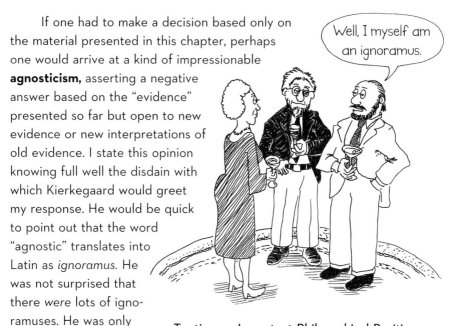

Well, I myself am an ignoramus.

Touting an Important Philosophical Position

Topics for Consideration

1. David Hume says, "There is no being whose nonexistence implies a con-tradiction." State as clearly as you can why Anselm and Descartes dis-agree with Hume. Then comment on the debate between the two sides.
2. Contrast the Platonic (hence rationalistic) features of the ontological proof with the empirical groundings of the cosmological proof. Regardless of your own opinion concerning the existence of God, which of the two approaches do you think would be more fruitful in settling the issue of God's existence or nonexistence?
3. Despite Darwin's and Hume's criticisms of teleological accounts of nature, it is in fact difficult to look at certain natural phenomena (such as the structure of the eyeball and the function of vision) without assum-ing that there are natural purposes or goals. Is this intuition enough to support the teleological proof of God's existence in your judgment?
4. Explain the sense in which the atheist Marx is more sympathetic to reli-gion than the atheists Richard Dawkins and Daniel Dennett. Is the athe-ist Sigmund Freud more sympathetic than Dawkins and Dennett?
5. Sigmund Freud thinks that religion is for the fainthearted. Contrast his view of religion with that of Søren Kierkegaard.

6. Take a position in the debate between W. K. Clifford and William James concerning the question of whether we have the right to hold beliefs in the absence of sufficient evidence.

7. David Hume would not deny that Teresa of Avila had the experiences she says she had. But he would argue that she was not warranted to describe them as she did (that is, as experiences that justified her belief in God). In your opinion, can an experience of the type Teresa describes be so strong as to authenticate itself?

Suggestions for Further Reading: Paperback Editions

Richard Dawkins, *The God Delusion* (New York: Houghton Mifflin Company, 2006). Many of the ideas in this book and the next have been treated in this chapter.

De Cruz, Helen and Johan De Smedt, *A Natural History of Natural Theology: The Cognitive Science of Theology and Philosophy of Religion* (Cambridge, MA and London: The MIT Press, 2015). An excellent short discussion of whether Darwinian theory of natural selection supports or undermines a belief in God but with an intentionally inconclusive conclusion.

Daniel C. Dennett, *Breaking the Spell* (New York: Penguin Books, 2006).

Sigmund Freud, *The Future of an Illusion,* trans. James Strachey (New York: Norton, 1989). An interesting but not terribly compelling introduction to psychoanalytic thought through a critique of the religious mind.

John Hick, *Philosophy of Religion,* 3rd ed. (Englewood Cliffs, NJ: Prentice-Hall, 1978). A short, clear introduction.

David Hume, *Dialogues Concerning Natural Religion* (New York: Hafner, 1960). Hume's famous posthumously published critique of religious reasoning. Short and quite accessible.

William James, *The Varieties of Religious Experience* (New York: Random House, Modern Library, 1994). Lucid and very understandable. A masterpiece by an astute and sympathetic observer of the religious mind.

Søren Kierkegaard, *Fear and Trembling,* either trans. Alastair Hannay (NY: Penguin Books, 1985) or the more traditional translation by Walter Lowrie (Garden City: NY: Doubleday, 1954). Kierkegaard's small gem.

Alvin Plantinga, ed., *The Ontological Argument* (Garden City, NY: Doubleday, 1965). A good summary of the arguments for and against Anselm's proof, from the eleventh century to our own.

John Searle, *The Mystery of Consciousness* (New York: New York Review Books, 1997). We have discussed a number of Searle's ideas in this chapter.

Notes

1. Bertrand Russell, *The Autobiography of Bertrand Russell. The Early Years: 1872–World War I* (Boston: Bantam Books, 1969), p. 43.

2. Ibid., p. 45.

3. Anselm of Canterbury, "Proslogium," in *The Age of Belief*, Anne Fremantle, ed., The Age of Belief. (New York: New American Library, 1954), pp. 88–89.

4. David Hume, *Dialogues Concerning Natural Religion* (New York: Hafner, 1960), p. 58.

5. The example is taken from Richard Taylor, "Introduction," in *The Ontological Argument*, ed. Alvin Plantinga (Garden City, NY: Doubleday, 1965), p. xv.

6. Immanuel Kant, *Critique of Pure Reason* (Garden City, NY: Doubleday, 1961), p. 358.

7. Norman Malcolm, "Anselm's Ontological Arguments," in Plantinga, *The Ontological Argument*, pp. 141–147.

8. See Alvin Plantinga, "A Valid Ontological Argument?" and Paul Henle, "Uses of the Ontological Argument," in Plantinga, *The Ontological Argument*, pp. 160–171, 172–180.

9. Malcolm, "Anselm's Ontological Arguments," p. 159.

10. Thomas Aquinas, *Summa Theologica*, in Fremantle, *The Age of Belief*, p. 153.

11. Helen de Cruz and Johan de Smedt, *A Natural History of Natural Theology: The Cognitive Science of Theology and Philosophy of Religion* (Cambridge, MA and London: The MIT Press, 2015), p. xvi.

12. Frederick Copleston, *Aquinas* (London: Penguin Books, 1955), pp. 110–122.

13. Aquinas, *Summa Theologica*, pp. 154–155.

14. John Hick, *Philosophy of Religion*, 3rd ed. (Englewood Cliffs, NJ: Prentice-Hall, 1983), p. 29. All subsequent quotes from this book will be cited in the text.

15. Heller quoted in *The Fresno Bee*, Fresno, California, March 14, 2008.

16. For a different interpretation of the Book of Job, see Carl G. Jung, *Answer to Job* (Princeton, NJ: Princeton University Press, 1973).

17. Marx discusses "ideology" in "A Contribution to the Critique of Political Economy," in *Marx and Engels: Basic Writings on Politics and Philosophy*, ed. Lewis S. Feuer (New York: Doubleday, 1959), pp. 43–44 and in "The German Ideology," in Feuer, pp. 247–248. The term "false consciousness" was coined by Marx's colleague, Friedrich Engels, in a letter, "Engels to Franz Mehring," Feuer, p. 408.

18. Karl Marx, "Toward the Critique of Hegel's Philosophy of Right," in Feuer, p. 263.

19. Herbert Marcuse, *Eros and Civilization* (Boston: Beacon Press, 1966), p. 74.

20. Sigmund Freud, *Civilization and Its Discontents* (New York: Norton, 1962), p. 19. Unless otherwise stated, all subsequent quotes from Freud in this chapter are from this source.

21. See, for example, Frederick Crews, *The Memory Wars: Freud's Legacy in Dispute* (New York: New York Review of Books Press, 1995).

22. The quotations from Darwin are from letter 12041, "Darwin, C. R. to Fordyce, John," May 7, 1879, and letter 12757, "Darwin, C. R. to Aveling, E. B.," October 13, 1880, in Cambridge University Library's Darwin Correspondence Project.

23. Adrian Desmond and James Moore, *Darwin* (New York and London: Norton, 1991), p. 479.

24. Richard Dawkins, *The God Delusion* (Boston and New York: Houghton Mifflin, 2006), p. 120. Page numbers of future quotations from the book will be included in the text.

25. Daniel C. Dennett, *Breaking the Spell: Religion as a Natural Phenomenon* (New York: Penguin Books, 2006), p. 163. Page numbers of future quotations from the book will be included in the text.

26. *Time* magazine, October 25, 2004, 62–72. Quoted by Dennett, *Breaking the Spell: Religion as a Natural Phenomenon* (New York: Penguin Books, 2006), p. 316.

27. Dawkins coined the term "memes" and Dennett picked it up from him. Memes are supposed to be cultural units that can be replicated, entering into competition with other memes, just as genes do in natural selection. The analogy has been criticized, primarily because it obliterates Dawkins's strong distinction between design and natural selection: Memes seem to be selected only after having been designed, which is the opposite of genes, which produce "design" only after having been "selected." The meme/gene analogy has become quite controversial. For example, see John R. Searle's critique in *The Mystery of Consciousness*, p. 105.

28. Ezra Klein, "Unpopular Mandate," *New Yorker* magazine, June 25, 2012, 30–33, p. 31.

29. Quoted by Dawkins, 78. The Dennett/Dawkins team and Gould have a long-standing antagonism. In a series of articles in the *New York Review of Books* in 1997, Gould called Dawkins's selfish gene theory "a logically flawed and basically foolish caricature of Darwin's radical intent" (NYRB, June 12, 1997, p. 34). In the same article, he calls Dennett's *Darwin's Dangerous Idea* a "limited and superficial book [that] reads like a caricature of a caricature. . . . Dennett manages to convert an already vitiated and improbable account into an even more simplistic and uncompromising doctrine" (p. 36). Ah, nature! Ah, naturalists, red in tooth and claw!

30. Alvin Plantinga, "Introduction" to *Naturalism Defeated? Essays on Plantinga's Evolutionary Argument against Naturalism*, ed. James Beilby (Ithaca, NY and London: Cornell University Press, 2002), pp. 8–9. Page numbers of future quotations from the book will be included in the text.

31. William James, *Pragmatism* (New York: World Publishing, 1961), p. 42. Unless otherwise stated, all subsequent quotes from *Pragmatism* in this chapter will be cited in the text.

32. Quoted in William James, "The Will to Believe," in *Pragmatism: The Classic Writings*, ed. H. S. Thayer (New York: New American Library, 1970), p. 191.

33. William James, "The Will to Believe," in *Philosophy of Recent Times*, Vol. 2, ed. James B. Hartman (New York: McGraw-Hill, 1967), p. 28.

34. William James, *The Varieties of Religious Experience* (New York: Random House, Modern Library, 1994), p. 379. All subsequent quotations from James in this chapter are from this source.

35. Chapter 21 of Teresa's *Book of Her Life*, quoted in E. Allison Peers, *Studies of the Spanish Mystics*, Vol. I (London: Sheldon Press, 1927), p. 197. All other quotations from St. Teresa are from this source.

36. Søren Kierkegaard, *Fear and Trembling*, trans. Walter Lowrie (Garden City, NY: Doubleday, 1954), p. 36. Unless otherwise stated, all subsequent quotes from Kierkegaard in this chapter are from this source.

37. *We* know the story, indeed, but Sartre's biblical knowledge fails him here. It was not an angel who spoke to Abraham but God himself.

38. Jean-Paul Sartre, *Existentialism and Human Emotions* (New York: Philosophical Library, 1957), p. 19.

39. William Barrett, *Irrational Man* (Garden City, NY: Doubleday, 1962), p. 262.

6

The Largest Airline in the Free World
Philosophy of Freedom

Just before the collapse of the Soviet Union, a TV commercial caught my attention. "TWA is the largest airline in the Free World." What information was being communicated in that commercial, and what information was being suppressed? The latter question is easy to answer. The suppressed truth in the commercial is this: "The official Soviet airline, Aeroflot, is the largest airline in the world. TWA is only the second largest." (Can you imagine *that* as a commercial?) Well, if we weren't supposed to think the hidden thought, what were we supposed to think? I take it that we were supposed to associate in our minds TWA/bigness/anti-totalitarianism/the Free World (hence **freedom**). These thoughts together were meant to loosen a few dollars from our pockets. (By the way, Aeroflot is still afloat; TWA, like the Soviet Union, has since gone under.) Here is the problem. In our culture, freedom is, on the one hand, so cherished that we are taught that it is worth dying for ("Live free or die"—motto on the New Hampshire license plate). Yet, on the other

Spend your money with us and strike a blow for freedom!

hand, it has been co-opted by the ideologues and moneymakers to the extent that it has become a meaningless buzzword. Yes, there is indeed a lot of talk in our society about freedom. We hear about it in TV commercials, in political speeches from the left, middle, and right, and we not uncommonly see reference to it on bumper stickers or license plates. In North Carolina the current plate informs us that this state is "First in Freedom."

When philosophers turn to the topic of freedom, they ask the following kinds of big questions:

- What do we mean by "freedom"?
- Does freedom exist, or is there only necessity?
- How is freedom possible in a world governed by natural laws?
- Can we ever know whether there is freedom?
- If there is freedom, is it an either-or proposition, or are there degrees of it? Can we do anything to maximize it or endanger it?
- Do any of these questions matter practically, or are they only of academic interest?

Determinism: Ancient Greek and Enlightenment Views

Determinism is the thesis that everything that occurs happens of necessity. This thesis first appears in the history of philosophy in the theories of LEUCIPPUS (ca. 460–? B.C.E.) and DEMOCRITUS (ca. 460–ca. 370 B.C.E.), who, at the culmination of a hundred years of philosophical speculation about the nature of reality (what we have called here "the pre-Socratic tradition"), concluded that every existing thing was composed of atoms in motion. These atoms moved inexorably along trajectories necessitated by the very nature of atoms and the nature of motion.

The single fragment of Leucippus's book that remains to us today says, "Naught happens for nothing but everything from a ground of necessity."

Democritus's view did not become the dominant one in his day, mostly because he stood not at the end of the history of science but on its threshold, and he could not appeal to any tradition of scientific authority to support his views. It would take another two thousand years before such a tradition could establish itself as authoritative. But when it did, Democritus's theory came to the fore with a vengeance. In the eighteenth century, armed with the prestigious discoveries of Sir Isaac Newton, a number of **Enlightenment** figures put forth new versions of Democritus's old argument. Foremost among them were the Baron HENRI D'HOLBACH (1723–1789) and PIERRE-SIMON LAPLACE (1749–1827). D'Holbach argued that the same principles that apply to the physical world must necessarily apply to the human brain, which was as much material in nature as were the moon and the stars. Therefore, every thought of every brain followed

There is a drunken ladybug on this leaf now. Therefore, on June 19, 2023, there will be a mudslide in Rangoon.

Pierre-Simon Laplace (1749–1827)

necessarily from the brain states that preceded those thoughts. Laplace held a similar view and went so far as to imagine a genius who knows all the laws of nature, and if the genius has one complete description of the universe at any given moment, then he can predict all future events and retrodict all past events. The "genius" has come to be known as "Laplace's demon."

D'Holbach and Laplace were very much children of their own age—the so-called Age of Reason—and as such, they were already members of the modern world. Ever since the seventeenth century, the advance of science has had an enormous impact on most fields of endeavor, particularly but not exclusively in the Western world. This influence has been either practical, in terms of the products that have been the direct result of scientific discoveries (e.g., air travel, weaponry, television, antibiotics, and face-lifts), or attitudinal (rejection by a great number of people—though obviously not by all—of the premodern belief that the earth is the center of the universe, that the earth is only four thousand years old, that spirits and ghosts exist, and that English is God's native language). Certainly, the triumphs of science have had a major effect on modern philosophy, which has taken great pains to either worship it, or be strongly supportive of it, or at least be consistent with it. This is particularly true within analytic philosophy, the philosophy that currently dominates the academies of the English-speaking world.

At the risk of oversimplification, I will say that one of the primary principles of science since the seventeenth century is that the most accurate explanations of events in the universe are expressed in terms of causal theories. In causal theories, the relation between a cause and its effect is understood to be a lawlike relationship—one that ideally could be expressed in mathematical equations of the type you studied in high school physics courses, for example, $f = ma$ (force equals mass times acceleration). Our person-in-the-street today may well believe that the earth orbits the sun, may believe that the solar system has existed for millions of years, and—having passed her high school physics class—may believe also that $f = ma$. However, this person-in-the-street also believes intuitively in a certain kind of freedom. If she holds this common idea of freedom, she believes that her decisions and actions are "up to her," that no matter what she decides or does, usually she "could have done otherwise" than what she did, and that therefore she is to a great extent responsible for her choices and actions. That is to say, the person-in-the-street believes in what will later in this book be identified as **indeterminism,** which involves the idea that some acts (namely, her own acts) could be different from what they in fact are, even if those different decisions and acts had been preceded by the very same history that they now have. Determinism could be provisionally defined as "same past, same future," meaning that if two events are preceded by identical past causal circumstances, then those two events will be identical. On the other side of the coin, indeterminism could be provisionally defined as "same past, different future," meaning that there is nothing in the past that necessitated a person's decision to choose A rather than B. Given exactly her past, she might have chosen B when in fact she chose A.

Let's make these ideas more concrete with a simple example. A moment ago, I typed the letter "A." Determinism says that, given my specific past up to that moment—that is, given the causal circumstances that constitute my past—my typing the letter "A" at that moment was a necessary consequence of that past. Indeterminism says that, given my specific past up to that moment, it was not necessary that I type the letter "A" at that moment.

Well, perhaps many a person-in-the-street holds the indeterminist view, but a lot of contemporary philosophers (again, especially many in the analytic tradition) find that such a conception flies in the face of science and that it is in fact positively mystifying. Let's look into this.

Hard Determinism: Modern Views

The key ideas of determinism are those of causality and necessity. According to this theory, every event in the world is caused, where to say that "X causes Y" is to say that if event X takes place, then event Y necessarily happens as well. **Hard determinism** is the view that determinism is true and that its truth rules out the possibility of freedom. If everything is necessary, then nothing is free.

B. F. Skinner

In the twentieth century, hard determinism was perhaps most clearly defended by B. F. Skinner (whom we have already met in Chapter 3). In his book with the telling title *Beyond Freedom and Dignity,* Skinner says:

> [M]any anthropologists, sociologists, and psychologists have used their expert knowledge to prove that man is free, purposeful, and responsible.
>
> This escape route is slowly closed as new evidences of the predictability of human behavior are discovered. Personal exemption from a complete

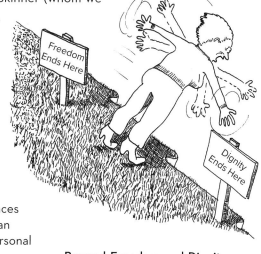

Beyond Freedom and Dignity

determinism is revoked as a scientific analysis progresses, particularly in accounting for the behavior of the individual.[1]

Skinner correctly associates the concept of freedom with the teleological model of explanation. You will recall from Chapter 5 that a teleological model is one that explains things in terms of goals, purposes, plans, and intentions. Skinner, an empiricist and a materialist, is suspicious of nonphysical, unobservable entities, so he wants to get rid of the teleological model of explanation. He has this to say about it:

> Physics did not advance by looking more closely at the jubilance of a falling body or biology by looking at the nature of vital spirits, and we do not need to try to discover what . . . plans, purposes, intentions, or the other prerequisites of autonomous man really are in order to get on with a scientific analysis of behavior.[2]

The Causal Model (Push from Behind)

The Teleological Model (Pull from Ahead)

Implementation of Skinner's Theories Would Empty the Prisons

Skinner knows that if he does away with the teleological model, he also overturns our moral and legal institutions, such as courtrooms and prisons. His theory is a radical one, and he is well aware of that fact.

Skinner wishes to replace the teleological model with a **causal explanation,** namely, with a *stimulus-response* model, based on Pavlov's famous experiment with his drooling dog: when you get ready to feed a steak to a dog, the animal begins to salivate as soon as it sees or smells the meat. Now, if you repeatedly ring a bell just before you serve the steak, eventually the dog will begin to salivate at the sound of the bell. We need no "dog psychology" to explain this fact and no references to purposes, plans, intentions, and goals. It can be explained in purely mechanical terms. Skinner believed he could extend the Pavlovian model to the human sphere, thereby overturning the traditional teleological model and placing us "beyond freedom and dignity."

Pavlovian Science

Sigmund Freud

Sigmund Freud was another important early-twentieth-century thinker in whose work many find a version of hard determinism, at least as it concerns any so-called decisions of any weight at all. The deterministic argument runs like this: An individual's personality has crystallized by the age of five years. One has no personal control over the formation of one's own personality, yet everything that happens to an individual after that age will be responded to by that already completed character structure. Furthermore, the bulk of one's motivational system is unconscious, structured by antisocial biological urges, painful childhood memories, unresolved emotional conflicts, fantastic desires, and fears, all of which have been repressed into the unconscious. The **ego** (more or less the conscious self) is nothing more than a façade, masking a ferocious struggle between the **id** (the antisocial, animal self that "wants it all now") and the **superego** (the irrational, nay-saying, guilt-spawning social con-science). According to this deterministic reading of Freud, all significant actions of the so-called normal person, as much as those of the psychotic, are unfree. And, as was the case with Skinner's deterministic scheme, there is no such thing as responsibility here. John Hospers, a philosopher who interprets Freud pretty much as a hard determinist, says:

The Standoff between the Id and the Superego

> But what is not welcome news is that our very acts of volition, and the entire train of deliberations leading up to them, are but façades for the expression of unconscious wishes, or rather, unconscious compromises and defenses.
>
> . . . .
>
> We may . . . say that a man is free only to the extent that his behavior is *not* unconsciously motivated at all. If this be our criterion, most of our behavior could not be called free: everything, including both impulses and volitions, having to do with our basic attitudes toward life, the general tenor of our tastes, whether we become philosophers or artists or busi-ness men, our whole affective life including our preferences for blondes or brunettes, active or passive, older or younger, has its inevitable basis in the unconscious. Only those comparatively vanilla-flavored aspects of life—such as our behavior toward people who don't really matter to us—are exempted from this rule.[3]

The little twist at the end of this paragraph shows that, in effect, Hospers does not interpret Freud as a strict hard determinist, because Hospers allows that, according to Freud, *some* conscious decisions—namely, those that don't matter at all—may not be caused by unconscious motives. So for Hospers, Freud is a hard determinist only where it matters.

British philosopher Richard Peters has pointed out that it is rather far-fetched to read Freud as claiming that *every* act is motivated by the unconscious. Suppose you and I are playing chess, and you see that my queen is unprotected. It's your turn, so you take my piece. We don't need to seek an unconscious motive to explain your act. We don't need to know anything about your unhappy childhood or your repressed sexual fantasies.

Some of these psychoanalytic topics *might* be pertinent to the question of why you like to play chess in the first place but not to the question of why, while playing chess, you decide to take my unprotected queen. Your ordinary conscious reasons, combined with a knowledge of the rules of chess, are perfectly adequate to explain your action.

In another of Peters's examples, he says that if a person explains why he is crossing the road by asserting that he wants to buy tobacco, this is a perfectly sound explanation under certain circumstances. (The person smokes, he is out of cigarettes, there is a tobacco shop across the street.) No unconscious motive or psychoanalytic theory is needed here (though an unconscious motive might be useful in explaining why the man smokes in the first place). On the other hand, if the man *rolls* across the street and explains his actions by saying that he's going to get tobacco, *this* explanation needs looking into. In such a case, a psychoanalytic account *might* be needed precisely because our normal account has broken down. Concluding his nondeterministic interpretation of Freud, Peters says:

> When Freud wants to describe goings-on of which it is appropriate to say that a man is acting, that he has a *reason* for what he does, and so on, he talks about the Ego; when on the other hand, he wants to say that a person suffers something, or is made or driven to do something, he speaks of the Id.[4]

Skinner and Freud were tremendously influential, each in his own way, but even if they appeared to have left a permanent mark on the way people think, their theories seem to be in decline today, mostly because of new discoveries of how the brain works. At least Skinner and Freud were bold enough to recognize that their views conflicted with major features of the traditional institutions of civilization, and they were brave enough (or stubborn enough) to condemn those institutions and practices that were in conflict with the principle of their respective versions of determinism. However, in the twenty-first century, few philosophers or scientists are willing to be so daring (or so foolish) as Skinner or Freud; consequently, few contemporary thinkers are willing to call themselves hard determinists. This does not mean that there are no determinists; to the contrary, a great number of contemporary philosophers are determinists. But they prefer to be called **soft determinists,** or, more commonly, **compatibilists,** because they believe not only that determinism is true (i.e., same past, same future) but also that determinism is compatible with freedom and that therefore they do not have to set about attacking the main institutions of civilization, nor all of the thinking patterns of the person-in-the-street.

Before saying how these compatibilists defend their view that determinism, freedom, and responsibility are interrelated concepts, let's discuss why they reject the indeterminist theory, usually called **libertarianism.** The theory is indeterminist in that it asserts the "same past, different future" thesis; it is libertarian in that it asserts the reality of **free will,** where free will involves either uncaused, undetermined choices, or choices caused by the agent himself, whose character is itself uncaused, or caused through free choice. (The term is only indirectly related to the political party that calls itself "libertarian"—an organization that defends individual liberty from governmental restraints.)

The Attack on Free Will

We have already seen that some philosophers reject indeterminism because the idea of a free action or even a free thought, conceived as an uncaused event, seems to contradict the main thrust of the scientific understanding of the natural world. But in addition to this, philosophers have also claimed that the very idea of such free action is wrong or even unintelligible. Here's one such argument: Let us imagine that Joe has decided to get a face-lift. He reached his decision after some hard thinking, which went something like this:

(a) On the one hand, I am mistaken for an old man because my face has fallen and is scoured with wrinkles.

(b) On the other hand, it is true that I am getting along in years, and these wrinkles and sagging jowls are the natural ravages of the hard life I have led.

(c) On the one hand, I dislike looking at myself in the mirror, because my fading image makes me sad about my lost youth.

(d) On the other hand, I dislike vain people and fear that my current unhappiness is an indication that I have become vain.

(e) However, despite this concern, I see no good reason for rejecting this opportunity to recover my good looks, since doing so will give me more self-assurance and make me more attractive for the "dating market."

At this point,

(f) Joe calls Dr. Evertight and makes an appointment for a cosmetic medical intervention.

Apparently, libertarians are committed to arguing that, at the end of processes (a) through (e), Joe *could* have decided to do otherwise, and choose

(g) *not* to call Dr. Evertight.

That is, they think that, given series (a) through (e), both (f) and (g) are possible (same past, different future). However, determinists argue that if series (a) through (e) can lead to both (f) or (g), then both (f) and (g) are purely irrational and arbitrary. That is, if series (a) through (e) has no necessary effect, then Joe himself has no control over his own actions—at least, no rational control. Determinists suggest that such a "free will" would not be worth having even if it were available.

A skeptical argument against free will that has proved to be influential was concocted by Galen Strawson.[5] Basically, Strawson argues that free will would be possible only if an individual could create her own character or if an individual's character could create itself, because the cause of our actions is our character. But we do not create our character, nor does our character create itself; it is created by outside influences. Strawson claims that an **infinite regress** would be set in motion by an attempt to show that character creates itself, because a decision to create one's own character would have to be made by a character that must have preexisted the decision.

Some of these arguments that are skeptical of free will are, in my opinion, impressive, and libertarians will have to work hard to undo their effects. But before we see how a libertarian might respond to these arguments, let us see how the compatibilists defend their next move, which is to claim that the kind of freedom they offer—one that is compatible with determinism—is objectively more reasonable and philosophically more respectable.

Soft Determinism (a.k.a. Compatibilism)

As we've already noted, philosophers who affirm the truth of determinism and deny that their deterministic views preclude the existence of freedom and responsibility are called soft determinists or compatibilists (I will use these terms interchangeably). This stance is quite common among a number of contemporary philosophers, especially in the analytic tradition, but its roots go back to Roman times. The Stoics (first century C.E.), St. Augustine (fourth century), Thomas Hobbes (seventeenth century), and Baruch Spinoza (seventeenth century) all defended versions of it.

What do we mean by "freedom"? Soft determinists ask this not so much as philosophers but as ordinary persons in everyday life. What we mean by freedom is the coincidence of will and capacity; that is, we are free to the extent that we are able to do and get what we want. If you ask me if I am free to go to the movies tonight, and I say that I am not, I am implying that I *want* to but *am not able to*. This is the sense in which the prisoners at San Quentin are not free. They are not free to leave if they want to. However, they *are* free to write their mothers. So, according to this commonsense definition, freedom is relative to context. One is both free and not free at the same time. Nevertheless, everyone is free sometimes. (No one has ever been so miserable as never to have gotten what he wants.)

I am determined to have a banana split.

A Soft Determinist

Some are freer than others or freer at certain periods of their lives than at others. And when one wants to do X and does X, then doing X is a free act, and one is responsible for that act.

Furthermore, in this definition, freedom is *compatible* with determinism. I sometimes do what I want to do, even if my will is determined according to Freudian or Skinnerian principles. So both freedom and necessity can exist in the same world.

But many people are dissatisfied with the soft determinist's definition of freedom as the coincidence of will and ability ("desire to do X" plus "ability to do X" equals "freedom to do X"). A wealthy heroin addict on this account freely engages in his addiction. This interpretation seems to trivialize the idea of freedom. Critics of soft determinism say that a more robust conception of freedom is required. If one sticks with the soft determinist's definition, according to which freedom comprises desire and ability, then it must be demonstrated that the agent's desires themselves are under his or her control. But it is not obvious that such self-control would be compatible with any form of determinism.

Some contemporary determinists, both soft and hard, respond to these criticisms, challenging them with one or the other of a couple of remarkable arguments. One of these arguments zeroes in on the demand that true responsibility presupposes true freedom, and true freedom exists only when the agent has true alternatives. In other words, says the libertarian, Samantha's act was a free act only if Samantha could have done other than she actually did do. In response to this claim, some compatibilists argue that the correct analysis of the phrase, "She could have done otherwise . . . ," is achieved by translating it into a hypothetical conditional phrase, such as this: "She could have done otherwise, *if she had wanted to.*" Then they assert that the phrase, "She could have done otherwise if she had wanted to," is compatible with determinism, because desires, wants, and intentions are *causes* of actions. Samantha's desires, wants, and intentions may well have been produced by Skinnerian or Freudian-type causal circumstances (or more likely just by the laws of neurochemistry), but she is still free in the most important sense of that word: she wants to do X, and she can do X. As determinist Ted Honderich says, "There is nothing about actions being voluntary in their initiation that conflicts with determinism. For determinism, voluntary actions are ones that have a certain kind of causal history, as distinct from any non-causal history."[6]

A rather different kind of compatibilist argument challenges the primary libertarian assumption—namely, the assumption that true moral responsibility is possible only if the agent has genuine alternatives. This argument uses what have come to be known as **Frankfurt-type examples** because Harry Frankfurt, a well-known compatibilist philosopher, first developed this line of attack.[7] Here is such an example:

> Imagine Jones is walking down a dark corridor in a castle. He comes to a fork, where there is a door on the left (A) and a door on the right (B). He goes through door A. But, unknown to Jones, door B was locked (by Black). So Jones could not have gone through door B. Nonetheless, Jones did go through door A on his own, not knowing door B was blocked. Black did not interfere with the deliberation process that led to Jones going through door A, even though Jones could not have done otherwise.[8]

Even if Jones could not have gone through door B, he is responsible for his decision to go through door A, say the Frankfurters, and therefore, the ideas of freedom and responsibility do *not* presuppose genuine alternatives. Shortly, we will see how incompatibilists or libertarians (I am using these two terms interchangeably, along with the term "indeterminist") might respond to such arguments. First, we will inspect one other variation on the theme of determinism, one set forth by British philosopher Ted Honderich, already mentioned earlier.

Honderich admits that he cannot prove that universal determinism is true. He concedes that recent developments in the field of physics called quantum mechanics (which we will inspect shortly) may seem to have raised questions about the determinist's thesis, but he suspects that eventually quantum theory itself will prove to support determinism. (He admits that his view on this topic is not popular among many physicists, and he insults these scientists by adding "perhaps it is not too much the worse for that [!]" [p. 75].) Well, on Honderich's own theory, he could not help insulting them. However, even if it turns out that he is wrong in thinking that the new physics will demonstrate support for determinism, Honderich points out that quantum theory applies only to the subatomic world, not the world of human-size objects or even brain-size objects, so Honderich will accept "near-determinism" (p. 76) if he must. What is rather new in Honderich's theory is his assertion that *all* the other parties in the debate about freedom and determinism are wrong. The indeterminists are wrong, because determinism is (probably) true. The hard determinists are wrong not only because they think determinism and moral responsibility are totally incompatible but also because they think we will have to give up virtually all of our commonsense views about human behavior and attitudes if determinism is true. The compatibilists are wrong because they think we will have to give up *nothing* if determinism is true. Honderich writes:

> Compatibilists say determinism leaves [moral responsibility] where it is. Incompatibilists say that determinism wrecks it. Both are wrong. Compatibilists are wrong because we know from our reflections that we have one way of holding people responsible, involving an image of origination, that is out of place if determinism is true. Incompatibilists are wrong because we know that we have one way of holding people responsible, involving only an idea of voluntariness, that goes perfectly well with determinism. (p. 113)

In other words, the libertarian and the hard determinist both think the *true* meaning of the idea of freedom is "origination" or uncaused thoughts and actions originated by the agent herself, while the compatibilist thinks that the *true* meaning of the idea of freedom is simply being able to do what you want to do. But in fact, *both* meanings exist and have installed themselves deeply in our psyches. According to Honderich, determinism says we can keep the latter meaning but must give up the former, and giving up the former involves a somewhat painful sacrifice. We can no longer blame or praise people's actions the way we normally do, and we will certainly have to abandon practices of punishment if their sole purpose is retribution (to dish out pain or impose restrictions on people because they deserve it), nor will we be able to praise or reward people for actions on the grounds that they were the result of "free choice" in the old, now discredited, sense. Neither can we be proud of ourselves for our freely chosen accomplishments.

But, says Honderich, punishment of antisocial behavior *is* justified if its purpose is to create examples and to remove from society individuals who have shown their willingness to harm others. Similarly, though we will have to give up some "life-hopes" (e.g., that we can become famous philosophers [or artists, or political leaders, or inventors, or porn stars] on our own justly deserved merits), we can still hope and strive to become any or all of these things. What we have to give up is the hope in an "open future, a future we can make for ourselves" (p. 94). Honderich asks, does this discovery produce dismay? He answers, "To speak for myself, it has certainly got me down in the past" (p. 95).

Prof. Honderich Mulls Over Determinism

There are strategies we can use to cope with our newly discovered determinism, says Honderich:

> To put the proposal in a nutshell, our new response should be this: trying *by various strategies to accommodate ourselves to the situation we find ourselves in—accommodate ourselves to just what we can really possess if determinism is true, accommodate ourselves to the part of our lives that does not rest on the illusion of Free Will.* We can reflect on what is perhaps the limited worth of what we have to give up, consider possible compensations of a belief in determinism, take care not to underestimate what we can have, and consider a certain prospect having to do with genuine and settled belief in determinism. (p. 126)

If Honderich is right, there are even certain consolations of deterministic philosophy:

> Determinism offers the compensation of an escape from a mordant kind of self-dislike and self-approval. (p. 129)

Honderich continues:

> What it all comes to, as perhaps a critic would say, is looking on the bright side, or putting a good face on things, or even making the best of a bad job. That is a bit unkind and perhaps not serious enough, but not far off the truth. (p. 131)

Don't worry? Be happy?

A similar conclusion is reached by Galen Strawson:

> As a philosopher I think the impossibility of radical free will, ultimate moral responsibility, can be proved with complete certainty. It's just that I can't really live with this fact from day to day. Can you, really?[9]

Indeterminism

We have seen that the opposite of determinism is called indeterminism. This is simply the view that determinism is false. There are several versions of this claim. In the twentieth century, a number of scientists and philosophers of science rejected the nineteenth-century conception of causality, according to which, saying that A causes B is to say that A is the **sufficient condition** of B (given A, B follows of necessity). They urged replacing this one-on-one billiard ball–type model of causality with a looser, more statistical model. For example, according to the newer conception, imagine that A is the sufficient condition of B or C or D or E (but not necessarily of any one of them as opposed to the others). That is, when A happens, one of the members of the series B through E necessarily happens. In the case of the occurrence of (say) E, A caused E, but E is not a *necessary* event. (Given A, there were other possibilities besides E.) When the meteorologist says there is a 90% chance of rain on Saturday, and Saturday comes and goes with not a drop of rain at all, this does not mean she was wrong. There was indeed a 90% chance of rain (i.e., in all of the other recorded data of periods with identical conditions to Saturdays', it has rained nine times out of ten), but this time, it didn't rain.

So, an indeterminist can argue either that (1) there are only random events, or (2) there are some random events, or (3) there are some uncaused events, or (4) some caused events are not necessary events. Probably the first possibility does not find many defenders, if any, except by parents of two-year-olds. (The thesis that there are only random events would be an extreme version of the thesis that the center does not hold.) Possibility 4 is probably the best one for explaining the truth of propositions like "Heavy smoking causes cancer." Not every case of cancer is caused by heavy smoking, and not every case of heavy smoking causes cancer, but nevertheless, heavy smoking (statistically) causes cancer. Indeterminists defend possibilities 2, 3, or 4, depending on which model of causality they work with.

Indeterminism has been given a new respectability because of recent developments in physics (which is somewhat ironic because the authority of determinism has usually been associated with its relationship to classical physics). Ever since the work of the Nobel Prize recipient Werner Heisenberg, it has been suggested that at the subatomic level of physical reality (i.e., at the most basic level) the causal model does not work and must be replaced with a statistical model. Let's explain this point by imagining a bird's-eye view of a pool table in a classical Newtonian world. If the ball is propelled here, and we know the exact force applied to it by the cue stick, the exact point of application of the force, and exactly the amount of friction provided by the felt tabletop, then in theory we can predict with accuracy the trajectory of the billiard

ball and its location at times t^1, t^2, t^3, and t^4. Now, if the Heisenbergian "principle of uncertainty" is true (and apparently most physicists think it is), then the same model will not work at the subatomic level. Imagine an electron instead of an eight ball. Even if we knew its mass, its location, its velocity, and its trajectory at times t^1, t^2, and t^3 (which we can't, by the way), we still could not predict with certainty the location of the electron at time t^4. It might end up at point Y or point X, even though there is a greater statistical probability of its ending up at X. This failure to be able to predict the fate of the electron is not merely a weakness in our human ability to know but is a fact about the nature of the subatomic world. It follows from this that the movement of our electron from t^3 to t^4 would be either an *uncaused event* or an occurrence that did not happen *of necessity*. If there are such events (as most physicists believe to be the case), then strictly speaking, determinism is false and indeterminism is true.

Libertarianism

Heisenberg himself waxed philosophical at this point and tried to derive a libertarian position from his indeterminism.[10] Libertarianism is indeed a version of indeterminism. It is the view that determinism is false and that freedom does exist; that is, some acts do not follow necessarily from their antecedents and in addition are freely chosen. Heisenberg hoped that the fact that some events in the brain are uncaused might be the scientific basis for a theory of freedom. But his critics pointed out that uncaused, or nonnecessary, subatomic events can hardly be called *free*.

A Free Act?

Rather, they are more correctly called *random events*. Similarly, a human act based on such an uncaused brain event would itself be a random and not a free event. If I intend to walk to the window to open it for fresh air, and if, upon arriving there, I have an uncaused brain event and throw myself through the window, we should not call this event a "free act." If a person walking through her living room cannot know whether she will get to the other side of it without kicking the dog or doing a backflip, she would be experiencing the very opposite of freedom. Freedom may well be considered the opposite of necessity. Yet there are not just two components of this formula but three.

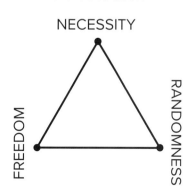

Well then, it seems that Heisenberg has not given us theoretical freedom. But at least his principle of uncertainty has broken the backbone of classical determinism by removing the scientific stamp of approval from it. This move should be worth something to the libertarians.

If the libertarians do not find much solace in Heisenberg's physics, they received a boost when in 1983 the highly respected philosopher, Peter van Inwagen, published *An Essay on Free Will*, in which he broke ranks with the majority of professional philosophers in the analytic tradition who were compatibilists. In that book, he presented a demonstration that he calls the Consequence Argument, which he summarizes as follows:

> If determinism is true, then our acts are the consequences of the laws of nature and events in the remote past. But it is not up to us what went on before we were born; and neither is it up to us what the laws of nature are. Therefore the consequences of these things (including our own acts) are not up to us.[11]

This argument, and similar ones by van Inwagen's followers, does nothing to prove free will (in that sense of a "deeper" freedom, sought by libertarians), but it does damage the analysis of "could have done otherwise" in terms of hypothetical conditionals ("She could have done otherwise, if she had wanted to"). According to van Inwagen, there is no robust meaning of "could have done otherwise" that is compatible with determinism, and if freedom and responsibility require a serious sense of alternative possibilities, then no one can ever be held responsible for what they do. If Samantha cannot change the past, and if all of Samantha's thoughts and actions are caused by the past, then there is no significant sense of the words "freedom" and "responsibility" in which she is ever free or responsible.

Well, then, are there such things as uncaused decisions and actions?

One problem for libertarians who believe that such thoughts and actions exist is that the traditions that insist on freedom have often been closely associated with the kind of dualism discussed in Chapter 4, a dualism that is generally unpopular among contemporary philosophers—especially those in the analytic tradition. Religious thinkers have attributed freedom of choice to the soul's domination of the body, where the soul is understood as a spiritual entity that has no dependence on the material world. René Descartes used the words "mind" and "soul" interchangeably, and, as you have seen, he produced a mind–body dualism whose problems are so formidable as to be considered unsolvable by most philosophers in his day and in ours. However, *if* his dualism were true, that would certainly be significant to the problem of free will. All bodies, including the human body, behave in terms of the laws of physics, but the mind can intervene in the natural system as a kind of first cause. An apple falls from the tree (at 32 feet per second squared, as Newton later proved), but a person's quick decision to reach out and catch the falling apple intervenes in the natural world.

But certainly the biggest problem with Descartes's theory is its inability to explain the *causality* between minds and bodies. How can a decision (a mental thing having no dimensionality and therefore taking up no space, having no size or shape) make a physical thing—such as one's arm—move? Not many contemporary philosophers want to be saddled with that problem.

I believe it is safe to say that most professional philosophers in the analytic tradition are materialists of one stripe or another, believing that ultimately there is only one kind of substance in the universe—physical matter. As you saw in Chapter 4, materialists struggle to figure out how mental events fit into this picture, and although many philosophical theories try to resolve this problem, I think it is easy to agree with Ted Honderich when he says, "It is very plain that the problems of the nature of consciousness and its relation to the brain are unsolved, or anyway remain in dispute" (p. 35). This problem spills over into the discussion of freedom and determinism, of course. Trying to solve the problem of freedom is very much like trying to solve the problem of consciousness. If there is only matter, both consciousness and freedom seem impossible. Yet most people are convinced that both exist. Perhaps you will recall from Chapter 4 that philosopher Colin McGinn claimed that we "have no idea what an explanation of consciousness would even *look like*." McGinn went on to say, "We are facing a problem that points to an enormous hole in our conceptual resources, a theoretical blind spot of epic proportions. This is why I refer to the problem as a *mystery*." [12]

Similarly, some libertarians admit that the problem of freedom is mysterious. They do not accept the compatibilists' views—mostly for reasons such as those of van Inwagen—but they are at a loss to account for freedom. Richard Taylor put it this way, "One can hardly affirm such a theory of agency with complete comfort . . . and wholly without embarrassment, for the conception of men and their powers which is involved in it, is strange indeed, if not positively mysterious." [13]

Peter van Inwagen himself says, "I conclude that free will remains a mystery—that is, that free will undeniably exists and that there is a strong and unanswered prima facie case for its impossibility" (p. 159). But before you embrace the mysterian view, perhaps we should look at some attempts to make sense out of free will. The diagram below summarizes most of what has been said about libertarianism so far. [14]

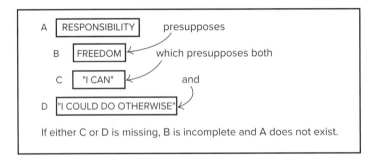

Letter D in this diagram, "I could do otherwise," is the feature of the system that challenges compatibilism. Libertarians reject the hypothetical conditional analysis of "could have done otherwise" ("I could do otherwise if I wanted to; but I don't want to, so I can't do otherwise"). Libertarians say that you also have to be free to *want* differently than you do. Also, the libertarians reject the analysis provoked by Frankfurt-type examples, according to which it is *not* true that genuine alternatives are needed for true freedom and responsibility. (Recall the case of Mr. Jones, who chose to enter door A rather than B and was responsible for that decision even though, unbeknownst to him, he could not have gone through door B because it was blocked.) Libertarians can respond that even though Jones could not go through door B, he did indeed have options; he could have chosen to remain standing or turn back and return to his point of departure. The warp and weave of the whole narrative of Jones's journey presupposes the model of genuine choices. The only reason we say that Jones is responsible for going through door A is because that act is placed within such a context of freedom in the sense of genuine alternatives. If Jones could not have entered door B or door A, nor have remained standing, nor have turned around, then it would never occur to us to hold him responsible for his acts. But the problem still remains: If there is freedom—if there is an open future—how could such freedom exist without overturning the laws of nature?

Some libertarians are attracted to the idea that free will is an emergent biological property that developed evolutionarily, that such powers of free thought and action "are ontologically emergent, while still being powers and properties of the biological organism," as Timothy O'Connor asserts.[15] Such an emergent property would be much more complex than the typical emergent properties discussed in science (such as liquidity being an emergent property present in neither oxygen nor hydrogen but present in certain combinations of those elements [H_2O]). Also, it is not clear that such a move provides much explanatory power—that is, it doesn't answer as many questions as it needs to—but if such a model even makes sense, perhaps it could be developed to overcome certain scientific objections to the idea of free will.[16]

Some critics of free will are willing to entertain the possibility of random uncaused thoughts (perhaps echoing the discovery of Heisenberg's subatomic particles), but they have claimed that such a model does not provide a theory of freedom and responsibility of the type libertarians desire. If saying that a person could have chosen otherwise than she did when she made a particular choice means that her choice could have gone against her personal desires, hopes, intentions, and reasons, then such a free choice would be purely arbitrary and have nothing to do with the agent. Libertarians have certainly wanted free will to be more than a series of random events. But one libertarian approach, which might be traced as far back as Aristotle, is open to the possibility that such "random thoughts" are indeed a significant part of human freedom. Aristotle concentrated on the process of deliberation in his discussion of free will. When a young man, call him Mike, deliberates, for example, about accepting a job offer in Oregon or Outer Mongolia, a number of ideas may cross his mind that might be correctly considered as "'arbitrary,' 'capricious,' 'random,' 'uncontrolled,' 'irrational,' 'inexplicable,' or 'matters of luck and chance,'" as Robert Kane says (p. 38). Yet, according to Kane, these random thoughts might make a difference in the decision Mike makes. Though Mike had no control over some of these thoughts and images, "he would be in control of how he reacted to those thoughts and imaginings once they did occur" (p. 65). Kane claims that the arbitrariness of the thoughts that enter into Mike's decision would not prevent his decision from being perfectly rational. This scenario does not give

**The Arnold Schwarzenegger
of the Free Will Debate**

the libertarians the full freedom that they desire, but, says Kane, "perhaps this is as much as libertarians can hope for" (p. 65). Professor Kane himself has, according to his deterministic opponent Ted Honderich, "laboured most manfully" to defend free will. (It may not have occurred to you that the defense of free will demands manliness.)

Honderich's defense of determinism concludes that "determinism is *very strongly supported,* and that certainly it has *not been shown to be false*" (p. 90). I suppose a defender of libertarianism such as Kane might use language similar to Honderich's and say, "Determinism is *very strongly rejected,* and certainly it has *not been shown to be true.* Indeterminism is *very strongly supported* and certainly it has *not been shown to be false.*"

Existential Freedom

What you have read here so far has described certain historical developments of the theme of freedom and determinism (e.g., by Democritus, Laplace, D'Holbach, Skinner, and Freud) or developments in the last fifty years within analytic philosophy. We will now briefly turn to a few dramatic developments within Continental philosophy, specifically, the existentialist perspective of JEAN-PAUL SARTRE (1905–1980) and SIMONE DE

BEAUVOIR (1908–1986), two Parisian intellectuals who philosophized together and were romantic, political, and cultural companions throughout their adult lives. Beauvoir was a founding mother of the European feminist movement and, like Sartre, a novelist and philosopher. Sartre published more philosophical texts than did Beauvoir, but since their deaths, a study of their works, letters, and journals indicates that much of Sartre's work was deeply influenced by Beauvoir and

Jean-Paul Sartre (1905–1980)

that she should have received more public acknowledgment from him for her contribution to the idea of existentialism than she did receive.[17]

Jean-Paul may have stolen some of the limelight that Simone deserved. At this point, I will not try to present a definition of existentialism, other than to say that it is a philosophy whose primary category for understanding and characterizing human action is that of freedom.

Simone De Beauvoir

You will find a more complete definition of existentialism in Chapter 10, which concerns the philosophy of art.

As has already been mentioned, there has not been much dialogue between the analytic and the Continental philosophical traditions. The general complaint from the analytic side is, to nobody's surprise, that Continental philosophers are not analytical enough; their positions are set out more as pronouncements than as arguments, and what passes as argument is presented not in careful logical form but in epigrams and outbursts. In addition to these general complaints, there are some specific reasons for the lack of interest that analytic philosophers have had in Sartre's existentialism. It has seemed too "literary" and therefore not "serious" enough (Sartre and Beauvoir expressed their philosophical views not only in essays and books but also in novels and plays, and he is at least as famous for the latter as for the former). Existentialism, like other Continental productions, has seemed to some to be more of a fad than a search for truth. (Sartre himself abandoned existentialism a few years after inventing it, fleeing it for Marxism; then, several years after writing a two-volume, thousand-page book defending his version of Marxism, he abandoned that philosophy as well. Did he do it freely?)

If we ignore these kinds of objections and look at the philosophies themselves, we may find more substantive reasons for the lack of dialogue between the analytic philosophers and existentialism. We see that analytic philosophy honors the kind of standards of objectivity to which science aspires and that admiration involves a move away from subjectivity and the authority of first-person accounts and toward anonymous objectivity (what the philosopher Thomas Nagel calls "the view from nowhere"[18]). On the contrary, in the middle of the last century, when Sartre created the term "existentialism," Continental philosophy was tremendously concerned with subjectivity and the authority of first-person accounts.[19] René Descartes, with whose work you are somewhat familiar by now, was the model for this concern, with his "I think, therefore I am." (Ironically, Descartes can be associated with certain strains of the analytic tradition too, in that one of his goals was to show that the only correct account of the physical world was provided not by philosophy, not by the Church, not by common sense, and not even by the individual, but by science. On the other hand, he tried to derive absolute objectivity—which is what he took science to be—from his foundation of "I think"—i.e., he derived absolute objectivity from absolute subjectivity.)

Both Sartre and our person-in-the-street discover freedom in the subjective experience of consciousness (an experience whose trustworthiness some determinists have argued against, as we have just seen); but the freedom that Sartre discovers in phenomenology is much more radical than that found in everyday life by the person-in-the-street, and indeed Sartre argues that the goings-on of everyday experience disguise from us the depth of our freedom. Consciousness, Sartre says, is "an impersonal spontaneity,"[20] created *ex nihilo* (out of nothing), a tireless creation that overflows the self. The self cannot cope with this "monstrous spontaneity" (p. 99) and searches for something like the Freudian unconscious to blame it on. But we do not need to invent an unconscious to explain these dis-

Monstrous Spontaneity

ruptions. They are parts of consciousness—but parts that we try to disguise from ourselves because they terrify us. "In fact," suggests Sartre, "perhaps the essential role of the ego is to mask from consciousness its very sponta-

neity" (p. 100). To illuminate this feature of consciousness, Sartre tells us about a patient of the psychologist Pierre-Marie Janet, "A young bride was in terror, when her husband left her alone, of sitting at the window and summoning the passers-by like a prostitute" (p. 100). This young woman, perhaps angry at her new husband's inattention, may have thought to herself, "I can have any man I want simply by beckoning him from my window." She is terrified by the possibility that has entered her mind—terrified that she might act on that possibility. This patient's "psychasthenic ailment," as Sartre calls it (p. 99), is actually only an exaggeration of the normal condition of the mind, because consciousness is "a vertigo of possibility," demonstrating that we are "monstrously free" (p. 100).

Sartre claims to have made the surprising discovery that something very much like a disconnection between consciousness and the rest of reality is the source of spontaneity, and when that spontaneity breaks through, the terrifying depth of our freedom is revealed. This revelation is not received with philosophical calm, however, but with something like terror. Think of the time you were driving at night in the rain on a narrow, dangerous road facing occasional oncoming traffic. One car coming at you has on its high beams. You "flash" your lights to ask the other driver to lower his, but he is oblivious. You are nearly blinded by the lights, and you are scared and furious. As the other car rushes toward you, you think, "I'll show him; I'll drive right into that idiot!" As you think this suicidal thought, you find that you have grasped your steering wheel hard. Why? To prevent yourself from driving into him. You are experiencing "the vertigo of possibility"—your own "monstrous freedom"—and you are terrified by it.

These ideas of Sartre derive not only from his own study of subjectivity but also from his inspiration by the Danish philosopher Søren Kierkegaard, whose acquaintance you made in Chapter 5. In 1844, Kierkegaard wrote a book called *Begrebet Angest,* sometimes translated as *The Concept of Anxiety* and other times as *The Concept of Dread.* Kierkegaard has been called the "Father of Existentialism," even though Sartre coined the term "existentialism" a hundred years later. Kierkegaard was one of several of Sartre's mentors, despite the discrepancy between Sartre's radical atheism and Kierkegaard's radical Christianity. Kierkegaard tells us that his little book is a "psychological deliberation on original sin."[21]

Kierkegaard imagines Adam in the Garden of Eden. Even though Adam is innocent and happy, there is a slight shadow cast over his contentment. But Adam cannot detect the source of his disquietude. Everything comes to a head when God commands Adam not to eat from the tree of knowledge. Perhaps it had not even crossed Adam's mind to do so, but once

God prohibits him from doing it, Adam knows he *can* do it (i.e., that he is free to do it); once he knows he can do it, he knows he *may* do it, and in fact that he probably *will* do it. So, for Kierkegaard, "original sin" is primarily the dread or anxiety of Adam when he confronts his own freedom—a dread each of us must experience when we confront *our* freedom.

Kierkegaard's theory is confirmed by Sartre by his own version of phenomenology, which, like Kierkegaard's Adam, reveals that anguish in the face of freedom is foundational to consciousness. When we look deeply into consciousness, we do not find a "self," but *angoisse*. The self that Descartes claimed to discover in consciousness as absolute is for

Sartre only a construct, an ongoing project that is re-created in each of our choices. Unhappily, it is usually (or perhaps always) one created in what Sartre calls **bad faith,** which is the attempt to flee from the freedom, anguish, and responsibility that define us.

If freedom is "a permanent structure of the human being,"[22] and if the recognition of freedom is inextricably bound up with anxiety, why aren't we all in a constant state of anguish? Sartre admits that the actual *experience* of anguish is rare and explains this rareness by turning to a common example— that of responding to the ringing of the alarm clock. The ringing is an invitation to begin the day. It announces the possibility of *my* going to work, says Sartre. But I perceive it not as a possibility but rather as a necessity. I *must* get up, dress, eat, because I *must* earn the money to pay for the food I eat at breakfast so I can go to work [!].

Getting caught up in these "necessities" distracts me from the truth that none of these is really necessary except relative to values and goals that I choose. They allow me to ignore the possibility of the refusal of work, of action, of life itself. Sartre says:

> In short, to the extent that I apprehend the meaning of the ringing, I am already up at its summons; this apprehension guarantees me against the anguished intuition that it is I who confer on the alarm its exigency—I and I alone. . . . There exist concretely alarm clocks, signs, tax forms, policemen—so many guardrails against anguish. But as soon as the undertaking is held at a distance from me, as soon as I am referred to myself, . . . then I discover myself suddenly as the one who gives its meaning to the alarm clock, . . . the one who makes the values exist in order to determine his actions by their demands. (pp. 76–77)

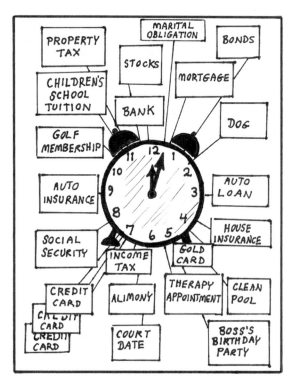

All this makes it difficult to imagine what the refusal to flee from freedom and anxiety would be like for Sartre—that is, what would count as "good faith" or "authenticity." Sartre's definition may or may not be of help: "A freedom which wills itself freedom is in fact a being-which-is-not-what-it-is and which-is-what-it-is-not, and which chooses as the ideal of being, being-what-it-is-not and not-being-what-it-is! (p. 798)"

It is this kind of writing that provokes peals of laughter, or rage, on the part of analytic philosophers. In fact, most of Sartre's presentation seems to be in a different philosophical world from that of Ted Honderich, Peter van Inwagen, or Robert Kane. Yet it seems to me that parts of Sartre's theory of freedom overlap with the ideas of Kane, especially the role of arbitrary thoughts and images in the construction of freedom and the creation through free choice of the persons that we are.

Perverse Freedom

Besides Sartre's existentialist theory, there is yet another radical theory of freedom in the literature, called "perverse freedom."[23] This theory appears not in a philosophical treatise but in a novel, Fyodor Dostoyevsky's *Notes from the Underground*. (Apparently a more literal translation would be *Notes from Under the Floorboards*, implying that the "underground man's" perspective on life is like that of a rat, looking up at life through the cracks in the floor.) The novel begins with the following curious passage:

The Man under the Floorboards

> I am a sick man. . . . I am a spiteful man. I am an unattractive man. I believe my liver is diseased. However, I know nothing at all about my disease and do not know for certain what ails me. I don't consult a doctor for it and never have, though I have a respect for medicine and doctors. Besides, I am extremely superstitious, sufficiently so to respect medicine, anyway (I am well-educated enough not to be superstitious, but I am superstitious). No, I refuse to consult a doctor from spite. That you probably will not understand. Well, I understand it though. Of course, I can't explain who it is precisely that I am mortifying in this case by my spite: I am perfectly well aware that I cannot "pay back" the doctors by not consulting them; I know better than anyone that by all this I am only injuring myself and no one else. But still, if I don't consult a doctor it is from spite. My liver is bad, well—let it get worse![24]

As the "argument" of the novel develops, we discover that the underground man takes deep offense at all the restrictions imposed upon his freedom by society and reality at large. He takes them as personal insults. He is offended by the demand that his acts be *prudent*. He is told that he is supposed to act in ways that are in his own best interest. If his liver is ailing, he is supposed to see a physician. If the weather in Moscow is bad for him, he is supposed to move to St. Petersburg. If his food doesn't agree with him, he is supposed to change his diet. But in these cases, according to him, *prudence* is a determining factor restricting his freedom. Therefore, he refuses to act for his own advantage, though he admits that there is one advantage, "the most advantageous advantage," on which he will act:

> One's own free unfettered choice, one's own caprice—however wild it may be, one's own fancy worked up at times to a frenzy—is that very "most advantageous advantage" which we have overlooked, which comes under no classification and against which all systems and theories are continually being shattered to atoms. And how do these wiseacres know that man wants a normal, a virtuous choice? What has made them conceive that man must want a rationally advantageous choice? What man wants is simply *independent* choice, whatever that independence may cost and wherever it may lead. And choice, of course, the devil only knows what choice.[25]

Encumbrances on Freedom

Furthermore, the underground man is offended by the demand that his actions be *reasonable*, that whenever he does anything he is supposed to have a reason for doing it. In that case, he believes, reason delimits his freedom. The underground man seeks a mode of action that is *unmotivated*. He seeks to perform acts for which there are no reasons. He says he is a "spiteful man." That is, his acts are motivated by spite, not by reasons. The Russian word is *zlost*, and apparently it means more than "spite"; it also means "whim" and "fancy," "contrariness" and "caprice." If someone points out to the underground man that operating from whim, fancy, or spite is itself to operate with a *reason*, is still to have a *motive*, the underground man will not object because to him, in those cases, the motive for his action is pure freedom. Indeed, we know from experience that children often do things out of spite, and when they do so, they are often trying to establish their independence from their parents.

But it is not only children who operate out of spite. In his book, *On Being Free*, Frithjof Bergmann gives us an excellent example of this spiteful freedom, which he has noticed in the film, "*Lawrence of Arabia.*"

> Still another parallel to the undergroundman's extreme idea of freedom appears in a scene in the film made after the life of T. E. Lawrence. It occurs in the last third of the film when Lawrence is already in command of a small but formidable Arab army [during World War I] with a long string of brilliant exploits to its credit. After a temporary setback, Lawrence is in the process of preparing a major and well-planned campaign that promises defeat to the Turks and glory and loot to his men. He needs troops, however, and the scene narrates his interview with a proud tribal leader. In its course Lawrence tries out reason after reason on the chieftain. "Your fame will spread far if you join me. There will be much money. This is your long-sought chance to get even with the Turks. Together we will lead your people out of their servility. We will lift them up out of their obeisance. You can be the father of a new, proud nation." The Arab sits unmoved and distant. Disdainfully he shakes his massive head to each of these reasons. But he knows full well what force they have, and he feels it. His gesture is a refusal, a fending off; really the sign of his determination not to surrender to their power. Eventually Lawrence's arsenal is exhausted. He has given every reason and all have been parried by the same shaking of the head. So both men sit through a silence, till Lawrence is just at the point of rising and taking his curt leave. Then at last the chief speaks: "I will join you," he says, "but not for fame, nor for money, not even for my people. Not for any of the reasons you have offered. I will do it but only because it is my whim."[26]

As extreme as this version of freedom is, it does capture something of the aboriginal attraction of the idea of freedom. As Bergmann says, "The idea of being totally unbounded, of yielding to no authority whatever (not even to that of reason), of acting without any encumbrances—that image seems close to the root-experience of freedom, . . . a distant memory of this expectation still glows behind all talk of liberation."[27] It also engages deeply with the idea of arbitrary thoughts and decisions playing a role in the structure of freedom, as we saw in Robert Kane and Jean-Paul Sartre.

Conclusion

So what are we to believe? What about determinism? There are some good reasons for taking it seriously, after all. At the macrocosmic level, physical bodies do seem to behave according to laws and to be, in principle, predictable. And because human beings are physical bodies (I do not mean that they are *merely* physical bodies), and because human behavior is to a great extent predictable, we might have a suspicion that determinism is true. Even Heisenberg's attack on determinism at the microcosmic level seems to replace determinism only with a randomness that may exist at the subatomic level but that leaves necessity unchallenged at the level of things the size of human bodies. (Not only that, but random human action might be worse than predetermined action.) Moreover, the belief in human freedom can seem a bit presumptuous, because it seems to entail the claim that in one otherwise insignificant minuscule corner of a cosmos so large as to overwhelm the understanding there

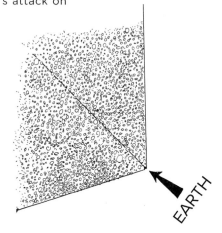

In One Small Corner of the Universe, There Is Freedom

exists a feature or quality (freedom) that may be nonexistent elsewhere in the cosmos.

Nevertheless, we do not *know* that determinism is true, even if we do not know that it is false. It may well be that freedom is an emergent characteristic of certain physical systems (in the same way that consciousness might be such an emergent characteristic). Again, we do not *know* that this, or any other, explanation of freedom is true, but there are some good reasons for believing in freedom nevertheless.

First, there is the experiential reason. A number of libertarians take it as a fact that we experience ourselves in the world as free, and we should reject this experience as illusionary only if we are given a very compelling reason to do so.

Second, there is a practical reason for rejecting determinism. If hard determinism is true, then no one is ever responsible for his or her actions, and there is no moral reason for ever praising or blaming anyone for any act whatsoever. Indeed, in this case, all of our moral and juridical institutions and ideas are wrong and should be dismantled, as Skinner suggested. I would think that the determinist's argument would have to be tremendously convincing for us to be willing to accept such radical consequences. The soft determinist's conception of freedom sometimes seems like a philosophical trick—a word game to solve serious problems.

I'm sorry I'm doing this to you, but I'm not responsible for my actions.

Furthermore, there is the practical problem of consistency. Is it really possible to make a belief in determinism consistent with our thoughts and actions in the world? Our normal understanding of reality and our discourse about it are loaded with concepts that presuppose notions of freedom and responsibility. As we saw in Chapter 3, when a determinist like Skinner finds it convenient to use these concepts in his more popular works, he likes to put the words denoting them in quotation marks (e.g., he says that a person can be made to "choose"). Skinner seems to be implying that he *could* restate these concepts in more appropriate, scientific language if he wanted to. But *could* he and with what consequences?

All right then, if there are good reasons for rejecting the deterministic claim, can we accept a form of libertarianism? If we do so, we do it at our own philosophical risk. The arguments for freedom seem no stronger than the arguments against freedom. It seems that each of us must make a decision for ourselves. This is, of course, a very ironic conclusion, and it very much invites the accusation that it begs the very question it is meant to resolve.

Topics for Consideration

1. Tie the hard determinism of Leucippus and Democritus to the discussion of the Mythos-Logos debate in Chapter 1.
2. Discuss the disagreement between John Hospers and Richard Peters concerning the correct interpretation of Freud's view of freedom.
3. Under what names does the theory operate according to which freedom is compatible with determinism? Explain how the compatibility of these apparently mutually exclusive ideas is possible, according to that theory.
4. Show how libertarianism stands in relation to (a) hard determinism, (b) soft determinism, and (c) indeterminism.
5. At this moment in history, apparently there is no scientific evidence that proves determinism to be true. Why, then, do so many philosophers seem so convinced that determinism is true?

6. Explain why the two formulas, "Same past, same future" and "Same past, different future," are used to distinguish between determinism and indeterminism.

7. Some determinists claim that the ability to do otherwise than what one in fact does ("could have done otherwise") is not a necessary condition of freedom. Explain this claim, and report how indeterminists respond to this claim.

8. What does Sartre mean by "monstrous freedom"?

9. Explain why the ever-present potential of perverse freedom can undermine the possibility of a *science* of human behavior.

Suggestions for Further Reading: Paperback Editions

Frithjof Bergmann, *On Being Free* (Notre Dame, IN: University of Notre Dame Press, 1977). A very articulate and carefully argued version of soft determinism.

Fyodor Dostoyevsky, *Notes from the Underground,* trans. Constance Garnett (New York: Dell, 1960). An amazing novelistic presentation of the idea of perverse freedom by one of the greatest fiction writers of all time.

Stephen Greenblatt, *The Swerve: How the World Became Modern* (New York and London: Norton, 2011). A study of the Roman determinist, Lucretius, who was inspired by the first atomist, Democritus. Beautifully written by an esteemed professor of literature.

William Hasker, *The Emergent Self* (Ithaca, NY: Cornell University Press, 1999). A defense of freedom as characteristic of the "emergent" self.

Ted Honderich, *How Free Are You?* 2nd ed. (Oxford, England: Oxford University Press, 2002). Honderich is a clear thinker who pulls no punches. The answer to the title's question? Not a whole heck of a lot.

Robert Kane, *A Contemporary Introduction to Free Will* (New York & Oxford, England: Oxford University Press, 2005). Clear and well written, covers all sides of the current arguments by analytical philosophers.

Robert Kane, ed., *The Oxford Handbook of Free Will* (Oxford, England: Oxford University Press, 2002). This is a big, state-of-the-art volume containing articles by many philosophers discussed in this chapter, such as Frankfurt, Kane, O'Connor, Strawson, and van Inwagen.

Jean-Paul Sartre, *Existentialism and Human Emotions,* trans. Hazel E. Barnes and Bernard Frechtman (New York: Philosophical Library, 1957). A popularization of the arguments for existentialism by the philosopher who coined the term.

Jean-Paul Sartre, *Transcendence of the Ego,* trans. Robert Kirkpatrick (New York: Farrar, Strauss and Giroux, 1957). Short, brilliant, but hard reading.

B. F. Skinner, *Beyond Freedom and Dignity* (New York: Knopf, 1971). A popularization of the arguments for behaviorism by its modern architect.

Richard Taylor, *Metaphysics,* 4th ed. (Englewood Cliffs, NJ: Prentice-Hall, 1992). A provocative and excellent book by a provocative and excellent philosopher. Read Chapter 4 for Taylor's defense of freedom.

Notes

1. B. F. Skinner, *Beyond Freedom and Dignity* (New York: Knopf, 1971), pp. 20–21.

2. Ibid., pp. 12–13.

3. John Hospers, "Meaning and Free Will," *Philosophy and Phenomenological Research,* Vol. 10, No. 3 (March, 1950), pp. 316–330.

4. Richard S. Peters, *The Concept of Motivation* (New York: Humanities Press, 1969), p. 69.

5. Galen Strawson, *Freedom and Belief* (Oxford, England: Oxford University Press, 1986), and "The Bounds of Freedom," in Robert Kane, ed., *The Oxford Handbook of Free Will* (Oxford, England: Oxford University Press, 2002), pp. 441–460.

6. Ted Honderich, *How Free Are You?* 2nd ed. (Oxford, England: Oxford University Press, 2002), p. 96. Page numbers of future quotations from this book will be included in the text.

7. Harry Frankfurt, "Alternate Possibilities and Moral Responsibilities," in Gary Watson, ed., *Free Will,* 2nd ed. (Oxford, England: Oxford University Press, 2003), p. 169.

8. This Frankfurt-type example is not by Frankfurt himself, but by Robert Kane, who, by the way, does not endorse Frankfurt-type arguments. Robert Kane, *A Contemporary Introduction to Free Will* (New York and Oxford, England: Oxford University Press, 2005), p. 89. Page numbers of future quotations from this book will be included in the text.

9. Galen Strawson, *Things that Bother Me: Death, Freedom, etc.* (New York: New York Review Books, 2018), p. 111.

10. Werner Heisenberg, *Physics and Philosophy: The Revolution in Modern Science* (New York: Harper & Row, 1962).

11. Peter van Inwagen, *An Essay on Free Will* (Oxford, England: Oxford University Press, Clarendon Press, 1983), p. 16. Page numbers of future quotations from this book will be included in the text.

12. Colin McGinn, *The Mysterious Flame: Conscious Minds in a Material World* (New York: Basic Books, 1999), pp. 61–62.

13. Richard Taylor, *Metaphysics* (Englewood Cliffs, NJ: Prentice-Hall, 1974), p. 57. Quoted by Kane, p. 47.

14. The ideas to which this diagram points are developed nicely in an early essay by Richard Taylor, "I Can," *Philosophical Review,* Vol. 69 (1960), pp. 78–89.

15. Timothy O'Connor, "Libertarian Views: Dualist and Agent-Causal Theories," in Kane, ed., *The Oxford Handbook of Free Will,* pp. 337–355, quote from p. 342.

16. See, for example, William Hasker, *The Emergent Self* (Ithaca, NY: Cornell University Press, 1999), and Timothy O'Connor, ed., *Persons and Causes: The Metaphysics of Free Will* (New York: Oxford University Press, 2000).

17. Beauvoir's most influential feminist work is *The Second Sex,* trans. Constance Borde and Sheila Malovany-Chevalier (New York: Knopf, 2009). The clearest statement of her commitment to existentialism is *The Ethics of Ambiguity,* trans. Bernard Frechtman (New York: Philosophical Library, 1948).

18. Thomas Nagel, *The View from Nowhere* (New York: Oxford University Press, 1986).

19. Phenomenology is the name of the philosophy that studies the nature of consciousness. Sartre sometimes called himself a phenomenologist.

20. Jean-Paul Sartre, *Transcendence of the Ego*, trans. Robert Kirkpatrick (New York: Farrar, Strauss and Giroux, 1957), p. 98. First published in French, 1937. Page numbers of future quotations from this book will be included in the text.

21. Kierkegaard wrote the book under the pseudonym Vigilius Haufniensis. See *The Concept of Dread*, trans. Walter Lowrie (Princeton, NJ: Princeton University Press, 1957), or *The Concept of Anxiety*, trans. Reidar Thomte and Albert B. Anderson (Princeton, NJ: Princeton University Press, 1980).

22. Jean-Paul Sartre, *Being and Nothingness: An Essay in Phenomenological Ontology*, trans. Hazel Barnes (New York: Washington Square Press, 1992), p. 73. First published in French in 1943. All future quotes from Sartre in this chapter are from this book. Page numbers of future quotations will be included in the text.

23. I have borrowed the term "perverse freedom" from Robert C. Solomon, *Introducing Philosophy*, 3rd ed. (New York: Harcourt, Brace, Jovanovich, 1985), p. 457.

24. Fyodor Dostoyevsky, *Notes from the Underground*, trans. Constance Garnett (New York: Dell, 1960), p. 25.

25. Ibid., p. 46.

26. Frithjof Bergmann, *On Being Free* (Notre Dame, IN: University of Notre Dame Press, 1977), pp. 21–22.

27. Ibid., p. 18.

7

Thou Shalt
Become Perfected
Ethics

The standard to which we appeal when we call some person or behavior "immoral" is usually a kind of spoken or unspoken principle that we assume most "decent" individuals (i.e., humane, civil, conscientious, responsible individuals) accept. Here are some examples of such principles: People should be fair in their dealings with other people. Institutions should be fair with people who fall under their authority. People should not cause unnecessary suffering. People should be prepared to help those who are in dire need (up to a point). People should keep their promises. There are disagreements about how these principles should be applied in specific contexts, but most individuals and institutions with which you deal probably accept these principles as reasonable. According to these and similar moral principles, some individuals and some acts are blatantly immoral, and, perhaps, certain institutions are immoral as well.

Most immoral people know that the acts they engage in are wrong in some sense or other. Of these people, some feel guilty, others deny the wrongness of their behavior and even take cynical delight in it, and others promise themselves they will mend their ways . . . after only one or two more episodes. We sometimes use the term "amoral" to describe those people who have no idea that their certain acts are wrong or who are indifferent to how their acts affect others. Amoral people are either incapable of keeping their behavior within moral limits or, in some perverse way, unwilling to do so. When a person's amoralism is massive, we say that he or she is a sociopath, and we think of the person as afflicted with a disease. There are probably more immoral acts and people than amoral ones, which is a good thing, because immoral people or moral people who sometimes perform immoral acts (e.g., pretty much all of us, on occasion) are at least capable of being influenced by moral reasoning. And moral reasoning abounds; there are many arguments among individuals and groups, for example, about whether U.S. initiation of the wars in the Middle East and extended participation in them is morally justified, whether abortion is immoral, whether suicide or euthanasia is moral. Oddly, most people on both sides of these arguments accept, in their own interpretations of them, all of the common moral principles that I've listed previously. In such cases, the question is, how should those principles be applied?

This is one place where moral philosophy or ethics comes into its own. But philosophy not only tries to show how moral principles are to be contextualized; it also looks into the status of moral principles themselves. Historically, many philosophers have tried to demonstrate the *source* of moral principles and their justification or to present whole ethical systems and justify them.

Historically, these are the kinds of "big questions" that moral philosophy has asked: What is the Good? What is the good life? What ought we to do? Are there such things as moral duties and obligations? Are there absolute moral values, or are moral values relative to time, place, culture, and the individual? Is there any reason to be moral at all? In ethics too we can ask the question—Does the (moral) center hold?

Ancient Greek Moral Philosophers

As so often, we will go back to ancient Greece to begin our study of moral philosophy. Ethical concepts have evolved greatly since Greek times, nevertheless, some modern moral concepts like "duty" do not seem to have had any direct counterpart in Greek thought. We will begin our discussion of ethics where so many philosophical discussions began—in Athens during the fourth century B.C.E.

Justice/Morality

Plato's major work, and one of the masterpieces of world literature, the *Republic,* opens with a discussion of *dikaiosyne,* an umbrella term for all conventions that command respect for the interests of other people. This concept covers much of what we mean in English by the term "morality," though the word *dikaiosyne* is usually translated as "justice." Unfortunately, the English term "justice" designates a

Justice!

much narrower concept than does the original Greek. So when the question is raised in the *Republic*, "Why should I be just?" the ensuing conversation probably makes more sense to us today if we read it as asking, "Why should I be moral?" Knowing what you already know about Socrates and Plato, you will not be surprised to find out that they thought this question could not be answered until we knew what *dikaiosyne* was. (Once again, the question "What is X?" is the key theme of the Platonic dialogue.)

Early in the first chapter of the *Republic*, we are shocked by the bald assertion of the sophist Thrasymachus, one of the protagonists of that dialogue, who informs us that "Justice is the advantage of the stronger." Thrasymachus explains his claim in the following passage:

> Don't you know then . . . that some states are under despots, and some are governed by a democracy, and some by an aristocracy? . . . Is not the strong power in each the ruling power? And each power lays down the laws so as to suit itself, a democracy, democratic laws, and a despotism, despotic laws, and so with the rest, and laying them down, they make it clear that this is a just thing for their subjects, I mean their own advantage; one who transgresses these they chastise as a breaker of laws and a doer of injustice. Then this is what I mean, my good friend: that the same thing is just in all states, the advantage of the established government. This I suppose has the power, so if you reason correctly, it follows that everywhere the same thing is just, the advantage of the stronger.[1]

So, according to Thrasymachus, "morality" is nothing but a concatenation of rules and conventions imposed upon a gullible community by those who command political power, and these rules and conventions are always contrived to be of advantage to the rulers. So the institutions that enjoin us to behave in ways that are truthful, honest, fair, equitable, open, helpful, and merciful are manipulated by those in power for their own use.

But Socrates gets Thrasymachus to admit that sometimes morality does *not* benefit those in power because sometimes those in power err concerning what is to their own benefit and that

Agent Reginald Smith, Internal Revenue Agency. We're levying a 2000% tax on income. How much did you earn today? (And remember, it would be immoral to lie about it!)

therefore morality cannot be *defined* in terms of benefit to the strong. Despite his concession, Thrasymachus nevertheless insists that being moral is a great disadvantage to the individual. Thrasymachus says:

> You must consider, my most simple Socrates, that a just man comes off worse than an unjust man everywhere. First of all in contracts with one another, wherever two are in such partnership, and the partnership is dissolved, you would never find the just man getting the better of the unjust, but he always gets the worst of it. Secondly, in public affairs, when there are taxes and contributions, the just man pays more and the unjust less from an equal estate; when there are distributions the one gains nothing and the other much. Again, when these two hold public office, the just man gets his private affairs, by neglecting them, into a bad state, if he has no other loss, and he has no profit from the treasury because he is just; besides, he is unpopular with friends and acquaintances if he will not serve them contrary to justice; but it is quite the opposite with the unjust man. (pp. 142–143)

So, for Thrasymachus, being immoral "is to one's profit and advantage." Socrates must prove the opposite—that being moral is profitable and advantageous and being immoral is unprofitable and disadvantageous. This argument will be difficult to establish in the face of Thrasymachus's examples. The truth of some of those examples grates on us. We all know cases of people who, because of their manipulative lifestyle and shady business practices, drive the cars *we* would like to drive, maintain great bank accounts, seem especially attractive to people, travel extensively, and in general, lead a life we could easily envy. We would *like* Socrates to be able to prove that, appearances to the contrary, these people are in fact miserable because of their immorality; but it is hard to imagine what kind of argument could demonstrate a priori that this class of people *must* be unhappy.

At the end of Book I of the *Republic*, Socrates, employing some very questionable rhetorical strategies, manages to befuddle Thrasymachus, who lapses into an angry silence. But the problem Thrasymachus posed does not disappear and in fact continues and intensifies in Book II. The second book begins with a discussion of three kinds of good:

1. Good in itself (e.g., harmless small pleasures)
2. Good for its consequences (e.g., taking medicine)
3. Combination of number 1 and number 2 (e.g., being healthy)

Socrates says that morality ought to be a number 3, but most people take it to be a number 2. We engage in moral behavior because we fear the consequences of *not* doing so. Glaucon, one of Socrates's companions, paraphrases what he takes to be the standard opinion about justice:

Thrasymachus Feels That Debating Socrates Is Not in His Interest

> They say, then, that to be unjust is good, and to suffer injustice is bad, and the excess of evil in suffering injustice is greater than the excess of good in being unjust; so that when people do and suffer injustice in dealing with one another, and taste both, those who cannot both escape the one and take the other think it profitable to make an agreement neither to do nor to suffer injustice; from this they begin to make laws and compacts among themselves, and they name the injunction of the law lawful and just. This, they say, is the origin and nature of justice, which is something between the best, namely to do wrong and not to pay for it, and the worst, to suffer wrong and not to be able to get vengeance. Justice, they say, is between these two, and they are content with it not as a good, but as honoured in the weakness of injustice; since one who was able to do injustice, if he were truly a man, would never make an agreement neither to wrong nor to be wronged—he would be mad to do so. Then this . . . is the nature of justice, Socrates, and such is its origin, as they say. (p. 156)

Glaucon illustrates his point with the story of the magic ring of Gyges. In the story, the man who possesses the ring is able to become invisible and

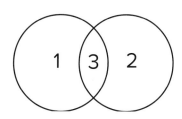

avoid the normal conse-
quences of his actions. He
seduces the queen, kills the
king, and takes over the
kingdom. The implication of
the story is that anybody
would do the same and
would be a fool not to. If
we condemn Gyges, it's
because we are envious or
don't want to be thought
of badly.

Gyges and His Magic Ring

At this point, another
companion, Adeimantus,
chimes in agreeing with Glau-
con. Morality is definitely a number 2. People praise it for the rewards it
brings. But the *appearance* of morality gets these rewards as well as the
actual morality, so the prudent person will be concerned with *reputation*,
not morality. (This view was later defended by the Renaissance political
philosopher, Niccolò Macchiavelli, in his book of 1513, offering advice to
political leaders called *The Prince*, in which he asserts that it is not necessary for the Prince to have piety, faith, honesty, humanity, and integrity. But
it is necessary for him to *seem* to have them.) At this point, Socrates apparently recognizes that he is facing some heavy artillery, and he responds the
way many of us do in such situations; he
changes the subject . . . or so it seems.

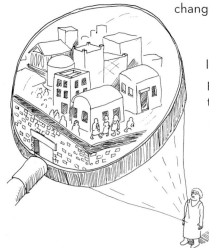

The City Is the Soul Magnified

City/Soul

In fact, Socrates concludes that the
problem has become so complex and
the details so unclear that it can be
resolved only by holding a magnifying
glass up to it. This metaphor becomes
the pretext for Socrates to present a
curious theory that will go on to
occupy a large part of the *Republic*
and will even give the book its
title. The theory comes in two
parts: first, that the problem of
morality can be resolved only by

coming to an understanding of the human Soul and, second, that such an understanding can best be achieved by studying the nature of the City (the Polis, the Republic) because, ideally at least, the City is the Soul writ large. The study of the ideal City will reveal to us the ideal Soul, and from that picture, we can deduce the nature of justice and an answer to the question of why one should be moral.

The Guardian Must Know the Difference between Friends and Enemies of the City

Socrates's analysis leads him to the following conclusion (summarized rather cursorily here). The ideal City contains three distinct classes. First are the rulers who know philosophy; hence they have beheld the "Platonic" essence of citizenship and, as a class, have the virtue of *wisdom*. Second, there is a military caste, called the guardians, whose job it is to protect the City from enemies, internal and external. The members of this class know *some* philosophical principles (otherwise they would not know the difference between friends and enemies of the City). The guardians can eventually be promoted to the ruling class if they prove their philosophical mettle. The collective virtue of the guardian class is *courage*. Finally, there is the class of artisans and workers. This class comprises the numerical majority of the City, but it is incapable of self-governance because it is incapable of philosophy. It must submit to the rule of reason imposed upon it by the ruling class. When it does so, its collective virtue is that of *moderation*.

Because the City is the magnification of the Soul, it follows that the Soul, though a unity in fact, can be analyzed into three components—reason, spirit, and appetite. The rational component, reason, finds itself constantly opposed to the appetitive component, which is what we might call the animal part of the psyche. This lower part of the Soul contains all the primitive lusts and irrational desires, which must be constrained if psychic peace is to be achieved. It is very much like the Freudian id, and this similarity is surely no coincidence because Freud was greatly influenced by Platonic philosophy. In fact, in one passage, Plato describes (in a most

"Freudianly" graphic way) the desires of the appetitive Soul as manifesting themselves in dreams. Discussing "lawless desires" as "those which are aroused in sleep," he says:

> whenever the rest of the Soul, all the reasonable, gentle and ruling part, is asleep, . . . the bestial and savage, replete with food or wine, skips about, and throwing off sleep, tries to go and fulfill its own instincts. You know there is nothing it will not dare to do, thus freed and rid of all shame and reason; it shrinks not from attempting in fancy to lie with a mother, or with any other man or god or beast, shrinks from no bloodshed, refrains from no food— in a word, leaves no folly or shamelessness untried. (p. 370)

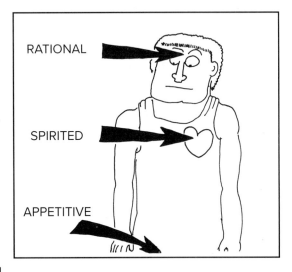

RATIONAL

SPIRITED

APPETITIVE

Perhaps not surprisingly, Plato metaphorically locates the appetitive aspect of the Soul "below the midriff" and the rational component of the Soul in the head. The spirited Soul Plato locates in the heart. We can view the battle of the psyche as the struggle between reason and lust for the allegiance of the spirit because spirit is the source of action. If the appetites persuade spirit to join them, then the individual will become lustful and unruly. If reason persuades spirit to side with it, then the individual becomes rational. Each of the components of the Soul has its own virtue (*aretê*), which manifests itself in the actions of the individual when each component is operating under optimal conditions. The virtue of reason is *wisdom*. The virtue of spirit is *courage*. The virtue of appetite is *moderation*. When the three parts of the soul operate under the rule of reason, the result is *justice* (*dikaiosyne*), and it would be clear to anybody whose Soul was in order why he or she should behave in a just (i.e., moral) manner. Why is this conclusion so clear? Because the opposite of justice, namely injustice, is *confusion*, with the part that naturally should be a slave trying to rebel against rational rule. Confusion is incompatible with *aretê*. The expression of human excellence is possible only when justice triumphs, that is to say, only when the individual takes into consideration the interests of other human beings and not only his own private interests. In other words, the individual discovers that it is in his interest to take others' interests seriously.

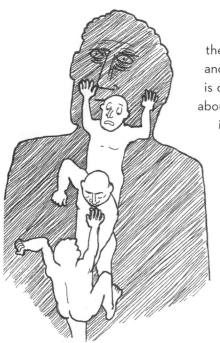

Confusion in the Psyche

Plato has Glaucon say, "Virtue [*aretê*] then, it seems, would be a kind of health and beauty and fine fitness of the soul; vice is disease and ugliness and weakness." What about Thrasymachus's question of whether it is more profitable to be just than unjust? Glaucon says, "The inquiry seems to me to become from now absurd." Why? Because Socrates has shown that the question "Why should I be just?" is identical to the question "Why should I be healthy?" This question is absurd, and anyone who asks it does not understand it (with the possible exception of Dostoyevsky's "underground man").

Let us turn once more to Plato's formula, "City equals Soul magnified." We saw that each of the three classes in the City has its virtue, and when each class seeks its virtue, the result is justice in the City. Both in the City and in the Soul, justice follows from certain rational principles that must be obeyed. The individual human behaves morally when he or she grasps these rational principles, seduces the heart to follow its rule, and, with the help of the heart, imposes a regimen on the passions. But there is a grating paradox when this model is applied to the City. Most people in Plato's good City are *bad*. That is, most of its inhabitants are congenitally incapable of discovering the rule of reason for themselves and of applying it to their own behavior, so it must be dictatorially imposed upon them.

So what's the big deal about being healthy?

cough sputter wheeze

Ethics must be grounded in *reason,* but reason itself is not a *force*—it has no binding power, and it must be *enforced.* As the contemporary British philosopher Bernard Williams puts it, "For Plato, the political problem of making the ethical into a force was the problem of making society embody the rational justification, and that problem could only have an authoritarian solution."[2]

Most People Are Bad

I suppose that today the majority of us in our most negative moments suspect that Plato is right—many people will not behave morally unless coerced to do so. But most people cannot accept Platonism as their own moral doctrine, not only because they don't agree with his elitism and its totalitarian implications but also because they are much less certain than he that there is an *absolute* Good and that the only sin is ignorance of it.

Egoism

Plato argued that being moral was in the interest of the individual (though he thought that, unfortunately, most people were too benighted to understand that truth). Plato believed that no one would ever knowingly operate in a way that ran counter to his or her own interests, and if we ever saw someone who was operating in that manner, that would simply be proof that he or she was *ignorant* of his or her best interests. We can call this belief the *egoistic* assumption in Plato's thought. I read Plato's egoism as comprising both **psychological egoism** (every act *is* motivated by self-interest) and **moral egoism** (every act *ought to be* motivated by self-interest). However, according to Plato's spokesman, Socrates, psychological egoism does not amount to the same thing as moral egoism, because people are usually wrong about what is truly in their best interest. At this point, philosophical education comes in and bridges the gap between psychological and moral egoism, because if people come to know which acts really are in their best interest, they will pursue those acts. For Plato, the claim that one *ought* to act in one's own interest entails the claim that one ought to act in the interest of others. It is the

> I would be glad to help you, but as far as I can determine, there's nothing in it for me. Make me an offer.

job of Socrates's philosophical discourse to demonstrate that hidden truth. (By the way, when we talk about self-interest here, notice that the appropriate term is **egoism** and not "egotism." If I call you an egotist, I am intentionally insulting you; I am calling you a name. If I call you an egoist, I am ascribing to you a view about motivation: "ego"—the Latin word for "I.") It is interesting to note that in this important respect, Socrates of the *Republic* and his antagonist, Thrasymachus, share the same egoistic view. The difference is that Thrasymachus thought that it is *not* in one's best interest to act morally, but Socrates thought that it is. Thrasymachus's egoism, then, creates an opposition between the individual and society (society's interests are not *my* interests), but Socrates's egoism does not. Socrates (like Karl Marx after him) tried to show that the interests of the individual are identical to the interests of the community.

The philosopher who is most famous for his direct commitment to egoism is THOMAS HOBBES (1588–1679). In his book *Leviathan*, Hobbes wrote, "of the voluntary acts of every man, the object is some good to himself."[3] Hobbes's view is what I have identified as psychological egoism. He believes it is simply a psychological fact (which for him as a materialist means a biological fact) that all

> We're all in this together!

> And you're for communism, too?

> Yes, but only for the elite. The workers are too stupid to get the point.

Karl Marx and Socrates Agree (Sort Of)

Love Thy Neighbor as Thyself

people always *do* act in ways that they take to be to their personal benefit. He agrees with Socrates that philosophical thinking can clarify what truly is in one's best interest. Hobbes's view, if true, rules out the biological possibility of *altruism* (ego = I, alter = other; egoism = I-ism, altruism = otherism). Altruism as a psychological theory is the claim that people sometimes do sacrifice their own interests for the interests of others, and as a moral theory, it is the claim that people sometimes ought to sacrifice their own interests for the interests of others. Altruism, which would be very foreign to the ancient Greek mentality, is a view we often associate with Christianity (though perhaps not correctly because Jesus tells us "Love thy neighbor *as thyself*" and "Do unto others as you would have them do unto *you*" [emphases added]. On the other hand, Jesus also said, "If any man cometh unto me and hateth not . . . his own life, . . . he cannot be my disciple" [Luke 14:26]. If altruism is *impossible*, then surely it cannot be a moral duty. (As Immanuel Kant said, "ought" implies "can.") Well, then, *is* altruism impossible? Is it ever possible to sacrifice one's own interests in order to act in the interest of another? Hobbes says sacrifice is possible *only if one perceives it to be in his interest to sacrifice his interests.* Certainly most of us are surprised by Hobbes's claim, because we tend to draw certain distinctions that he rejects. For example, in the case of a person who, at great risk to his own life, saves a drowning child from the surf, consider the kinds of explanations he might give after the fact:

I saved her because . . .

A. I saw that she would drown if I didn't go in after her.
  (Somebody had to do it!) (responsibility)
B. I recognized that it was my duty to try and save her. (duty)
C. Only an animal would have stood by and
  let her drown. (natural sentiment)
D. I know that family, and I love that little girl. (love)
E. Her father helped me once when I was down and out. (debt)
F. Well, I don't know why I did it. I'm as surprised as you are. (?)
G. My conscience would have plagued me for the rest of my
  life if I hadn't tried. (guilt)
H. I didn't want people to say that I was a coward. (reputation)
 I. I hoped I would get some recognition out of all this. (reputation)
J. I wanted to satisfy a need I have to help others.
  (self-aggrandizement—perhaps
  out of guilt or feelings of inferiority)
K. I wanted to achieve a benefit for myself. (Hobbesian honesty)
L. I wanted a pleasant sensation. (hedonism)

ALTRUISM ↑

↓ **EGOISM**

Hobbes says that reasons A through J are really versions of K, and indeed K is a version of L because he defines "benefit" in terms of pleasure. ("*Pleasure . . .* or *delight,* is the appearance or sense of good, and *molestation* or *displeasure,* the appearance, or sense of evil."[4]) Hobbes's definition means that his egoism is a form of psychological **hedonism,** which is to say that we are motivated by the desire for pleasure.

How does Hobbes know that human action is always motivated by self-interest? Surely this claim purports to be an empirical one—one that

ought to be the *result* of a scientific investigation. Yet Hobbes has not only failed to conduct a scientific investigation, he has in fact subverted the possibility of any such investigation. Truly, scientific theories must always be open to possible refutation if new disconfirming data are discovered. This has come to be known as the **principle of falsifiability** (associated with the British-Austrian philosopher of science, Sir Karl Popper). In other words, for a thesis to be a truly scientific view, its defender must be able to state the conditions under which it would be admitted that the hypothesis had been refuted. For example, obviously, Isaac Newton would admit that his theory of gravity was false if, all other things being equal, repeated instances were reported and confirmed of heavier-than-air objects hovering, floating, or rising. Precisely, what makes Newton's theory so convincing is the fact

Things Going Up

that no such events have been confirmed, but what makes his theory *scientific* is that we know what it would be like for it to be false.

Now, in the face of the principle of falsifiability, what is the status of Hobbes's thesis? What kind of data, if discovered, would refute Hobbes's view? I think the answer to this is: *none*. No matter what possible counter-evidence we could imagine, Hobbes would claim that his theory can account for it. For example, let's try to imagine an event that we believe to be paradigmatic of altruism. What about the case of the young soldier who throws himself on the grenade, thereby saving the lives of his comrades at the cost of his own life? Such heroic events are possible (in fact, they have happened). Are these possibilities not evidence of altruism, hence evidence against Hobbes's egoism? Not at all, Hobbes would say. If the soldier sacrificed his life, it was because (whether foolishly or not) he construed it as being in his interest

> Wow! A chance to earn a medal!

Mommy! Flower for you.

Thanks, dear. (What's the hidden agenda here?)

to do so. ("He knew he would be dead either way and preferred to be remembered as a hero," "He was raised in such a way that his concept of self-esteem was intimately tied up with the performance of heroic acts," or "He thought people would like him," and so on.) Hobbes probably believed that it was to his theory's credit that it could be applied to any possible contingency, but we see that the opposite is true. Indeed, any theory that accounts for every possible case accounts for no case at all. Or, to put it slightly differently, any "theory" that is compatible with every possible state of affairs is no theory at all, because real theories must exclude some possibilities. Confucius is supposed to have said, "If the mind is *too* open, everything falls out." The same goes for theories.

If Hobbes had stated his proposition differently, we might have more sympathy with it. What if Hobbes had said, "There is more self-interest in most motivation than is usually admitted. One should be generally suspicious when estimating an agent's intentions. One should ask, 'What's in it for the agent?'" Then Hobbes would be admitting the possibility, though not the likelihood, of altruistic acts, and the question concerning which acts are egoistic and which are altruistic would be an *empirical* one (i.e., one to be determined by *evidence*). As it stands, however, it is hard for me to take Hobbes's thesis totally seriously when trying to construct a moral picture for oneself.

Utilitarianism

A historical connection exists between Hobbes's hedonism and a very influential contemporary moral theory called **utilitarianism.** This view was first put forth in the late eighteenth and early nineteenth century by the British philosopher JEREMY BENTHAM (1748–1832). Then it was criticized and revised by his somewhat wayward disciple, JOHN STUART MILL (1806–1873). The essential difference between traditional hedonism and utilitarianism is that the former was egoistic in nature and the latter is social. That is that utilitarian hedonism requires that I include the interests of others when determining my own interests.

The Calculus of Felicity

Bentham, who may not have been one of the deepest philosophers in the Western tradition, was certainly one of the most practically oriented and influential. He had an active hand in the reformation of the British legal system of his day. Agreeing with Hobbes, Bentham began his philosophy with the assumption that, like it or not, we humans are all governed by a desire for pleasure and an aversion to pain. Unlike Hobbes, however, he did not conclude that therefore altruism was either impossible or unwise. Again like Hobbes, he believed we are endowed with reason and that therefore it is possible to give moral advice on how one should pursue the goal of the "pleasure principle" (Freud's term).

Bentham formulated his advice in what he called "the calculus of felicity." According to it, pleasure can be catalogued into seven categories, and this catalogue provides a rational analysis of pleasure. The seven categories are:

1. Intensity—how intense?
2. Duration—how long?
3. Certainty—how sure?
4. Propinquity—how soon?
5. Fecundity—how many more?
6. Purity—how free from pain?
7. Extent—how many people are affected?

On a scale of one to ten, this is a "ten" in all categories.

According to Bentham, whenever you consider performing any action, you can analyze its value in terms of these categories and contrast it with its alternatives. For example, say you need to study for tomorrow's chemistry examination, but it turns out that today promises to be the most glorious day of the year. The beach positively beckons. Try out the calculus of felicity on such a decision—between studying for a chemistry midterm and going to the beach with some friends. Obviously, the beach party will be strong in some categories (1, 3, 4, and 6) and weaker in others (2 and 5). Studying will be weak in most categories but strong in a few (2, and 5 and 7 also, if others have an interest in your succeeding in

Beach Guilt

college). Are the assets of studying strong enough to overcome its deficits in the face of the fun enticing you to the beach? (Of course, the guilt you would experience at the beach has to be taken into consideration too.)

We can imagine that if Bentham had lived in today's world of inexpensive calculators, he would have invented a pocket "calculator of felicity." There is something silly about the image of someone punching the values of various acts into a calculator, but Bentham thought that his calculus of felicity was actually the schematization of something we do semiconsciously (hence often poorly) anyway and that once we become experienced in manipulating these figures, we would be able to do it intuitively.

Looking back at the calculus of felicity, take note of category 7, "extent." It is this category that makes utilitarianism a form of *social* hedonism. One must consider the pleasures and pains of others and not only one's own. In fact, what Bentham and Mill call "the principle of utility" stresses precisely this aspect, which allows for the possibility of altruism in utilitarianism—"the greatest amount of happiness for the greatest number of people." If an act I am about to perform will bring about a great amount of happiness for a large number of people, then I should perform it even if it brings mostly misery to me.

Besides this social aspect of utilitarianism, there is also a democratic bias built into it—especially in Bentham's version. When it comes to evaluating acts in terms of the pleasure they will produce, Bentham firmly believed in the "one person, one vote" principle. Each person's judgment is as important as every other's. No one—be he your parent or the state—has the right to *inform* you that you are or are not having fun. According to Bentham, "Prejudice apart, the game of push-pin is of equal value with the arts and sciences of music and poetry. If the game of push-pin furnishes more pleasure, it is more valuable than either."[5]

The Quality of Pleasure

John Stuart Mill thought of himself as a disciple of Bentham, but he was clearly concerned about the implications of some of Bentham's formulations of utilitarianism. Mill feared that an adherent of the calculus of felicity might conclude that pushpin (or watching football on TV) *is* better than the arts and sciences, and Mill knew in his heart that such a conclusion is simply not true. Utilitarianism would have to be rewritten in such a way as to be able to demonstrate that the reading of Shakespearean sonnets is better than some of its alternatives. Part of the problem is that the calculus generates a purely quantitative analysis, and Mill was convinced that quality in pleasure was even more important than quantity. Furthermore, he feared that a literal application of the calculus of felicity would, over a number of generations, completely erode culture.

You are now enjoying yourselves! This is an official proclamation!

Fascistic Hedonism

What if you offered the following proposition to the electorate of a particular state: "It has been determined that the teaching of Shakespeare in the schools of this state costs each taxpayer $25 every five years. Now, the state would like to know if you taxpayers would prefer to continue paying $25 a person for the next five years of Shakespeare instruction or would prefer a rebate of $25 in the form of four cases of beer per voter." Mill was afraid that, given the tenuous foothold that culture has among the masses and given Bentham's "one person, one vote" principle, Shakespeare would lose out. In a number of generations, no one would even remember who Shakespeare was. (In fact, a

Go Niners!

Shakespeare or the NFL?

Tough Benthamite Decisions

similar proposition was presented to the voters of California in 1978. It was called "Proposition 13." The voters went for the beer.)

In order to counteract the possibility of this "leveling down" of culture, Mill insisted that it was part of our human heritage to have desires higher than those that lent themselves to analysis in terms of the calculus of felicity. He wrote:

> Few human creatures would consent to be changed into any of the lower animals for a promise of the fullest allowance of a beast's pleasures; no intelligent human being would consent to be a fool, no instructed person would be an ignoramus, no person of feeling and conscience would be selfish and base, even though they should be persuaded that the fool, the dunce, or the rascal is better satisfied with his lot than they are with theirs.[6]

Apparently, Mill felt that the "lower" desires (those of animals and perhaps the most biologically basic human desires) could be adequately dealt with in terms of the quantitative analysis provided by the calculus of felicity but that the "higher desires" could be talked about only in terms of *quality*, something no calculus could evaluate. According to Mill:

> It is quite compatible with the principle of utility to recognize the fact that some kinds of pleasure are more desirable and more valuable than others. It would be absurd that, while in estimating all other things quality is considered as well as quantity, the estimation of pleasure should be supposed to depend on quantity alone.
>
> If I am asked what I mean by difference of quality in pleasures, or what makes one pleasure more valuable than another, merely as a pleasure, except its being greater in amount, there is but one possible answer. Of two pleasures, if there be one to which all or almost all who have experience of both give a decided preference, irrespective of any feeling of moral obligation to prefer it, that is the more desirable pleasure. If one of the two is, by those who are competently acquainted with both, placed so far above the other that they prefer it, even though knowing it to be attended with a greater amount of discontent, and would not resign it for any quantity of the other pleasure which their nature is capable of, we are justified in ascribing to the preferred enjoyment a superiority in quality so far outweighing quantity as to render it, in comparison, of small account.[7]

Mill's objection is perhaps summed up in this famous line: "The uncultivated cannot be competent judges of cultivation."

**The Uncultivated Cannot Be
Competent Judges of Cultivation**

One can certainly be sympathetic to Mill's concerns. Bentham's calculus does seem to be a bit crass, and in a democracy, there is always the danger of every standard falling to the lowest common denominator. But Mill's solution to these problems brings about problems of its own. Mill can be accused of abandoning democracy for elitism and of abandoning hedonism altogether. The basis of the charge of elitism must be obvious. If one must demonstrate "competence" before one is granted a vote, then on many issues, only a small minority will have the right to express an opinion. This minority will probably tend to be the best educated, wealthiest, and most powerful segment of society. (In the United States, we have accepted a compromise version of Mill's solution. We are not a "participatory democracy" but a "representative democracy." Not everybody votes on all issues; rather, we elect representatives who in theory are, by virtue of their excellent education and their paid staff of assistants, competent to decide certain issues concerning which we ourselves have no competence. However, in some states, the citizens reserve the right, through the initiative process, to bypass those representatives on certain matters. This is how the system works in theory, though of course not always in practice.)

Let us now look at the charge that Mill has abandoned hedonism. In itself, this charge is perhaps not so devastating, though Mill himself would have been displeased by it. Mill accepts the basic principle of hedonism—the sole criterion of value is pleasure—but he also claims that some pleasures are *better* (more valuable) than others. We must ask—More valuable according to what criterion? It can't be just "pleasure" because some pleasures

POLLING PLACE
(only the competent will be allowed to vote*)

* Sheriff Billy Joe Bob will determine competency.

are *better,* and "better" here no longer means "more intense, purer, more lengthy, more certain, more imminent," and so on. Rather, it means "has more quality." But what is this elusive thing called "quality" that only the "competent" can recognize? In an odd way, we seem to have returned to the Platonic doctrine of *aretê* because one of the English translations of that word is "quality." But perhaps this result isn't so bad after all. In fact, most contemporary utilitarians feel no need to defend hedonistic principles. Rather than talking about "pleasure," they prefer to stick to the broader terms like "happiness," "interests," "well-being," and "human flourishing," without trying to "cash them out" in terms of specific ingredients.

Utilitarianism's Problems

On the face of it, utilitarianism is plausible. It does indeed appear that morality must essentially have something to do with promoting happiness and well-being and with minimizing unhappiness and misery. It would be odd to claim that some act was good even though it brought nothing but unhappiness and misery to absolutely everybody. Therefore, there must be something right about the opposite view (that an act is good if it brings happiness and well-being to everyone), which just happens to be utilitarianism's view. Still, some serious problems arise with utilitarianism. One of them has to do with its "consequentialist" nature (we will deal with this topic later in this section), and the other has to do with notions of *justice* and *meritoriousness.*

The problem of justice and meritoriousness can be revealed in a fictitious example. Suppose you had to go to court for failing to pay a few parking fines. You are alone in a small courtroom with the judge, the bailiff, and the court reporter. After the bailiff reads the charge ("failure to pay three fines for expired parking meters"), you respond ("Guilty, your Honor"), and she announces her judgment: "I find you guilty on all charges. The punishment will be that you shall suffer death at the hands of a firing squad." "What?!!" you scream. "Death for three lousy parking tickets??" The judge leans forward and whispers, "I know you don't deserve this punishment, but there has been a rash of murders in our community, and a study has just been released demonstrating that immediately after an execution, the crime rate drops substantially. Unfortunately, we don't have any convicted murderers on our hands right now. But we do have you, and there is every reason to believe that if we execute you, the public good will be served. Hence, even though my decision may seem unfair to you personally, it will certainly promote the greatest amount of happiness for the greatest number of people.

So it is the only judgment I can really reach in good conscience."

Take another example (one that appears in almost every critical discussion of utilitarianism and that even has a name—"the case of Sam"). Sam, a basically normal, rather nondescript but "nice" human being, goes to the hospital to visit his only living relative, his senile, sick aunt. His visit coincides with five medical emergencies at the hospital. One person needs a liver transplant, another a spleen transplant, another a lung transplant, another a new heart, and a fifth a new pineal gland. Each of the five patients is a tremendously important, much-loved person whose

Sam Visiting His Sick Aunt

death would bring a great deal of grief and actual physical discomfort to a great number of people. Sam's death, on the other hand, would be mourned by no one (except possibly by his aunt in her lucid moments). The top members of the hospital administration, all strict utilitarians, lure Sam into an operating room, remove all his vital organs, and distribute them to the other needy patients, thereby operating (literally) in accordance with the principle of utility: the greatest amount of happiness for the greatest number of people.

The reason these fictitious cases are so jarring is that they go so radically against our intuitive sense of justice and meritoriousness. Neither the parking meter violator nor Sam deserves the fate dished out by the executing judge and the hospital staff. Because these cases are compatible with utilitarianism, either something is wrong with our intuitive sense of justice or something is wrong with utilitarianism. Most people are probably more likely to jettison a *theory* than to go against their sense of justice.

Many contemporary utilitarians have recognized this problem and have tried to adjust utilitarian theory to correspond more with our intuitions. To this end, they have drawn a distinction between *act utilitarianism* and *rule utilitarianism*. Act utilitarianism is the traditional form. According to it, one must perform the specific *act* that will produce the greatest amount of happiness for the greatest number of people. Rule utilitarianism says, to the contrary, that in contemplating one of two acts, a person should perform that act governed by a (hypothetical) rule whose general obedience would produce the greatest amount of happiness. According to rule utilitarianism, even if a particular self-serving deceit or lie may go undetected, and hence cause no one any unhappiness, nevertheless I probably should not engage in it because, generally, lying and deceiving cause more unhappiness than happiness. It also means that the executing judge and the hospital administrators cannot proceed as they desire because the rule governing their acts would be something like this: "If the lives of a number of people (or even a few exceptional people) can be saved by sacrificing an innocent bystander, the sacrifice should be performed." But members of a community who knew that they might be set upon by the authorities and arbitrarily killed or disemboweled would be members of a community of fear, one whose citizens would be loath to set foot on the streets in daylight.

One critic has argued that rule utilitarianism can lead to unpalatable consequences. He asks—What about the Dutch family during World War II who defied the Nazis by hiding Jews in their attic? According to rule utilitarianism, would they be required to answer truthfully if the Gestapo came to their house looking for Jews (on the grounds that lying generally creates more unhappiness than does honesty and that therefore one may not lie)? But surely the rule utilitarian can operate according to the general rule: "Lying is wrong, except when directed to evildoers in order to save the lives of innocent people." The problem here is that one begins to suspect that the clever, self-serving rule utilitarian can think of a general rule to rationalize all sorts of questionable behavior. ("Shoplifting from large department stores is okay as

A Community of Fear

long as one doesn't get caught and no one ever finds out.") Such rationalizations would surely begin to unravel rule utilitarianism.

So the modification of traditional utilitarianism (or act utilitarianism) to rule utilitarianism may allow the utilitarian to meet the objection that utilitarianism does not square with our sense of justice and meritoriousness, but there was another related objection concerning utilitarianism's "consequentialist" nature. Notice that according to the view we are now studying, no act is good or bad in and of itself. Rather, an act is good or bad only in terms of its *consequences*. Acts that result in happiness, well-being, and flourishing are good; acts that result in the opposite are bad. Now, there is a certain prima facie plausibility to this view, but at some point it too runs up against the moral intuition of many, because a lot of us feel that certain acts, such as wanton cruelty, are

YELP!!

Mama! Isn't that bad?

Depends on its consequences

Consequentialism: The moral worth of act X depends on the consequences of X.	Nonconsequentialism: The moral worth of act X depends exclusively on act X.

bad in and of themselves regardless of their consequences. We also feel that some acts—those performed out of moral duty—are right independent of their consequences. The philosopher who most clearly defended a moral doctrine based on this kind of reasoning was Immanuel Kant.

Duty-Oriented Morality: Immanuel Kant

Immanuel Kant, whose epistemology we inspected briefly in Chapter 3, took a strictly nonconsequentialistic view of ethics. For him, the empirical consequences or results of an act had nothing whatsoever to do with the moral worth of the act. In fact, according to him, any attempt to justify an act by appealing to its consequences immediately removes the act from the ethical sphere. In order to demonstrate this point, Kant distinguishes between two kinds of "oughts" or "shoulds"—a *moral* ought, which he calls a **categorical imperative,** and a merely *practical* ought, which he calls a **hypothetical imperative.** Let's illustrate this distinction. Suppose I say to you, "You know, you really ought not to come to class with your shoes untied, with your fly open, and eating ice cream that is melting down your arm and dripping off your elbow." You ask, "Why not?" I say, "Because you look like a fool when you do that!" You approach me and whisper in my ear, "That's exactly the impression I *want* to give. Actually, I'm an undercover agent tailing a suspected terrorist who is in your class." I respond, "Oh! Well, in *that* case, you *ought* to do just as you are doing because you appear to be a *perfect* fool." This conversation contains examples of hypothetical imperatives. The imperative (ought) can be placed in the "then" clause of a hypothetical conditional sentence.

Undercover Agent

IF you don't want __X__ ,

$\underbrace{\qquad\qquad\qquad\qquad}$
hypothesis

THEN you ought to __Y__ .

$\underbrace{\qquad\qquad\qquad}$
condition

In hypothetical imperatives, the ought can be defeated by rejecting the if clause of the hypothesis ("Oh, but I *want* to look like a fool. . . ."). This analysis shows what's wrong with the following exchange:

Fran: "You ought not to steal my car."
Jan: "Why not?"
Fran: "Because they'll put you in jail."

Jan can always rejoin, "Oh, but I *want* to go to jail. I've decided that I can't afford life on the outside. I'd like to have the state provide me with room and board. Having seen the TV series, *Orange Is the New Black,* I even think my social life would improve in prison. Therefore, it seems to me that the most certain way of achieving my goals is to steal your car." Fran now seems to be in the curious position of having to assert, "Oh, in that case, you *ought* to steal my car."

According to Kant, a truly *moral* ought cannot be conditional upon any individual's desires. It must be *absolute*— that is, universal and exceptionless—or as he calls it, "categorical." Are there any such moral demands, and how would we demonstrate their existence? According to Kant, there are indeed such moral oughts, and once we have discovered them we can discern what our moral duty is.

They are rooted in a certain fact about human nature, namely, the fact that we are *rational* beings. (Notice that utilitarianism is rooted in the fact that we are *passionate* beings—that we have desires. Kantianism is rooted in a very different fact about us—that we have reason. Kantianism, like Platonism, contains more than the subtle implication that reason should override desire.)

The principle behind the categorical imperative is a principle that every rational agent must accept. Refusing to do so would be tantamount to abandoning one's rationality, leading to "the obliteration of one's dignity as a human being." Let us state the categorical imperative: "Act only according to that maxim by which you can at the same time will that it should become a universal law."[8] A related version of the categorical imperative (call the first one "version A" and this new one "version B") states, "Act as if the maxim of your action were to become by your will a universal law of nature." These two versions of the categorical imperative presuppose that it is possible to state the general principle behind any act you may consider performing. Before engaging in an act (such as helping your neighbor fix her flat tire), you can ask, "What principle (maxim) governs this act?" In this case, it might be "It is good to help one's fellow human in distress." Now, according to version A of the categorical imperative, we are to universalize our principle to see if any logical contradiction appears in that universalization. In other words, is the world conceived by the universalization of my principle illogical in the way that a game would be illogical and hence unplayable if its rules contradicted each other? Is there any logical contradiction in the idea of a world in which everyone always helps a fellow human in distress?

A World in Which Everyone Repairs the Neighbor's Flat Tire

If so, I cannot will such a world without contradiction. Version B of the categorical imperative yields what we might call an empirical or a material criterion of self-contradiction rather than a logical criterion. It says, imagine a world in which everyone always helps fellow humans in the same manner that the moon always orbits the earth, that is, out of necessity. Would such a world be factually possible? For example, imagine a world called "World X" in which everyone was obliged to help others in need. There is no logical contradiction caused by this obligation in World X. Now, imagine a world called World Y in which everyone is obliged to fly (like a bird) to help others. This is a materially impossible world because—as it turns out—no one but birds that can fly like a bird. So, I can will World X but not World Y. If so, I can will such as World X without contradicting myself. In the case of helping one's neighbor, it appears that there is no contradiction, either logical or material, under either test. So far, then, the conclusion is that there is no moral law preventing me from helping my neighbor. I *may* help her, but (so far) nothing says that I *must* help her.

Now let's try it in the negative. What if I don't feel like helping out my distressed neighbor? If I'm a Kantian, I must ask these questions in order to find out whether I am duty-bound to assist her:

1. Can I conceive of a logically consistent world in which nobody helps out others in distress? (version A)
2. Can I conceive of a materially consistent world in which nobody helps out others in distress (i.e., for psychophysical reasons, they couldn't help each other even if they wanted to)? (version B)

In the first case, there seems to be no logical self-contradiction. It's not like trying to conceive of a world full of square circles. (So far, I'm off the hook. Let her fix her own flat tire!) But according to Kant, in the second case—version B—there is a contradiction. Based on his speculations about human nature, he concluded that human beings are interdependent. Only pathologically are they ever truly solitary individuals. (This view he shares with the ancient Greeks and, as you will see, with Hegel and Marx.) Not only would a maxim denying the duty to help others prevent human babies from surviving, but even "rugged individuals" need support. For Kant, this claim is an empirical one, not a logical one.

Because human life cannot flourish without mutual assistance, version B of the categorical imperative says I have a moral duty to help my neighbor. (Darn! There goes my football game.)

Let's try these principles out on some other cases. Let's suppose that you owe a friend five dollars, and to your annoyance, he pressurizes you to repay. So

LAW OF THE LAND
Everyone must kill someone

you say to yourself, "If I kill him, I won't have to repay the debt." But as a true Kantian, you first check to see if you could universalize the principle governing the proposed action. You ask yourself, what if everyone accomplished his goals by killing someone? Could there exist a universal law, "Everyone ought to kill someone"? This would be an impossible law, because if everyone complied with it, there would be no one left to comply with it. In this case, it is the material contradiction that kicks in. Therefore, we are duty-bound not to kill as a way of solving problems. OK, then, what if you lie to your friend, telling him that you already repaid the debt? Can the principle behind this proposal be universalized? Could there be a general law, "Everyone ought always to lie"? Obviously not, because it would be impossible even to state the law without breaking it. This is a *logical* fact. Therefore, we are duty-bound not to lie. Well, what if you repay the five dollars, then steal them back? Can the principle behind this act be universalized? Imagine a general law saying, "Everyone ought always to steal." But this, too, is an impossible law for both logical and material reasons because the concept of stealing is parasitical upon the concept of *property*.

Where Theft Is the Law of the Land

If everyone always steals, there can be no property; there can only be temporary possession, that is, stuff passing from person to person. So we are also duty-bound to refrain from stealing. (If you are a true Kantian, it's beginning to look as though you will have to pay your debt!)

Kant's Strengths and Weaknesses

Some interesting things are going on in duty-oriented morality. There is some genuine insight and there are some serious problems, too. Let's talk first about the positive features. Kant's moral philosophy recognizes that an essential aspect of morality is the need to view the world, including one's own actions, from the point of view of others. We need to climb out of our own shoes and stand in the shoes of other people. (This view Kant shares with utilitarianism and with Jesus's "golden rule," though the latter two moral codes are based on the universalizability of desire, and Kant's is based on the universalizability of reason. So Kant doesn't ask, "If everyone behaved like that, how would *you* like it?" He doesn't really care what you *like*. Rather he asks, "If everyone behaved like that, would the standards of reason and dignity still be maintained?" The individual is forced out of subjectivism and selfishness, because he realizes that it is unreasonable to demand for himself special exemption from universal laws.) Kant's principles

Standing in Someone Else's Shoes

are fine tools for revealing hypocrisy—that of others or oneself. If it is wrong for someone to take my property without my permission, then it is wrong when I take the property of another person without permission. I am a hypocrite if I claim that it is theft when you take my stereo but that it is simply redistribution of wealth when I take your stereo. Kant is correct. If it is wrong for you to take mine, then, in circumstances that are identical in all relevant respects, it is wrong for me to take yours.

I cannot tell a lie. She's over there.

But the problems with Kant's theory lie in the same area as do its strengths. There is something too absolutist about his view. If a heavily armed madman, frothing at the mouth, asks me if I know where Sue Smith is, and I realize that he intends to kill her if he finds her, my moral intuition tells me that I *ought* to lie—in fact, that it would be immoral to tell the truth. Yet Kant says that I must tell the truth even to a murderous madman, on the grounds that the principle behind lying cannot be universalized without contradiction.

Critics of Kant have pointed out something that was mentioned in connection with rule utilitarianism, namely, that it is possible to generate modified rules that can be universalized, such as this one: "One ought to lie when doing so will save the life of an innocent person." Kant argued against such modifications on the grounds that they destroy the universalizability of the rule by making it more context bound, but many critics find this argument unpersuasive and point out that Kant believed in capital punishment for capital crimes; hence, Kant himself was modifying his injunction against killing. It does seem that only by accepting in principle the possibility of modifying Kant's general rules can we save his moral philosophy from absurdity.

Kant thought that acts whose principle cannot be universalized cannot in any way commit us to moral obligation. This belief seems correct for reasons mentioned previously. (Reminder: If an act is declared to be bad when *you* perform it, then an act that is the same in all relevant respects must be bad when *I* perform it, in exactly the same way that if this figure → △ is a triangle when *you* draw it, then it must also be a triangle when *I* draw it.) But from this principle, how can we generate the concept of *duty*, which is so close to Kant's heart? Surely we don't have a moral obligation to perform every act whose maxim can be generalized. (I like to smile when I see birds. The maxim behind that act might be "It is good to express joy in the presence of pretty things." This maxim *can* be generalized without contradiction, but it's hard to believe that therefore we all have a moral obligation to smile at birds, to whistle in the dark, or to clear our throat before scratching our nose.)

The Moral Obligation to Smile at Birds

Kant agrees. He does not argue that we have a duty to perform every act whose maxim can be universalized, only that such acts are morally permissible. What gives an act *moral* worth is not simply the fact that it *can* be universalized but also the fact that it was chosen as a moral act. Our duty is not only that of performing any specific acts but also to choose only acts that can be universalized; and what makes them *moral* is that we choose them in order to be performing our duty. In the first sentence of his *Foundations of the Metaphysics of Morals* (1785), Kant says, "Nothing in the world—indeed nothing even beyond the world—can possibly be conceived which could be called good without qualification except a *goodwill*" (p. 9). What he means by "goodwill" is the *will* to do one's duty. The same act—let's again say the act of helping your neighbor fix her flat tire—may be moral, morally neutral, or even immoral, depending on its motivation. (Here we see the big difference between utilitarianism, which is con-

Expectation of Reward

Pity

Duty

Three Different Motives for Helping Your Neighbor Fix Her Flat

sequentialist in nature, and Kantianism, which is *nonconsequentialist*. That is, for Kant, the act's moral worth is not only determined by its *results* but also by its *intention*.) The act is immoral if my motivation is to deceive her into thinking that I'm a nice guy so she will bestow favors on me. It is morally neutral if the reason I helped her is because I felt sorry for her. (Mere *feelings* can never be the basis of morality, according to Kant.) The act is moral only if my motive for performing it is the desire to do my duty. Kant is surely right to think that the agent's intention must be considered when assigning moral worth (an act motivated by pure greed is not *morally* worthy even if it happens to benefit

I find you disgusting. But I'm going to help you anyway

A Kantian Hero

many). But there is something disturbing going on here. Kant thought that the Good Samaritan who helped the wounded stranger because the Samaritan's heart went out to the suffering human being had not performed a peculiarly moral act; yet he thought that a Good Samaritan who *loathes* people, including the man he helps, yet helps him nevertheless out of a sense of duty, is a *moral* man. A coldness lurks in the heart of this doctrine. Perhaps feelings cannot be the sole criterion of moral worth, but they certainly enter into the picture in a big way. A truly good person must have sympathy and empathy for a fellow human being. Thank goodness this icy side of Kant's moral philosophy can be ignored without damaging his insights about universalizability.

Kant's Third Formulation

Kant presented his categorical imperative in several forms. His third formulation runs like this: "Act so that you treat humanity, whether in your own person or in that of another, always as an end and never as a means only" (p. 47). Apparently Kant thought that this formulation was simply another way of stating his first version, which itself was an expression of the principle of universalizability. Whether such an identity between the two versions exists is certainly debatable. Kantian specialist Allen Wood argues that the first two versions (A and B) of the categorical imperative are meant to be not the equivalent of the third version but rather steps leading to it and that this third version is the essence of Kant's moral philosophy. Because Wood believes that this third version holds good on its own, he minimizes the problems in the first two versions on which critics dwell.[9] In any case, it appears to be true that the principle of universalizability prohibits one from using other people for one's own ends. At any rate, Kant is suggesting that any-one who is committed to rationality is

Using People as Pawns

also committed to treating other people as "ends in themselves" and not as pawns in one's own game of personal advantage. To verify Kant's suggestion, we will have to summarize in a very cursory manner some complicated arguments that he presents in his *Foundations of the Metaphysics of Morals*.

Kant believed that, if there were no *persons* in the world, only *things*, there would be no *values*. Nothing would be worth anything more or less than anything else. There are values in the world only because there are persons—that is, individual entities that have not only desires (animals, too, have desires) but also rationality and freedom. Something is valuable only relative to a human goal. Then, as the source of values, humans have *dignity*, which Kant defines as something so valuable that nothing could transcend it in worth. Therefore, to claim one's status as a human—that is, to claim one's dignity—one must value above all else that which bestows dignity and humanness on one, that is, rationality, freedom, and autonomy. One must value absolutely the rationality, freedom, and autonomy not only of oneself but also of individuals other than oneself. Or, in Kant's words, one must treat them as ends in themselves.

There are some striking features of Kant's position here. Despite his argument's highly abstract nature, its conclusion squares with the very wide-spread moral intuition that it is wrong to use (exploit) people for one's own benefit. Furthermore, if that conclusion is accepted, it can be the basis of taking positions on such morally loaded topics as euthanasia, abortion, racism, equal rights, and feminism. But, of course, some difficulties remain. First, it seems to me that the ecological crisis we humans have provoked must force us to realize that any adequate moral code today will have to be one that demonstrates some responsibility to the natural world. A doctrine like that of Kant, which says that nature has value only as a means to human ends, must seem to us today to be not just a bit arrogant but perhaps ironi-cally even dangerous—ironic because that doctrine is itself not conducive to human ends. Second, arguments as abstract as that of Kant are hard to evaluate and are not always very compel-ling. (Pointing this out, of course, does *not refute* Kant's argument.) Third, the difference between using people as a means and treating them as ends-in-themselves is not always clear. Kant says we may not treat peo-ple "as a means only." How about as a means *mostly?* For example, I must admit that one of my main motivations in teaching philosophy is to earn a living for myself. Does that prove that I am using my students as means to satisfy my own ends? What if I am deeply committed to teaching my students philosophy but try along the way to extort money and sex from them? Fourth, real-life situations often present us with dilemmas in which no matter what we do, our act can be interpreted as using someone. For example, the existentialist philosopher Jean-Paul Sartre demonstrates an example of a genuine moral dilemma. He cites the case of one of his students who, during the German occupation of France, approached him for advice. The young man came to Sartre under the following circumstances:

> His father was on bad terms with his mother, and, moreover, was inclined to be a collaborationist; his older brother had been killed in the German offensive of 1940, and the young man, with somewhat immature but generous feelings, wanted to avenge him. His mother lived alone with him, very much upset by the half-treason of her husband and the death of her older son; the boy was her only consolation.
>
> The boy was faced with the choice of leaving for England and joining the Free French Forces—that is, leaving his mother behind—or remaining with his mother and helping her to carry on. . . . Who could help him choose? Christian doctrine? No. Christian doctrine says, "Be charitable, love your neighbor, take the more rugged path, etc., etc." But which is the more rugged path? Whom should he love as a brother? The fighting man or his mother? Which does the greater good, the vague act of fighting in a group, or the concrete one of helping a particular human being to go on living? Who can decide *a priori*? Nobody. No book of ethics can tell him. The Kantian ethics says, "Never treat a person as a means, but as an end." Very well, if I stay with my mother I'll treat her as an end and not as a means; but by virtue of this very fact, I'm running the risk of treating the people around me who are fighting, as means; and, conversely, if I go to join those who are fighting, I'll be treating them as an end, and, by doing that, I run the risk of treating my mother as a means. . . . You will say, "At least, he did go to a teacher for advice." But if you seek advice from a priest, for example, you have chosen this priest; you already knew, more or less, just about what advice he was going to give you. In other words, choosing your adviser is involving yourself. The proof of this is that if you are Christian, you will say, "Consult a priest." But some priests are collaborating, some are just marking time, some are resisting. Which to choose? If the young man chooses a priest who is resisting or collaborating, he has already decided on the kind of advice he's going to get. Therefore, in coming to see me he knew the answer I was going to give him, and I had one answer to give: "You're free, choose, that is, invent." No general ethics can show you what is to be done; there are no omens in the world.[10]

From this story we see that, even accepting Kant's categorical imperative in any of its forms, we still might be confronted with real moral situations in which Kant's philosophy is of little help to us. In fact, Sartre himself accepted Kant's view that to claim our status as human beings we must recognize ourselves and others as autonomous, free, and rational, but Sartre obviously held that ultimately our freedom overrides our rationality. Ultimately, our freedom, not our rationality, generates values. Kant would surely see this Sartrean view as a form of subjective irrationalism (more on Sartre in the next chapter).

Kantianism Today?

A number of contemporary philosophers still call themselves utilitarians, but very few are willing to call themselves Kantians. However, this does not mean that Kantianism is dead. First, Kantianism still lives (and lived long before Kant) as an aspect of everyday morality. Kant's categorical imperative is in many ways a highly technical rendition of the moral wisdom that parents have imparted to their children from time immemorial, "How would you like it if someone did that to you?" This idea is also expressed in Jesus's golden rule: Do unto others as you would have them do unto you. I have pointed out that when Kant refined this principle, he may have overreacted in removing individual desire and moral sentiment from the formula, replacing them with "reason" (logic); but he nevertheless seems to have captured the essence of the universalizability of the age-old principle. In fact, it may well be that each of the historical ethical movements that we have inspected in this chapter (Platonism, egoism, utilitarianism, and Kantianism) is derived from one of several main moral intuitions that altogether make up what we might call the common moral map that most of us follow and that the real job is to see if each part of this map can be made consistent with all the other parts, without creating contradictions and therefore moral dilemmas.

But, to pursue the question I raised above, if there are so few recognized "Kantians" in professional philosophy, what is the status today of Kant's moral theory? We will take a brief look at a contemporary view that has descended from Kant's moral philosophy.

Contractualism

Contemporary versions of **contractualism** have been defended by both JOHN RAWLS (1921–2002) and T. M. SCANLON (1940–). In Chapter 9, you will study Rawls's theory of justice, and perhaps you will notice certain similarities between that theory and some of Kant's main principles. Here, we will look at a simplified version of Scanlon's contractualism, which is sometimes characterized as "morality by agreement." According to the contractual formula that Scanlon suggests, "thinking about right and wrong is, at the most basic level, thinking about what could be justified to others on grounds that they, if appropriately motivated, could not reasonably reject."[11] Now, the contractual formula may appear so obvious as to be tautological. In other words, someone might say that going on a killing spree is wrong, and therefore, no one could "reasonably reject" a rule against it. But for Scanlon, it's the other way around. Rather than the idea of "reasonable rejection" being derived from moral views, moral views are derived from the idea of reasonable rejection (as in Kant). We live in a world with other human beings, and we want to be able to justify ourselves to them. We do this by showing that we have good reason for comporting ourselves the way we do. Justifiability is the basis of moral motivation, not sentiment, self-interest, or utility (again, as in Kant).

When Scanlon says that our acts must be motivated by reasons, he means *good* reasons. Perhaps that qualification does not need to be added, because the phrase *"rational person"* may cover the problem. A rational person is one who is motivated by good reasons rather than bad ones. If you fall out of a boat, you have good reason to want to swim toward shore, and we need no further explanation of your act of swimming than that. We *would* need a further explanation if you tried to *fly* to shore, however. For example, says Scanlon, we all recognize that everyone needs privacy; hence, nobody could reasonably reject a principle granting the *right to privacy*. Also, we know that people have good reason to avoid suffering and premature death and to hope "that their lives go well in other respects" (p. 86). Similarly, people have reason to want the freedom to pursue their own projects and be near friends and family. Therefore, there is a *right to the pursuit of happiness without unreasonable restriction* that could not reasonably be rejected. Also, we know that people have "strong reasons to want to be able to rely on assurances they are given, and to have control over what happens to their own bodies. We therefore think it is reasonable to reject principles that would leave other agents free to act against these important interests" (p. 204). So we can add that we owe to each other *the right to move freely without fear of physical assault, battery, rape, or murder,* and an obligation *not to lie or break promises* (though, unlike in Kant's theory, this obligation is not absolute).

The examples I have listed so far are negative, being obligations requiring us *not* to act in certain ways against others. Scanlon also deduces certain principles that put us under a positive obligation to *perform* certain acts. One is designated as the "Rescue Principle": "If you are presented with a situation in which you can prevent something very bad from happening, or alleviate someone's dire plight, by making only a slight (or even moderate) sacrifice, then it would be wrong not to do so" (p. 224). Contractualism cannot tell us how much sacrifice is required in any specific case, but it does require a

The Rescue Principle: "A Slight or Moderate Sacrifice . . . "

judgment concerning this from each of us. Another principle that no one could reasonably reject is the "Principle of Helpfulness": "If you can be of great help to someone and save that person a great amount of effort without placing any significant hardship on yourself, then you should render aid" (p. 224).

As was mentioned earlier, there are connections between Scanlon's theory and that of Kant. Some commentators go so far as to call Scanlon a "neoKantian."[12] We can see this possibility if we write Scanlon's contractual formula in Kantian language: "So act that the principle governing what you do could be justified to others on grounds that they, if appropriately motivated, could not reasonably reject" (p. 373). In this form, Scanlon's formula sounds remarkably like Kant's categorical imperative, despite Scanlon's occasional insistence on the differences between them. There are other similarities as well. For example, Scanlon offers a formula for deciding how far one's obligations extend: "If C counts in favor of my ø-ing in conditions S, then it counts in favor of ø-ing for any other person whose situation is similar in relevant respects" (p. 373). (The symbol "ø-ing" represents any verb designating an action, such as "helping," "shooting," "eating," or "truth-telling.") This looks to be the same kind of principle of universalizability to which Kant appeals over and over.

Scanlon believes, however, that the main thing wrong with Kant's system is its formalism. It appeals almost exclusively to the logic of rules and tries to derive moral standards from the very nature of rationality. But, says Scanlon, if rationality and morality were so closely equated, it would mean that people who rejected Kant's ethics (or other kinds of ethical standards) are irrational. In fact, "the fault involved in failing to be moved by moral requirements does not seem to be a form of incoherence" (p. 151). The person who does not understand that murder, rape, and torture are wrong seems more in need of a cure than of a correction of his logic. There seems to be a distinction in ordinary language between rationality and reasonableness according to which the former is more cold and calculating than the latter, and Scanlon thinks that this distinction between rationality and reasonableness is important. Kant appears to think that he can derive morality from the very nature of rationality, which itself is not a part of morality. It may appear that Scanlon is doing something similar, but the big difference is that he thinks that the nature of reasonableness itself is already complicit with morality. A person who searches for reasons for his actions has already taken into consideration the concerns of others, which is already to engage in morality. In Scanlon's theory, we are forced to consider seriously the concerns of other people and not just the laws of logic, and this gives his theory substance.

Virtue Ethics

We will once again return to ancient Greece for the roots of our last moral theory, Virtue Ethics, because ARISTOTLE (384–322 B.C.E.) is seen to be the founder of this school of thought that has experienced a revival in contemporary philosophy. Aristotle looked at every object in the universe teleologically—that is, in terms of goals, purposes, and functions—and thought of every object as struggling for self-realization, thereby producing a metaphysics that many would call outdated in today's post-Darwinian world. However, though most of us no longer think in terms of the "purpose" or "function" of the human being, we do treat most human activity teleologically, talking of behavior as motivated by reasons, purposes, and intentions rather than merely by causes (with the exception of accidents and other unintentional events or processes, such as heartbeats), so Aristotle's goal of self-realization may make more sense in the case of the human being (more than when he speaks of acorns having the goal of becoming an oak tree).

Moral Bad Luck

Aristotle writes:

> . . . a human being's function we posit as being a kind of life, and this life as being activity of soul and actions accompanied by reason, and it belongs to a good man to perform these well and finely, and each thing is completed well when it possesses its proper excellence.[13]

The English word "excellence" was used here to translate the Greek word *aretê*, which you have already run into, sometimes translated as "virtue." For Aristotle, there are two kinds of virtue: intellectual and moral. Intellectual virtue is acquired partly by having a good brain and using it to fullest advantage in your educational studies. Moral virtue requires the development of good habits that result in "states of character"—that is, in dispositions to act in certain ways—and these states of character are virtuous for Aristotle if they result in acts that are in accordance with "a golden mean of moderation." For Aristotle, a "mean" is a position taken between two extremes; he calls one extreme "deficiency" and an opposite extreme "excess." Both extremes are vices, and the mean is a virtue. For example, when it comes to facing danger, one can act with excess, that is, show too much bravado (foolhardiness), or one can act deficiently, showing too much fear (cowardliness). Or one can act with moderation—courage. (General George Custer was certainly no coward, but was he courageous or foolhardy?)

An important feature of Aristotle's "virtue ethics" is the realization that the golden mean is not simply an arithmetical issue. (It would be an error to think that the mean is halfway between excess and deficiency, so all you really need is a ruler.) Rather, the necessary choices cannot be made scientifically; they are always context-bound and made through trial and error. For example, concerning giving alms, stinginess is *deficiency*, wastefulness is *excess*, and generosity is a *virtue*. When Aristotle says that the generous person gives away just the right amount, that amount is always relative to what he can afford. Moreover, the generous man here does not give money to just anybody, but to the right person, in a timely manner, and for a good reason. Giving generously to a drunken spendthrift is not a virtuous act, hence is not true generosity. By the way, when Aristotle talks about a generous *man*, he means man. Women are incapable of true self-realization because, according to Aristotle, females have incomplete souls. Modern virtue theorists simply jettison Aristotle's sexism, along with his racism, elitism, approval of slavery, and emphasis on military virtues. In fact, a large number of such contemporary theorists are, coincidentally, women philosophers. This list includes Rosalind Hursthouse, G. E. M. Anscombe, Martha Nussbaum, Susan Wolf, Iris Murdoch, and Philippa Foot, among others.

Following Aristotle's claim that ethics cannot be an exact science, modern virtue ethics seems to reject the idea that morality can be codified (i.e., set forth in a list of binding rules, like a legal code) because its idea of a moral agent is always contextualized in historical situations, hence, in a sense, relativized. As virtue theorist John McDowell says, "Occasion by occasion, one knows what to do, if one does, not by applying universal principles but by being a certain kind of person: one who sees situations in a certain kind of way."[14]

Besides rejecting as artificial the kind of program of codification and absolutism that we found in Kant, virtue ethics also mounts an attack on the consequentialism of the utilitarians. Elizabeth Anscombe, one of the pioneers of modern virtue ethics, writing in the mid–twentieth century, argued that because it is impossible to know all the consequences of any act, consequentialism is empty because it cannot advocate any act at all except the most simple and uncontroversial ones. She says that a consequentialist has no footing on which to say "This would be permissible, this not"; because by his own hypothesis, it is the consequences that are to decide, and "he has no business to pretend that he can lay it down what possible twists a man could give doing this or that. . . .[H]e has no right to say he will, in an actual case, bring about such-and-such unless he does so-and-so."[15]

The virtue theorists are convinced that one of Kant's major errors was to characterize the emotions as always irrational and hence as an enemy of moral effort, never as a motive of moral effort. In contrast, Aristotle had said that virtuous actions are performed with the *right* feelings and emotions behind them. Sometimes we *should* feel love, sometimes we *should* feel righteous indignation, or even anger, as we act in the world. The Kantian agent that acts only out of duty is a hollow individual. Coldness of heart is a vice, no matter what the coldhearted agent's motives are.

Unforeseen Consequences of Kicking Puppies

Like every moral theory, virtue ethics has had its critics. A primary one is the charge of circularity in defining "practical wisdom," an idea that is central to Aristotle's explication of this quality. According to the *Nicomachean Ethics*, "Excellence [*aretê*] is a disposition issuing in decisions, depending on intermediacy [i.e., means] of the kind relative to us, this being determined by a rational prescription and in the way in which the wise person would do it" (p. 117, sec. 1107a1). It sounds as though "virtue" is defined as "what a virtuous person does." (Other translations have "as a man of practical wisdom would determine it." The Greek word for "the man of practical wisdom" is *phronimos*.) Indeed, Aristotle does believe that to a large extent, virtue is learned by imitation. Robert Louden, for instance, asks, "But who are the *phronimoi*? And how do we know one when we see one?"[16]

Several virtue theorists have responded, trying to establish that virtue can be defined in ways other than by observing virtuous agents. One interesting solution is provided by Martha Nussbaum, who suggests that much can be learned about what Aristotle called practical wisdom by reading the kind of fiction that deals with precisely situations in which this kind of wisdom is tested. In her book *Love's Knowledge*, the key literary heroes seem to be the ancient Greek dramatists, as well as Dickens, Proust, and, most saliently, the American-English novelist of the late nineteenth and early

Martha Nussbaum Interviews Aristotle

twentieth centuries, Henry James (brother of the philosopher William James). Nussbaum states her project clearly:

> My aim is to establish that certain literary texts (or texts similar to these in certain relevant ways) are indispensable to a philosophical inquiry in the ethical sphere: not by any means sufficient, but sources of inquiry without which the inquiry cannot be complete.[17]

Conclusion

I shall not attempt to reach any conclusion concerning ethical theory until we have examined some attacks on its foundation in the next chapter.

Topics for Consideration

1. Socrates does not deny that the immoral person is able to take advantage of the moral person in matters of money and business, yet ultimately, according to Socrates, the moral person wins out over the immoral one. Why?
2. What psychological and sociological presuppositions are there behind Socrates's simile, "The soul is like the city"? How successful is that simile in your view?
3. In this chapter, it is argued that the truth of Hobbes's egoism can never be established empirically (i.e., by appealing to evidence). Defend or attack that view.
4. Can you reconcile John Stuart Mill's apparently contradictory views that (a) pleasure is the sole criterion of value and (b) some pleasures are better than other pleasures?
5. Can rule utilitarianism resolve the dilemma presented to the principle of utility ("greatest amount of happiness for the greatest number of people") in "the case of Sam"?
6. Why does Kant think that the only morally right actions are those whose "maxim" can be universalized?
7. Explain how utilitarianism and Kantianism, respectively, would treat each of these cases:
   A. The case of a physician assisting the suicide of a terminally ill patient.
   B. The case of a person of modest means stealing money from a careless millionaire who will never know he's been robbed.
   C. The case of a woman lying to her dying father who urges her to promise that she will not marry anyone of a religion different from that of the father.
   D. The case of a person offered a large sum of money to execute another person whom everyone detests.

8. Defend or attack Kant's view that it is always wrong to use other people for one's own purposes.
9. If morality is really "by contract," as Scanlon seems to hold, are there no moral truths except those upon which we reach agreement?
10. According to Aristotle, why can ethics never become an "exact science"?
11. In the list of moral philosophies you have studied in this chapter, which would you classify as **moral realism** and which as moral relativism or subjectivism?

Suggestions for Further Reading: Paperback Editions

Gilbert Harman, *The Nature of Morality* (New York: Oxford University Press, 1977). A book on the topic of this chapter by an important American philosopher.

Immanuel Kant, *Foundations of the Metaphysics of Morals,* trans. Lewis White Beck (Indianapolis, IN: Bobbs-Merrill Publishing, 1976). A classic of moral philosophy; certainly not easy on the face of it, but short! And now that you are somewhat familiar with the argument, you can follow most of this important book.

Plato, "Republic," in *Great Dialogues of Plato,* trans. W. H. D. Rouse (New York: New American Library, 1956). Particularly Book I, where Plato presents the moral debate between Socrates and the Sophists, and Books II, III, IV, and V, where he develops the analogy between "the soul" and "the city."

Jean-Paul Sartre, *Existentialism and Human Emotions,* trans. Bernard Frechtman and Hazel Barnes (New York: Philosophical Library, 2000). Sartre promised to write a big book on ethics. He never did. This will have to do. It is short and readable.

T. M. Scanlon, *What We Owe to Each Other* (Cambridge, MA and London: Harvard University Press, 1998). A bit tough for beginners, but Scanlon is a good, clear thinker and expresses himself well, so a little work will pay off.

Allen W. Wood, *Kant's Ethical Thought* (Cambridge, England: Cambridge University Press, 1999). A readable but detailed and technical attempt to correct errors that the author thinks most interpreters of Kant (including people like me) have made.

Notes

1. Plato, "Republic," in *Great Dialogues of Plato,* trans. W. H. D. Rouse (New York: New American Library, 1956), p. 137. Unless otherwise stated, all subsequent quotes from the *Republic* in this chapter are from this edition.
2. Bernard Williams, *Ethics and the Limits of Philosophy* (Cambridge, MA: Harvard University Press, 1985), p. 27.
3. Thomas Hobbes, *Leviathan: Or the Matter, Forme and Power of a Commonwealth Ecclesiasticall and Civil* (New York: Collier Books, 1962), p. 105.
4. Ibid., pp. 49–50.

5. Jeremy Bentham, "The Rationale of Reward," in *The Works of Jeremy Bentham* (Edinburgh, Scotland: Tait, 1838–1843), vol. II, sec. i, p. 253.

6. John Stuart Mill, *Utilitarianism* (New York: E. P. Dutton, 1951), p. 10.

7. Ibid.

8. Immanuel Kant, *Foundations of the Metaphysics of Morals* [1785], trans. Lewis White Beck (Indianapolis, IN: Bobbs-Merrill Publishing, 1976), p. 39. Page numbers of future quotations from this book will be included in the text.

9. Allen W. Wood, *Kant's Ethical Thought* (Cambridge, England: Cambridge University Press, 1999).

10. Jean-Paul Sartre, *Existentialism and Human Emotions* (New York: Philosophical Library, 1957), pp. 24–28.

11. T. M. Scanlon, *What We Owe to Each Other* (Cambridge, MA and London: Harvard University Press, 1998), p. 5. Page numbers of future quotations from this book will be included in the text.

12. For example, Gary Watson, "Some Considerations in Favor of Contractualism," in *Contractarianism/Contractualism*, ed. Stephen Darwall (Oxford, England and Malden, MA: Blackwell Publishing, 2003), pp. 249–269, p. 259.

13. Aristotle, *Nicomachean Ethics*, trans. Sarah Broadie and Christopher Rowe (Oxford, England and New York: Oxford University Press, 2002), p. 102, sec. 1098a.

14. John McDowell, "Virtue and Reason," collected in *Virtue Ethics*, eds. Roger Crisp and Michael Slote (Oxford, England: Oxford University Press, 1998), pp. 141–162, pp. 161–162.

15. G. E. M. Anscombe, "Modern Moral Philosophy," collected in Crisp and Slote, *Virtue Ethics*, pp. 26–44, p. 38.

16. Robert B. Louden, "On Some Vices of Virtue Ethics," collected in Crisp and Slote, *Virtue Ethics*, pp. 201–216, p. 212.

17. Martha Nussbaum, *Love's Knowledge: Essays on Philosophy and Literature* (New York and Oxford, England: Oxford University Press, 1990), pp. 23–24.

8

Different Strokes for Different Folks
Six Critiques of Traditional Ethical Theories

(1) Existentialism

At the end of the previous chapter, we saw that in a certain sense, Jean-Paul Sartre's existentialism challenges the possibility of any moral code or system. Sartre and Simone de Beauvoir's philosophy makes this challenge despite the fact that at one level, Sartre accepts Kant's moral views, as we see in a passage such as this one:

> I am responsible for myself and for everyone else. I am creating a certain image of man of my own choosing. In choosing myself, I choose man. . . . Certainly, many people believe that when they do something, they themselves are the only ones involved, and when someone says to them "What if everyone acted that way?" they shrug their shoulders and answer, "Everyone doesn't act that way." But really, one should always ask himself, "What would happen if everybody looked at things that way?" There is no escaping this disturbing thought except by a kind of double-dealing. A man who lies and makes excuses for himself by saying "not everybody does that," is someone with an uneasy conscience because the act of lying implies that a universal value is conferred upon the lie.[1]

This reference to the universalizability of acts is the Kantian side of Sartre's moral views. He goes on to say, "Therefore though the content of ethics is variable, a certain form of it is universal. Kant says that freedom desires both itself and the freedom of others. Granted."[2]

In spite of granting the Kantian premise, Sartre has demonstrated very convincingly, in the example of the young man who came to Sartre for advice, that when moral values conflict, no moral formula can resolve the opposition. The young man simply had to invent, that is to say, choose. Sartre has radicalized Kant's view that the source of value is always the human being, and he has prioritized freedom over rationality. If Sartre is right, then reason cannot compel anyone to behave in one way as opposed to another, because reason can be an authority only if one *chooses* to authorize reason. Once I decide that reason has value, then reason can force me to behave only in ways for which I can give cogent reasons. But what if rather than valuing reasons, I—like Dostoyevsky's

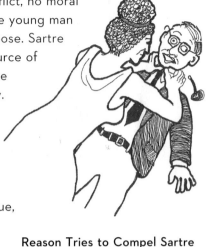

Reason Tries to Compel Sartre to Do the Right Thing

underground man (see Perverse Freedom in Chapter 6)—choose *unreason* to guide me? Then I do not need to, nor can I, give *reasons* for my choice. So we see that even though Sartre accepts many of the same facts about humans that Kant does (that humans are free and autonomous), he draws exactly the opposite conclusion from that of Kant. Because we are free and autonomous, we cannot be *naturally* rational. We are rational only by choice. Or to put it another way, if we are free, then no moral code can be binding on us.

(2) Hume and the Naturalistic Fallacy

Sartre was certainly not the first philosopher to challenge the foundations of morality. Already in the eighteenth century, David Hume had exploded a bombshell whose reverberations are still heard up through our time. This explosive device has come down to us in the form of a simple five-worded phrase: "No 'is' implies an 'ought.'"[3] What Hume meant by this phrase is that no moral claims whatsoever could be derived from any merely *factual* claims. Let's clarify this point by choosing a moral principle with which almost everyone would agree: "It is morally wrong to torture innocent children just for the pleasure of doing so." Now, Hume's point is this: If someone challenges this claim and says, "How do you know this principle to be true?" what demonstration can we give him? The utilitarian will say that the act is wrong because it goes against the principle of utility ("the greatest amount of happiness for the greatest number of people"). But what if the utilitarian is asked why we should accept the principle of utility? Bentham answered that we should do so because "Nature has placed mankind under the governance of two sovereign masters, *pain* and *plea-sure*. It is for them alone to point out what we ought to do."[4]

But even if Bentham's factual claim is true and we are all motivated by the desire for pleasure, does it follow logically that we *ought* to be? What if most people, or even

I enjoy doing this. Therefore, I am morally obliged to continue.

Aii, Aii, more!

Faulty Logic

all people, derived great pleasure from cruelty? Would it follow in some moral sense that people *ought* to be cruel? Of course not. So the utilitarians' claim that we *ought* to adopt the principle of utility because we all *do* desire happiness simply doesn't work, and left unanswered is our question as to why we ought not to torture innocent children.

Kant would answer that we ought not to do so because such behavior conflicts with the categorical imperative. But why should we follow that principle? Kant says we must do so because we are rational. But Hume's point is that even if we *are* rational, it does not follow that we *ought* to be. Hence, from his point of view, the question of why we ought not to torture children is still unanswered.

In the twentieth century, Hume's moral skepticism influenced the important Cambridge moral philosopher GEORGE EDWARD MOORE (1873–1958), usually called G. E. Moore. Moore pointed out that the concept of good cannot be *defined* in terms of any "natural" quality, such as "pleasure," "happiness," or "survival value." (What Moore called a "natural quality" is more or less the same as Hume's "factual claims," his "is"). In a true definition, such as "A sister is a female sibling," it would be nonsense to question the predicate of the subject—to ask, for example, "Yes, but *is* a sister a female sibling?" Of course, she is—that's what "sister" means. (Or try these: "*Is* a bachelor an unmarried male?" "*Is* a triangle a three-sided figure?")

Yet when we turn to attempted definitions of the word "good," curious things happen. For example, the hedonist tries to define "good" in terms of *pleasure*. Yet the question "*Is* pleasure good?" is not nonsense in the way that the question "*Is* a square four-sided?" is nonsense. (E.g., what about Hitler's pleasure? Is it necessarily good?) A similar result is obtained when social Darwinists try to define "good" in terms of survival value. The question "Yes, but *is* survival always good?" is not nonsense. (Being willing to betray one's friends may have survival value in some situations, but that doesn't necessarily make treachery good.) The same thing is true of religious attempts to define "good" in terms of obedience to God's will. The question "But *is* it always good to obey God?" at least makes sense, even if we don't know the answer. (Think of God's instruction to Abraham to kill his innocent son.) So the result is that all attempts to define "good" in terms of any existing facts whatever result in a fallacy. Moore called it "the naturalistic fallacy." Pointing it out was his way of affirming Hume's dictum "No *is* implies an *ought*." (Moore's own view in his *Principia Ethica* was that the good is some "nonnatural" simple quality that cannot be analyzed but that can be recognized. Hardly any moral philosophers have agreed with Moore's mysterious claim or even been able to make much sense out of it.) So the question remains: If we cannot derive our moral values from any facts in the world, from where can we derive them? This question threatens any attempt to ground morality in objectivity.[5]

The Good as a Nonnatural, Unanalyzable, Simple Quality

(3) Logical Positivism

In Chapter 3, we saw that Hume had influenced a group of twentieth-century philosophers who came to be known as the logical positivists. Their views are no longer fashionable, but in their day, they were tremendously influential, and ghosts of their ideas still abound. They are worth studying for this reason and also, more pertinent to the point of this chapter, because they mounted one of the most powerful attacks on the possibility of moral philosophy to be carried out by any group of philosophers.

In Chapter 3, we saw that the positivists' attack on ethics derived from their theory of meaning, according to which there are only two kinds of genuine propositions: analytic and synthetic. Remember, according to the positivists, analytic propositions are true by definition, mere tautologies, telling us nothing about reality, only something about how concepts are related (e.g., "All circles are round"). Synthetic (or empirical) propositions can be confirmed or refuted only by some actual or possible observation. Only these propositions are truly about reality. Any putative proposition that is neither analytic nor synthetic is cognitively empty or

The Three Possibilities According to the Logical Positivists		
ANALYTIC True by definition "Unicorns have one horn."	SYNTHETIC Established by observation "Pickles are sour."	NONSENSE . . . . . . "Twas brillig." "God loves you."

nonsense. A sentence like "Torturing innocent children is immoral" is not analytic; that is, it is not true simply by virtue of the meaning of its words (as is proved by negating the sentence and seeing that the negation, "Torturing innocent children is *not* immoral," is not a self-contradiction in the way that the sentence "A sister is not female" *is* self-contradictory).

On the other hand, neither is our sentence empirical. That is,

Find the Immoral Part

there is no observation, actual or possible, that could confirm or refute the sentence. If we watched a brute torturing a small child, we would feel horror, revulsion, and fury, but there would be nothing we could point at and say, "There it is! *That's* the immoral part" (in the way that we *can* say, "That's the yellow part" or "That's the heavy part"). So what *is* the status of our moral claim, according to the positivists? Because it is cognitively empty, it is merely expressive. A British member of the school of logical positivism, philosopher A. J. Ayer, who as a young

SIR ALFRED JULES AYER (1910–1989)

man went to Vienna to study positivism, claimed that moral language was simply a disguised display of emotion, often coupled with "commands in a misleading grammatical form." So the sentence "Torturing is immoral" really means something like this:
Only the third part of this division could have truth value; therefore, the whole sentence "Torturing is immoral" can be neither true nor false. It expresses what Ayer called "a pseudoconcept."

Logical positivism inspired many in its day, and we still see its influence here and there, for example, in B. F. Skinner's conception of science, but positivism's rather shocking views about morality need not distress us too much. The consensus today is that we do not have to take logical positivism all that seriously. It offers some good tools for analysis, but it is fairly obvious that its theory of meaning is much too restrictive. Furthermore, it suffers from a deadly internal defect. If every proposition is analytic, synthetic, or nonsense, what is the status of the proposition that *asserts* that every proposition is analytic, synthetic, or nonsense? It is not analytic, because its negation does not lead to a self-contradiction. It is not synthetic, because no observation would tend to confirm it or refute it. What status is left for it except that of nonsense according to its own criterion? Perhaps Professor Jon Wheatley was writing an obituary when he said, "Logical positivism is one of the very few philosophical positions which can be easily shown to be dead wrong, and that is its principal claim to fame."[6]

So what is the ultimate impact of these various philosophical assaults on the foundations of morality? Notice that, each in its own way, the Sartrean, Humean, and positivistic critiques are indeed just that—assaults on the *foundations* of morality. Sartre tries to show that the foundations of morality must be subjective and unstable. Hume and

The Assault on the Foundations of Morality

the positivists try to show that morality cannot have its foundation in any true facts about the world. But what if talk about the *foundations* of morality turns out to be misconceived? At the end of Chapter 3, we saw that the attempt to discover the foundations of knowledge might have been completely wrongheaded. It was suggested there that knowledge may prove to be more like a net or a spiderweb than like a house. The same is true in ethics. As the influential British moral philosopher Bernard Williams says:

> the foundationalist enterprise, [that] of resting the structure of knowledge on some favored class of statements, has now generally been displaced in favor of a holistic type of model, in which some beliefs can be questioned, justified, or adjusted while others are kept constant, but there is no process by which they can all be questioned at once, or all justified in terms of (almost) nothing. In Neurath's famous image, we repair the ship while we are on the sea.[7]

Repairing the Ship while on the Sea

According to Williams, the same is true of ethics. "The aim of ethical thought," he says, "is to help us to construct a world that will be our world, one in which we have a social, cultural, and personal life."[8] Now, for *that* activity, no foundation is needed. By virtue of being human, we find ourselves engaged in it willy-nilly. That is why Williams prefers a version of Aristotle's moral question over that of Socrates. Williams takes it that Socrates's ethical question is "How should *one* live?" This theoretical question is abstract in nature. It tends toward foundationalism. Aristotle's question is more concrete. He asks, "How should *we* live?" Socrates's question presupposes some abstract human nature in universal conditions; Aristotle's question presupposes a concrete psychological and communal social situation in which *we* actually find ourselves engaged on a daily basis.

But before we can accept this pragmatic solution to the problem of ethics, we must address another objection to morality, an objection that seems to threaten even a pragmatic solution: the problem of cultural relativism.

(4) Cultural Relativism

Here we must talk about another kind of twentieth-century assault on the possibility of ethics, one that has come not from the field of philosophy but from the social sciences. Associated with some important names in anthropology and psychology, cultural relativism denies that there can be any absolute or objective moral values on the grounds that moral values are the products of individual cultures, which differ from one another in such a fashion that the values central to each society differ from one another. In a famous article of 1934, the anthropologist Ruth Benedict wrote:

> We recognize that morality differs in every society and is a convenient term for socially approved habits. Mankind has always preferred to say, "It is

morally good," rather than "It is habitual," and the fact of this preference is matter enough for a critical science of ethics. But historically the two phrases are synonymous.

The concept of the normal is properly a variant of the concept of the good. It is that which society has approved. A normal action is one which falls well within the limits of expected behavior for a particular society.

Anthropologists Attacking Moral Philosopher

. . . .

Those individuals whose characteristics are not congenial to the selected type of human behavior in that community are the deviants, no matter how valued their personality traits may be in a contrasted civilization.[9]

Benedict's views were echoed a generation later by the psychologist B. F. Skinner, who said:

What a given group of people calls good is a fact: it is what members of the group find reinforcing as the result of their genetic endowment and the natural and social contingencies to which they have been exposed. Each culture has its own set of goods, and what is good in one culture may not be good in another. To recognize this is to take the position of "cultural relativism." What is good for the Trobriand Islander is good for the Trobriand Islander, and that is that. Anthropologists have often emphasized relativism as a tolerant alternative to missionary zeal in converting all cultures to a single set of ethical, governmental, religious, or economic values.[10]

The views of Benedict and Skinner resonate with ideas we have all heard about and that to many people (especially to many college students) seem quite correct—namely, that "good" must always mean "good for her" or "good for them" or "good for me," but never just *good.* What is good for one person or culture is not necessarily good for another, and therefore, there can really never be any genuine moral *reasoning,* only "acknowledgment" of others' "good." ("I hear what you're saying.") And the data from

It is <u>wrong</u> to take things that do not belong to you!

I acknowledge your space on that.

the social sciences sometimes do seem to support such a relativism. (It is not "good" for me to worship cows, but it is "good" for Hindus to worship cows, because cow manure provides both fertilizer and fuel for Hindu society.)

It cannot be denied that this kind of relativism is healthy in struggling against puritanical "uptightness" and dangerous ethnocentric arrogance. ("Our values are right, and we'll impose them on you if we have to kill you to do it!")

But our relativism runs up against problems when we turn to questions like these: Must we withhold moral judgment about Nazi "brutalities" on the grounds that we are *not* members of a Nazi culture? Exterminating six million people is "good" for Hitler but not for me? This "different strokes for different folks" philosophy seems dangerously hollow here. So let's go back and take a closer look at what ethical relativism is saying. Under scrutiny, its thesis becomes less clear. Is the cultural relativist saying, (1) "There are no universally held moral values" or (2) "No value or set of values can justifiably be recommended for all people"? These are very different claims. Let's look at each of them.

A Texas Cow Worshipper

There Are No Universally Held Moral Values

Notice that this first claim is an empirical one. In theory, at least, it is capable of confirmation or refutation through scientific investigation. Now, there are several things to say about it. If it is meant to be interpreted *individually*, saying that there never has been a moral value accepted by *absolutely everybody*, then, no doubt, the claim is true but not very impressive. (Just because one person—Cronus perhaps—broke the law against eating one's children doesn't mean there is something wrong with the law.) Then what about interpreting the relativist's thesis culturally rather than individually? Certainly not *all* social scientists are in agreement concerning the truth of this version of the claim. For example, the eminent anthropologists Alfred Kroeber and Clyde Kluckhohn argued that certain universal values have been accepted by all cultures: No culture tolerates indiscriminate lying, stealing, or violence within the in-group. The incest taboo is virtually universal. No culture places value on suffering as an end in itself. Every culture ceremonializes death. "All cultures define as abnormal [those] individuals who are permanently inaccessible to communication or who fail to maintain some degree of control over their impulsive life."[11] Kroeber and

Cronus Eating His Children (After Francisco Goya)

All Cultures Define as Abnormal Those Individuals Who Are Permanently Inaccessible to Communication

Kluckhohn do not deny that what *counts* as lying, stealing, or violence might be culturally defined, but they think that these values are universals behind the particulars.

The social psychologist Solomon Asch holds a similar view. He claims that every society despises cowardice and honors bravery. In every society, modesty, courage, and hospitality are encouraged. Even in cultures where acts that are horrible to us are routinely performed, it is often possible to find that the disagreement between their culture and ours is really more of a debate about apparently empirical facts than it is a debate over values. Ancient Chinese cultures commonly engaged in infanticide (leaving unwanted infants exposed to die in nature). But Asch claims that in that culture, infants were not considered human until their first year. The ancient Chinese and we may actually be seen to agree on the value of human life but to disagree on the facts concerning what constitutes a human being.

At least *those* kinds of disagreements are not just disagreements of taste and hence are debatable and, in principle, resolvable—though perhaps not easily, as is seen in the amount of passion engendered by the debate over abortion in our own culture. Again, to a great extent, this debate is not over the value of human life—both parties are probably more or less in agreement over that—but over the facts concerning what constitutes a human being. Still, I don't want to be seen as oversimplifying a complicated issue. The question "What is a human being?" *looks* like a straightforward question that could be answered either with a dictionary-type definition or with some empirical research. But, in fact, the concept "human being" is probably one involving a complex concatenation of facts and values and does not admit of a purely scientific determination. In an odd way, it is probably a socially negotiable concept, and we are in the midst of a rather painful, protracted debate over it right now. Perhaps we always have been.

For example, it has not always been clear to all cultures whether to treat women, strangers, and minorities as fully human or whether to treat volcanoes and winds as if they are adversarial entrepreneurs.

So then, if the thesis of cultural relativism is that there are no values held by all or by most cultures, that thesis is probably false. What about cultural relativism's second formulation?

Cutting a Deal with a Volcano

There Is No Value or Set of Values Recommendable for All People

The thesis that no value or set of values can justifiably be recommended for all people cannot be the conclusion drawn from a legitimate scientific investigation. Even if, contrary to the implication of the foregoing discussion, it did turn out that no values are universally held, it wouldn't follow from that fact that no value is *worthy* of adoption by all. (This is another version of the is/ought problem.) Even if we found out that all people enjoyed inflicting suffering on others, it wouldn't follow that they *ought* to inflict suffering on others. In *this* sense, anthropology has nothing to offer to moral philosophy. In *this* sense, it doesn't matter what people from other cultures do. We can't deduce what they *ought* to do from their current or past practices. But there *is* a sense in which anthropology is helpful to moral philosophy.

All People Enjoy Inflicting Suffering on Others

We've already pointed out that the study of the values of other cultures can have a salutary humbling effect, cutting into our tendency to assume that the values of *our* culture are somehow "natural," hence superior. But also, if we accept Kroeber's and Kluckhohn's claim that the universals they listed obviously have survival value, that they are "necessary conditions to social life," *and* if we accept as a moral principle the view that "human life should prevail and flourish," then anthropology, sociology, and social psychology can help us think clearly on behalf of our own moral reasoning.

(5) Ethics and Feminism

Is there after all a fundamental flaw in traditional Western ethics—that of being inappropriate for more than half of the human race? The question we are asking is this: is moral philosophy, as it is traditionally expounded, biased toward androcentrism (male-centeredness)? Does it fail to take into account the experience of women and to take advantage of the moral insights derived from female experience? A good number of **feminist** critics of moral philosophy think the answer to these questions is yes.

Certainly, there is good reason to believe that women's experience is in some significant ways different from men's experience. Novelists,

... A really great ethics ...

Except it's inappropriate for half the human race!

psychologists, and sociologists have confirmed this suspicion. It is difficult to establish to what extent, if any, these differences can be traced to fundamental distinctions between the brains and bodies of females and males, as opposed to differences in the way females and males are treated from birth forward. In our culture, for instance, each sex is immediately assigned a color (pink, blue) and toys (dolls, trucks), as well as behavioral models (passive, active).

However, regardless of the extent to which the differences in experience between females and males can be traced to biological or social distinctions, the question still remains—Is it possible that the experience of girls and women can provide insight into moral life that has been ignored by traditional ethical discourse? Furthermore, is it possible that the same "patriarchal" moral discourse not only has ignored women but also has participated in their oppression and perpetuated a bias against them? In some ways, it would seem so.

Let us begin with this question: What differences exist in the experience of women that might be morally significant? An important step toward answering that question was provided by Carol Gilligan in 1982 with the publication of her book *In a Different Voice: Psychological Theory and Women's Development.* One of Gilligan's techniques was to interview children using a set of questions developed by the psychologist Lawrence Kohlberg. When Kohlberg performed the tests in the 1960s, it seemed to him that girls did not

All right now, let's see who gets the doll and who gets the truck ...

The Assignment of Toys

Patriarchal Discourse

prove to have as clear a sense of justice as did boys, nor the same deductive capacity for deriving moral conclusions. There has been a whole literature based on the claim that women have a less-developed moral sense than men. The German philosopher ARTHUR SCHOPENHAUER (1788–1860) wrote:

> women remain children their whole life long . . . the fundamental fault of the female character is that it has *no sense of justice*. This is mainly due to the fact . . . that women are defective in the powers of reasoning and deliberation.[12]

According to psychologist OTTO WEIN-INGER (1880–1903), "A woman cannot grasp that one must act from principle; as she has no continuity, she does not experience the necessity for logical support of her mental processes."[13] Probably the most egregious case comes from (no surprise!) Freud, who wrote:

> I cannot evade the notion (though I hesitate to give it expression) that for women the level of what is ethically normal is different from what it is in men. Their superego is never so inexorable, so impersonal, so independent of its emotional origins as we require it to be in men. Character-traits which critics of every epoch have brought up against women—that they show less sense of justice than men, that they are less ready to submit to the great exigencies of life, that they are more often influenced in their judgements by their feelings of affection or hostility—all these would be amply accounted for in the modification of the formation of their superego. . . . We must not allow ourselves to be deflected from such conclusions by the denial of the feminists, who are anxious to force us to regard the two sexes as completely equal in position and worth.[14]

"Because He Thought So Highly of the Penis, He Thought Women Did Too"
(Germaine Greer on Otto Weininger)

I hesitate to give this thought expression!

Gilligan replicated Kohlberg's interviews and reinterpreted the data. In one interview, she posed the following question to a girl and a boy, both eleven years old: If Heinz cannot afford the medicine for his sick wife, and the pharmacist refuses to lower the price, should Heinz steal the medicine in order to save his wife's life? The boy, Jake, is sure that Heinz should do so and is able to produce a principle ("life is worth more than money") and a logical argument applying that principle. Amy, on the other hand, is less sure. She thinks it's wrong for Heinz to steal the drugs but insists also that it is wrong for the pharmacist to withhold them. She refuses to apply the rules of logic to the case—in fact, in a way she refuses the hypothesis. She thinks if we could talk with the pharmacist and make him understand the situation, he would freely donate the drugs.

Jake's Solution

Is Amy's answer an example of retarded moral development? Is Amy incapable of understanding the abstract concept of justice, of applying a principle to the case, and of drawing deductive conclusions from it? Gilligan does not believe that these conclusions are the correct lessons being taught here. She sees the girl's account as concentrating, not on "a contest of rights," but on "a network of relationships on whose continuation they all depend."[15] In short, Amy *does* refuse to apply abstract principles in a mathematical fashion to unrealistic scenarios as a solution to a human problem. She contextualizes and concentrates on the pragmatics of relationships between human beings.

A number of feminists (I say a *number* because there is no such thing as *the* feminist position; in fact, a few have disagreed with some of Gilligan's views.[16]) think Amy got it right. They think that Amy is right to reject the typical extreme-case scenarios in which moral philosophy is often argued (e.g., "the case of Sam"). She is right to stress relationships over rules, and she is right to demand more information regarding the context. That is, she is correct to see moral judgments as *emergent,* flowing out from an understanding of a real situation.

Amy's Solution

Why would women have such different moral experiences? Agnes Heller believes that precisely women's historical confinement to the home and exclusion from the broader world of commerce, industry, travel, and war in Western society has made their lives more similar over the generations and has given them more close-up insight into real human relations. They have had to learn to create and manage small communities involving real people, people with all their virtues and foibles. Because ethics must ultimately be about human relations—with other humans or with nature—women may indeed have special insights into this sphere.[17]

Does this special insight mean that women are morally superior to men? Not necessarily so. (Though in Victorian England they were thought to be morally superior, and this supposed superiority was both used against them—they would have to be confined to the home to protect their purity—and used to try to liberate them—they should be given the vote in order to influence society morally.) Nevertheless, special insight means that women might be afforded a unique perspective from which to criticize male-dominated ethical theory and to develop their insights systematically into a moral view.

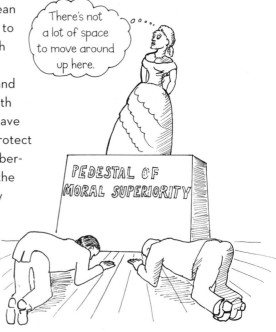

Victorian Virtue

Six Critiques of Traditional Ethical Theories

The feminist criticism of patriarchal ethics has two prongs. First, as philosopher Alison Jaggar says, feminist ethics "seeks to identify and challenge all those ways, overt but more often and more perniciously covert, in which Western ethics has excluded women or rationalized their subordination."[18] Second, it seeks to develop an ethics inspired by, or at least consistent with, the actual moral experience and intuition of women.

Concerning the first point, some feminists are worried that a masculine tendency toward abstract thought may allow *theories* to be distanced from actual human *life*. Conceptions of morality derived from such alienated thought may have "permeated human social life and institutions in a way that leads to a distorted and dangerous sense of human priorities; to a morality, in fact, that may be seen as underlying such things as militarism," feminist philosopher Jean Grimshaw says. Women's lives, Grimshaw asserts, may "provide the space for questioning the sorts of priorities that see human lives as easily dispensable in the service of some abstract idea or great cause; that see care for others or a life devoted to serving others as relatively unimportant."[19] Furthermore, precisely because women have to a great extent been historically excluded from the commercial and industrial world and from "world-historical events," they ironically may be in the best position to criticize the morality of the capitalist market economy. Such social commentators need

not be professional philosophers. Long-dead female novelists like George Eliot (a.k.a. Mary Anne Evans) in *The Mill on the Floss* (1860) can be very instructive on such topics.

The second point, the development of a feminist ethics, is still undergoing formulation. An interesting suggestion for it comes from Mary Raugust and is based not on an "ivory tower" perspective from a professor's chair at a university but on a workplace perspective. Raugust was director of the Kennedy Aging Project; she sets forth her proposal for a feminist ethics in seven tenets.[20]

First Tenet: The central priority of ethics is the concept not of individual rights but of relationships with other human beings. (Here Raugust

seems to be agreeing
with Amy's intuitions as
opposed to that
of Jake.)

Second Tenet:
The principal goal of
ethics is not to respect
and maximize autonomy
and liberty of individual
humans (as in Kantian
and Sartrean ethics),
rather it is "the giving and
receiving of care appropriate to specific persons and
their situations." (The feminist philosopher who has
pursued this feature of ethics
in detail is Nel Noddings, in
*Caring: A Feminine
Approach to Ethics and Moral
Education.*[21] For her, "caring" involves setting aside one's own concerns in
order to put oneself into the experience of another person as far as possible.
Such a definition of "caring" does seem to get at the very heart of morality.)

Moral Edicts from the Ivory Tower

Third Tenet: Interdependence over individualism. (Again, this seems to square with Amy's
intuition.)

Fourth Tenet: The "other" with whom
one deals morally must be distinctly personi
fied and not an impersonal, faceless
abstraction. (The object of the critique
here seems to be particularly
Kantianism, in which the moral subject has no particular characteristics at all, but also utilitarianism,
wherein the "greatest happiness" is established
formulaically.)

Fifth Tenet: Moral judg-
ments emerge from actual
situations and are not
derived by applying logical

Immanuel Kant as a Faceless Abstraction

formulas to general principles. (Once again in line with Amy's intuition and anti-Kantian and antiutilitarian.)

Sixth Tenet: Feminist ethics are "accepting rather than transformative." (To this extent, they agree with the biblical precept "Judge not . . ." but disagree with another biblical precept—the one that graces Chapter 7 as its title—"Thou shalt become perfected." This tenet is another anti-Kantian thrust in that Kant saw ethics as an engagement in self-improvement.)

Seventh Tenet: Feminist ethics will be a morality of *virtues* rather than primarily one of *justice*. (We have already seen that Virtue Ethics entails a rejection of

the main thrust of Western ethics in the modern period. It is an ethics based on social contextualization where moral behavior is analyzed in terms of propensities to act virtuously: courage, self-control, generosity, amiability, truthfulness, wittiness, friendliness, modesty, and so on. This description seems much closer to Amy's way of approaching the "case of Heinz and his sick wife" than to that of Jake.)

Amy Triumphant

(6) Ethics and Deep Ecology

A powerful attack on traditional Western moral philosophies has come out of an intensified version of the environmental movement calling itself **deep ecology.** It challenges the *anthropocentrism* of Western ethics, that is, its human-centeredness. We have seen, for example, that both Kant and Sartre find the source of value exclusively in *human* characteristics: Kant in reason and Sartre in freedom. Utilitarianism advocates "the greatest amount of happiness for the greatest number of *people*." Now, it is true that utilitarianism *can* be extended to cover other animals that are capable of sensing pain, and in

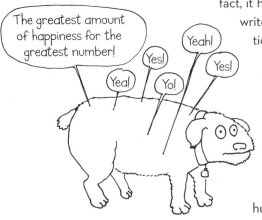

Flea Liberation

fact, it has been so extended by some writers supporting "animal liberation."[22] But such an extension is not sufficient for the loosely knit conglomeration of activists, writers, poets, and philosophers known as "deep ecologists." Nor are they satisfied with the views of those conservationists who argue that it is in the interest of humans to defend nature. To the deep ecologists, even this view is spawned by a human arrogance that sees all of nature as created exclusively for human use and consumption and, all too often, for human despoliation. Deep ecologists point out that throughout the long existence of the human race (say a million years), only a minority of humanity has held an anthropocentric view of the universe. Most hunter-gatherer societies had "eco-centric" religious views involving a sacred sense of the earth. This sense survived into the historical period in certain **pantheistic** religions, and echoes of it are found in the pre-Socratic philosophies we looked at briefly in Chapter 1. In the theories of Thales, Anaximander, Pythagoras, Heraclitus, Parmenides, and Democritus, humanity held no special position in reality. Deep ecologists seem to agree with Martin Heidegger that something went wrong in ontological thinking with the advent of the sophists and Socrates, who abandoned cosmic speculation and introduced the human being as the center of reality and meaning. A similar development took place in the Judeo-Christian tradition when its holy writ introduced the claim that the animal and vegetable world was placed under "man's" dominion for "his" use. (Not every thinker in that tradition has drawn the same anthropocentric conclusions from the Scriptures. The medieval Jewish philosopher, MOSES MAIMONIDES [1135–1204], pointed out that even before God created Adam and Eve, he created nature and saw that it was "good." Also, certain strands of religious mysticism like the medieval cult of divine light seem to be ecocentered. And in seventeenth-century Holland, the Jewish philosopher Baruch Spinoza was a notable exception to the Western anthropocentric tradition. He is revered by a number of the deep ecologists, as we will see.)

The deep ecologists hold a view called "biocentric" or "ecocentric egalitarianism," explained by the Norwegian philosopher ARNE NAESS (1912–2009) (one of the architects of the movement and the one who named it "deep ecology"), with these words:

> The earth does not belong to humans. . . . Humans only inhabit the lands, using resources to satisfy vital needs. And if their nonvital needs come in conflict with the vital

The Fifth Day

needs of nonhumans, then humans should defer to the latter.[23]

Naess, along with fellow deep ecologist George Sessions, formulated the principles of the movement while sitting on the desert floor in Death Valley on a camping trip in April 1984, which they developed into the following eight points:

Arne Naess

1. The well-being and flourishing of human and nonhuman life on Earth have value in themselves (synonyms: intrinsic value, inherent worth). These values are independent of the usefulness of the nonhuman world for human purposes.
2. Richness and diversity of life forms contribute to the realization of these values and are also values in themselves.
3. Humans have no right to reduce this richness and diversity except to satisfy vital needs.
4. The flourishing of human life and cultures is compatible with a substantially smaller human population. The flourishing of nonhuman life *requires* a smaller human population.

(6) Ethics and Deep Ecology **325**

Death Valley, 1984

5. Present human interference with the nonhuman world is excessive, and the situation is rapidly worsening.

6. Policies must therefore be changed. These policies affect basic economic, technological, and ideological structures. The resulting state of affairs will be deeply different from the present.

7. The ideological change will be mainly that of appreciating life quality (dwelling in situations of inherent value) rather than adhering to an increasingly higher standard of living. There will be a profound awareness of the difference between bigness and greatness.

8. Those who subscribe to the foregoing points have an obligation directly or indirectly to try to implement the necessary changes.[24]

As we see, the first of the eight principles holds that life in all its forms has intrinsic value, as opposed to mere instrumental value. (We can say that X has instrumental value if it leads to value Y. Remember Plato's example: Medicine has instrumental value, because it leads to good health, and health has intrinsic value.) Now, we might want to ask Naess how he *knows* that all life forms have value in themselves. Why should we believe this assertion, which, if true, puts us under a certain kind of moral obligation to respect all life forms? (And, if we are going to abandon Kantian, Sartrean, and utilitarian anthropocentrism, why stop with *life* forms? Edward Abbey, a radical wilderness defender who has actually influenced both deep ecology and the related activist movement Earth First!, once said: —a kind of Platonism in reverse.)

Naess, as a professional philosopher, is well aware of the "naturalistic fallacy" and the need to avoid it. Yet he claims that (living) nature *is good* in and of itself. How does he then avoid the illegitimate logical move from "is" to "ought"? Naess has an answer that we will develop in several stages. First, he rejects the fact/value distinction as an arbitrary philosophical conceit. When we look at certain life forms (and ecological systems of life forms) with the correct form of wonder—the very wonder with which Western philosophy began among the ancient Greeks and one that continues to be found in many strands of nature poetry—we discover a certain *intuition* in us that every living being has the same right to exist and to flourish that we humans have. In this intuition are both rational and extrarational factors—perhaps poetic or even spiritual factors. This intuition seems capable of provoking what Freud once referred to as an "oceanic" experience—a feeling of connectedness with the whole of reality—that might be the basis of certain kinds of mysticism. It gives us a new

Animal Rights

sense of self wherein we realize that we are not simply enclosed within our epidermis (the way potatoes might be held in a sack) but that our skin is a sensuous surface connecting us with the rest of the world, a world that in fact is now realized to be *a part of us*—part of the self.

Next, given this new broader definition of the self, Naess is satisfied to return to the Aristotelian moral maxim of *self-realization* as the highest goal. "Maximizing self-realization" will then be the moral demand of deep ecology—but now we understand that maxim to mean that we are personally committed to realizing our own undeveloped potentialities *and* that this realization in turn commits us to letting other life forms realize theirs. (Naess is of course aware of the possible conceptual and factual conflicts that may arise. A good deal of the technical literature of deep ecology is directed toward the practicalities of resolving "disputes" among the conflicting vital needs of different species and ecological spheres.)

Despite this carefully thought-out moral defense, Naess says that he prefers to base deep ecology on *ontology* rather than on ethics. Apparently, deep ecologists can turn to certain traditional Asian philosophies for inspiration here. Deep ecologists Fritjof Capra, physicist and Gary Snyder, the well-known poet of the Californian Sierra Nevada are influenced by Buddhism, for instance. But Naess and Sessions seem to turn mostly to Spinoza for their inspiration.

A quick glance at *Ethics*, the main work of BARUCH SPINOZA (1634–1677), might reveal no obvious reason why radical late-twentieth-century ecologists should find inspiration in him. His format is that of Euclid's books on geometry, with definitions, axioms, propositions,

Baruch Spinoza (1634–1677)

corollaries, and conclusions, each ending in a "Q.E.D." (*quod erat demonstrandum* = "which was to be demonstrated"). His vocabulary is that of Cartesian metaphysics (substances, essences, mind, body, attributes, modes), and his passion is from the medieval philosopher Maimonides, who advocated an "intellectual love of God." Where in all these do we find a deep ecology?

We can answer this question by examining an error that Spinoza claims to detect in Descartes's main idea—an error concerning the definition of *substance*.

Descartes had said, "By substance we can conceive nothing else than a thing which exists in such a way as to stand in need of nothing beyond itself." Then Descartes had gone on to say, "And in truth, there can be conceived but one substance which is absolutely independent, and that is God," which he called "infinite substance."[25] Despite this admission that by definition there could exist only *one* kind of being that was absolutely independent, Descartes (in a contradictory manner, according to Spinoza) proceeded to distinguish between "infinite substance" and "finite substances"—the latter divided into corporeal substance (body) and mental substance (mind). This radical dualism led Descartes to his notorious mind–body problem and his universally scorned pineal gland solution.

Spinoza avoided this embarrassment by accepting Descartes's definition of substance (as that which is absolutely independent) and taking seriously the inference that there could be only *one* such substance. (If there were two, they would limit each other's independence.) Furthermore, because finiteness would constitute a limitation on God's absolute independence, Spinoza defined God as having infinite attributes. So once again one arrives at the conclusion that there can be but one substance, because any substance other than God would have to possess attributes that have already been defined as belonging to God.

Let's look at a schematized comparison of the systems of Descartes and Spinoza:

There ain't room enough in this cosmos for both of us!

FIRST SUBSTANCE

2nd SUBSTANCE

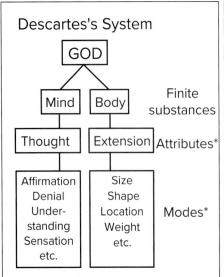

Descartes's System

GOD

Mind | Body — Finite substances

Thought | Extension — Attributes*

Affirmation
Denial
Under-
standing
Sensation
etc.

Size
Shape
Location
Weight
etc.

Modes*

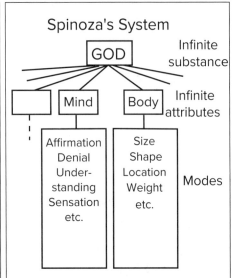

Spinoza's System

GOD — Infinite substance

[ ] | Mind | Body — Infinite attributes

Affirmation
Denial
Under-
standing
Sensation
etc.

Size
Shape
Location
Weight
etc.

Modes

*An *attribute*, for Descartes, is a characteristic that is the *essence* of a substance (i.e., that is essential to it). For Spinoza, an attribute is a characteristic that to the human intellect *seems* to be an essence. A **mode** is a specific modification of an attribute (i.e., a characteristic of a characteristic).

The Unrequited Love of Nature

Now, you still might be wondering what this discussion has to do with *ecology*. In fact, to derive deep ecology from Spinoza, its architects had to use Spinoza's principles against some of his own conclusions, because Spinoza personally believed that the human exploitation of the animal world was philosophically justifiable. What principles are these? That secret becomes revealed when we discover that Spinoza equates "infinite substance" not only with God but also with *nature*. According to Spinoza, the true philosopher attempts to transcend the purely human perspective and view reality *sub specie aeternitatis*, that is, from the perspective of reality itself. From this perspective, one comes to realize that the human has no privileged position in the cosmos, the human has no more nor less dignity than anything else in nature. One must come to love everything, which is to say, to love God (because one must either love every-thing or nothing at all). The *love of God* is tantamount to the *knowledge of God,* which is to say, a philosophical knowledge of nature. As the British Spinoza scholar Stuart Hampshire says, "To Spinoza, it seemed that men can attain happiness and dignity only by identifying themselves, through their knowledge and understanding, with the whole order of nature."[26]

For Spinoza, it is not easy to achieve this wisdom. He says, "But all things excellent are as difficult as they are rare."[27] Yet once one has that wisdom—an understanding of the whole order and of one's connectedness with it—one achieves a state of bless-edness and joy. In one of the most marvelous lines in the history of West-ern philosophy, Spinoza says, "There cannot be too much joy: it is always good; but melancholy is always bad."[28] It is this joy that Naess wishes to tap, and it is this prom-ise, rather than the demand for self-sacrifice, that motivates the ethics of the deep ecology movement.

Can There Be Too Much Joy?

Can a Moral Code Be Derived from Nature?

Conclusion

My own conclusions concerning the topic of moral philosophy are cautiously skeptical. We cannot know what "the Good" is, not for Plato's reasons (that too much ignorance and too many obstacles exist), but because there is no such thing as "the Good"—in about the same sense as there is no such thing as "the Real," according to John Austin. Concerning the question "What is the good life?" we can perhaps be more positive but only if we make some utilitarian-type assumptions about human desires and goals. If we do (and I see no reason not to), then I think that both Aristotle and the utilitarians can be very instructive for us. It should be possible to create a general theory of what is most likely to contribute to a life of happiness—a theory showing in such a life the approximate role of the pursuit of pleasure, the development of potentialities, creative expression, commitment to other persons (including family, friends, and lovers), commitment to causes and a professional life, acceptance of social responsibilities and personal obligations, respect for nature as well as the "virtues" (courage, honesty, temperance, etc.) in one's life.

But it should be understood that though such a theory can be normative (i.e., can guide us in our decision making and in forming our habits), it cannot make anyone either good or happy. Socrates was wrong to think that if one *knew* the good, one would necessarily *become* good. Unfortunately, it is possible to know what one ought to do (to know what one's obligations are), to know what would be a good thing or the right thing to do, yet to do the opposite. A moral theory can be part of an argument meant to motivate a certain kind of thinking and acting, but philosophy by itself cannot create right action. (In my view, Plato and Socrates were wrong about that, too.) If one's only reason for behaving in a certain way comes from a philosophical theory, one will probably not find oneself behaving in the desired way very often. And even if one is already motivated by extraphilosophical reasons to engage in a moral form of life, a moral theory can be a guide but not a final source of judgment. Sartre is right to say that a theory never makes moral judgments, only a human being does. He has also shown us that in real life, moral problems are often caused by "conflicts of ideals" (the name of an excellent book on this topic written by Luther Binkley) and not by questions like "Should I be moral?" or "Why should I be moral?"[29] No ethical theory will be able to solve these real conflicts, and we should not expect one to do so.

The moral skeptics (Hume, the logical positivists, the cultural relativists, the existentialists) were right to say that it is impossible to discover the *foundations* of morality, and those philosophers who claimed to do so (Plato, the hedonists, the utilitarians, Kant) were, in my view, wrong to think that they had succeeded. But this admission is not so disastrous after all. It is true that a house without foundations would be in a sorry state, but morality is not a house. Just as many philosophers today have concluded that foundationalism is wrong in epistemology (see

You *will* be good!

ETHICS

Moral Theory Cannot Make You Good

Conclusion in Chapter 3), so it is beginning to look as though it is wrong in moral philosophy. Earlier, I quoted Bernard Williams as saying that the role of philosophy in this region is not to discover the foundations of morality but "to help us construct a world that will be our world, one in which we have a social, cultural, and personal life."[30] In this quest, I believe (following the legal philosopher Christopher Stone) that a kind of moral pluralism is required.[31] We should not feel that this quest must be guided by only one principle (e.g., a hedonistic one, a utilitarian one, or a Kantian one). Rather, we should develop some system of "moral mapping." A Kantian principle of universalizability can be very useful vis-à-vis our relations to other humans yet be fairly useless, and even destructive, vis-à-vis the natural world. A kind of Spinozistic "deep ecology" principle may be needed to reveal the intrinsic value of the natural world, but that same principle might not be as informative concerning my relations to other people as would be the views set forth by the feminist moralists. The decision as to when one moral map should be set aside and another made to "kick in" would not itself be purely the function of a philosophical theory, though philosophical speculation can guide such a decision. So here, as elsewhere, if we do not expect *too* much of philosophy, she can be an excellent companion.

Topics for Consideration

1. In what way does Sartre agree with Kant, and in what way does he disagree with him?
2. Explain why Hume would have more trouble justifying the claim "Killing people is wrong" than the claim "Murdering people is wrong."
3. How would you argue against a logical positivist who told you that the sentence "Torturing children is immoral" was cognitively empty (i.e., nonsense)?
4. The Nazis claimed to believe that exterminating certain peoples was morally justifiable. From the perspective of a cultural relativist, would it be immoral to invade Nazi Germany to prevent that extermination?
5. What feminist objections do you find to the moral philosophies of Kant and the utilitarians?
6. Combining the ideas of Baruch Spinoza and Arne Naess, explain the deep ecologists' conception of selfhood, and contrast this with the traditional view.

Suggestions for Further Reading: Paperback Editions

Alfred Jules Ayer, *Language, Truth, and Logic* (New York: Dover, 1952). A short, clear statement of the logical positivists' critique of tradition philosophy, including ethics.

Simone de Beauvoir, *The Ethics of Ambiguity,* trans. Bernard Frechtman (New York: Citadel Press, 1970). A careful analysis of existentialistic ethics by one of its best practitioners.

Jean Grimshaw, *Philosophy and Feminist Thinking* (Minneapolis, MN: University of Minnesota Press, 1991). Well written and forceful.

Alasdair MacIntyre, *After Virtue: A Study in Moral Theory* (Notre Dame, IN: University of Notre Dame Press, 1981). The best contemporary presentation available of an ethics based on virtue by one of America's ablest philosophers imported from Britain.

Jean-Paul Sartre, *Existentialism and Human Emotions,* trans. Hazel E. Barnes and Bernard Frechtman (New York: Philosophical Library, 1957). A short, readable account of Sartre's views on morality in about 1946.

George Sessions, ed., *Deep Ecology for the Twenty-First Century* (Boston, MA: Shambhala Publications, 1995). The best access to the works of the deep ecologists.

Bernard Williams, *Ethics and the Limits of Philosophy* (Cambridge, MA: Harvard University Press, 1985). A beautifully presented argument against foundationalism in ethics by an important twentieth-century British philosopher.

Notes

1. Jean-Paul Sartre, *Existentialism and Human Emotions* (New York: Philosophical Library, 1957), pp. 18–19.

2. Ibid., p. 47.

3. David Hume, *A Treatise of Human Nature,* eds. L. A. Selby-Bigge and P. H. Nidditch (Oxford, England: Clarendon Press, 1978), pp. 469–470.

4. Jeremy Bentham, *An Introduction to the Principles of Morals and Legislation* (Darien, CT: Hafner, 1970), p. 1.

5. Currently a debate is in progress concerning the validity of Moore's claim to have discovered a logical fallacy in naturalistic ethics. A group espousing "analytical naturalism" defends the possibility that "some moral properties are identical to natural properties." (See Susana Nuccetelli and Gary Seay, "Does Analytical Moral Naturalism Rest on a Mistake?" in *Ethical Naturalism: Current Debates,* eds. S. Nuccetelli and G. Seay [Cambridge, England: Cambridge University Press, 2012].) Though there is disagreement among the various individuals in this debate, most participants on all sides agree that Moore's generalization is too broad. For example, Nuccetelli and Seay argue that Moore cannot prove that *all* attempts to substitute natural properties for moral properties fail, though they admit that Moore's challenge puts the onus of defending such substitutions on the analytic naturalist in each case.

6. Jon Wheatley, *Prolegomena to Philosophy* (Belmont, CA: Wadsworth, 1970), p. 103.

7. Bernard Williams, *Ethics and the Limits of Philosophy* (Cambridge, MA: Harvard University Press, 1985), p. 113.

8. Ibid., p. 111.

9. Ruth Benedict, "Anthropology and the Abnormal," *Journal of General Psychology,* Vol. 10 (1934), pp. 72–74.

10. B. F. Skinner, *Beyond Freedom and Dignity* (New York: Bantam Books, 1972), p. 122.

11. Alfred Louis Kroeber and Clyde Kluckhohn, "Values and Relativity," in *Culture, a Critical Review of Concepts and Definitions,* Papers of the Peabody Museum, Harvard University, Vol. 47, No. 1 (1952), pp. 174–179.

12. Arthur Schopenhauer, "On Women," in *Self and World: Readings in Philosophy,* ed. James A. Ogilvy (New York: Harcourt, Brace, Jovanovich, 1973), pp. 395–396.

13. Otto Weininger, *Sex and Character* (London: W. Heinemann, 1906), p. 149.

14. Sigmund Freud, "Some Psychic Consequences of the Anatomical Distinction between the Sexes," in *The Complete Psychological Works of Sigmund Freud,* Vol. XIX, trans. James Strachey (London: Hogarth Press, 1968), pp. 257–258.

15. Carol Gilligan, *In a Different Voice: Psychological Theory and Women's Development* (Cambridge, MA: Harvard University Press, 1982), p. 30.

16. See Judy Auerbach, Linda Blum, Vicki Smith, and Christine Williams, "Commentary on Gilligan's *In a Different Voice,*" in *Feminist Studies,* Vol. 11, No. 1 (Spring 1985).

17. Agnes Heller, "The Emotional Division of Labour between the Sexes," *Social Praxis,* Vol. 7, No. 3/4 (1980).

18. Alison M. Jaggar, "Feminist Ethics: Some Issues for the Nineties," *Journal of Social Philosophy,* Vol. XX, No. 1-2 (Spring/Fall 1989), pp. 91–107.

19. Jean Grimshaw, *Philosophy and Feminist Thinking* (Minneapolis, MN: University of Minnesota Press, 1986), p. 194, 196.

20. Mary C. Raugust, "Feminist Ethics and Workplace Values," in *About Philosophy*, 6th ed., ed. Robert Paul Wolff (Englewood Cliffs, NJ: Prentice-Hall, 1996), pp. 78–82.

21. Nel Noddings, *Caring: A Feminine Approach to Ethics and Moral Education* (Berkeley, CA: University of California Press, 1984).

22. See Peter Singer, *Animal Liberation* (New York: Random House, 1990). See also Tom Regan, *The Case for Animal Rights* (Berkeley and Los Angeles, CA: The University of California Press, 1983).

23. Arne Naess, "The Deep Ecological Movement: Some Philosophical Aspects," in *Deep Ecology for the Twenty-First Century,* ed. George Sessions (Boston, MA: Shambhala Publications, 1995), p. 74.

24. Ibid., p. 68.

25. René Descartes, "The Principles of Philosophy," in *The Essential Descartes*, ed. Margaret D. Wilson (New York and Scarborough, Ontario: New American Library, 1969), p. 323.

26. Stuart Hampshire, *Spinoza* (London: Faber and Faber, 1951), p. 61.

27. Baruch Spinoza, "Ethics, part V, prop. XLII," in *The Rationalists: Descartes, Spinoza, Leibniz,* trans. R. H. M. Elwes (New York: Doubleday Anchor, 1974), p. 406.

28. Ibid., part IV, prop. XLII. (Following Hampshire's translation, I have rendered *hilaritas* as "joy" rather than as "mirth.")

29. Luther Binkley, *Conflict of Ideals: Changing Values in Western Society* (New York: D. Van Nostrand, 1969).

30. B. Williams, *Ethics and the Limits of Philosophy*, p. 111.

31. Christopher D. Stone, *Earth and Other Ethics: The Case for Moral Pluralism* (New York: Harper & Row, 1987).

9

Let Them Eat Cake
Political and Social Philosophy

The distinction between political and social philosophy is fairly arbitrary, one that some philosophers refuse to draw at all. My approach in this chapter is that the key issue in political philosophy is the legitimacy of government and that of **social philosophy** is the problem of justice—two topics that clearly overlap each other. Political philosophy concerns itself with the proper organization of human beings into groups governed by law or by instinct. It asks questions about legitimate and illegitimate political power: Why are citizens of political collectives (nations, states, townships, etc.) bound to submit to the laws of these collectives? What legitimately holds the collectives together: blood? land? birth? consent? contract? If consent or contract, must such agreements be formal, or may they be informal? "Social philosophy," as I use the term here, already presupposes a state of legitimate authority and asks what role that authority has in the distribution of goods and services to the various citizens of the collective. To what extent may the state determine fair apportionment, and to what extent may it not? What principles are in play to justify these determinations?

Political Philosophy

In a famous passage, Jean-Jacques Rousseau, the eighteenth-century Swiss philosopher, once wrote, "Man is born free; and everywhere he is in chains." This idea is an appropriate one with which to begin a discussion of political philosophy. In a significant sense, we, like the beasts of the field and the birds of the sky, are "born free." It was once believed

Everywhere We Are in Chains

337

RULES

I. CLOTHING
A. YOU MUST WEAR CLOTHES ON ALL SOCIAL OCCASIONS.
B. SUCH CLOTHING MUST COVER ALL PRIVATE PARTS (AS DEFINED BELOW)
C. CLOTHING MUST BE SUCH AS TO AVOID PROVOKING SHOCK OR OUTRAGE.

II. NOISE
A. NOISE MAY BE MADE, BUT ONLY UNDER CERTAIN CONDITIONS
1. IT IS SENSIBLE NOISE
2. IT DOES NOT ANNOY GREAT NUMBERS OF PEOPLE.
3. IT IS APPROPRIATE NOISE

III. SNEEZING

that some people were born to be slaves to others or to be their natural servants, but in our culture, we no longer believe that. We are not born with any natural masters (though it is possible, as we saw in Chapter 5, that we are born with a *supernatural* master, but even most theories that argue for a supernatural lord also hold that he created us as free beings). Yet, Rousseau says, everywhere we are in chains. Well, that view is surely a bit exaggerated, but look at it this way. In civilized society, rules govern almost every aspect of our behavior—rules tell us what we have to wear, how we must behave with other people, where we can and cannot go, how fast we must do it, in what circumstances it is all right to say certain things but not others and whether we must give birth if we find ourselves with an unwanted pregnancy. Furthermore, all these rules are enforced by an implied threat of immediate violence and eventual loss of property, freedom, and in some cases, even life. Just breaking a fairly simple rule, such as that against jaywalking—if you persist in breaking the rule numerous times in sequence contrary to the advice of a passing "peace officer"—can produce billy clubs, body searches, and handcuffs. So, in a sense, Rousseau is right. We perform all our acts looking up the barrel of a gun. This point raises one of the key questions in political philosophy—*Why should we put up with it?* This is just a rhetorical way of posing some of the big questions in this area, such as these:

- Are we naturally political, or is the political body a mere artifice? (If the latter, is it a necessary one, or could we do without it?)
- Is there a real distinction between legitimate and illegitimate authority? If so, how can we draw that distinction?
- Is revolution ever justified when political legitimacy is challenged and if so, under what conditions?

Performing Our Acts Looking Up the Barrel of a Gun

Plato

We begin once more with Plato. We started with him in our discussions of epistemology, ontology, and morality; we saw his influence in philosophy of religion; we will begin with him again in Chapter 10 on art. This is because, for better or for worse, Plato determined the course of Western philosophy. In some respects it is true, as Alfred North Whitehead said that the history of Western philosophy is a series of footnotes to Plato. Consciously or unconsciously, philosophers seem to have spent an inordinate amount of time either trying to achieve Plato's ideals or trying to escape from them. But precisely because so much has already been said here about Plato, we will not have to deal with him extensively now. Instead, I will give a cursory sketch of his political views, using them to set the stage for later developments in political philosophy.

THE REPUBLIC

PLATO

1) *Metaphysics*
Aristotle

2) *The Manual*
Epictetus

3) *Enneads*
Plotinus

4) *On Free Will*
Augustine

5) *The Divisions of Nature*
John Scotus Eriugena

6) *Proslogium*
Anselm of Canterbury

The History of Philosophy as a Series of Footnotes to Plato

Plato shared the typical Greek view that we are *naturally* social beings. But the "naturalness" of our sociality stems from a natural weakness on our parts as individuals. As individuals, we are not self-sufficient. As we saw in Chapter 7, from our necessary dependence on each other, Plato deduces a kind of natural division of labor along class lines, with skilled laborers and artisans forming one class, a military police caste forming another, and philosophers forming a third, the ruling class, which is created by promoting older members of the military caste. The lower class is incapable of philosophy (though there is no clear explanation in the *Republic* why some people are capable of it and others are not—it seems that these abilities and disabilities must be congenital). He suggests that those unfit from birth or habit for the rule of reason must be forced or tricked into submitting to it. The work and productivity of the laboring class are needed

Guppies Are Self-Sufficient at Birth. Humans Are Not.

by society, and these workers must be rewarded for their output. Hence, they are allowed to have families, are paid salaries, and are allowed to wear gold and silver decorations. The military caste is capable of philosophy, so its members are able to understand that their virtues of courage and determination are their own rewards. In a remarkable passage, Plato has Socrates describe to Glaucon the conditions in which the two upper classes will live:

> "Then besides this education any sensible man would say that we must provide their lodgings and their other property such as will not prevent them from being themselves as good guardians as they can be, and such as will not excite them to do mischief among the other citizens. . . . First of all, no one must have any private property whatsoever, except what is absolutely necessary. Secondly, no one must have any lodging or storehouse at all which is not open to all comers. Then their provisions must be so much as is needed by athletes of war, temperate and brave men, and there must be fixed allowances for them to be supplied by the other citizens as wages for their guardianship, so much that there shall be plenty for the year but nothing over at the end. They must live in common, attending in messes as if they were in the field. As to gold and silver, we must tell them that they have these from the gods as a divine gift in their souls, and they want in addition no human silver or gold; they must not pollute this treasure by mixing it with a treasure of mortal gold, because many wicked things have been done about the common coinage, but theirs is undefiled. They alone of all in the city dare not have any dealings with gold and silver, or even touch them, or come under the same roof with them, or hang them upon their limbs, or drink from silver or gold. In this way . . . whenever they get land of their own and houses and money, they will be householders and farmers instead of guardians, masters and enemies of the

I've been very courageous!

You mean, ... that's it? No medals? No glory?

Congratulations

Virtue Is Its Own Reward

rest of the citizens instead of allies; so hating and hated, plotting and plotted against, they will spend all their lives fearing enemies within much more than without, running a course very near to destruction, they and the city together. For all these reasons," I said, "let us agree on this manner of providing our guardians with lodging and all the rest, and let us lay it down by law. What do you say?"

"I agree wholly with you," said Glaucon.[1]

Furthermore, we are told that for the "guardians" (the military and ruling castes), there will be no families as such: "No one must have a private wife of his own, and the children must be common, too, and the parents shall not know the child nor the child its parent" (*Republic*, p. 255). So sexual relations will be by lottery—though there is a hint that the lottery is rigged and that the rul-

ers know who is sleeping with whom. Hence, the upper classes will produce children according to **eugenic** principles.

Plato prescribes a kind of absolute **communism** but only for the upper classes. This system will protect them from the greed that perme-ates the lower, more ignorant class; and as we saw, greed is allowed to motivate the work-ers and the artisans and is always contained and con-trolled by the philosopher rul-

LOVE LOTTERY
Step up and try your luck

And I say the lottery is rigged!

ers and their military allies. Like Karl Marx, some 2,250 years later, Plato saw society as *natural* but capable of being undermined by greed, if not structured in such a way as to contain it. (The difference between Plato and Marx is also striking, of course. For the latter, the destiny of the human race is associated with the communism of the working class; for Plato, that class is so benighted that it [and only it] is incapable of communism.)

In the *Republic,* a character named Adeimantus points out that the ideal city Socrates is describing may, through its totalitarian practices, be immune to the dangers of *greed,* but it can still be corrupted by *envy.* The lower class will envy the upper classes because of their power and intelligence, and the upper classes will envy the lower class because life at that level just seems more *fun.* In order to answer this objection, Plato has Socrates make a very curious suggestion, one that plagues political science to our day. (Indeed, Socrates admits that he is quite embarrassed to have to make the suggestion.) The suggestion is that all

Greed and Envy: Two Forces That Can Undermine the Republic

members of the City—including the rulers—be told a lie about why they must accept the order of things. Plato calls it a "noble lie," and it is introduced in the *Republic* when, with some trepidation, Socrates says:

Here goes, then, although I don't know how I shall dare, or what words to use. Well, I will try first to convince the rulers themselves and the soldiers, then the rest of the city; and this is the story. The training and education we were giving them was all a dream, and they only imagined all this was happening to them and around them; but in truth they were being moulded and trained down inside the earth, where they and their arms and all their trappings were being fashioned. When they were completely made, the earth their mother delivered them from her womb; and now they must take thought for the land in which they live, as for their mother and nurse, must plan for her and protect her, if anyone attacks her, and they must think of the other citizens as brothers also born from the earth.

"I am not surprised," [Glaucon] said, "that you were shy of telling that lie!"

Socrates Trying to Get People to Believe the Noble Lie

"There was good reason for it," I said, "but never mind, listen to the rest of the fable. 'So you are all brothers in the city,' we shall tell them in our fable, 'but while God moulded you, he mingled gold in the generation of some, and those are the ones fit to rule, who are therefore the most precious; he mingled silver in the assistants; and iron and brass in farmers and the other craftsmen. Then because of being all akin you would beget your likes for the most part, but sometimes a silver child may be born from a golden or a golden from a silvern, and so with all the rest breeding amongst each other. The rulers are commanded by God first and foremost that they be good guardians of no person so much as of their own children, and to watch nothing else so carefully as which of these things is mingled in their souls. If any child of theirs has a touch of brass or iron, they will not be merciful to him on any account, but they will give him the value proper to his nature, and push him away among the craftsmen or the farmers; if again one of them has the gold or silver in his nature, they will honour him and lift him among the guardians or the assistants, since there is an oracle that the city will be destroyed when the brass or the iron shall guard it.' Now have you any device to make them believe this fable?" (pp. 214–215)

This passage is very curious and even quite discouraging. It is curious because, as has been mentioned, part of the job of the *Republic* was to destroy the authority of myth in the Greek world (particularly the mythical stories told by Homer and Hesiod) and to replace mythical authority with the authority of *reason* (i.e., philosophy), yet here Plato is required to create a *new* myth to keep the City cohesive. And it is discouraging because Plato is admitting that reason itself is not strong enough a force to bind the City together. It is especially striking that even the rulers must be lied to, despite the fact that humans are supposed to be naturally social. Plato raises a specter that has haunted some thinkers even in our century: the idea that perhaps a society can remain vibrant and vital only if it has a myth about itself that it can tell itself. And unfortunately, these myths are usually tribalistic, nationalistic, and ethnocentric, hence often aggressive, arrogant, xenophobic, racist, and imperialistic. The great twentieth-century sociologist

Each Culture Must Have Its Own Myth

Émile Durkheim thought that when a society loses the capacity to tell itself such a myth, **anomie** (a sense of loss of meaning and direction) sets in. Anomie leads to both cultural and individual suicide, according to Durkheim.

You will remember that Plato, through Socrates's voice, told us that the city (the Republic) was "the soul writ large." Here, he seems to be implying that for Reason to control the other parts of the soul—the spirited and the appetitive parts—there must also be another "Noble Lie." Without such a lie, apparently the individual would not be happy or even satisfied.

Anomie

Thomas Hobbes

In the modern period, a number of important philosophers addressed "the big questions" of political philosophy. Thomas Hobbes's book *Leviathan* (1651) had as one of its main goals the resolution of the problem of politics, and we shall turn to it now.

Recall from Chapter 7 that Hobbes had a very distinctive view of human motivation, a view now called "psychological egoism," according to which all human actions are motivated by self-interest. Hobbes's political views presuppose the truth of psychological egoism, and even though that theory was rather soundly criticized in our earlier discussion as an unsuccessful account of individual human actions, it must be said that it is probably more acceptable as a political model or perhaps a political metaphor. When we think not of individuals but of foreign policies of various nations, it is difficult to believe that they are *not* motivated by what their framers conceive as the interest of the nation; or when we think of negotiations between labor and management groups, it is hard to imagine them as motivated by pure altruism.

Altruistic Labor Negotiations

So perhaps Hobbes's psychological egoism is a little less offensive here than in a discussion of morality, though here, too, its harshness may taint Hobbes's political views. Like the authors of the American Declaration of Independence, Hobbes begins his essay with the assumption that all people are equal. But his reasons for this assumption are very different from those of the Founding Fathers, who believed that our equality was a kind of moral state into which we were all created by our maker. Hobbes asserted the thesis of equality as a purely physical fact. Even the strongest or smartest among us is not so strong or so smart that two or three weaker, dumber ones could not overcome him or her. One may have some slight advantage over another but not enough to make a difference in the long run. We humans are, after all, more or less the same.

Now, given the fact that human nature is selfish, power-mongering, and equally distributed, Hobbes tries to imagine what human beings would be like in a "state of nature," that is, in a condition prior to any civil state, any rule by law. Concerning such a condition, Hobbes says:

> From this equality of ability, ariseth equality of hope in the attaining of our ends. And therefore if any two men desire the same thing, which nevertheless they cannot both enjoy, they become enemies; and in the way to their end, which is principally their own conservation, and sometimes their delectation only, endeavor to destroy, or subdue one another.
>
> . . . .
>
> Whatsoever therefore is consequent to a time of war, where every man is enemy to every man; the same is consequent to the time, wherein men live without other security, than what their own strength, and their own invention shall furnish them withal. In such condition, there is no place for industry; because the fruit thereof is uncertain: and consequently no culture of the earth; no navigation, nor use of the commodities that may be imported by sea; no commodious building; no instruments of moving, and removing, such things as require much force; no knowledge of the face of the earth; no account of time; no arts; no letters; no society; and which is worst of all, continual fear and danger of violent death; and the life of man, solitary, poor, nasty, brutish, and short.[2]

Hobbes's Five Dwarfs Plus Two

To this bleak and depressing picture, Hobbes now adds:

> To this war of every man, against every man, this also is consequent; that nothing can be unjust. The notions of right and wrong, justice and injustice have there no place. Where there is no common power, there is no law: where no law, no injustice. Force, and fraud, are in war the two cardinal virtues. Justice, and injustice are none of the faculties neither of the body, nor mind. If they were, they might be in a man that were alone in

the world, as well as his senses, and passions. They are qualities, that relate to men in society, not in solitude. It is consequent also to the same condition, that there be no propriety, no dominion, no *mine,* and *thine* distinct; but only that to be every man's, that he can get; and for so long, as he can keep it. And thus much for the ill condition, which man by mere nature is actually placed in; though with a possibility to come out of it, consisting partly in the passions, partly in his reason. (pp. 101–102)

So Hobbes's view is this: Concepts like right and wrong, justice and injustice, and "mine and thine" (property) are concepts generated by *law,* hence dependent on law. In the absence of law, these concepts cannot be meaningful. Furthermore, the concept of law is itself dependent upon *power.* A law with no power behind it is not authoritative, because it cannot be enforced. This view is called **legal positivism,** and according to it, justice is whatever legality *calls* just, and what is legal has been established as legal by the powers that be and for just as long as they are able to enforce the law. According to this tradition (pretty much

> # Power
> $\downarrow$
> # Law
> $\downarrow$
> Justice/Injustice
> Right/Wrong
> Property/Theft

the tradition of Thrasymachus and Macchiavelli), talk about "unjust laws" simply doesn't make much sense. (In this tradition, calling a law *morally* unjust doesn't carry any weight, because the "moral sphere" is just a fantasy, the mental projection of an ideal legal system where the power of the rulers is replaced by the power of an imagined God.)

Notice at the end of the previous anxiously pessimistic passage there was one glimmer of hope. Hobbes said, "And thus much for the ill condition, which man by mere nature is actually placed

Legal Positivism

in; though with a possibility to come out of it, consisting partly in the passions, partly in his reason."

The *passionate* part of our self desperately desires to survive. (How else could we acquire power and enjoy pleasure?) And there is a *natural right* to attempt to do so. Hobbes writes:

> The RIGHT OF NATURE . . . is the liberty each man hath, to use his own power, as he will himself, for the preservation of his own nature; that is to say, of his own life; and consequently, of doing anything, which in his own judgment, and reason, he shall conceive to be the aptest means thereunto. (p. 103)

Notice that for Hobbes, there is only *one* natural right, not a great group of them, as we find in our Bill of Rights, Declaration of Independence, and Constitution. Perhaps the best way to state Hobbes's view is to say that no one can reasonably fault or condemn the actions of another person who believes that these actions are required for her personal survival.

I have, then, a natural right to protect myself against you, and this right entails the subsidiary right to use violence against you, if I see violence as the most effective form of self-protection. Now, unfortunately for me, *you* also have a natural right to try to preserve yourself, with the following consequences:

> And because the condition of man . . . is a condition of war of every one against every one; in which case every one is governed by his own reason; and there is nothing he can make use of, that may not be a help unto him, in preserving his life against his enemies; it followeth, that in such a condition, every man has a right to every thing; even to one another's body. And therefore, as long as this natural right of every man to every thing endureth, there can be no security to any man, how strong or wise so ever he be, of living out the time, which nature ordinarily alloweth men to live. (p. 103)

**Two People Pursuing
Their Natural Right**

Hobbes assumes that in a state of nature there will be a general scarcity of goods. Because not enough goods exist for everyone's survival and flourishing in such a state of nature, each becomes an enemy of all others. In this condition, even though I have a *right* to try to survive, in fact, there isn't much likelihood of my lasting very long.

So, based on our passions alone, we would not survive long enough to enjoy the goal of the natural right. But at this point, our *reason* comes into play. It is associated with what Hobbes calls "natural law."

A LAW OF NATURE . . . is a precept or general rule, found out by reason, by which a man is forbidden to do that which is destructive of his life, or taketh away the means of preserving the same; and to omit that by which he thinketh it may be best preserved. (p. 103)

Because none of us has much chance of survival if we each blindly pursue our own natural right, we must appeal to our reason and the "natural law" that reason discovers:

And consequently it is a precept, or general rule of reason, *that every man, ought to endeavor peace, as far as he has hope of obtaining it; and when he cannot obtain it, that he may seek, and use, all helps, and advantages of war.* The first branch of which rule, containeth the first, and fundamental law of nature; which is, *to seek peace, and follow it.* The second, the sum of the right of nature; which is, *by all means we can, to defend ourselves.*

From this fundamental law of nature, by which men are commanded to endeavor peace, is derived this second law; *that a man be willing, when others are so too, as far forth, as for peace, and defence of himself he shall think it necessary, to lay down this right to all things: and be contented with so much liberty against other men, as he would allow other men against himself.* For as long as every man holdeth this right, of doing any thing he liketh; so long are all men in the condition of war. But if other men will not lay down their right, as well as he; then there is no reason for anyone, to divest himself of his: for that were to expose himself to prey, which no man is bound to, rather than to dispose himself to peace. (pp. 103–104)

So the idea of natural right is the foundation of Hobbes's *social contract.* My natural right justifies my use of violence against you, if I perceive the use of such violence as being in the interest of my survival. Unhappily for me, *your* use of violence against me is equally justified. So I agree to renounce my right to use violence against you, if you agree to renounce your right to use violence against me. However, our contract is conditional, because each of us will break it the moment we think the other is not going to hold to it. This contract does not provide a very stable peace, especially if Hobbes is correct in attributing to each of us a selfish and power-mongering nature. If I see any advantage to myself in breaking the contract, I will

None of Us Can Sleep Easily

do it. None of us can sleep very easily. In fact, none of us dares sleep at all in this tenuous peace.

The solution to this dilemma requires another step in the contract. All of us must agree to transfer our right to violence and our right to sovereignty over ourselves to a mutually agreed-upon sovereign (a parliament or a monarch), which now has absolute political authority over us. In exchange for absolute power (including an army), this sovereign promises to pass laws that create a state of peace. Basically, the sovereign promises to restrain and punish anyone who breaks the initial part of the contract and uses violence against any other member of this newly created artificial body, the state.

The Sovereign

Hobbes realizes that there are no guarantees that the sovereign won't abuse its absolute power. In fact, it's almost certain the sovereign *will* do so, given his, her, or their egoistic propensities. Nevertheless, even abused authority is better than no authority, according to Hobbes. Furthermore, it is hoped that the sovereign will use both its passion (the egoistic side) and its reason (the natural law) and realize that a peaceful state is beneficial to *it* as well, because otherwise the angry populace may revolt and kill the sovereign. Notice, however, that in Hobbes's political system, revolt is never legitimate *unless it succeeds* because only power legitimates for Hobbes. However, not even the legitimate absolute tyrant can pass a law that succeeds in taking away my natural right. This is because that right is inalienable except by my uncoerced consent. No law can remove my right to resist law, if the law tries to deprive me of my life.

So, returning to "the big questions" with which we began this chapter, we see that for Hobbes, the state is an artifice (a monster, a "Leviathan") and a *necessary* one. Legitimate authority is empowered authority. Political bodies themselves determine what counts as just or unjust, so in one sense they cannot be unjust. Yet even when they create a *sense* of injustice, they are almost always better than their alternative. For this reason, we accept the gun constantly aimed at us and the

Leviathan—The Best Show in Town

threat of state violence. No matter how brutal the state is, it is the best show in town. Its alternative is chaos, misery, and death, a condition wherein life is "solitary, poor, nasty, brutish, and short." *Any* state is better than no state. You may not like politics, but according to Hobbes, only because of politics does the social center hold. When the social contract that creates political authority fails, human life is plunged into an abyss. "Things fall apart, the centre cannot hold."

John Locke

Locke, writing fifty years after Hobbes, used much of the same language as Hobbes did but with very different meanings. For example, Locke too discusses a "state of nature," but for him, this would be the *moral* state into which all of us are born by virtue of being God's creatures. Hobbes had obviously intentionally kept God out of political theory, not because Hobbes was an atheist (he may or may not have been), but because he thought God belonged no more in political science than he did in physics and because Hobbes was sick of tyrants justifying their power by something called "divine right." But though Locke was also against the so-called divine right of kings, he had no qualms against grounding his political theory in a religious belief. For him, God's power plays a role similar to that of secular power in Hobbes's theory, so for Locke, God created humans and gave them basic rights, the right to "life, health, liberty, and possessions." Each of us is born into a moral "state of nature" in which these rights are ours along with certain moral obligations that Locke calls the "law of nature," which, as

in Hobbes's philosophy, is a law of
reason. (Notice, however, that
otherwise Hobbes's "law of
nature" is very different from
Locke's "law of nature.")

Locke writes:

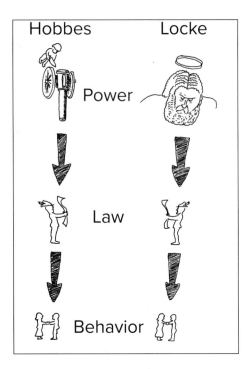

> To understand political power
> right, and derive it from its
> original, we must consider what
> state all men are naturally in,
> and that is a state of perfect
> freedom to order their actions
> and dispose of their posses-
> sions and persons as they think
> fit, within the bounds of the law
> of nature, without asking leave
> or depending upon the will of
> any other man. . . .
> The state of nature has a
> law of nature to govern it
> which obliges every one; and
> reason which is that law, teaches all mankind who will but consult it that,
> being all equal and independent, no one ought to harm another in his life,
> health, liberty, or possessions; for men being all the workmanship of one
> omnipotent and infinitely wise Maker—all the servants of one sovereign
> master, sent into the world by his order, and about his business—they are
> his property whose workmanship they are, made to last during his, not one
> another's, pleasure; and being furnished with like faculties, sharing all in one
> community of nature, there cannot be supposed any such subordination
> among us that may authorize us to destroy another, as if we were made for
> one another's uses as the inferior ranks of creatures are for ours.[3]

Hobbes had made a particular point of claiming that there is no such
thing as "natural property." Property itself could be created only by laws. In
the state of nature, there were no laws. Hence, for Hobbes, property is, as
Marx was later to call it, a "legal fiction." But, as we have seen, for Locke,
God's law creates *natural* property. Let's look at this curious idea. According
to the biblical account, God created the earth and provided it with natural
resources for the benefit of humankind. As was indicated earlier, Locke, like
Hobbes, was anxious to counter monarchical claims of divine right to property, and he used the biblical account to do so, then added a philosophical
touch of his own. In his *Two Treatises of Government,* Locke wrote, "The
earth and all that is therein . . . belongs to mankind in common . . . and . . .
nobody has originally a private dominion, exclusive of the rest of mankind"
(p. 134). Now, the one uniquely natural piece of property we each have is

our own body. The property right we have to our bodies can be extended to that which is created by our bodies' labor.

Though the earth and all inferior creatures be common to all men, yet every man has a property in his own person; this nobody has any right to but himself. The labour of his body and the work of his hands, we may say, are properly his. Whatsoever then he removes out of the state that nature hath provided and left it in, he hath mixed his labour with, and joined to it something that is his own, and thereby makes it his property. It being by him removed from the common state nature hath placed it in, it hath by this labour something annexed to it that excludes the common right of other men. For this labour being the unquestionable property of the labourer, no man but he can have a right to what that is once joined to, at least where there is enough and as good left in common for others. . . .

It will perhaps be objected to this that "if gathering the acorns, or other fruits of the earth, etc., makes a right to them, then any one may engross as much as he will." To which I answer: not so. The same law of nature that does by this means give us property does also bound that property, too. "God has given us all things richly" (I Tim. vi. 17), is the voice of reason confirmed by inspiration. But how far has he given it us? To enjoy. As much as any one can make use of to any advantage of life before it spoils, so much he may by his labour fix a property in; whatever is beyond this is more than his share, and belongs to others. . . .

I think it is plain that property in that, too, is acquired as the former. As much land as a man tills, plants, improves, cultivates, and can use the product of, so much is his property. . . .

Nobody could think himself injured by the drinking of another man, though he took a good draught, who had a whole river of the same water left him to quench his thirst; and the case of land and water, where there is enough for both, is perfectly the same. (p. 134, 136, 137)

Then one may accumulate as much "natural property" as one can use, without its spoiling so long as one leaves enough for everyone else. This idea reveals a tremendous attitudinal difference between Locke and Hobbes. Hobbes's political philosophy presupposes a condition of *scarcity*.

Locke's philosophy presupposes a condition of *abundance*. Locke's picture of human nature is much more generous than that of Hobbes.

The State of Nature
(According to Hobbes)

The State of Nature
(According to Locke)

We might consider the possibility that Locke and Hobbes are both right. Under conditions of abundance, altruism, generosity, and magnanimity might be natural virtues; under conditions of scarcity, stinginess and cold-heartedness might be natural. When I was a boy growing up in the fifties, there was a campaign to get people to build backyard A-bomb shelters. At that time, there was a lot of talk con-cerning a hypothetical postnu-clear attack scenario when social order had bro-ken down and the food and water supply had been contami-nated with radiation. The typical question was: Would you have the right to shoot your neighbor who had foolishly failed to build a shelter for himself and was now trying to get into your

**Protecting Your Backyard A-Bomb Shelter
from Covetous Neighbors**

already crowded shelter? The consensus was that you would be justified in doing so. This was Hobbes's world, not Locke's. And I suppose that if your neighbor tried to get hold of the gallon of uncontaminated water that would keep you and your children alive, you might well defend it with violence.

Back to Locke's concept of "natural property." When he turns to his analysis of money, he says, "And thus came in the use of money—some lasting thing that men might keep without spoiling, and that, by mutual consent, men would take in exchange for the truly useful but perishable supports of life" (p. 144). So there is nothing wrong with hoarding money or passing it along to your sons and daughters so long as you leave enough for others, because "gold and silver may be hoarded up without injury to anyone" (p. 144). This doctrine was very convenient for Locke and his well-to-do friends and somewhat counteracted the radicalness of his view that the land belongs to whoever tills it. But it failed to recognize that the excessive accumulation of wealth is a form of power that can be used to undermine the moral state of equality into which we were all supposed to be born. It is well known that Locke's political philosophy was one of the major blueprints for the American Founding Fathers. Some think that Locke's failure to combat the possibility of unjust accumulation of wealth infected our own political system. (Later we will talk again of economic justice in the "good society.")

Locke believed that his theory of our natural moral status (the state of nature) entailed a theory of justifiable punishment. He wrote:

> And thus in the state of nature one man comes by a power over another; but yet no absolute or arbitrary power to use a criminal, when he has got him in his hands, according to the passionate heats or boundless extravagancy of his own will; but only to retribute to him, so far as calm reason and conscience dictate, what is proportionate to his transgression, which is so much as may serve for reparation and restraint; for these two are the only reasons why one man may lawfully do harm to another, which is

that we call punishment. In transgressing the law of nature, the offender declares himself to live by another rule than that of reason and common equity, which is that measure God has set to the actions of men for their mutual security; and so he becomes dangerous to mankind, the tie which is to secure them from injury and violence being slighted and broken by him. Which being a trespass against the whole species and the peace and safety of it provided for by the law of nature . . . *every man hath a right to punish the offender and be executioner of the law of nature.* (pp. 124–125)

So in the state of nature, each of us has the right to our "life, liberty, health, and property." If any person violates the rights of others, that person alienates him- or herself from the state of nature and thereby forfeits his or her own natural rights. The person has thus *earned* a punishment, which ought to be meted out. On the principle that "the punishment must fit the crime" (Gilbert and Sullivan), even capital punishment is possible in the state of nature:

> By the same reason may a man in the state of nature punish the lesser breaches of that law. It will perhaps be demanded: with death? I answer: Each transgression may be punished to that degree and with so much severity as will suffice to make it an ill bargain to the offender, give him cause to repent, and terrify others from doing the like. Every offence that can be committed in the state of nature may in the state of nature be also punished equally, and as far forth as it may in a commonwealth. (p. 126)

(Those who are against capital punishment today may find Locke's views too harsh, but keep in mind that he was very progressive for his time on this score, because in the eighteenth century, dozens of crimes could be punished with death. Locke has at least reduced capital punishment to apply to one crime only—murder.) We see here that Locke's theory of justice is *retributive* (the criminal has earned the punishment with his acts and we owe it to him) and *preventative* (he and others who are aware of his punishment will be restrained from committing similar crimes). In terms of *distributive* justice, Locke's state of nature is a meritocracy. That is, one may own only as much property as one merits by virtue of one's labor (or inherits from the labor of one's ancestors).

In Thomas Hobbes's political theory, the conditions under which the citizens would probably revolt were pretty predictable, but there could be no such thing as *legitimate* revolt because legitimacy is determined by law, and the sovereign has been given the authority to create law by the social contract. In Locke, however, a very clear doctrine of legitimate revolution exists, once again grounded in our God-given moral condition, the state of nature. Locke wrote:

> There is, therefore, secondly, another way whereby governments are dissolved, and that is when the legislative or the prince, either of them, act contrary to their trust.
>   . . . The legislative acts against the trust reposed in them when they endeavour to invade the property of the subject and to make themselves or any part of the community masters or arbitrary disposers of the lives, liberties, or fortunes of the people.
>   . . . Since it can never be supposed to be the will of the society that the legislative should have a power to destroy that which every one designs to secure by entering into society, and for which the people submitted themselves to legislators of their own making. Whenever the legislators endeavour to take away and destroy the property of the people, or to reduce them to slavery under arbitrary power, they put themselves into a state of war with the people who are thereupon absolved from any further obedience. (p. 233)

So the function of the political state is to guarantee our moral state. In this sense, the political state is potentially superior to the state of nature because the latter lacks impartial judges, precise laws, and sufficient power to uphold the moral law. The *justification* of the political state is the consent of its citizens. The citizens consent to submit to political authority only with the proviso that such political authority will do whatever is necessary to protect our natural rights. This proviso is Locke's "social contract." But the citizen is bound to the contract only as long as the government upholds its end of the contract. Locke thought that the populace should not go lightly into a condition of revolt. Because of the seriousness of such a condition, all sorts of attempts should be made to correct the abuses of power before a revolution is declared. But if the state not only fails to uphold the citizens' rights to life, health, liberty, and property but also becomes the violator of those rights, then revolution is justified.

Locke was writing at a time when King James II tried to impose Catholicism in Britain, which provoked "the Glorious Revolution," a bloodless civil war that ended in a parliamentary victory and the flight of the king. It is somewhat ironic that the next use of Locke's doctrine of

What? The cost of postage stamps has gone up a penny? That's it! To the barricades!

Revolution Should Not Be Entered into Lightly

legitimate revolution was by the American colonists, revolting against the British government of King George III. The Founding Fathers wrote in the American Declaration of Independence:

We hold these truths to be self-evident, that all men are created equal; that they are endowed by their Creator with certain unalienable rights; that among these are life, liberty, and the pursuit of happiness. That, to secure these rights, governments are instituted among men, deriving their just powers from the consent of the governed; that, whenever any form of government becomes destructive of these ends, it is the right of the people to alter or to abolish it, and to institute a new government, laying its foundation on such principles, and organizing its powers in such form, as to them shall seem most likely to effect their safety and happiness.

As I mentioned before, the United States is sometimes thought of as a giant Lockean experiment, containing all the best features of Locke's political theory (government justified by consent of the citizens, basic rights guaranteed by law, recognition of moral and legal equality, and the recognition of the right to revolt if government abrogates its duties) and also suffering from some of the defects of his theory (the contradiction of separating religion and politics, yet grounding political rights in a theological conception of the human being, the lack of a theory of distributive justice based on anything other than merit or inheritance, the failure to recognize that the accumulation of power in the form of wealth can jeopardize the democratic foundations). Attempts have been made to address some of these problems through the passage of laws legalizing labor unions and creating a graduated income tax, among others.

Jean-Jacques Rousseau

JEAN-JACQUES ROUSSEAU (1712–1778) stands approximately to the French Revolution as Locke stands to the American Revolution, though the United States probably continues today to be more a Lockean experiment than France does a Rousseauian one. (And the Soviet Union was probably even less of a Marxian experiment.)

Rousseau, like Locke, believed that all humans are born free and autonomous and that the only legitimate government is one that preserves and maximizes that condition. Again, like Locke, he believed that such legitimacy can come about only through consent to a social contract. However, he believed that such legitimacy in fact existed nowhere in his time and that even the English parliamentarians deceived themselves concerning their own freedom. In fact, we began this chapter with Rousseau's words: "Man is born free, and everywhere he is in chains." Indeed Rousseau thought that men were born both free and good but that society had imprisoned them and had corrupted their goodness. Let's take a look at his diagnosis of the political situation of his time and his prescription for it.

Men Are Born Good but Are Corrupted by Society

Consistent with the theories of Hobbes and Locke, Rousseau begins his analysis with an account of the "state of nature." Like Hobbes, and unlike Locke, Rousseau claims that in a condition outside the social order, there would be no *morality* (no "ought," no "duty"). However, it is possible to talk about *virtues* in the state of nature. For example, Rousseau takes it that *self-love (amour de soi)* is a *natural virtue*, a natural good.

Anyone who lacks it is in some sense perverted and is incapable of truly moral development. (Notice that Jesus's moral teaching—"Love thy neighbor as thyself"—also presupposes self-love as a necessary condition of morality.) Similarly, according to Rousseau, we have (contrary to Hobbes's claim) a natural pity or pain at the misfortune of others. Unfortunately, traditional societies pervert the first of these virtues (self-love) and invert the second (pity). Self-love is turned into *pride* (*amour propre*), and pity is transformed into its opposite—delight in others' misery.

Amour de Soi?

Pride results from anxious reflection about oneself and the need to feel superior. This need induces one to compare oneself forever with others, to the extent that one finds one's most exquisite pleasure in the misfortune or inferiority of others. Pride and envy are encouraged everywhere by traditional social organization, but in truth, they prevent one from developing into a full person. This speculation leads Rousseau to the view (in *Émile*) that a truly correct education of a child would require the child to be as far from society's corrupting influences as possible. The child

Pleasure Derived from the Unhappiness of Others

should be reared in as nearly a "state of nature" as can be arranged (hence, the understandable but misleading attribution to Rousseau of the philosophy of "back to nature"). In this primary state, the child will be allowed to develop his or her own natural virtues. Such a child, left to his or her own devices, learns through *trial and error*, not theories, through *facts*, not words, through *sensations and feelings*, not abstractions. This child is freed from the necessity of holding "opinions" and lives a happy, self-sufficient, timeless existence, unaware of artificial needs or worries about the future.

The child will be taught to read, but the only book allowed in his or her education will be *Robinson Crusoe!* Those who have read only *Émile* sometimes think that Rousseau was calling for the abolition or minimalization of the state and demanding a "return to nature" for all. But they have failed to see that, for Rousseau, if one remained at the state of natural virtues, one would fail to develop fully one's humanity. The state of natural virtues must be developed into a moral state, and morality and politics go hand in hand. The move from natural virtuousness to morality involves the development of our social being. Only by filling out the social side of our nature (which was necessarily underdeveloped in childhood) can we find our fullest freedom. But if society is to be a *natural* extension of the self, it must be consistent with our natural virtues and with our *free* and *rational* status. (A society founded on sheer force would be both unnatural and unjust.) The natural and just society will be constituted by the social contract, which Rousseau describes:

Child Reading *Robinson Crusoe*
(Classic Comics Version)

> The clauses of this contract are so determined by the nature of the act that the slightest modification would make them vain and ineffective; so that, although they have perhaps never been formally set forth, they are everywhere the same and everywhere tacitly admitted and recognized. . . .
>   These clauses, properly understood, may be reduced to one—the total alienation of each associate, together with all his rights, to the whole community; for, in the first place, as each gives himself absolutely, the conditions are the same for all; and, this being so, no one has any interest in making them burdensome to others.

Moreover, the alienation being without reserve, the union is as perfect as it can be, and no associate has anything more to demand: for, if the individuals retained certain rights, as there would be no common superior to decide between them and the public, each, being on one point his own judge, would ask to be so on all; the state of nature would thus continue, and the association would necessarily become inoperative or tyrannical.

Finally, each man, in giving himself to all, gives himself to nobody; and as there is no associate over which he does not acquire the same right as he yields others over himself, he gains an equivalent for everything he loses, and an increase of force for the preservation of what he has.

If then we discard from the social compact what is not of its essence, we shall find that it reduces itself to the following terms:

"Each of us puts his person and all his power in common under the supreme direction of the general will, and, in our corporate capacity, we receive each member as an indivisible part of the whole."

At once, in place of the individual personality of each contracting party, this act of association creates a corporate and collective body, composed of as many members as the assembly contains voters, and receiving from this act its unity, its common identity, its life, and its will.[4]

A number of problems leap out at us from this statement. First, notice that Rousseau completely rejects the notion of *representative democracy*. According to him, a true democracy must be a *participatory democracy*; all citizens must vote on all issues of public interest:

Sovereignty, for the same reason as makes it inalienable, cannot be represented; it lies essentially in the general will, and will does not admit of representation: it is either the same or other; there is no intermediate possibility. The deputies of the people, therefore, are not and cannot be its representatives: they are merely its stewards, and can carry through no definitive acts. Every law the people has not ratified in person is null and void—is, in fact, not a law. The people of England regards itself as free; but it is grossly mistaken; it is free only during the election of members of parliament. As soon as they are elected, slavery overtakes it, and it is nothing. The use it makes of the short moments of liberty it enjoys shows indeed that it deserves to lose them. (p. 240)

Also, notice that Rousseau is saying a legitimate political body must be very limited in size, because all its members must be capable of convening at regular intervals. Rousseau was from Switzerland, and his model is similar to the democracy of the local Swiss cantons (though they did not completely legalize voting for women on national issues until 1981, and as late as April 29, 1990, the male citizens of the town of Appenzell denied the vote to women in local elections!) or of the town meetings of New England. A country as massive as the United States could not possibly be a true

The Hills Are Alive with the Sound of Democracy

democracy for Rousseau—at least, not in his own day. Ironically, today, with our sophisticated technology, it would be at least theoretically possible to engage every American on every vote. Imagine that Monday evenings were set aside for politics. For three hours, the TV stations would be dedicated to debating the political issues, followed by a vote in which each legal voter would punch his or her Social Security number into a computer and would vote on each issue. These votes would be instantly tallied and the results known immediately.

Another problem in Rousseau's political schema is the apparent contradiction between his claim that only in the political body does

Monday Evening TV

one find one's true freedom and his assertion that one must transfer all of one's rights to the whole political body and accept as one's own will what he calls "the general will." Rousseau was aware of the problem. He wrote:

> When the State is instituted, residence constitutes consent; to dwell within its territory is to submit to the Sovereign.
>
> Apart from this primitive contract, the vote of the majority always binds all the rest. This follows from the contract itself. But it is asked how a man can be both free and forced to conform to wills that are not his own. How are the opponents at once free and subject to laws they have not agreed to?
>
> I retort that the question is wrongly put. The citizen gives his consent to all the laws, including those which are passed in spite of his opposition, and even those which punish him when he dares to break any of them. The constant will of all the members of the State is the general will; by virtue of it they are citizens and free. When in the popular assembly a law is proposed, what the people is asked is not exactly whether it approves or rejects the proposal, but whether it is in conformity with the general will, which is their will. Each man, in giving his vote, states his opinion on that point; and the general will is found by counting votes. When therefore the opinion that is contrary to my own prevails, this proves neither more nor less than that I was mistaken, and that what I thought to be the general will was not so. If my particular opinion had carried the day I should have achieved the opposite of what was my will; and it is in that case that I should not have been free. (p. 250)

In other words, in consenting to live in a state (and tacit consent is given by mere residency ["love it or leave it"]), one is not only consenting to abide by the will of the people but also recognizing that that will *is* the state. Therefore, every vote is a vote for the general will, even if one's vote on any particular issue is overridden. So even if I vote "no" on Proposition P, and Proposition P wins the majority of the votes, then I have actually voted *for* P in a general sense, despite voting against it in fact. Therefore, I can happily follow it as a law even if I thought it was a bad idea when it was first proposed. Or, to put it another way, all legitimate political activities must

The General Will

transcend individual opinion and selfish desire. The only nondespotic way of determining the general will is through a democratic act determined by majority rule. Therefore, not only am I bound by the outcome of such an act, but I also recognize that its outcome is my desire qua social being.

Of course, Rousseau's readers must decide for themselves if this explanation is a real insight or mere **sophistry.** (Only one vote per person, please.)

John Stuart Mill

We have just seen that according to Rousseau, individuals come into their full humanity precisely by alienating their individual wills to the general will (or by submitting it to the general will, thereby identifying their individual wills with the general will). Three-quarters of a century after Rousseau and on the other side of the Channel from him, John Stuart Mill (1806–1873), whose utilitarian moral philosophy has already been discussed, had a political agenda that was exactly the opposite from that of Rousseau. Mill saw his goal as that of distinguishing between the public and the private. He believed there was a realm that was genuinely the concern of society (and hence of the body politic).

But he also believed there was a realm that was genuinely the concern of the individual, and in that realm, politics had no business. Even if with 100 percent unanimity the "general will" approved of interfering in the legitimately private sphere, it could interfere only by doing violence to the truly human charter. On this, Mill wrote:

The Private versus the Public

> Let us suppose, therefore, that the government is entirely at one with the people, and never thinks of exerting any power of coercion unless in agreement with what it conceives to be their voice. But I deny the right of the people to exercise such coercion, either by themselves or by their government. The power itself is illegitimate. The best government has no more title to it than the worst. It is as noxious, or more noxious, when exerted in accordance with public opinion, than when

in opposition to it. If all mankind minus one, were of one opinion, and only one person were of the contrary opinion, mankind would be no more justified in silencing that one person, than he, if he had the power, would be justified in silencing mankind.[5]

In order to draw the distinction between the public and the private, Mill formulated a principle he called "the principle of liberty." Mill began his essay, *On Liberty*, with this assertion:

> The object of this essay is to assert one very simple principle. . . . That principle is, that the sole end for which mankind are warranted, individually or collectively, in interfering with the liberty of action of any of their number, is self-protection. That the only purpose for which power can be rightfully exercised over any member of a civilized community, against his will, is to prevent harm to others. His own good, either physical or moral, is not a sufficient warrant. He cannot rightfully be compelled to do or forbear because it will be better for him to do so, because it will make him happier, because, in the opinion of others, to do so would be wise, or even right. These are good reasons for remonstrating with him, or reasoning with him, or persuading him, or entreating him, but not for compelling him, or visiting him with any evil in case he do otherwise.[6]

In other words, the body politic, the general will, or whatever one wants to call political authority, can legitimately restrain the action of individual members of the society only if those actions harm other members of the society. What Mill is ruling out here is what is called "state paternalism." Or, to put it another way, he is ruling out "victimless crime." That is, the state has no right to criminalize behavior it deems harmful to the agent but to no one else. This principle means that drunkenness or drug abuse in the privacy of one's home cannot be a crime, nor prostitution, nor the reading of pornography, nor the refusal to wear a helmet while riding one's motorcycle, among other activities.

State Paternalism or Government as Daddy

Mill's principle strikes an intuitive chord with me. I could do or say or think certain things that I claim are nobody's business but my own and over which society has no legitimate authority. Nevertheless, there seem to me to be serious problems with Mill's principle. First, from a historical perspective, we might detect an ideological component of Mill's principle. It supports a cherished middle-class Victorian

**A Drunken Male Prostitute Riding His Motorcycle
without a Helmet in the Privacy of His Own Home**

dream, the vision of separate spheres—a peaceful private home life isolated from the noisy, combative competition of the ongoing industrial revolution—hence the English aphorism "A man's home is his castle." Social critics have recently attempted to burst this bubble, pointing out the intimate connections between hearth, factory, and imperial militarism.[7] Second, even granting a possible Victorian domain of separate spheres, the social world has become much more complicated since Mill's time. Social welfare schemes and tax schemes have become so entwined today that the motorcyclist who foolishly opts to forgo a helmet in the name of "coolness" no longer involves just himself when he enters the hospital for brain surgery. Rather, the price of his surgery is charged partially to *me*, the taxpayer.

This situation is also somewhat true concerning the abuse of alcohol and drugs. And some studies conclude that there is a significant connection between the pornography industry and violent crimes. If so, then the demarcation between the private and the public begins to deteriorate. Furthermore, a conceptual difficulty exists with Mill's notion of "harm to others" that emerges as soon as we try to define "harm." If we construe it as purely "physical harm," we shall have circumscribed it too narrowly, because it will exclude theft and fraud. As the late American philosopher Richard Taylor wrote:

> If we say, for example, that *harming* a man consists not merely of injury to his body, but to any of his deepest interests then of course we bring such

things as theft and fraud within its meaning. Men do have a deep interest in the security of their property as well as of their persons. But unfortunately, men have *other* deep interests as well which no believer in freedom supposes for a minute should never be foiled.

Thus, there are men who have a deep interest in such things as religion, patriotism, public manners, the preservation of wildlife, and so on, without end. Now if we say that no one shall be permitted to do anything that would foil, frustrate, or damage any such interest held by anyone, this will be about equivalent to saying that no one may do anything at all. The whole of the criminal law would be summed up in saying that all actions are prohibited. And a principle having that consequence can hardly be called a principle of liberty.[8]

The solution will have to be that actual courts of law must determine exactly what constitutes harm, using the concept of criminal law to make the appropriate distinctions. The problem with that approach is that the principle of liberty was meant by Mill to determine criminal law, not the other way around, or the whole process becomes circular.

Mill extended his principle of liberty to encompass such areas as freedom of thought, expression, and assembly. No government, not even a pure democracy, can legitimately legislate against these rights, according to Mill. He would have approved of the American idea of a "Bill of Rights" that in fact, if not in principle, somehow transcends public opinion. It is clear that, for him, democracy was the best form of government. But it was not an end in itself; rather it was the most likely means of guaranteeing the interests of both the public and the private domains. And these, contrary to Rousseau, not even democracy could override.

This is the doctrine of laissez-faire or "hands off" (literally, in French, "leave alone"). There are certain realms where government has no business except to protect the existence of precisely those realms. Otherwise, government must "butt out" of them. Mill extended this doctrine of laissez-faire throughout his social philosophy. Not only must there be no state interference in the inner life and harmless activities of the citizens, but in general, "Laissez-faire . . . should be the general practice: every departure from it, unless required by some great good, is a certain evil."[9] Among other applications, this doctrine means that, in most respects, the government ought to keep its hands off the marketplace, allowing a system of free enterprise unhampered by state controls. Even though Mill is thought of as "the saint of liberalism," the doctrine of laissez-faire is now usually associated with the economic policy of conservatism. Still, despite Mill's enthusiasm for economic laissez-faire policy, Mill thought that deviations from it were required:

> But if the workman is generally the best selector of means, can it be affirmed with the same universality, that the consumer, or person served, is the most competent judge of the end? Is the buyer always qualified to judge the commodity? If not, the presumption in favor of the competition of the market does not apply to the case; and if the commodity be one, in the quality of which society has much at stake, the balance of advantages may be in favour of some mode and degree of intervention by the authorized representatives of the collective interest of the state.
>
> Now, the proposition that the consumer is a competent judge of the commodity can be admitted only with numerous abatements and exceptions. He is generally the best judge (though even this is not true universally) of the material objects produced for his use. These are destined to supply some physical want, or gratify some taste or inclination, respecting which wants or inclinations there is no appeal from the person who feels them; or they are the means and appliances of some occupation, for the use of the persons engaged in it, who may be presumed to be judges of the things required in their own habitual employment. But there are other things of the worth of which the demand of the market is by no means a test; things of which the utility does not consist in ministering to inclinations, nor in serving the daily uses of life, and the want of which is least felt where the need is greatest. This is peculiarly true of those things which are chiefly useful as tending to raise the character of human beings. (pp. 952–953)

Such a policy of legitimate state intervention not only justifies for Mill a governmental subsidy of the arts, but it could also be used in today's world to protect citizens from the contamination of dangerous pesticides and to protect the environment from the competition of vicious profiteers who see their short-term profit as necessitating the destruction of the natural world. To quote Mill once more: "The uncultivated cannot be competent judges of cultivation" (p. 953).

Social Philosophy

The problem of justice is the key issue of social philosophy. This problem is usually seen as having to do with fairness and desert (deservedness) in meeting the claims of citizens and in the distribution of goods and services. The big question here is—What is the state's legitimate role in these activities? We will look at three views concerning this issue: the communist solution, the **minimal-state** solution, and **liberalism.** I will view liberalism as located between the other two positions, though I do not mean to imply that

because communism and minimalism are extremes relative to liberalism, therefore they could not be true. Indeed, these two "extreme" views are not the most extreme possible in any absolute sense. Such extremes would be these: On the one hand is a kind of statism that holds the state and only the state totally responsible for the fair distribution of goods and services to its citizens and says only it can determine the legitimacy of the citizens' claims. On the other hand is an **anarchistic** position, claiming that the state itself is illegitimate, hence can never play a role in fair distribution or in responding to legitimate claims of individuals.

Communism

The political philosophy of Karl Marx (1818–1883) was greatly influenced by his early contact with the metaphysics of G. W. F. HEGEL (1770–1831), whose theory of reality is distinctly organicistic. (**Organicism** is the opposite of atomism: **Atomism** says that reality is composed of individual, simple units—that the individuals are more real than the whole, which is somehow actually only an abstraction. Organicism says that the whole is more real than the parts; the whole is an organic unity, and the parts depend completely on the whole. Hence, the parts are somehow less real than the whole.) In Hegel's version of organicism, the so-called individuals are themselves just points of intersecting relations of power within the system, so in a certain sense, each individual is really a microcosmic mirror of the macrocosm—a reflection of the whole system.

The Individual as a Point of Intersecting Relations of Power

Marx's Materialism   Marx rejected Hegel's grandiose metaphysical schema, but he too tended toward organicism. Not only did he see the human race as ecologically closely related to nature (according to one story, Marx had written to Charles Darwin asking for Darwin's permission to let Marx dedicate *Das Kapital* to him, but Darwin declined the honor, saying that his own theory had caused him enough trouble without being blamed for Marx's theory as well), but Marx also saw the individual human as ecologically related to his or her society. Society is not merely the totality of individuals; rather, it is an organic whole that in certain ways creates the individual. Therefore, for Marx, there can be no question of individual rights that somehow supersede social rights.

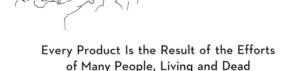

Every Product Is the Result of the Efforts of Many People, Living and Dead

Everything that an individual does is a result of the efforts of many people, living and dead. Hence, all products are in that sense *social* products and belong to society. (This view is closer to Rousseau's than to Mill's.)

Historical societies have been unjust, according to Marx, almost from the very beginning (even though the most aboriginal social arrangements, hence the most natural ones, were forms of primitive communism). This unjustness is because a minority of individuals managed to wrest power and material wealth from their communal source, thereby setting up systems of privilege and generating social institutions that would guarantee those privileges—protected at first by armed thugs called "police" or "army," eventually by social institutions and internalized guilt. (Marx thought that this grabbing of power and wealth was somehow "unnatural." Some of his Hobbesian critics claim it was all *too* natural.) Ever since the original power grab, the history of the social world has always been the history of the quest for material justice. This quest has taken on the guise of class antagonism and sometimes of class warfare, where the interests of the majority (a dispossessed working class: slaves, serfs, laborers) are pitted against the interests of the privileged minority. Marx's optimistic teleological conception of history tells him that the interests of the majority *must* finally triumph.

The Interests of the Few versus the Interests of the Many, According to Karl Marx

Marx's materialistic organicism, based as it is on categories from economics and sociology rather than physics, is such that the socioeconomic structure of society is a very powerful determinant of the individual in society. So the problem is not simply that unjust socioeconomic structures of power create unfair conditions for individuals; rather, they create *mutilated individuals*. For example, Marx writes:

> The alienation of the worker in his object is expressed as follows in the laws of political economy: the more the worker produces the less he has to consume; the more value he creates the more worthless he becomes; the more refined his product the more crude and misshapen the worker; the more civilized the product the more barbarous the worker; the more powerful the work the more feeble the worker; the more the work manifests intelligence the more the worker declines in intelligence and becomes a slave of nature. Labor certainly produces marvels for the rich, but it produces privation for the worker. It produces palaces, but hovels for the worker. It produces beauty, but deformity for the worker. It replaces labor by machinery, but it casts some of the workers back

into a barbarous kind of work and turns the others into machines. It produces intelligence, but also stupidity and cretinism for the workers.[10]

You Are What You Make

According to Marx's positive, optimistic conception of human nature, humans are naturally creative, productive, artistic, aesthetic beings who must express their being in their products. (Humans thus objectify their subjectivity.) Marx prefers the name *Homo faber* (man the maker) over *Homo sapiens* (man the knower) because, for him, all *knowing* follows upon *doing* and *making*. So another effect of unjust socioeconomic systems is that the individual's selfhood is stolen from her. She does not produce as a natural outlet of her creative urge; rather, she is forced to sell her work to another person. Her work is stolen from her and becomes a part of an economic system that is hostile to her own interests. This effect is what Marx calls "alienated labor," and here is what he says about it:

> What constitutes the alienation of labor? First, that the work is *external* to the worker, that it is not part of his nature; and that, consequently, he does not fulfill himself in his work but denies himself, has a feeling of misery rather than well being, does not develop freely his mental and physical energies but is physically exhausted and mentally debased. The worker therefore feels himself at home only during his leisure time, whereas at work he feels homeless. His work is not voluntary but imposed, *forced labor*. It is not the satisfaction of a need, but only a *means* for satisfying other needs. Its alien character is clearly shown by the fact that as soon as there is no physical or other compulsion it is avoided like the plague. External labor, labor in which man alienates himself, is a labor of self-sacrifice, of mortification. Finally, the external character of work for the worker is shown by the fact that it is not his own work but work for someone else, that in work he does not belong to himself but to another person.[11]

Marx's Vision of Society So what would a just society look like for Marx? (Or what *will* it look like? He thought its advent was inevitable.) First, its social production must be addressed to what he calls *true needs* rather than *false needs*. True needs derive from our real nature as biological and social beings (e.g., the need for food, shelter, clothing, medical care, love, and education). False needs are any artificial needs of the

False Needs

privileged that are at the expense of the true needs of the majority, any exaggeration of true needs that are instilled in some while others go without (the need for mansions, luxurious clothes, and gourmet excesses) or the instillment of economic needs in the masses whose real goal is not satisfaction but profit for the privileged owning class (planned obsolescence: lightbulbs that burn out in a month, razors that go dull and are to be thrown away, pantyhose that tear after one wearing, automobiles whose bumpers collapse in collisions at five miles per hour). Second, the foundations of social production (natural resources, means of production, means of distribution) must not be privately owned but must be socially owned and democratically controlled. Third, social production must be such that individual workers are not forced to enter into streams of specialization that constrain the natural abundance of the creative urge. No one may be objectified in a specific role— become *the* waiter, *the* teacher, *the* janitor, *the* physicist, or even *the* neurosurgeon. Marx does not mean that no one can *specialize*. (Who wants to have one's brain operated upon by one's hairdresser or by one's philosophy teacher?) A person may spend years training to learn neurosurgery, but still, one does not become *the* neurosurgeon. (In today's America, perhaps one also becomes a golfer?)

Karl Marx Inspects a Triumph of Capitalism

In a famous passage in which Marx announces the abolition of "the division of labor," he says:

> In communist society, where nobody has one exclusive sphere of activity but each can become accomplished in any branch he wishes, society regulates the general production and thus makes it possible for me to do one thing today and another tomorrow, to hunt in the morning, fish in the afternoon, rear cattle in the evening, criticize [art, literature, and poetry] after dinner, just as I have a mind, without ever becoming hunter, fisherman, shepherd or critic.[12]

Under these conditions, the motto of justice will be "from each according to his ability, to each according to his need." Here we will have the recovery of true human nature, the release of the human creative potential, and for the first time, *true* individuality, because true individuality requires "true consciousness" (recognition that the needs of the individual and the needs of the society are identical) and unconstrained creativity—which is really where individual differences come into play. Marx has no trouble handing these new humans over to a democracy.

Criticisms of Marx's View   Many of Marx's ideas are impressive. In my view, he is right that much of world history has been characterized by the power and privilege of a few, supported by the misery of many, and I think he is also right that any complete theory of the just society must include the concept of **distributive justice** (the fair distribution of socially produced wealth or the fair distribution of scarcity). But Marx's system is itself fraught with problems.

First, consider Marx's tremendously optimistic picture of human nature. As opposed to pessimists like Freud and Hobbes, Marx thought we are naturally social and naturally workers. (Freud thought we were natural egoists and natural bums, so our true nature would have to be suppressed if civilization was to flourish.) According to Marx, we are naturally cooperative. Competition and selfishness are primarily the result of unhealthy social arrangements. Now, one can *hope*

that Marx was right, but the evidence available to you and me is not always on the side of his argument. His response to this charge is that such evidence comes to us from cultures of alienation and is being evaluated through a fog of alienation (your fog and my fog). But because all cultures *have* been alienated to one degree or another, according to Marx, what evidence can he point to in order to establish that people are basically "good"?

A second objection concerns the mystification of the working class. Why should we accept Marx's claim that the destiny of the human race is the destiny of the working

Trying to See through the Fog of Alienation

class? Why should a particular class of oppressed, alienated, and unhappy people contain the hidden meaning of human history? (And are we sure that human history has a *meaning*, a *telos*?)

A third criticism concerns Marx's essentially Platonic claim that, in the truly human society, the interests of the individual and those of society will be identical. Certainly, Marx is right that every effort must be made to reduce the opposition between these two, but isn't there a suspicion, as critic Alan Brown says, that

> the only way in which the individual interests can be reconciled with collective interests is for those collective interests to *replace* the individual's own self interests in his own consciousness? . . . Consider the problem of congested traffic in rush hours. There is a collective interest in everyone using public transport, since this would be so much more convenient.

Does History Have Goals?

The individual has to curtail his own behavior to achieve a *second-best* solution—he would prefer that he should use his car and everyone else the bus.[13]

Civic-Mindedness

And finally, what about Marx's willingness to accept democracy as valid only "after the revolution"? He would reject as factitious the Western democracies of the contemporary world on the grounds that the voters in them are all alienated ideologues in a state of **false consciousness** who misunderstand their own interests and those of the human race. Marx will only give the vote to those nonalienated communalists in true consciousness who will be the second- or third-generation product of the revolution; yet their

The Newly Hatched True Human Being

creation will depend on an interim "dictatorship of the **proletariat**"—an absolute totalitarianism that will guide the newly revolutionized society for several generations until the "new human" has been fully hatched. Because at that point social classes will be no more, class struggle, exploitation, and the need for the state as an instrument of exploitation will have disappeared, and the dictatorship of the proletariat will simply "dissolve itself," voluntarily stepping down and handing its absolute power over to "the people."

Doesn't one have to be a bit *naive* to accept this vision? Is one simply a capitalist lackey if one observes that, unfortunately, Lord Acton was probably more accurate than Marx? (Acton: "Power corrupts; absolute power corrupts absolutely.")

These criticisms matter because of Marx's organicism. He believed that no piecemeal corrections of injustice can succeed. If the game is rotten, then every possible move in the game is rotten. The whole thing must be swept away, or there will be injustice forever. So, according to Marx, we must accept his judgment in all these issues: We must become revolutionaries or be ourselves condemned eternally as reactionaries, lackeys, and mouthpieces of the forces of injustice.

The Minimal State

At the opposite pole from Marx's communist society (or "communalist" society) is the idea of the minimal state. This state would have the legitimate power to prevent the use of force and fraud and to punish such uses but, without the express consent of all adult citizens, could not have the legitimate power to tax or confiscate property in order to perform any actions above and beyond these minimal duties. No public works or systems of aid to the needy would be justified.

Such a minimal state has been defended in a much-read and greatly discussed book by ROBERT NOZICK (1938–2002), called *Anarchy, State, and Utopia*. The starting point for Nozick's defense is Locke's "state of nature," in which, as we have seen, individuals have a natural right to "life, liberty, health, and property." Nozick holds the view that only a minimal state can defend these rights without itself becoming a violator of them. The reason the minimal state is the maximum state allowed is that any more extensive state must finance its projects through taxation, and if this taxation is not consented to by some individuals, it will violate their rights. Of course, the minimal state taxes its citizens for the protective services it offers them, and only those who pay the tax receive the benefits. According to Nozick, beyond this, unconsented taxation is on a par with forced labor. It makes the government part owner of you (because on the Lockean principles from which Nozick's argument proceeds, you own yourself, and your labor is an extension of yourself) and is indistinguishable from semislavery.

Nozick criticizes both socialism (of which communism is a version) and liberalism (which, like socialism, claims that fairness demands some kind of redistribution of wealth) on the grounds that they are what he calls "patterned" theories of justice rather than historical theories. That is, they impose a certain kind of pattern on the distribution of goods (e.g., Marx's "from each according to his ability, to each according to his need") that has nothing to do with the *history* of the goods distributed. This distribution would be fine, says Nozick, if goods fell from heaven like manna. But, in fact, most goods come to us with a history. They are already encumbered, already owned—purchased, traded, earned, or received as a gift. Those goods,

or "holdings," are covered by an absolute right to them by their owners—a right whose overriding would be unjust. This right pertains if the initial acquisition was just and if all subsequent transactions with it are just (e.g., if I own an object by virtue of having made it or purchased it with money that is legitimately mine and the like). Furthermore, people have a right to transfer holdings. I can trade or give away things I own (which means there is a right to inheritance). Finally, people have a right to demand rectification. In an anarchy (Hobbes's "state of nature"), I have a right to defend myself and my

Goods Falling Like Manna from Heaven

property against those who would injure me or my holdings, steal from me, or defraud me, and I have the right to punish those who do so. In a minimal state, I give up the right to punish others personally, by my own hand, but I do have the right to demand that the state perform these protective and punitive functions (though there are no other demands I can make on the state).

The implication of the minimal state concept is that *only* an unrestricted capitalism can produce a just society and that any state that prohibits "capitalist acts between consenting adults" is a tyranny. Nozick seems to recognize that one consequence of his view is that some people will amass great wealth and power while others will struggle in poverty. But he believes that this unfortunate side effect of his system is nevertheless consistent with justice. On the first page of his book, Nozick says that he knows many readers will reject his conclusions, which are "so apparently callous toward the needs and sufferings of others." Throughout his argument, he does little to alleviate this concern, though he does make a gesture in its direction by subscribing to Locke's proviso that, in acquiring property, "one must leave enough for others." Says Nozick:

Thus a person may not appropriate the only water hole in a desert and charge what he will. Nor may he charge what he will if he possesses one, and unfortunately it happens that all the water holes in the desert dry up, except for his. This unfortunate circumstance, admittedly no fault of his, brings into operation the Lockean proviso and limits his property rights.[14]

In a footnote, Nozick adds, "The situation would be different if his water hole didn't dry up, due to special precautions he took to prevent this" (p. 180).

Not surprisingly, Nozick's theory has delighted a number of people whose political posture is decidedly to the right. But most of the literature that his book has inspired has been critical. Still, the sheer volume of this literature is an impressive testimony to the significance of Nozick's book. It's as if political writers see Nozick's arguments as important enough to require a response.

Pleased by Nozick's Views

Numerous critics attack the notion of *rights* on which Nozick's libertarian utopia is based. The first sentence of his book is "Individuals have rights, and there are things no person or group may do to them (without violating their rights)." These rights are the right against coercive interference in one's affairs and the right to property. Where did one get these rights? Nozick does not really tell us; yet for him they are absolute and override any other moral claims. A typical strategy against Nozick is to insist that the existence of such rights cannot be merely presupposed but must be demonstrated. One group of critics simply denies that such absolute rights

Once upon a time in a far distant land there existed witches, unicorns, and natural rights....

exist at all. For example, Alasdair MacIntyre, a prominent British philosopher, says, "Belief in them is one with belief in witches and unicorns."[15] Another British philosopher, Alan Brown, says that claiming that I have a *right* to something is simply an elliptical way of saying that "all things considered, there is a good moral reason to respect or promote my freedom in this case" (p. 106). Therefore, rights cannot be absolute or foundational; rather, they are derived from other moral deliberations. Other philosophers have agreed with Nozick that there are basic rights but claim that *his* list of them is arbitrary. For instance, Ronald Dworkin (1931–2013) says:

> I agree that rights ought not to be violated. But sometimes claims of rights conflict, and I see no reason why Nozick's right to property is exclusive of other rights, or why it is necessarily more important than others.[16]

Another kind of criticism attacks the purely utopian (hence impractical) nature of Nozick's argument. For example, Nozick claims that only a *historical* theory of acquisitions can be truly just and also claims that *current* entitlement to holdings is just only if original acquisition was just. But what is original acquisition? Adam's and Eve's? Certainly, most current holdings are historically

Adam and Eve and the Original Acquisition

traceable to items that were once the spoils of war or of other forms of removal by force or intimidation. My county was once the territory of the Miwok Indians. I don't know if the Miwoks wrested this land from an earlier prehistoric people, but I do know that the Miwoks did not simply bestow the land on the European settlers who are my ancestors. In today's world, does *anybody* have just entitlement to his or her property derivable from an original acquisition? Amazingly, Nozick seems to admit that these historical facts undermine his historical theory and force us to accept some form of "patterning." He says, "Although to introduce socialism as the punishment for our sins would be to go too far, past injustices might be so great as to make necessary in the short run a more extensive state in order to rectify them" (p. 231). Critic Alan Brown concludes from Nozick's hedging:

> So Nozick's theory is essentially Utopian in the worst sense of the term: it has no practical relevance. Like the Garden of Eden before the Fall it can offer no insight into the problems of what we are to do here and now, since we are left ignorant of what principles are to inform our choice. The theory has application nowhere. (p. 99)

Liberalism

Somewhere in the theoretical spectrum between the communistic utopia of Marx and the minimalist utopia of Nozick we can find the idea of "the liberal state." It has been heartily defended by Nozick's colleague at Harvard, JOHN RAWLS (1921–2002), in his book *A Theory of Justice.*[17] The liberal state is pretty much what exists today in the Western democracies: a large degree of free enterprise with capital and many of the natural resources in private hands but regulated by the state in order to foster low inflation and high employment. Tax-financed social security tries to control poverty for those who cannot work or for whom no work exists. The presupposition behind liberalism is that society is necessarily much more complex than it is seen to be in either Marxian or Nozickian utopias—that it is necessarily a cooperative enterprise and that therefore its products and wealth are partially the result of cooperation (and that therefore all members of the cooperation—the stakeholders—have a claim to a fair share of the products and the wealth, as in Marx) and also that there will necessarily be competition in both producing and obtaining the goods (and that therefore some members of the cooperative—those who contribute most to it—have a claim to unequal portions of the products, as in Nozick). Any adequate theory of justice will have to balance these legitimate claims and find a formula for dismissing illegitimate claims. Rawls thinks that such a theory, once formulated, could apply to a democratic capitalist society or a democratic social-

Cooperation but Also Competition

ist society. In any case, society must have a public school system, must be dedicated to equality of economic opportunity, must have social security, and must define a minimum standard of living below which its citizens will not be forced to accept.

Rawls's conception of justice is "justice as fairness." Besides guaranteeing that all citizens will get a reasonable share of the social goods, the doctrine of fairness consists of a set of constraints on what people may do to each other in the pursuit of those goods. On the one hand, Rawls thinks that no *theory* of justice can be justly forced down people's throats—the correct theory would have to be one that rational people would somehow arrive at by themselves. On the other hand, Rawls is pretty sure he knows what such a theory would look like. Justice would be whatever was chosen by rational, self-interested, unenvious people who knew that they would have to inhabit the society created by their mutual agreement but who did not know what personal characteristics they would bring to that society (i.e., they wouldn't know their race, their physical and mental abilities, their inheritances, or their social

Justice as Fairness

backgrounds). Such people, Rawls says, would choose the following principles in the following order:

1. Equal and maximum liberty (political, intellectual, and religious) for each person consistent with equal liberty for others.
2. Wealth and power to be distributed equally except where inequalities would work to the advantage of all and where there would be equal opportunity to achieve individually advantageous positions.

If these principles are true, then it follows (unlike in Nozick's theory) that the only society that can be just is a liberal society that partially redistributes wealth and income for the benefit of its most disadvantaged members.

I know that $e = mc^2$, that Charlemagne was crowned Holy Roman Emperor on Christmas Day, 800 C.E., that the first person singular of the present subjunctive of the Spanish verb "hacer" is "haga." ... I know everything (except my name, age, weight, race, parents, bank account, I.Q., friends, and education).

A Rawlsian Citizen

Notice that Rawls's theory, like that of Plato, begins with a political myth—a "noble lie." In Plato's myth, people are told that their memories of their past are really only memories of a dream and what they believe of themselves is in fact false. Similarly, Rawls's myth establishes what he calls a "veil of ignorance," in which the facts we know about ourselves are set aside (our psychological, physical, social, and racial characteristics). The myth also supposes that we are not envious and that we rationally pursue our own self-interest. If you tell Rawls that his myth is *only* a myth, that none of it is true, he will respond that it is merely a philosophical device for use as an analytic tool to demonstrate the rationality of a certain kind of society. (In this respect, his "original position" [as he calls the status of his mythical negotiators behind their

Students Wearing the Veil of Ignorance (Proudly)

veil of ignorance] is very much like the "state of nature" in traditional contract theories.) Rawls's veil of ignorance allows the political philosopher to acknowledge the intuitive fact that some inequalities in a naturally evolving society are unjust, because they are undeserved. It is unjust that some should have to suffer through life because they were born with less and that others are surrounded by excessive amounts of goods due to the mere accident of birth. The veil allows Rawls to arrive rationally at a conclusion that he intuits to be true, namely, that the society can be just only if it partially redistributes wealth for the benefit of its most disadvantaged. In short, it shows how a just society requires that we all be transformed from Hobbesian egoists into Kantian universalists. The veil purports to show that if we were forced to enter into a society that we would negotiate with others, denuded of all the characteristics that were ours merely by accident of birth, we would choose the liberal society.

Though Rawls's theory strikes a responsive chord in many of its readers, you will not be surprised that it has also found its share of critics. Many are suspicious of any theory that sets out to determine the most rational of all possible societies and concludes that it just happens to be the type inhabited by the theory's author.

A specific criticism says that Rawls ignores our natural gambling nature. Rawls thinks that his liberal society is superior to a utilitarian society because the latter is compatible with slavery (a *few* miserable, hardworking slaves might produce the greatest amount of happiness for the greatest number of people), but slavery is incompatible with liberalism because negotiators in the "original position" would not risk opting for slavery as they themselves might end up as slaves. But, ask the critics, wouldn't some people risk the low odds of being designated a slave if the odds for a great benefit from such a system were high enough?

Yet another criticism is that no contract is legally binding if the signers of it are kept in ignorance of their own real interests; yet *all* signers to

Rawls's social contract are ignorant of even their personal identity. So, on this account, Rawls's contract, produced behind the "veil of ignorance," is invalid. Finally, we should remind ourselves of Nozick's main criticism of Rawls. Nozick says that it would be okay to divide the goods according to some patterned formula of equality "if goods fell from heaven like manna." But it is unjust to divide up the pie equally when it is known who contributed to it and who in fact owns it. Nozick asks: How do the people in the "original position" get the *right* to divide up the pie as they do? (But of course it could be asserted that *the right to fair treatment* is as basic as Nozick's *right to property*.)

Conclusion

I began this chapter by noting that much of our behavior is controlled by rules and laws enforced by a not-so-subtle threat of the use of force against violators. The question was posed: Why do we put up with it? Well, I think at one level we can accept Hobbes's answer to this question: Putting up with the regulation of our behavior by a threat of force is better than the radical alternative—anarchy, a state of social existence in which the center does not hold. But this conclusion doesn't mean (as it seems to for Hobbes) that we should settle for just *any* form of government. Exactly what we can reasonably expect from a government depends very much on whether the Hobbesian (and Freudian) picture of the self is true. Is the self essentially a selfish atom, naturally seeking only its own gratification and acting cooperatively only when forced to do so? Or is the self naturally social, cooperative, and sympathetic to the plight of others, as Locke and Marx would have us believe?

The Self as a Selfish Atom

If the former picture is true, the political state *is* an artificial creation, and a culture without excessive repression (and also excessive guilt, in the Freudian account) is impossible. Furthermore, some kind of "noble lie" or myth will be required to keep the citizens in line. If the latter, more optimistic picture is true and we are naturally social, then society is not artificial or necessarily excessively repressive, and reason, rather than myth, should be able to represent, explain, and justify social values to its citizens. But which picture is correct?

This is a tough question. One could spend a lifetime pondering it and testing different hypotheses concerning it (though Freud thought the issue could be settled in twenty minutes of observing children's play in the sandbox). My own view is that no believable account of human nature corresponds to one or the other of these pictures. But in a situation of scarcity, Hobbes is more or less right, and in situations of abundance, Locke is more or less right.

The Noble Lie Keeping Citizens in Line

The British anthropologist Colin Turnbull in his book *The Mountain People* has described the effect of virulent scarcity on a particular culture, the Ik. These people seem to have no sympathy for each other, they are selfish and vicious—parents withhold food from their children, children steal from their parents and take advantage of the feebleness of their grandparents. Yet in his later book, *The Forest People*, Turnbull describes another culture, the BaMbuti, Pygmies of the Congolese rain forest, who have a fairly easy time filling their basic material needs and whose members are social, cooperative, and sympathetic. Turnbull's data don't *prove* anything, but they can give us hope that when our fundamental material needs are met, a more positive aspect of human nature can be activated. Turnbull's descriptions also lead us to fear that when these basic needs

Children at Play

are not met, a more sinister side of human nature may be activated. And if *that* fear is true, then the government's role cannot be simply that of protecting us from each other (following Hobbes) but must also be that of promoting a certain moral or spiritual state (following Locke). On my hypothesis—though not explicitly on Locke's—the government must also promote a certain level of material well-being but not in an authoritarian mode. Hobbes, Locke, and Rousseau are right to say that the key concept of legitimacy is *consent*, though it is problematical exactly how this concept is to be understood. One of the primary features of political theory must be the development of a theory of consent.

A discussion of consent leads us to the topic of *justice*, which is a key concept of social philosophy. My own conclusions are not offered up as being trouble-free. Any position one takes on this important topic involves its author in serious problems. Still, that difficulty does not excuse us from thinking this problem through to the best of our ability and reaching some tentative conclusions; here are mine. I agree with Marx when he says that a just society cannot be one in which an oppressed majority (that is to say, most of the members of the society), is constrained to support a system of privileges for a nonproductive minority. Everyone who hopes to benefit from social productivity should contribute to it. But Marx (in contrast to Mill) needs to be criticized for his view that the individual has no legitimate rights vis-à-vis society, and he was wrong to think (if he did think) that society must be founded on *one* view of human good—that of productivity. Liberalism (Mill and Rawls) is to be applauded for its view that the state must be open to as many views of human good as are compatible with each other. Nozick correctly reminds us that the goods that offer themselves to us for consumption, purchase, or trade do not fall from heaven like manna. We cannot create justice by simply taking away from some to give to others without considering entitlement—that is, without considering that some people have legitimate claims of ownership or control of certain goods by virtue of having legally produced them, purchased them, or inherited them. But "**entitlement**" is not an absolute category.

I find Rawls convincing when he sides with Marx against Nozick in holding that a just society cannot be based on entitlement alone but that claims of entitlement must be balanced with claims of need or social victimization and that therefore the just society must be committed to an ongoing partial redistribution of wealth to guarantee that the least advantaged in society are not forced to fall below a certain agreed-upon standard of living and are provided with opportunities to rise above their position of disadvantage—not only because it is morally right to do so, but also because otherwise that vicious (Hobbesian) side of human nature may be activated that can make human relations dangerous for all.

Topics for Consideration

1. Most features of Plato's justification for his ideal republic are unappealing or even repulsive to citizens of modern democracies. Why? Do you find anything correct in his account?

2. Do you agree with Plato that no culture can survive without some kind of myth (or "noble lie") justifying its mission?

3. Despite using similar language, Hobbes and Locke have very different justifications of government. Discuss the differences in their respective answers to the question of why we should submit to a rule of law, and take a position one way or the other. (Or hammer out a compromise between them.)

4. Why does Rousseau think that participatory democracy is the only *true* democracy? What is his critique of representative democracy?

5. Contrast as clearly as you can the difference between Rousseau and Mill on the topic of the private and the public realms.

6. Pick out the feature in Marx's theory of social justice that you like the most and the feature that you like the least. Explain your judgment. How are these two features related in Marx's theory?

7. Contrast the kind of social fairness defended by Nozick in his account of the minimal state with that defended by Rawls in his account of the liberal state. Which view is more in line with *your* conception of fairness?

Suggestions for Further Reading: Paperback Editions

Alan Brown, *Modern Political Philosophy: Theories of the Just Society* (New York: Penguin, 1986). A clear summary with insightful commentary.

Thomas Hobbes, *Leviathan: Or the Matter, Forme and Power of a Commonwealth Ecclesiasticall and Civil* (New York: Collier Books, 1962). The old cynic's famous treatment of government and humanity—long, often tedious, somewhat difficult in its seventeenth-century English but contains lightning bolts of brilliance. Especially see Part I, Chapter 13 through Part II, Chapter 18 for topics discussed here.

John Locke, "The Second Treatise of Civil Government," in *Two Treatises of Government* (New York: Hafner, 1964). The "bible" of modern government that inspired the American Declaration of Independence. Surprisingly readable.

David McLellan, *Karl Marx* (New York: Viking Penguin, 1976). Short, excellent account in the Modern Masters series.

John Stuart Mill, *On Liberty* (Chicago, IL: Henry Regnery, 1955). Somewhat difficult reading because of the artificiality of Mill's Victorian style but short and impressive.

Robert Nozick, *Anarchy, State, and Utopia* (New York: Basic Books, 1974). Big and formidable, but Nozick is a good writer.

Karl Popper, *The Open Society and Its Enemies,* 5th ed. (Princeton, NJ: Princeton University Press, 1971). A heavy-handed but very interesting attack on Plato's politics in Volume I and on Marx's politics in Volume II by one of this century's foremost philosophers of science.

John Rawls, *A Theory of Justice* (Cambridge, MA: Harvard University Press, 1971). Sometimes pretty technical for a beginner but a good read.

Richard Taylor, *Freedom, Anarchy, and the Law,* 2nd ed. (Buffalo, NY: Prometheus Books, 1982). A short, highly readable account of the basic issues raised by Hobbes, Locke, Rousseau, and Mill.

Notes

1. Plato, "Republic," in *Great Dialogues of Plato,* trans. W. H. D. Rouse (New York: New American Library, 1956), pp. 216–217. Subsequent quotes from the *Republic* in this chapter are from this edition.

2. Thomas Hobbes, *Leviathan: Or the Matter, Forme and Power of a Commonwealth Ecclesiasticall and Civil* (New York: Collier Books, 1962), pp. 98–99, 100. Subsequent quotes from Hobbes in this chapter are from this source.

3. John Locke, "The Second Treatise of Civil Government," in *Two Treatises of Government* (New York: Hafner, 1964), pp. 122–124. Subsequent quotes from Locke in this chapter are from this source.

4. Jean-Jacques Rousseau, *The Social Contract and Discourses,* trans. G. D. H. Cole (London: J. M. Dent and Sons, 1982), pp. 174–175. Subsequent quotes from Rousseau in this chapter are from this source.

5. John Stuart Mill, *On Liberty* (Chicago, IL: Henry Regnery, 1955), pp. 23–24.

6. Ibid., p. 13.

7. See, for example, Leonore Davidoff and Catherine Hall, *Family Fortunes: Men and Women of the English Middle Class, 1780–1850* (London: Hutchinson, 1987); and Dorothy O. Helly and S. Reverby, *Gendered Domains: Beyond the Public and Private in Women's History* (Ithaca, NY: Cornell University Press, 1992).

8. Richard Taylor, *Freedom, Anarchy, and the Law: An Introduction to Political Philosophy* (Englewood Cliffs, NJ: Prentice-Hall, 1973), p. 58.

9. John Stuart Mill, *Principles of Political Economy* (New York: Longmans, Green, 1929), p. 950. Subsequent quotes from Mill in this chapter are from this source.

10. Karl Marx, "Economic and Philosophical Manuscripts," in *Marx's Concept of Man,* ed. Erich Fromm, trans. T. B. Bottomore (New York: Frederick Ungar, 1969), p. 97.

11. Ibid., pp. 98–99.

12. Karl Marx, "German Ideology," in Fromm, *Marx's Concept of Man,* p. 42.

13. Alan Brown, *Modern Political Philosophy: Theories of the Just Society* (New York: Penguin, 1986), pp. 117–118. Subsequent quotes from Brown in this chapter are from this source.

14. Robert Nozick, *Anarchy, State, and Utopia* (New York: Basic Books, 1974), p. 180. Subsequent quotes from Nozick in this chapter are from this source.

15. Alasdair MacIntyre, *After Virtue* (Notre Dame, IN: University of Notre Dame Press, 1981), p. 67.

16. "Interview with Ronald Dworkin," in *Men of Ideas: Some Creators of Contemporary Philosophy,* Bryan Magee (London: British Broadcasting Corporation, 1978), p. 254.

17. John Rawls, *A Theory of Justice* (Cambridge, MA: Harvard University Press, 1971).

10

But Is It Art?
Philosophy of Art

The urge to produce art seems to be as old as the human race. If you compare the thirty-thousand-year-old representations on the cave walls at Altamira or Lascaux with the images of typical prime-time TV production—or worse, with graffiti on men's room walls in the bus depot (or worse yet, if such is possible, with the drawings in this book)—you may think that there has been a downward spiral since the times of our Cro-Magnon ancestors. But at least there have been some great moments in between!

What are human beings doing when they create "art"? Are their works frivolous or even dangerous distractions, or do they exhibit something deep and essential about human nature? And what is the relationship between art and "reality"? Is art a mirror held up to the beauty of nature, or is it a poor imitation of reality, as some philosophers have held? Or is art a spiritualization and enrichment of nature—an improvement upon the world—as other philosophers have asserted? Or is it something that has nothing to do with anything but itself ("art for art's sake")? These are some

Early Graffiti

of the big questions in the philosophy of art. Whatever answers exist to these questions, it is not surprising that for thousands of years people have been provoked to philosophize about art, because, for better or for worse, art has been such a pervasive part of human experience.

But, hold on! Maybe we are already moving too fast. Perhaps these queries presuppose a more basic question: What *is* art? Old Socrates would have said that if we can't answer that question, we don't stand a chance with the others. Let's see if the analytic school of philosophy can do us some good here, because what seems to be needed is precisely an analysis of the concept of art.

Analytic Philosophy of Art

A number of contemporary aestheticians write under the rubric of "analytic philosophy of art."[1] Such a title indicates to us that we will see in their work analysis of certain key aesthetic concepts, such as *mimesis* (imitation), representation, expression, aesthetic experience, and certainly the concept of art itself. We will turn to these philosophers now to see what they have to say about all these. Once we have sorted out some of the *conceptual* problems about art, we will look at some of the *cultural* issues that art raises.

One tool that analytic philosophers often use in their investigations is the distinction between *necessary* and *sufficient* conditions, as that distinction applies to various concepts under study. Let me remind you that a necessary condition is one that *must* hold for anything to be an example of concept *x*. For instance, for person *p* to be correctly designated as a "sister," that person must necessarily be a female and necessarily be a sibling. The fulfillment of these two conditions together is *sufficient* to guarantee that *p* is a sister, and therefore, the necessary and sufficient conditions give us what might be called an essential definition

It doesn't look like me.

Picasso Paints Gertrude Stein

of the idea of a sister. Is such an analysis available for the idea of art? A number of theorists in various traditions have thought so. The ancient Greeks were pretty sure that art is **mimesis** or an artificial copy of nature (as we will see shortly when we look at Plato's views on art). This belief lasted for a long, long time, but it is now obvious to us that artworks are rarely mere copies of nature and that some artworks aren't copies of anything.

Changing the translation of mimesis from "imitation" to "representation" looked much more hopeful in the quest for art's necessary conditions, until the advent of nonrepresentational art, whose rather sudden appearance on the artistic scene shows that neither imitation nor representation is a necessary condition of art. Furthermore, the millions of snapshots and videos lying around our houses nowadays—and straining our computers' memories—prove that representation fails to be a necessary condition of art but that is not a sufficient condition either.

Analysis of Expressionism

A number of theorists have produced variations on the theory of **expressionism,** claiming that expression of emotion is a necessary condition of art. According to most versions of expressionism, the artist's intention is to communicate the emotions of his soul to the souls of the audience. Count Leo Tolstoy produced a famous version of this argument. Tolstoy's favorite emotions were religious in nature. Perhaps R. G. Collingwood's *The Principles of Art* (1938) represents the most articulate version of this school's argument. According to it, a work of art must communicate to an audience the emotion that the artist is feeling and generate in the audience in an individualized way the same emotions. (The "individualized"

component means to rule out things such as generic greeting cards—"To whom it may concern: I deeply feel your loss.") In some expressionist definitions, the artwork must not only communicate these emotions and generate empathy with them but also clarify them to the audience.

But most philosophers of art hold that such a definition fails. It is true that many works are expressive, but there is no guarantee that the audience feels the same emotion that the artist feels (if in fact the artist actually feels that emotion). Some art may arouse deep feelings that are nothing like the feelings of the artist. Certainly not all art intends to be expressive—some art wants to shock, and some art just wants to be beautiful. Therefore, the expressive theory cannot generate a successful essential definition.

Analysis of Formalism

Formalism represents another attempt to define art. Perhaps one of its most famous articulations is found in Clive Bell's book of 1914, simply called *Art*. It has been said—even by people who disagree with Bell's theory—that this volume is a modern classic.[2] Despite the book's title, Bell intended his theory to cover only the visual arts and perhaps music. Some of Bell's followers generalized the thesis to cover the whole of art. Bell's theory was that what turns an artifact into a work of art is its display of "significant form." For him the *content* of the work was indifferent to its artistic qualities and sometimes even distracted from the value of the significant form. One major advantage of Bell's theory is that it accounts for some of the new forms of art that appeared at the beginning of the twentieth century, such as cubism and abstract art. The main problem with the theory is that it provides no compelling definition of its key idea, "significant form." How do we decide whether a work's formal qualities (shapes, color relationships, designs, relations of part to part and part to whole) are significant? (The attempt to answer this question might have reached the depths of absurdity when the nineteenth-century formalist Robert Zimmerman exclaimed, "The large beside the small pleases; the small beside the large displeases.")

Another problem is that the theory has no room for the great number of items that most of us would call bad art. That is, "significant form" is an evaluative and not a descriptive term. Therefore, anything that is not good art (i.e., does not exhibit significant form) is not art at all.

Some formalists have tried to correct this last problem by saying that

The large beside the small

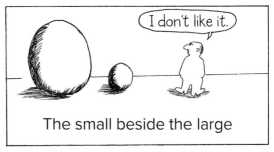

The small beside the large

the *function* of art is to exhibit significant form, and a necessary and sufficient condition of art is the artist's *intention* to exhibit such form. Does this solve the problem of why Andy Warhol's painting *Brillo Box* is art, but the Brillo box itself is not? Perhaps, but it's hard to imagine that Warhol's intention when he painted the box was to exhibit significant form. It's hard enough to pick out significant form, much less to detect an artist's intention. Also, this retreat into intentionalism goes against the main impetus of the inspiration of formalism, which was to reject any feature of the work of art that was not immediately perceptible. And, you will recall, this restriction included even the work's content—what the work is about.

A later group of thinkers, attracted to formalism but believing that the deletion of "content" from the definition of art is a mistake, developed a theory they call "neo-formalism," according to which the function of art is to marry form and content in satisfying ways. Certainly this formulation applies to much that we call art. (The art historian Heinrich Wölfflin, in his book *Principles of Art History* [1932], argued that the main formal characteristic of renaissance art is the triangle, and of baroque art, the off-centered cross, or X.) But, ironically, much of modern art seems not to be about anything, which is why there are so many works called "Untitled"; and even more ironically, as contemporary philosopher of art NOËL CARROLL (born 1947) points out, there are works that seem to have neither form nor content, such as John Cage's composition that he calls 4'33" (four minutes, thirty-three seconds), which is

> comprised of a set of instructions: a pianist is to sit at a piano and open a score, but not to strike the keys. The performance consists of all the ambient sounds that occur within the ensuing interval of four minutes and thirty-three seconds. If someone coughs and scrapes [a] chair along the floor, that is part of the piece. If a cellular phone rings, or a moving van rumbles past outside, that too is part of the piece. (p. 119)

Music by John Cage

There is also such a thing as **aleatoric art,** in which the artist engages in actions that produce arbitrary and chance results (and sometimes collateral damage).

A Jackson Pollock Wanna-Be Launches His Career

Analysis of the Aesthetic Experience

A number of philosophers of art believe that a definition of art can be derived from something they call "the aesthetic experience." Such an experience takes place when certain features of an artwork (or, inconveniently, certain features of nature) produce sensations and moods that are found in no other way. The character of this experience is not always agreed upon. Sometimes it is described as achieving a kind of distance, or as seeing in a certain way, or as wonder,[3] or awe, or as a unique kind of joy, or reverie, or disinterest, in the sense of an escape from worldliness. Apparently, each of us (or at least each of us who has a sensitive soul) is supposed to be able to identify this experience by thinking of our feelings, sensations, and moods as we listen to, or read, or watch, or look at our favorite works of art.

There are basically two versions of this theory: that of the objectivists, who concentrate on the features of the artwork that provoke the aesthetic experience, and the subjectivists, who concentrate on the experience itself. Both seem to agree, however, that the definition of art is something like this:

A work of art is an artifact that provokes an aesthetic experience.

The "artifact" part of this definition is required to distinguish between art and nature, since nature can also produce this experience (starry nights, sunsets and sunrises, mountains, waterfalls, and even some large holes, e.g., the Grand Canyon). Those who fear that this definition fails to allow a place for bad art—which apparently does not produce aesthetic experiences or does so only in people with really bad taste—prefer the modified definition:

> A work of art is an artifact that was created with the *intention* of provoking an aesthetic experience.

(When my son was four years old, he had the right artistic intention but had uneven results.)

Besides the problems mentioned earlier with intentionalism, an additional problem with the intention-based definition of aesthetic experience is that many works of art were intended to glorify God, or to be beautiful, or to scare people into better behavior, or—in some cases—to make demons run away. Neither definition provides a necessary condition and perhaps not a sufficient condition either. My only hesitation here is my lack of clarity on exactly what the much-touted "aesthetic experience" is. As GEORGE DICKIE (born 1927) says, "In short, it is thought [in these theories] that substantive guidelines for art criticism and appreciation can be derived from the nature of a certain kind of psychological state. If there is no such psychological state, this approach is in serious difficulty" (p. 31).

We have just looked at ideas on representation, on form, and on aesthetic experience. I think it is fair to say that none of them provides a satisfactory essential definition of art (i.e., a definition in terms of necessary and sufficient conditions). But that does not mean that these categories have proved to lack interest for philosophers of art. For example, even if the idea of representation is incapable of generating a successful definition of art, it does cover the key idea in a vast amount of both historical and contemporary art; so analytic philosophers have found it useful to analyze the very idea of representation in order to help characterize all the art that can correctly be called representational. Here we will temporarily detour away from the attempt to define art and see what kind of discussions about representation have been generated in the twentieth and twenty-first centuries.

Analysis of Conventionalism

In an interesting development in this pursuit, at least one important analytic philosopher has concluded that all artistic representation is a form of **conventionalism.** You read paintings in the way that you read a text, said NELSON GOODMAN in his *Languages of Art* (1968). Learning to read is mastering a code. You have to learn the alphabet, forms of print (upper-case and lowercase letters, etc.), and coordination of sounds with letters and combinations of letters. Therefore, the debate over objectivism versus subjectivism is misguided, according to Goodman. Images in artworks are objective in the sense that anyone who knows the code can understand the images; they are subjective in that the images themselves are not reproductions of anything that exists in reality, and only those who know the code can figure them out. If you learn the artistic codes of your culture, you will understand how to read a painting. So-called realistic art is simply art whose code we are used to. Images in art stand for (represent) objects or people, but do not copy them.

Goodman's book has been widely read and discussed, but he seems to have very few takers. There are certainly many features of art that are best explained as conventional codes (the haloes in religious paintings, pictures of devils and angels, or mythical creatures, and, some people think, even developments like perspective and foreshortening). But most discussants claim that Goodman has exaggerated the similarity between artistic images, on the one side, and words and numbers, on the other. For example, it has been said that if conventionalism were true, the depiction of sounds and smells should be possible, but it doesn't look as if they are. Also, children are able to recognize the images of real objects long before they learn systems of decoding. If "realism" is arbitrary and culturally determined, why do we have as much luck as we do recognizing people, nature, and objects represented in the art of alien cultures?

Analysis of Realism

Goodman may have thought that the debate between objectivists and subjectivists had been resolved, but not all art theorists agree.

Both philosophers and historians have been very interested in the question of whether there can be such a thing as "realism" in art. Recently, philosopher JOHN HYMAN (born 1960), in *The Objective Eye* (2006), has defended the idea of realism in art history and what he calls "the defensible residue of the resemblance theory of depiction" (p. 111). His view is at the opposite end of the spectrum from that of Goodman. Hyman's argument involves an attack on the view—initiated by Plato but apparently accepted by most art theorists today—that the images produced by artists are *illusions*. But Hyman's argument goes well beyond art to strike at the heart of a philosophical tradition (also beginning with the ancient Greeks), according to which perception itself produces illusion—in the more radical versions, a lot of illusion, and in the more moderate versions, only some illusion. For example, we are often told that a coin lying on a table has the appearance of an elliptical shape, rather than a round shape, if viewed from the edge of the table. This appearance is called illusory by many philosophers, who also say that so-called realist artists paint not the real shape of the coin but its elliptical shape, and therefore, they must be copying the illusion and not the reality; therefore, all realistic art is a version of **trompe l'œil.** Hyman denies the implications here. A

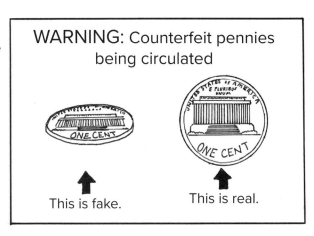

WARNING: Counterfeit pennies being circulated

ONE CENT

This is fake.

ONE CENT

This is real.

coin lying on a table does have what he calls an **occlusion shape,** which is the shape relative to an implicit line of sight. But the occlusion shape is not an illusion; it is part of reality, not of deception. Hyman writes, "The relationship between an object's occlusion shape and its three-dimensional shape . . . is a geometrical relationship between two properties, both of which are real, and both of which belong to the same object" (p. 235). Understanding this goes a long way toward grasping the idea of realism in art. Hyman is resisting the "recent resurgence of subjectivism in the theory of art" (p. 127), which he blames primarily on the widespread effects of the publication in 1956 of E. H. Gombrich's brilliant *Art and Illusion,* in which Gombrich stressed the roles of ambiguity in reading the world at large and especially in reading imagery. Gombrich further claimed that a good part of reading both the world and imagery involves projection on the part of the viewer, and he discussed, among other features of perception, "the beholder's share in the illusion of space."[4]

Gombrich talks about "the inherent ambiguity of all images" and of the reasons why we are so rarely aware of this ambiguity. "Ambiguity . . . can never be seen as such. We notice it only by learning to switch from one reading to another and by realizing that both interpretations fit the image equally well" (p. 249). Gombrich also attributes a large part of the way we read art to conventionalism, though, unlike Goodman, he does not reduce the whole of art to coding. He says of conventions that "it is their totality which makes up what we call 'style' in painting" (p. 291).

Hyman does what he can to repair the damage he thinks Gombrich has done. He argues well and forcefully, but the late Mr. Gombrich is not easily vanquished. For example, Hyman takes umbrage at Gombrich's claim that the bathroom mirror is "an instrument of illusion." How did Gombrich get in so much trouble with Hyman? Gombrich asked his readers to approach a steamed-up bathroom mirror after a hot shower and to draw a circle in the moisture around the hazy reflection of the face that they see on the mirror's surface. He guaranteed the readers that they would be surprised to discover that the size of the reflected face is only half as large as the size of their face. (The laws of physics and optics easily explain this phenomenon.) Gombrich also pointed out that the face in the mirror is inverted. That is, if I am shaving with the razor in my left hand, it is as if the "person in the mirror" has the razor in his *right* hand. Gombrich says that we are unaware of this illusion unless we disengage from practical affairs. (You can't shave *and* see the illusion at the same time, just as you can't see the "duck" *and* the "rabbit" at the same time.) Hyman responds in an annoyed tone, "The simple fact is that when I see my face in a flat mirror, I see it reversed. But *what* I see is nothing other than my face" (p. 125). Gombrich's view is that Hyman does *not* see his face in the mirror—what he sees is the *reflection* of his face—and that reflections are, by their nature, illusory. So, who's right? It seems to me that the reason so many people shave badly or put on makeup badly is because they don't

I always shave the little left-handed guy in the mirror first.

realize that the image in the mirror is of a person who would be standing twice as far from them as they think. Is that mistake based on an illusion?

Hyman makes a more convincing argument in his defense of the idea of realism in representative art, an idea that some art critics—perhaps under the influence of writers such as Goodman and Gombrich—have almost abandoned as laughable. Hyman concedes that the old definition of realism as "fidelity to nature" has been permanently rejected, and he understands that many different kinds of mutually incompatible art have been called "realistic," including Greek sculpture in the fifth and fourth centuries B.C.E., Dutch painting in the 1600s, and French painting in the mid-1800s. He insists, however, that if we concentrate not on *content* but on *technique,* we will find the idea of realism to be accurate and useful. He focuses on three areas. First, "pictorial accuracy." Looking at two early Greek vases depicting running male figures, Hyman points out that the later depiction is more anatomically accurate; the painter of the later vase has correctly reported his knowledge that "when a man runs, his forward arm is in fact opposite his forward leg" (p. 195). The earlier painter either did not notice this fact or did not care about it. By the way, this possibility of purposely ignoring a well-known fact is important in the history of art. The ancient Egyptian painters certainly knew that the human eye observed from the front does not look the same as the eye observed in profile, but for reasons of their own, they didn't feel it was right to depict that distinction in their paintings. (Perhaps they were not trying to depict eyes but symbolize them.) But, according to Hyman, whatever their reasons, artists who ignore this fact produce less-realistic portraits than those who do not.

A second element of realistic art pointed out by Hyman is what he calls "animation," which involves mobility and other related characteristics. Again, the difference between ancient Egyptian statues and early Greek statues demonstrates an evolution toward realism in this respect, and the later Greek statues show yet a further realistic development. It wasn't until the seventeenth century that the Spanish court painter Diego Velázquez, in his *Fable of Arachne,* mastered this skill, showing the motion of a rapidly turning spinning wheel. (Typically, Hyman chastises Gombrich for saying that Velázquez has produced a perfect illusion here. Hyman says, *"The motion of the wheel can actually be seen and need not be inferred from any other cues"* [p. 204].[5] Gombrich would surely point out that nothing is moving on the canvas, so what we have is the illusion of motion. Something that isn't moving appears to do so.)

The third category employed by Hyman in his quest for realism he calls "modality." He writes:

The overarching idea of modality is the key to understanding the evolution of realism in pictorial art. For the principal measure of realism—that is, realism in technique—is the range of questions we can ask about a picture's content: Is this man angry or impassive? Is he despondent or alert? Is he Semitic or Egyptian? Is he young or old? Is he fat or thin? Is his cloak made of linen or of wool? Is he standing in the shade or in the sun? Is he running, walking, jumping, or standing still? (p. 200)

I think Hyman is right about this. My son's *Meatball at Sunset,* though surely the work of a genius (Lake Wobegon: "where all children are above average"), ranks low in "modality." By the way, though Hyman defends the idea of artistic realism, he does not claim that realistic art is *superior* to nonrealistic art.

We have taken this little side journey into the concepts of representation, symbolism, and realism in order to show that topics such as these are of interest to analytic philosophers, even if they have been rejected as **definiens** of art. Let us now return to the philosopher's dream of defining the concept of art in terms of necessary and sufficient conditions. Why has it proved so difficult to realize this goal? Have philosophers not tried hard enough or probed deeply enough? Or are they on the wrong track?

Wittgenstein

In our quest for the definition of art, we now turn to a discussion very different from those we've seen so far. This view stems from the work of the Viennese philosopher LUDWIG WITTGENSTEIN (1889–1951), who studied and taught at Cambridge. Wittgenstein is hardly a household name among the general public. We dealt with him briefly in Chapter 1, but you probably had not heard of him before taking a philosophy class. Nevertheless, many people believe he proved to be one of the two or three greatest philosophers of the twentieth century, certainly one of the most influential.

We will examine two areas of Wittgenstein's thought on art that have proved especially instructive. One has to do with Wittgenstein's discussion of the "open-endedness" of certain concepts; the other concerns his notion of a language as a "form of life." As can be seen, neither of these two topics

Ludwig Wittgenstein

contains any specific reference to art; yet their application to the problems of the philosophy of art has generated much interest and controversy of late. However, before we can apply Wittgenstein's ideas to art, we will have to spend some time developing the key Wittgensteinian notions.

Open Concepts

Wittgenstein believed that over and over again in the history of philosophy, thinkers had been deceived by taking a particular successful model of clarity and trying to force all of language and thought into the mold of that one model. He called this error linguistic bewitchment of the intellect. A clear example of this kind of error is the attempt to come up with a general theory of meaning based on certain examples from mathematics or logic. For instance, take the definition of a triangle: "A triangle is a three-sided closed figure." Now, assuming standard meanings for words like "side" and "closed," this definition is exhaustive. Any candidate for the term "triangle" must meet this criterion. There can be a variety of kinds of triangles (isosceles, right, obtuse), but each one must be a three-sided closed figure. This feature, which can be called "the essence of triangularity," is the feature common to all possible triangles. The search for necessary and sufficient conditions of concepts was inspired by this kind of clarity.

In order to destroy the illusion that a successful theory of meaning can be based on such a model, Wittgenstein asks us to consider the concept of "game." However, he does not ask us to *philosophize* about the concept; rather, he asks us to *look* at all the activities we call "games" in order to see whether we discover anything they all have in common.

> Consider for example the proceedings that we call "games." I mean board-games, card-games, Olympic games, and so on. What is common to them all?—Don't say: "There *must* be something common, or they would not be called 'games'"—but *look and see* whether there is anything common to all.—For if you look at them you will not see something that is common to *all*, but similarities, relationships, and a whole series of them at that. To repeat: don't think, but look!—Look for example at board-games, with their multifarious relationships. Now pass to card-games; here you find many correspondences with the first group, but many common features drop out, and others appear. When we pass next to ball-games, much that is common is retained, but much is lost— Are they all "*amusing*"? Compare chess with noughts and crosses. Or is there always *winning and losing*, or *competition* between players? Think of patience. In ball games there is winning and losing, but when a child throws his ball at the wall and catches it again, this feature has disappeared. Look at the parts played by *skill and luck*; and at the difference between skill in chess and skill in tennis. Think now of games like

ring-a-ring-a-roses; here is the element of amusement, but how many other characteristic features have disappeared! And we can go through the many, many other groups of games in the same way; can see how similarities crop up and disappear.

And the result of this examination is: we see a complicated network of similarities overlapping and criss-crossing: sometimes overall similarities, sometimes similarities of detail.[6]

Notice what Wittgenstein means when he refers to characteristics like "amusing," "winning and losing," "competition," and "skill and luck." Take the term "amusing." Is it the case that everything that is amusing is a game and that all games are amusing (or "fun" or "enjoyable")? Exactly who must be amused? Must the players be amused as well as the spectators, if there are spectators? Imagine a professional baseball game on the last day of the season between the two last-place teams. Only a handful of fans have made the mistake of showing up to see what turns out to be the most sloppily played game of the season in the most miserable weather of the year. It is quite possible that you could interview every person in the stadium and discover that nobody was having any fun. Nevertheless, it certainly would not follow that, because no one was having fun, no game of baseball was being played. (And the fact that the game was a *professional* game doesn't keep it from being a game either.) In fact, I am sure that I have played games of Monopoly that went on so long that, toward the end, no one was enjoying the game. It was just that no one wanted to be the first to admit that the game was not fun. Finally, it is simply absurd to say that the only way of establishing that a particular activity is a game would be to interview people to find out whether anybody was having a good time.

Similar fates await any attempt to define games in terms of "winning and losing" or "skill and luck." Just look at ring-around-the-rosy. There is no winning or losing there; how much skill or luck do you need just to fall down? (Ring-around-the-rosy, by the way, is one of those games whose *origins,* at least, are hardly amusing. It probably derives from the period when the Black Death swept England. The "rosy" is the red ring around the mortal sores or, in some theories, the rosary. Thank goodness the sinister meaning of the last line, "Ashes to ashes, we all fall down," usually escapes our children.)

What about "competition"? Consider the game my son invented when he was five years old (probably along with every other five-year-old boy), called "hit-the-ball-against-the-wall." With whom was he competing? Perhaps he was competing against himself. But surely there's a difference between the case of the boy who plays to see how many times he can hit the ball without missing and the case of the boy who pretends he is first Tom, then Bill. When "Tom" misses the ball, it is "Bill's" turn to hit it. In this latter case, the boy really is competing against himself. When I was small, my cousin talked me into playing a game *he* invented. He called it "push-the-boy-down-the-stairs." There may or may not have been competition involved in that game.

Push-the-Boy-Down-the-Stairs

It might be suggested that all games have *rules* in common by virtue of which they are called games. It is probably true that all games have rules (a possible exception is the Caucus race in *Alice's Adventures in Wonderland*), but so do all sorts of other things that are not games—crossing the street, giving a lecture, attending a movie, and so on. In fact, in a significant sense all recognizable human activities are rule-governed. In the face of this fact, some of my students like to say that, after all, everything *is* a game, especially school. (To this, I usually reply that Aztec jai-alai was also a game, and the loser was decapitated; some games are more serious than other games.) And in fact, it is curious that almost any activity can be *made* into a game. (When I was a kid and had to mow the lawn, I used to pretend that the unmowed grass was "the Nazis." I still shave that way sometimes. I knew a man who drove home in the commuter traffic pretending he was a pilot in a bombing squadron. I found this out once when he forgot I was with him; as he pulled into his suburban driveway, he put his fist to his mouth as if he were talking into a microphone and muttered, "Lame Duck, Lame Duck; clear runway number five for a crash landing!") The fact that any activity can be made into a game proves that not all activities *are* games. Eric Berne wrote a book about how people try to escape responsibility for their actions.

He called it *Games People Play*. It was a success precisely because the activities he listed were not really games. My favorite in his list was the "game" he called "see-what-you-made-me-do!" There *is* a ritualized, gamelike quality in the activities of people who scapegoat, but if you buy a book called *Party Games,* you will never find "see-what-you-made-me-do!" in it. If you could find such a game, then Berne could not have included it in *his* book.

Games People Play

As we saw in Chapter 1, Wittgenstein's conclusion concerning the undefinability of the concept "game," despite the many similarities among games, is this:

> I can think of no better expression to characterize these similarities than "family resemblances"; for the various resemblances between members of a family: build, features, colour of eyes, gait, temperament, etc. etc. overlap and criss-cross in the same way.—And I shall say: "games" form a family. (p. 32)

"Game," then, is an "open concept." We cannot state the necessary and sufficient conditions for something's being a game. That is, we could never close the concept with a specific definition in the way that we *can* do with "triangle," because it is always possible, and even likely, that at a later date we will want to include a new activity under the concept "game."

You may have already guessed what this discussion of games has to do with art. Those who seek an exhaustive definition of the word "art" may be in the same bind as those who seek to define the word "game." Wittgenstein himself only hinted at this conclusion. It has been explicitly drawn by a follower of his, MORRIS WEITZ (1916–1981) in an influential article, "The Role of Theory in Aesthetics." Professor Weitz defines the term "open concept" in the following way:

> A concept is open if its conditions of application are emendable and corrigible; i.e., if a situation or case can be imagined or secured which would call for some sort of *decision* on our part to extend the use of the

concept to cover this, or to close the concept and invent a new one to deal with the new case and its new property. If necessary and sufficient conditions for the application of a concept can be stated, the concept is a closed one. But this can happen only in logic or mathematics where concepts are constructed and completely defined. It cannot occur with empirically-descriptive and normative concepts unless we arbitrarily close them by stipulating the ranges of their uses.[7]

According to Weitz, then, questions like "Is Andy Warhol's *Elvis* art?" cannot be answered by appealing to an already established definition; rather, a *decision* is called for: shall we extend the concept "art" to cover this case? Apparently, the reasons one can give to justify one's decision to apply or withhold the title "art" must have to do with what Wittgenstein calls "family resemblances." (*Is* "push-the-boy-down-the-stairs" similar enough to other activities we call games to justify our extending the term "game" to cover this case also?)

GENUINE ELVIS ART
on Black Velvet

Hmm. This calls for a decision.

If Weitz's Wittgensteinian account of the concept of art is correct, at least he will have explained what is surely one of the most puzzling features of contemporary art. He will have explained why the current crisis in art need not undermine the very concept of art itself. Only in our day could a pile of gravel be dumped onto the floor of an art museum and be given the title *The Gravel Pile*. Only in our day could people seriously interested in art read the title and slowly circle the pile, gazing studiously at it, arguing among themselves about its artistic merit. Old Socrates would have said that if one could not define art in such a way as to give its essence, and thereby give absolute reasons for calling something "art" or for declaring it not to be art, then one had no right to claim to know anything about art. But Weitz's analysis allows *all* the museum visitors to be certain that Vermeer's *Woman Reading a Letter beside a Window* is art, and it also allows them to argue rationally about the status of Robert Barry's work of **conceptual art** (his work: *All the things I know but of which I am not at the moment thinking*—1:36 P.M., 15 June, 1969, New York).

Some philosophers found Weitz's argument liberating, and many still do, but others chafed at what they took to be a restriction that could put them out of business, particularly those who had Platonic passions to find the essence of art and lock it up in a definition. (As George Dickie says, Weitz's essay "paralyzed most philosophers of art" [p. 79].) Some fought back. In 1965, MAURICE MANDELBAUM (1908–1987) challenged Weitz's analysis by directly attacking Wittgenstein's claims about the concept of "family resemblances." Mandelbaum began by pointing out what he took to be an error on Wittgenstein's part. By concentrating on only those features of family resemblances that are exhibited and hence visible, Wittgenstein had failed to notice an implicit feature that all families have in common, namely, a genetic heritage, which could provide the necessary conditions for family resemblance. Mandelbaum imagines people inspecting a series of photographic portraits and noticing what they take to be "family resemblances" among individuals in the photos, when in fact the similarities are pure coincidence and have nothing to do with family connections. About this case, Mandelbaum says that at best we could call this a *metaphorical* family resemblance. He says, "What makes the difference between a literal and a metaphorical sense of the notion of 'family resemblance' is, therefore, the existence of genetic connection in the former case and not in the latter."[8]

Similarly, in calling the relationship among games a "family resemblance," Wittgenstein can only present his examples as metaphorical family resemblance, because he has presented no genealogical evidence to back up his claim. Thus, according to Mandelbaum, Wittgenstein has made a similar error in his attempt to define games. He has failed to look behind the scene to find a figurative aspect similar to the genetic component used to explain family resemblance. Mandelbaum asserts:

> In the case of games, the analogue to genetic ties *might be* the purpose for the sake of which various games were formulated by those who invented and modified them, e.g., the potentiality of a game to be of absorbing non-practical interest to either participants or spectators. (p. 221, emphasis added)

Apparently, for Mandelbaum, this *purpose* (which is a kind of intention) is in fact a definiens for the concept "game."

Because a number of philosophers of art, perhaps grasping at straws, found this argument empowering, let us pause to inspect it. Mandelbaum finds a common denominator in all games, namely, a purpose (a kind of *intention*). I have already suggested that any definition of art that makes an intention the definiens is problematical, and that would also be the case in an attempted definition of game. For example, notice that Mandelbaum does not know whether the purpose he lists was the original purpose of games (he says, it "might be"). Also, according to Mandelbaum, is the way we will be able to tell that a particular activity is a game by interviewing each player to see if he or she shares the supposed intention that assures that the activity is a game? That is, must each player of a contemporary game share the purpose of the game's inventor or modifier? If so, the proposed definition fails, because some people play games for pure revenge, others for profit, and others because their mommies told them they *had* to play or else!

A more charitable analysis of Mandelbaum's definition might accept this "purpose" as a necessary condition but not a sufficient condition. I am not convinced that Wittgenstein would have denied that "game" has necessary conditions. Speaking of language, he says, "I am saying that these phenomena have no one thing in common which makes us use the same word for all" (p. 31). He is not denying that a group of phenomena might have one thing in common; rather, he is denying that there is something in common *by virtue of which we call them all* language. So, saying, for example, "One thing games have in common is that they are played" may be true but not very helpful, because saying this simply shifts the weight from the concept "game" to the concept "play." It may also work to say "Games have in common that they are rule-guided." I think Wittgenstein's near obsession with rules evinced in *Philosophical Investigations* after his discussion of games supports the view that he thinks that one thing that games do have in common is that they are rule-guided. However, he may well think that "rule" is an open concept too. ("A rule stands there like a sign-post. . . . The sign-post is in order—if, under normal circumstances, it fulfils its purpose." [pp. 39–41]) Even if we could say that a game is a rule-guided activity, that would not distinguish games from other kinds of rule-guided activities, and there are so very many activities that are rule-guided (maybe all of them). Similarly, Mandelbaum's "definition," even if successful in finding a necessary condition, cannot fulfill the philosopher's dream, because it can't determine which activity is a game and which is not. And for the same reason, he can't determine what is art and what is not.

NOËL CARROLL (born 1947) also criticizes Wittgenstein, and through him, Weitz. Carroll thinks there is something wrong with what he calls "the family resemblance method."[9] However, it should be mentioned that, contrary to Carroll's wording, Wittgenstein does not at all think of "family resemblance" as a *method*. He uses the analogy between family resemblances and games descriptively (to shed light on how we make certain determinations about commonality), not prescriptively (to instruct people on how to do something). Carroll's objection to what he calls this "method" mirrors Mandelbaum's thesis about the genetic common denominators that create real family resemblances. This genetic history could be expressed biologically in terms of necessary and sufficient conditions; therefore, Wittgenstein must be wrong. On the other hand, Carroll says, if Wittgenstein did not really mean "*family* resemblances," he must have simply meant "resemblances," and in that case, the idea is too vague to be useful, because there are always *some* resemblances between any two things (if only the fact that they are both *things*).

In Wittgenstein's defense against both Mandelbaum and Carroll, I would like to suggest that for Wittgenstein, the idea of "family resemblance" is intended as an analogy or a metaphor, and that as such, it does not entail the biological connections on which Mandelbaum and Carroll insist. (If I say, "Your lips are like roses," I am not committed to the claim that your lips would flourish if we apply dung to your roots in the spring.) Nor are analogies infinitely open to interpretation, which seems to be Carroll's other worry. Analogies are indeed open to different interpretations—and perhaps this is a source of confusion in Wittgenstein's analogy ("When he says my lips are like roses, is he saying my lips are red, or dewy, or delicate, or beautiful, or all those things?")—but the interpretations should be restricted by context. Only a person with very bad interpretive skills would think, "Yellow roses exist; therefore he's telling me my lips are yellow and thorny."

Carroll writes, "And yet we *are* able to identify art—to classify candidates as artworks—with a very high degree of consensus. The question of how we manage to do it remains pressing" (p. 249). Well, despite Carroll's reservations about Wittgenstein's family resemblance model, certainly philosophers of art who follow Wittgenstein's lead believe that his discussion of games as a "family" provides the structure for pursuing this question as it applies to art. Let's see what that structure might be. We'll try it with "game." (Take note that the analysis I am about to present does not employ the metaphor of family resemblances; that analogy is not essential to Wittgenstein's point, as far as I can tell.) Say that A = competition, B = skill, C = luck, D = amusement, and E = winning and losing; these are characteristics of possible activities. Then we can imagine five different activities—let's number them 1 through 5—each with a set of four characteristics:

1 ABCD	It seems that Wittgenstein is suggesting that if we witnessed any of these five activities we would probably be correct to recognize them as games, even though there is no one common denominator throughout by virtue of which we recognize them as games.[10]
2 ABCE	
3 ABDE	I don't think Wittgenstein means to say that every game must have at least four of these five characteristics. Will three do? Nor would he say that exhibiting any four of these guarantees that we are dealing with a game. I can't tell whether this is an ambiguity in Wittgenstein's "theory" (he would be
4 ACDE	loath to call his remarks a theory) or if it indicates an ambiguity in the concept of games. Even with four characteristics, we
5 BCDE	could imagine some ambiguity, and we could argue about some of them. For example, activity 2 might be a battle ("war

games" may or may not be games, and wars may in some respects be game*like*, but they are certainly not games), and activity 4 might be "push-the-boy-down-the-stairs." Are the reality shows on television games? They have a lot of A, B, C, D, and E. But they also have a lot of F (= prestaging). Is a staged game a game? And the ambiguity in the concept of art may be more radical than that in game, which is why some people (but surely not all) are willing to consider the claims of conceptual artists that they can designate as a work of art a concept, such as "All the squirrels I have ever dreamt about (which in my case would be an an empty concept, as far as I know)."

Another complaint that Noël Carroll directs against "the Neo-Wittgensteinians" is that they confuse the *concept* of art with the *practice* of art. It is possible, Carroll believes, for the concept to be closed (i.e., for it to be definable in terms of necessary and sufficient conditions) while the practice remains open and unconstrained. But it seems to me the constraints imposed by the definition of x also constrain the practice of x. For example, if religion were defined as "the worship of God" (it isn't, by the way), then the practice of religion would be constrained by the conditions of that definition.

It is interesting, by the way, that when Carroll turns to his own theorizing about art, he makes it clear that he has pretty much abandoned the quest for a definition. Carroll refuses to rule out the possibility that, sometime in the future, some philosopher will construct a perfectly adequate, all-encompassing definition of art. On the other hand, he says, we can't presuppose that such a thing will happen. He admits that "many of our concepts are not governed by essential definition. So why suppose that art is?" (p. 266). Furthermore, he admits, even if someone does construct such a definition in the future, it's clear that we are not using that future definition now to identify works of art.

Carroll calls his own theory "the historical narrative approach." It is not offered as a definition, rather as a way that we can (usually) judge whether something is a work of art. He says:

> When an artwork is challenged or likely to be challenged, our response is not a definition, but an explanation. . . . This explanation takes the form of a historical narrative. If the narrative is an accurate and reasonable one, this generally suffices to establish that the candidate is an artwork. . . . Where we can weave the candidate into the ongoing history of art as we know it, we are disposed to classify an artifact as an artwork. (pp. 254–255)

It seems to me that searching for a historical narrative in which to put a new work of art is quite similar to looking for that work's family antecedents.

A Form of Life: The Artworld

It is perhaps ironic that the most serious challenge to Morris Weitz's Wittgensteinian analysis of the concept of art comes from a group of philosophers who are themselves deeply influenced by Wittgenstein. They base their challenge on an aspect of Wittgenstein's philosophy different from the one that inspired Weitz. The basic position of these philosophers of art was laid down in articles by ARTHUR DANTO (1924–2013) and George Dickie (whom we met earlier). This view is called "the institutional theory of art." It began with a mental experiment of Danto's concerning what he called "visually indistinguishable pairs." This experiment asks us to imagine any famous painting (say, Leonardo da Vinci's *Mona Lisa*) and then to imagine another painting that is visually indistinguishable but the result of pure accident. Then, we are to ask ourselves—What makes the first painting art and the second nonart? It must be some *context* that determines the distinction, and that context is what Danto called "an artworld." He wrote, "To see something as art requires something the eye cannot de(s)cry—an atmosphere of artistic theory, a knowledge of the history of art: an artworld."[11]

Professor Dickie takes Danto's idea of "an artworld" and interprets it in the light of the following remark of that of Wittgenstein: "And to imagine a language means to imagine a form of life" (p. 8). Wittgenstein insisted that we always consider language as a *social* activity. Similarly, Dickie stresses the social context of art and of the discourse about art. He believes that if we *do* place art in its social context, we will be able to define art adequately despite Weitz's assurance of the wrongheadedness of such attempts. Here is Dickie's definition: "A work of art in the classificatory sense is (1) an artifact (2) upon which some person or persons acting on behalf of a certain social institution (the artworld) have conferred the status of candidate for appreciation."[12] Dickie's definition is based on an analogy between the institutional nature of "the artworld" and other social institutions. For example, a particular round, white, hidebound pellet becomes a "strike" when it has that status conferred upon it by an umpire; an adult male human and an adult female human become "married" when they have that status conferred upon them by a member of the clergy or justice of the peace; the author of a particular action becomes "guilty" when that status is conferred upon him by a jury or a judge. Similarly, a particular object becomes "art" when the title is conferred upon it by some member of the artworld, usually the artist who created the artifact, but sometimes the "artist" can confer that status on "ready-mades," as the twentieth-century French **dadaist** artist Marcel Duchamp did in the case of urinals and snow shovels. (In fact, Dickie tells us that it is the work of Duchamp and his followers, Rauschenberg, Warhol, and Oldenburg, that inspired his new definition of art.) Professor Dickie summarizes his argument, saying, "The main point I am trying to make is that something is art because of the place it has in a certain social system."[13]

Dickie's view has been influential among contemporary aestheticians, but not all of them are satisfied that he has refuted Weitz's claim that art is an open concept. A number of critics have complained that Dickie's move of having the artworld confer the status of art upon an artifact presupposes a structure of authority that is in fact missing in the so-called artworld. A university confers a degree upon a graduating student; the president of the United States confers freedom on a jailed criminal by pardoning him; the pope removes from a priest the right to say mass by excommunicating him; a general confers the status of hero on a soldier by awarding her a medal for bravery; but in each of these cases an established and definable authority gives these institutions or individuals the right to make such conferrals. In the artworld, there is no such authority.[14]

Similarly, B. R. TILGHMAN implies that Dickie's definition really comes down to claiming that "it's art if the artist says it's art," and he claims that such a definition "is altogether wide of the mark; the real issue of understanding and appreciation is not touched."[15] Nevertheless, Tilghman agrees with Dickie in stressing the social nature of art. Tilghman quotes Wittgenstein's *Lectures and Conversations,* where Wittgenstein says, "The words we call aesthetic judgments play a very complicated role, but a very definite role, in what we call the culture of a period. To describe their use or to describe what you mean by a cultural taste, you have to describe a culture."[16]

My own objection to Dickie's theory is twofold. First, even if it escapes other criticism, the definition of art provided by the institutional theory is trivial. Aristotle, whose definition of a human is "the rational animal"—a definition that provides two necessary conditions that together constitute a sufficient condition—mocked trivial definitions that denote nonessential commonality, such as "the human is the bashful animal" (i.e., only humans can blush) or "the human is the animal capable of developing corns" (i.e., only humans wear shoes that are too tight). Surely neither of these definitions gets at the *essence* of humanity—if there is such a thing. Well, it hardly gets to the essence of art to say that something is art because someone in the artworld agrees that it is. Also, the definition as proposed is circular, because the word "art" is used to define the word "art." (Dickie now admits that the definition is circular, but says that it is "not viciously so" [p. 92]. In other words, he believes the definition is informative and not a mere tautology.)

My other objection is that Dickie's definition does not seem capable of ruling out fraud. In every other institutional setting, fraud is identifiable—at least in theory. There are fraudulent marriages, counterfeit bills, plagiarized documents, and shoplifting in addition to shopping. But the "artworld" produces items that are clearly meant to flout the artworld and mock it. Even the Wizard of Oz might find someone in the artworld who would declare the Wizard's fraud to be art. (When his shenanigans are discovered by Toto, the Wizard finally admits to the Strawman, "I cannot give you a brain, but I can give you a diploma."[17])

Finally, I want to report on a contribution to this discussion of art made by TIMOTHY BINKLEY (born 1943) another contemporary philosopher deeply influenced by Wittgenstein. Binkley completely disarms Dickie's definition by making the following stipulation: "I hereby create a prodigious class of pieces of art by specifying everything to be art."[18] If Dickie's definition allows *everything* to be art, what is the point of drawing the distinction? Binkley wants to return to Weitz's Wittgensteinian claim that art is undefinable. However, he finds that Weitz's specific account makes art seem too tame. Binkley says that the family resemblances of "games" allow us to discriminate clear cases of games from clear cases of nongames, but the recent history of art indicates that this is not the case with art. He says that art is "radically open, radically indefinable." This conclusion is exciting—but it is also a little scary. A few years ago in an art gallery in London I saw a work that was composed of a large rectangular block of clear plastic with a complete standing cow inside it. The cow's body had been sliced like large crosscuts of sausage, and the slices were separated within their plastic tomb so that all of its internal organs were on exhibit. "Is this art?" I asked myself, and a queasy feeling of repulsion came over me. I felt at that moment that the center—at least, *my* center—might not hold.

The Neuroscience of Aesthetic Experience

In Chapter 4, we saw an interest on the part of Western philosophers in the recent advances in neurology and the role that science might play in the philosophy of mind. In Chapter 5, we inspected the recent function that neuroscience is playing in the study of religious belief. Perhaps it is not surprising that philosophers of art have also begun looking to neurobiology for insight. A recent impressive attempt to take advantage of breakthroughs in the study of the brain by relating them to traditional problems of aesthetics appears in a short book by G. Gabrielle Starr, called *Feeling Beauty: The Neuroscience of Aesthetic Experience.* Starr is a professor of English at New York University and a dean of the College of Arts and Science at that institution. During a recent leave of absence, she worked with

After Hieronymous Bosch's "The Cure for Madness," ca. 1485

neuroscientists in a lab setting, testing ideas about aesthetic experience.

Ironically, in some ways, Starr's book is old-fashioned, perhaps more like a seventeenth- or eighteenth-century book than one of the twenty-first century. In those early days, there were numerous publications about the nature of the aesthetic experience, about beauty, the sublime, and the ugly. As time passed, it was denied by some theorists that there was any sensation that could correctly be called "the aesthetic experience,"[19] and it was claimed that no theoretically useful definition of the beautiful, the sublime, or the ugly could be formulated. As the title of Starr's book indicates, she is very much interested in beauty and the nature of the aesthetic experience. Given that her work is on the cutting edge of a science that did not exist in the eighteenth and nineteenth centuries, it is striking that Starr appeals to many very traditional aestheticians to support her conclusions. Her goal in writing this book is to understand how "the neural underpinnings of aesthetic experience . . . can reshape our understanding of aesthetics and the arts,"[20] to help "explain the relations among the Sister Arts" ["music, painting, and poetry"], to provide "a reinterpretation of the relations among" those different forms of art (p. 69) and to establish "the idea of aesthetics as a coherent discipline" (p. 21).

Starr's primary method is to work in a laboratory with neural scientists, seeking reaction from volunteer participants who are shown various works of art while undergoing a study of the brain, using an "fMRI, a noninvasive tool for the indirect measurement of brain activity" (p. 23). Apparently, the main parts of the brain that are pertinent to Starr's study are found in what is called "*the default mode network*," defined by Starr in various ways, first as "an interconnected set of brain areas that contributes to our sense of self-identity, as well as to our ability to imagine other worlds and other people, among other functions" (p. xv).[21] Later, it is characterized as "an interlinked set of brain regions often implicated in self-assessment, forward planning, autobiographical memory, and ideas of self" (p. 46). It also activates "processes underlying self-concept, social life, and a heightened sense of both the external world and its internal, subjective representation" (p. 34). Also, there is evidence that "the default mode network is involved in social cognition" (p. 60). This is an interesting family of concepts for the aesthetic experience to be associated with, if Starr's theory is correct.

Starr points out that in response to most images shown to the participants, including most of the visual art they were shown, activity in the default mode network decreases as attention to specific perceptual objects increases. However, in response to the "most powerfully moving images," key components of the network were strongly activated. This fact "offers strong evidence for the involvement of the default mode network in intense aesthetic experience" (p. 62). Because that network encompasses so many important functions, Starr can write that "visual art might strike a person so strongly that it engages this system of integration between different worlds of experience" (p. 64), suggesting that "aesthetic emotions make us newly aware of being ourselves and being in the world. . . . Neurally speaking, art moves us by harnessing a key system with extraordinary resources, a system that not only helps make us who we are but also helps us be aware of who we are" (p. 66).

I find this to be eye-opening. However, there may be a logical or definitional problem here to be sorted out. If one sets out to prove that X exists (here, "X" is "aesthetic experience"), that X is caused as a response of Y to Z (here "Y" is "activation of the default mode network" and "Z" is "powerfully moving images"), then one should be able to define or characterize each of these components, X, Y, and Z, independently of the other two. Yet, as far as I can determine, Starr defines X in terms of Y and Z. This seems a bit circular. Starr admits that an image of something disturbing (a person throwing himself off the top of a building) or ugly (an engorged tick) counts as a powerful image. Does it count as an aesthetic experience? If it can be shown that the category "aesthetic experience" can be defined independently of the category "powerfully moving images," then I think that Starr's discovery is very exciting, as it indicates that aesthetic experience itself intensifies our lives and in some ways makes them deeper.

Starr believes she is able to demonstrate the relations among the Sister Arts by showing experimentally that each provokes similar responses in the default mode network. If Starr's theory is correct, does that mean that "beauty" is an unchanging objective fact? Not according to her. She says, "Aesthetic value changes over time (what is beautiful now may not seem so always, what was understandable may now be incomprehensible)" (p. 18). This assertion rescues Starr from the "old-fashionedness" of which I accused her earlier. The eighteenth- and nineteenth-century aestheticians almost to the individual tried to define beauty objectively and define aesthetic experience in terms of the appreciation of beauty (or of other powerful objects of perception, such as the sublime, or the ugly, which they also defined). For Starr, the aesthetic experience does not produce *knowledge*; rather, it produces a "restructuring of values," which results in "no new 'facts' but rather sets the stage for new *configurations* of knowledge" (p. 15).

Concerning her appeal to a number of "old-fashioned" thinkers about art (e.g., Blaise Pascal, Baruch Spinoza, Joseph Addison, Francis Hutcheson, and William Hogarth, all born in the seventeenth century; Immanuel Kant, Johann Winckelmann, and Edmund Burke, all born in the eighteenth century), we may ask why they make repeated appearances in a book about neuroscience. Perhaps we can say that a (slightly sup-pressed) thesis of this book is that neurological studies of the experience of art support certain earlier aesthetic theories, to the disadvantage of critics of these theories.

According to Starr, if we were able to study our own reception of powerful aesthetic objects from a neurological point of view, we would probably see how our default mode networks light up the screen. In her book, she provides four specific examples of powerful aesthetic objects: Elizabeth Bishop's poem, "At the Fishhouses" (pp. 95–97), John Keats's poem, "Ode on a Grecian Urn" (pp. 103–118), Ovid's "Metamorphoses" (pp. 118–127), and a specific set of Bluegrass musical pieces played by masters of the genre (pp. 129–132). If she is right, Starr will have helped us see how power and beauty relate to other important experiences in our lives. What more can we ask from an art critic?

I will now end the overview of analytic philosophy of art and the neuroscience of aesthetic experience, and we will spend the rest of our time looking at some philosophical issues of historical and cultural significance that art has raised.

Plato, Freud, and Art

Our discussion of the philosophical significance of art and of its cultural ramifications, as with so many of our discussions, will begin with Plato's views. You may or may not have anticipated that these views would be decidedly negative. His indictment of art, based on the metaphysics of the Simile of the Line (see Chapter 2), can be stated in three parts. There is an *ontological* objection, an *epistemological*

Forms	} INTELLIGIBLE WORLD	THE GOOD
Concepts		
Particular objects	} VISIBLE WORLD	THE SUN
Images		

Review of Plato's Simile of the Line

objection, and a *moral* objection. The ontological objection has to do with Plato's view that art is imitation (mimesis). This was the standard Greek view, and it went unchallenged by all the greatest Greek thinkers on the subject. But what is art an imitation *of*? Well, according to Plato, art must be imitating the world as it *appears,* not the world as it *is.* Artists imitate "particular objects." If so, then art itself must be consigned to the realm of "images" (being a copy of "particular things," which are themselves but copies of higher things). In Book 10 of the *Republic,* Plato says that mimetic art is "thrice removed from the truth." It is a copy of a copy of a copy.

Because most of us today do not approach art under the influence of the Simile of the Line, and because we are no longer satisfied with the view that art is simply imitative, we probably do not feel that Plato's ontological objection is very forceful. Therefore, to be able to understand his point better, consider the following example. Imagine a novel by someone like Charles Dickens that begins with this line: "It was a foggy day in London." Now, precisely *what* day was a foggy day? June 21, 1836? August 7, 1829? Obviously, the sentence does not refer to *any* real day. Strictly speaking, the sentence is false, or at least, its

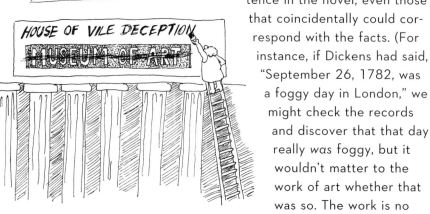

status has nothing to do with the truth. Such is the case with *every* sentence in the novel, even those that coincidentally could correspond with the facts. (For instance, if Dickens had said, "September 26, 1782, was a foggy day in London," we might check the records and discover that that day really *was* foggy, but it wouldn't matter to the work of art whether that was so. The work is no better or worse as a work of art if that sentence is true. Similarly, medieval and renaissance paintings of Jesus would be none the worse off as paintings even if it were proved that Jesus never lived.)

It follows that works of art are what they are by virtue of being *illusions*. The success of Dickens's novels depends upon his creating the illusion that he is describing real events and real people, just as the success of a realistic painting depends upon the artist's creating the illusion that these blotches of color are clouds, mountains, houses, people, and the like. So, for Plato, the function of art is always to deceive. It always draws attention away from reality (the Forms) and toward illusion (images). Plato

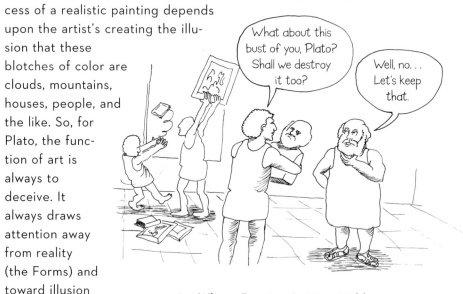

Art Whose Function Is More Noble

did not deny that an art whose function was more noble might be ontologically justifiable, but it seemed to him that almost all art was deceptive in the way just described.

Plato's *epistemological* objection is directed against both the work of art and the artist. The work of art, being false, does not give us any true knowledge of the world, and the artists do not know what they are doing. They cannot give the Logos.

Plato's *moral* objection is multifaceted. First, if Plato has established that the pursuit of knowledge is the pursuit of the Good, and if art produces ignorance, then art is immoral. Second, art seems to concentrate on the flaws in human and divine nature and often depicts great men and gods doing immoral things. Here Plato had in mind Homer and the Greek tragedies. How much respect can you have for a God like Zeus, who cheats on his wife and then lies to her when she asks him where he's been? Or can he be admired when on other occasions he is henpecked and even cuckolded by her? And what about the story of Odysseus in the underworld? When Odysseus meets the ghost of Achilles, Odysseus tells this honored hero of the Trojan War how much he envies him as prince among the dead. Achilles responds despairingly, "I'd rather be a serf or labouring man under some yeoman on a little farm than be king paramount of all the dead." How can you inspire courage in young men so that they will fight to defend their country if a role model like Achilles says it is better to be a live coward than a dead hero? If the people have flawed gods and heroes to imitate (even *tragically* flawed ones), the people themselves cannot be

Achilles and a Horrified Odysseus

A perfect example of madness is, of course, Don Quixote.

A Real Tyger Burning in the Forests of the Night

expected to try to achieve perfection.

And because we forget that art is an illusion, we do appeal to it for examples of ideal cases. Ask yourself how many times in the past week some of your own teachers have used an example from fiction to make a point. "A perfect example of madness is, of course, Don Quixote," "Hamlet exemplifies the feelings of indecision from which we all suffer," "Picasso's *Guernica* analyzes the horrors of war." But, in truth, a madman named Don Quixote never existed, nor did Hamlet have any *real* feelings of indecisiveness; not even bombed horses look like Picasso's horse, and real "tygers" do not burn in the forests of the night.

This brings us to the third and most important of Plato's moral objections to art. Art does not appeal to the highest faculty of the soul, "Pure Reason." (How could it? It must deal with *images*.) Rather, it appeals to the basest part of the soul, the emotions. Plato, like Freud after him, was very suspicious of the irrational passions. Both Plato and Freud believed that in the darkest recesses of the soul is a cauldron of sexuality and violence—unruly emotions. These passions are antisocial and destructive of the individual. One of the most difficult jobs we face is reining these passions under our control instead of surrendering to their control. It is interesting that both Freud and Plato point to dreams as proving the existence of this part of the psyche, which Freud calls "the id" and Plato calls "the appetitive

Philosophy appeals here.

REASON

Action appeals here.

COURAGE

Art appeals here.

PASSIONS

The Structure of the Soul

soul." You will remember from Chapter 7 that, in the *Republic,* Plato represents Socrates as discussing "the lawless desires" that are "born in everyone." They are "aroused in sleep," and, being "bestial and savage . . . and rid of all shame and reason," they do not shrink from desiring incest and bloodshed, and they "leave no folly or shamelessness untried."[22]

According to Plato, the way to control this part of the soul and thereby to prevent dreams of violence and sex is to live moderately, eat and drink little

Preventing Violent and Sexual Dreams

before retiring, think philosophical thoughts before sleeping, and above all, *avoid art!* Precisely the reason we like art is that it titillates the passions and provokes us. Sophisticated people are provoked by Bach, unsophisticated people by Western shoot-'em-up movies; but in some strange sense, the content is identical. We could almost say, in Plato's name, all art is pornographic.

Before you condemn Plato's view, ask yourself where you stand on this controversial claim from a contemporary debate of our own: "Violence on screens perpetuates violence in society. Children who spend a great deal of time watching TV are less sensitive to violence and are more prone to solve their own problems by resorting to violence." If you agree with that passage, you are siding with Plato, for television is *the* contemporary art form; and all of Plato's objections—ontological, epistemological, and moral—apply vividly to the bulk of what we see on our screens, including the commercial messages.

Before leaving Plato and his objections to art, let's return for a moment to the comparison between Plato and Freud. You may have noticed earlier a striking similarity between Plato's doctrine of innate ideas and parts of Freud's psychoanalytic theory. For both thinkers, liberation comes when we remember the past, a past buried deep in our unconscious. Also, both men divided the soul into three aspects: for Freud, the id, the ego, and the super-ego; for Plato, the appetitive, the spirited, and the rational portions. Now, in their suspicion of art, we have found another similarity. Freud's theory of art is interesting in itself, but a brief discussion of it will shed light on Plato's similar theory.

Freud's theory of instincts (*Triebe*, better translated as "drives" or "impulses") changed substantially over the

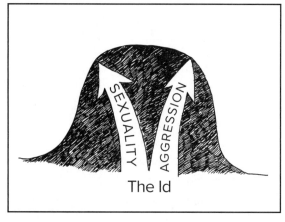

The Id

forty-year period of his work, but I'll try to present a representative version of it. The sexual and aggressive drives contained in the id are irrational and antisocial. If rationality and society are to survive, these passions must be controlled. The rational component of the psyche (the ego) is not by itself capable of containing the explosiveness of the id, so it must ally itself with the harsh irrationality of the superego. (For this alliance, the psyche pays a high price in terms of unconscious guilt.) Together they form a barrier that blocks the animal drives and returns them to their source. There they are "deanimalized" and redirected into socially acceptable forms of creativity: art, religion, philosophy, law, science, and morality—"higher culture." Freud calls this process **sublimation.** It produces a cultural product that is a substitute gratification for the primary aim from which the drive was deflected. Yet the cultural product never completely loses its original (sexual or violent) nature. For example, imagine a little boy with a particularly strong aggressive drive. His idea of fun is to tear flesh, maim, and make people

Sublimation

bleed. We can't afford to let him loose on the streets, so we send him to medical school, where he may sublimate his hostility into science and become a surgeon. He is now able to tear flesh, maim, and make people bleed and thereby receive wealth, prestige, and respectability. Freud believed that one could successfully sublimate one's animality into science (he believed that he and Einstein, at least, had done so), but apparently Freud was suspicious of artistic sublimation, even though he personally had a great reverence for art. His investigation of two of his favorite artists, Leonardo da Vinci and Michelangelo, did not alleviate his suspicions. Arnold Hauser has summarized Freud's most pessimistic estimation of art in this passage:

> Both neurosis and art are essentially purposive; they are not only the expression of a failure and resignation in the face of reality, but also a kind of escapism. They represent partly an outcome of, partly a means of withdrawal from the real. "Every neurosis," says Freud, "has the result, and therefore probably the purpose, of forcing the patient out of real life, of alienating him from actuality." As far as the work of art is concerned, there can be no doubt about the existence of such a purpose. Neurosis and art equally reject reality, but neurosis does not deny it, only tries to forget it; art, on the other hand, tries both to deny and to replace it. The artist's attitude is, therefore, in this respect at least, more akin to insanity than to neurosis.[23]

> Furthermore, the artist's product, unlike the scientist's, doctor's, or lawyer's, is still too close to its source in unconscious fantasies. Fantasies are guided by the infantile pleasure principle and have refused to submit to the reality principle. Therefore, art is not a rational response to the demands of reality but an irrational denial of reality. Freud's approach is just another, more complicated way of stating Plato's objection to art.

Aristotle and Art

Despite Plato's tremendous influence on Western philosophy, very few of his followers have agreed with his condemnation of art. In fact, the first philosopher after Plato to come to art's defense was Plato's most important student, Aristotle. We have already seen in Chapter 3 that Aristotle, though in many respects faithful to his master, ultimately rejected Plato's doctrine of Forms as too "otherworldly." Aristotle believed that the world we are born into is the real world and not just a shadow of a

more ultimate world. He brought Plato's philosophy down to earth by claiming that the Forms must be "imbedded in matter." He believed that the distinction between Form and matter was only an *intellectual* distinction, a distinction that could be drawn in theory but not demonstrated in reality. His theory does not have the bias against "the visible world" that we saw in Plato; thus, Aristotle could accept Plato's claim that art deals in mimetic images without thereby condemning art.

There is another comment about Aristotle's metaphysics that is pertinent here. The late British philosopher SIR ISAIAH BERLIN (1909–1997) liked to apply the story of the fox and the hedgehog to philosophers. The hedgehog has one *big* idea, and the fox has many small ideas. (Berlin said that

The Hedgehog and the Fox and Their Respective Collections of Ideas

the Russian novelist Tolstoy was a fox who wanted to be a hedgehog.) According to Berlin's criterion, then, Plato is a hedgehog and Aristotle is a fox. That is to say, Aristotle's metaphysics is more piecemeal than that of Plato. This means that his discussion of art was less under the domination of some central, overriding philosophical idea; therefore, Aristotle could consider art more as an autonomous activity (though not completely so because no Greek would consider *any* activity as independent of moral and political implications).

So Aristotle met Plato's ontological objection to art by rejecting Plato's hierarchical ontology. Yet he never denied that art is *mimesis*, imitation. Then what is art an imitation *of*?

Aristotle, who was particularly interested in poetry and drama, tells us that art imitates an *action*. But it does not imitate an *action* in the way that the writing of history imitates actions, simply recounting particular events (the second stage on Plato's line). Art is superior to history, because it *theorizes* about actions (the third stage on the line). It does not tell us what *has* happened; rather, it tells us what *can* happen. Art deals with universals and not with particulars, so it is more philosophical than history is. So we see that Aristotle has also answered Plato's epistemological objection to art. Nevertheless, I must point out that, for Aristotle, art is still inferior to philosophy. It is, as it were, on the third level of the line and cannot achieve the fourth level. Aristotle believed, as Plato did, that the fourth level can be achieved only by philosophy.

What about Plato's moral objection to art? Aristotle agreed with Plato's claim that art appeals to the passions, and even though Aristotle was less suspicious of the passions than was Plato, he too believed that they can be wild, unruly, and dangerous. However, rather than holding that art encourages the passions to take control away from reason, Aristotle believed that art *purges* the passions. Let's read Aristotle's famous passage about this purgation (*catharsis*).

> An emotion which strongly affects some souls is present in all to a varying degree, for example pity and fear, and also ecstasy. To this last some people are particularly liable, and we see that under the influence of religious music and songs which drive the soul to frenzy, they calm down as if they had been medically treated and purged. People who are given to pity or fear, and emotional people generally, and others to the extent that they have similar emotions, must be affected in the same way; for all of them must experience a kind of purgation and pleasurable relief. In the same way, cathartic [songs and] music give men harmless delight. We must therefore make those who practice *mousikê* [poetry and music] in the theater perform these kinds of tunes and songs.[24]

Keep in mind that, unlike the more domesticated audiences of today, when Athenians went to the theater, they laughed, moaned, shrieked, beat

Greek Audience

their chests, and tore their hair as the drama unfolded. It is easy to see why Aristotle claimed catharsis to be the function of art in such a context, but before you decide between him and Plato, ask yourself again whether you think that watching violence on television and in the movies *replaces* real violence or *stimulates* it. And perhaps you'll be even more confused when you ask yourself the same question concerning sex in films and literature. Does pornography replace sexual activity or encourage it? Does it replace sexual crimes or provoke them?

Regardless of your opinions concerning these topics, I think you may be somewhat disappointed with parts of Aristotle's defense of art when you read the passage that follows his description of catharsis:

> There are two kinds of spectator: the one kind is a free and educated man, the other, the vulgar kind, is made up of mechanics and general laborers and other such people; these too must be provided with contests and spectacles for their recreation. Their souls are perverted from their natural state; so there are perversions of melody and songs that are tense and corrupted. Every man takes pleasure in what is naturally akin to him, and we must therefore allow the performers to use this kind of *mousikê* with this kind of spectator in view.[25]

We see here that the experience of catharsis is most needed by "mechanics and general laborers" and other such "vulgar" people. Plato had worried about the effects of art on the aristocracy as well as on the plebeians.

Aristotle seems to see the production of art as a way of pacifying the masses (another "opiate of the masses"?). This view appears to conflict with his claim that art is philosophical.

There is a final point. Despite Aristotle's defense of art against Plato's

attack, it is clear to any reader of both authors that Plato has much more feeling for art than does Aristotle. In fact, ironically, Plato is a poet and artist par excellence, but no one will ever accuse Aristotle of being that. Aristotle never felt the stirring of passion produced in the sensitive soul by the confrontation with art. Plato had done so and was fearful of it. When he drummed the artists out of the *Republic*, he said he did so with tears in his eyes.

Marx and Art

The debate about the relation between art and justice, initiated by Plato, was reopened in the work of Karl Marx. Marx never wrote a treatise on art, but he was obviously fascinated by it and very concerned over it, because references to art and art theory are scattered at significant places throughout his philosophical, sociological, and economic works. The attempt to reconstruct his ideas about art is complicated by the fact that two separate strands of thought concerning art run through Marx's writings, and these strands sometimes seem at odds with each other. On the one hand is his claim that the need for artistic expression and aesthetic enjoyment is an essential aspect of human nature. On the other hand is his assertion that art and aesthetics are components of ideology and as such are political captives. The first assertion sides with those traditional authors, such as Kant and Tolstoy, who extoll art. The second claim sides with Plato's condemnation of art. We shall examine both strands and see whether they can be made consistent with each other.

Marx's view is that human beings cannot be studied in a vacuum but must always be studied in their relation to the world. The world of human beings is composed of relations to nature, to fellow humans, and to the products of their hands and minds. Under optimum conditions, these relations are positive. They are productive, artistic, aesthetic, and creative. Wherever those relationships are ruptured, humans are alienated from their world and hence from themselves. (In Chapter 9, we took a look at "alienated labor.") Marx wrote that man is independent only "if he affirms his individuality as a total man in each of his relations to the world, seeing, hearing, smelling, tasting, feeling, thinking, willing, loving—in short, if he affirms and expresses all organs of his individuality."[26] For Marx, the fully *human* being is essentially an artist who approaches the world aesthetically and forms things "in accordance with the laws of beauty."[27] From this point of view, we can say that the goal of **Marxism** (or at least as envisioned by the *young* Marx) was the liberation of *Homo artisticus,* the human being as artist. ROBERT C. TUCKER (1918–2010) has characterized this aspect of Marx's conception of communism in the following passage:

> What will remain is the life of art and science in a special and vastly enlarged sense of these two terms. Marx's conception of ultimate communism is fundamentally *aesthetic* in character. His utopia is an aesthetic ideal of the future man-nature relationship, which he sees in terms of artistic creation and the appreciation of the beauty of the man-made environment by its creator. The acquisitive and therefore alienated man of history is to be succeeded by the post-historical aesthetic man who will be "rich" in a new way. . . .

Economic activity will turn into artistic activity, with industry as the supreme avenue of creation, and the planet itself will become the new man's work of art. The alienated world will give way to the aesthetic world.[28]

However, this general theory, which turns all truly human productivity into artistic and aesthetic acts, does not tell us anything about the difference between artistic production and nonartistic production in history up to Marx's own time. When we look not to Marx's future communist society, where all are artists, but to the present and the past, where only some are artists, we run up against Marx's theory of ideology. To understand this theory, we must first remember Marx's distinction between the *foundation* and the *superstructure* of society. Marx says:

> In the social production of their means of existence men enter into definite, necessary relations which are independent of their will, productive relationships which correspond to a definite stage of development of their material productive forces. The aggregate of these productive relationships constitutes the economic structure of society, the real basis on which a juridical and political superstructure arises, and to which definite forms of social consciousness correspond. The mode of production of the material means of existence conditions the whole process of social, political and intellectual life. It is not the consciousness of men that determines their existence, but, on the contrary, it is their social existence that determines their consciousness.
>
> . . . .
>
> Then an epoch of social revolution opens. With the change in the economic foundation the whole vast superstructure is more or less rapidly transformed. In considering such revolutions it is necessary always to distinguish between the material revolution in the economic conditions of production, which can be determined with scientific accuracy, and the juridical, political, religious, aesthetic or philosophic—in a word, ideological forms wherein men become conscious of this conflict and fight it out.[29]

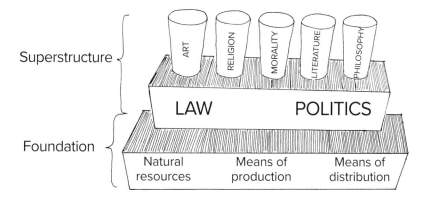

Furthermore, Marx added, "The ideas of the ruling class are in every epoch the ruling ideas."[30] That is to say, "ideology"—including art—is a justification of the power of the ruling class.

"The Ruling Ideas of Each Age . . ."

"Ideology" is Marx's term for the myth of self-aggrandizement that each socioeconomic system necessarily (if unintentionally) creates by monopolizing and controlling the form and content of the spiritual productions of its creative members. These products become a form of unconscious political propaganda. The theory of ideology clearly applies to artistic as well as philosophical and political ideas. That is, artists also express the values of the ruling class that supports them; therefore, artists, intentionally or not, endorse and perpetuate the status quo. Medieval art glorified God and condemned worldliness, thereby reflecting the values of the papal authority that ruled over the Christian world. Renaissance painting depicted religious themes as well as mythological allegories, the faces of the Medici, and great military victories, thereby affirming the values of the ruling elite who provided the artists' livelihood. The amazing treatment by Johannes Vermeer and the northern baroque artists of light and air in Dutch drawing rooms, kitchens, and studies was a celebration of the values of the bourgeoisie who bought those paintings. The lovely nineteenth-century English landscapes of Constable left one with the feeling that all's well with the (bourgeois) world. John Constable beautiful *Dedham Vale* shows the lush English countryside leading down the valley to the peaceful village of Dedham, whose church spire we see glimmering in the sun. We do *not* see the jute factories in which tubercular children are slaving twelve hours a day in order to be able to add a few pieces of bread to their parents' table and add their "surplus labor" (profit) to the sumptuous table of the capitalist mill owner. Again, art, like religion, is an opiate. Even the most beautiful art, the greatness of the classics, is ideology.

But I must add a further complication. For Marx, the material foundations of society, from which all art emerges, are fractured in terms of antagonistic classes. That is, one class

Portrait of Louis XIV (after Hyacinthe Rigaud)

Laws establishing aristocratic privilege (e.g., antipoaching laws)

Property ownership by the nobility

Art as Ideology

owns the material wealth of the society, and a dispossessed class must sell its labor to this owning class. The interests of the one class are not the interests of the other. The interests of the ruling class will always be expressed as the dominant ideas in any historical period, but the interests of the disadvantaged class may find cultural expression too. So for every expression of the socioeconomic foundation in terms of a cultural form, there can be a counter-expression as well. After all, the morality of the aristocrat is not the morality of the serf, nor are their ideas the same, nor their religion, nor their art. Cultured art may be the portrait of the king; counterculture art may be a caricature of him, drawn on a wall accompanied by scatological graffiti or, among the working class imbued with class consciousness, a political poster or a mural by José Orozco or Diego Rivera. But apparently from the perspective of the theory of ideology, it must be admitted that counterculture or revolutionary art, like mainstream art, is propaganda. (Of course, Marx would say that the propaganda of the revolutionary working class is not ideology, because ideology is always a form of illusion, and the proletariat is the one class that does not need illusion. But this claim itself seems ideological. Left-wing propaganda can be just as ideological as right-wing propaganda.)

As if his approach to art were not complicated enough, Marx also held that some socioeconomic systems were inherently antagonistic to art, specifically capitalism. Marx says, "Capitalistic production is hostile to certain branches of spiritual production, for example, art and poetry."[31] Capitalism is hostile to art because "the bourgeoisie has stripped of its halo every occupation hitherto honored and looked up to with reverent awe. It has converted the physician, the lawyer, the priest, the poet, the man of science, into its paid wage-labourers."[32] In capitalism, says Marx:

> Only that wage-labour is productive which produces capital. . . . For example, Milton, who wrote *Paradise Lost* for £5 sterling, was an *unproductive labourer.* On the other hand, the writer who turns out stuff for his publisher in factory style, is a *productive labourer.* Milton produced *Paradise Lost* for the same reason that a silkworm produces silk. It was an activity of *his* nature. Later he sold the product for £5 sterling.[33]

In capitalism, to be productive is to put out a commodity. But art is not a commodity. It is a necessary expression of true human essence. Therefore, art and capitalism are incompatible.

Another sense in which capitalism is hostile to art has to do with the division of labor. Marx and his collaborator Friedrich Engels say:

> The exclusive concentration of artistic talent in particular individuals, and its suppression in the broad mass which is bound up with this, is a consequence of the division of labor. . . . [The issue is not] that each should do the work of Raphael, but anyone in whom there is a potential Raphael should be able to develop without hindrance. . . . In a communist society there are no painters but at most people who engage in painting among other activities.[34]

So far, Marx's theory seems to be the following: the artistic impulse is a natural and necessary expression of human nature. In a truly human and humane community (i.e., in communism), each individual would find an artistic form of expression "according to the laws of

JOHN MILTON (1608-1674)

beauty," some reaching great heights of artistic excellence but all achieving a satisfactory expression of the aesthetic urge. However, the artistic impulse has historically been co-opted at times and sometimes suppressed. The artistic urge has also been corrupted and twisted into a conduit of political propaganda. The artistic form of expression will be liberated only in a postrevolutionary communist society where humankind's creative birthright will be restored to it.

But a problem arises with this interpretation (not to mention the problem of deciding whether there is any good reason to think Marx is right). If we look at Marx's actual examples, we see that he extolls the very artists whom, it would seem, his theory should condemn. Obviously, Milton and Raphael, the two artists referred to in the preceding passages, are not being denigrated by Marx; rather, it is implied that he holds them in high esteem, yet these are two artists whose work is essentially religious. Furthermore, if we look at the list of artists Marx admired (Balzac, Dickens, Cervantes, and Heine) and consider the fact that every year Marx reread the complete works of Goethe, Shakespeare, and Aeschylus, we discover that his own taste in art was decidedly traditional.

Karl Marx Contemplates Raphael's Madonna Del Granduca

How does Marx's personal preference in art square with his theory of art as ideology? Marx himself seems to have realized the tension between his general theory of culture as

Romeo, Juliet, and the Profit Motive

ideology and his personal aesthetic taste. He explained the apparent inconsistency by saying that art is more in bondage to the economic substructure in some epochs than in others. Art can have a relative autonomy if the economic system is not highly developed, if it is not especially hostile to art, and if there are a number of intermediary connections between material production and artistic production. Marx uses Greek art and Shakespeare as exemplifying the possibility of uneven development between economy and art. Apparently, Marx felt that neither the form nor the content of the works of Aeschylus and Shakespeare could be explained purely by the structure of the socioeconomic relations in their day. Such an admission seems to amount to a major qualification of the theories of materialism and ideology. Some might even pose the question as to whether it marks a total abandonment of those theories.

Indeed, after Marx's death in 1888, his collaborator, Friedrich Engels, admitted that perhaps he and Marx had overstated the dependence of culture on economics. And Marx himself was so upset by the exaggerations of certain French Marxists that he uttered to Engels, "All I know is that I am not a Marxist."[35]

Existentialism and Art

Existentialism is a twentieth-century philosophical movement that has had a great interest in art. The term "existentialism" was coined by Jean-Paul Sartre (as we saw in Chapter 6), but the philosophy itself derives from certain currents in the nineteenth century, especially from the thought of Friedrich Nietzsche and Søren Kierkegaard. The task of defining existentialism is complicated by the great variety of philosophers called existentialists and by the many discrepancies among their views. One can sympathize with those who finally abandon in exasperation the task of defining existentialism as a philosophy, settling for calling it "a shared mood" or "an attitude," but I think the task is really not that hopeless. Sartre himself has tried to define existentialism in a simple, relatively successful manner. I will follow his lead.

Existentialism: A Shared Mood

Sartre says that an existentialist is any philosopher who has as a guiding idea the view that, in the case of human beings at least, "existence precedes essence." Now, traditionally in philosophy, it has been held that the opposite is so, that "essence precedes existence." To sort out this debate between Sartre and the philosophical tradition, we have to return to Plato and Aristotle. In Greek thought, "essence" is associated with "nature" (as when we ask, "What is the nature of the beast?") and with "Form" in the Platonic sense. The Platonic doctrine, with which we are familiar, holds that a natural object or a human being exists only as a copy of a Form, so for Plato, "essence precedes existence." As we saw, Aristotle tried to bring Plato's Forms down to earth, pointing out that "Form" with a capital "F" was really "form" with a small "f." In other words, the Form of a knife is actually related to its *shape*, which is related to its *function*. (What would a knife with flabby edges be like? Well, it wouldn't be a knife, because it couldn't function as a knife.) So to say that "essence precedes existence" is to say that first the nature and function of a thing exist, then the thing exists.

Sartre agrees that this formula is true of artifacts, such as knives—or a *need* for that function exists—and he seems to agree that it is true of natural entities too. For instance, in the case of a knife, first the human being conceives of a *function* (fig. 10.1). He *needs* something that will cut the bread. Then he creates an object that fulfills this function (fig. 10.2). Therefore, the knife's essence precedes its existence. It is perhaps less clear how this analysis applies to natural objects, such as oak trees, mountains, and pussycats, but I suppose we can say that there really is a thing called the species "cat" (i.e., there is a "cat nature") and that, to be a cat, a thing must fulfill certain criteria of "catness." (This all sounds very Platonic, except that nowadays we would try to explain "cat nature" in terms of genetic codes: e.g., "A cat is a feline with 19 pairs of chromosomes.") Now, the *old* picture of the human being, that is, the preexistential picture, treats the human being the same way as it treats the cat or the knife. First, there is God. He conceives of the human being. ("What I need is one like me, only smaller, weaker,

Fig. 10.1

Fig. 10.2

Fig. 10.3

Fig. 10.4

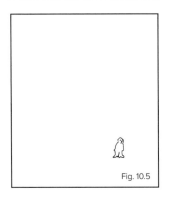

Fig. 10.5

and dumber" [fig. 10.3].) Then, Michelangelo-style, he creates one (fig. 10.4). The creature is truly human only insofar as it fulfills certain divine criteria. Actions falling outside these criteria will be viewed as "inhuman" or even "insane." Then along comes Friedrich Nietzsche with his bad news: "God is dead!" If we erase God from the picture, all we get is the scene in fig. 10.5, which is the human condition according to the existentialists. The human being is, as Kierkegaard said, in "absolute isolation" and, as Sartre says, "abandoned." Sartre asks:

> What is meant here by saying that existence precedes essence? It means that, first of all, man exists, turns up, appears on the scene, and, only afterwards, defines himself. If man, as the existentialist conceives him, is indefinable, it is because at first he is nothing. Only afterwards will he be something, and he himself will have made what he will be. Thus there is no human nature, since there is no God to conceive it.[36]

This account seems to make existentialism atheistic and would appear to rule out Kierkegaard's inclusion in its ranks. And indeed Nietzsche and Sartre, along with many other existentialists, are radically atheistic; but a few pages beyond the passage just quoted, Sartre himself says, somewhat contradictorily perhaps, "even if God did exist, that would change nothing" (p. 51). And, like Kierkegaard, Sartre uses the case of Abraham as an exemplification of the human condition. For Kierkegaard, the human condition is one of absolute isolation. In his despair, the human calls out for God's help, but instead of an answer there is only silence. (The Swedish film director Ingmar Bergman, deeply influenced by Kierkegaard, titled one of his movies *The Silence*.) For Kierkegaard, if there were no God, this silence would be bad enough; but in fact it is worse because there *is* a God. A qualitative abyss gapes open between man and God. As in Sartre's philosophy, the human is left alone, forlorn, dreading the total freedom that is his, despairing over the immense task of assuming the responsibility for the world he must create. If you agree with this picture, you are an existentialist.

From its first moments in the writings of Kierkegaard and Nietzsche, existentialism has always been fascinated by art. However, twentieth-century existentialists do not simply philosophize about art in a technical manner; many of them actively produce art. Sartre, Simone de Beauvoir, and Albert Camus not only produced systematic treatises on philosophy but also wrote novels, short stories, and plays. Nietzsche wrote poetry; Miguel de Unamuno wrote novels, plays, and poetry. And the novelists Franz Kafka and Fyodor Dostoyevsky are often included in the ranks of the existentialists. In order to see how existentialism theorizes about art, we will briefly inspect the work of two twentieth-century American existentialists, Arturo Fallico and Maurice

The World Confronts Us Like a Work of Art

Natanson. I have selected them not because they are well known (they are not), but because their books are readable and at the same time they are good representatives of the technical philosophizing about art that emerges from the phenomenological-existential school.

In ARTURO B. FALLICO's (1914–1982) book *Art and Existentialism,* he says, concerning the possibility of an existentialistic aesthetic, "We must try to see what we can learn about the condition of man from the art phenomenon, and about the art phenomenon from the existential condition of man."[37] One of the main themes in his book is that in some sense the world confronts us like a work of art, but there is also a sense in which the world confronts us quite differently from a work of art, and there is something about art and human existence that we can learn from each of these phenomena. The sense in which the world confronts us like a work of art is that our lived-in world is fundamentally aesthetic rather than scientific. The hegemony of science over the modern mind may make us forget this fact, but actually the world presents itself in terms of experienced qualities of the type better described in the language of the art critic than the language of the physicist. To the unjaded eye, the world looks like a spontaneous work of art. Under the impact of this insight, Fallico, with Nietzsche, talks about the possibility of "the aesthetic transformation of our experience" becoming our individual existential project. He approvingly quotes Nietzsche, who said, "To the extent that man is artist, he is already delivered from his ego and has become a medium through which the true subject celebrates his redemption in illusion." In *The Birth of Tragedy*, Nietzsche tells a story, which he calls "an old legend," about King Midas, who

> hunted a long time in the woods for the wise Silenus, companion of Dionysos, without being able to catch him. When he had finally caught him the king asked him what he considered man's greatest good. The daemon remained sullen and uncommunicative until finally, forced by the king, he broke into a shrill laugh and spoke: "Ephemeral wretch, begotten by accident and toil, why do you force me to tell you what it would be to your greatest boon not to hear? What would be best for you is quite beyond your reach: not to have been born, not to *be*, to be *nothing*. But the second best is to die soon."[38]

In the context of Nietzsche's version of existentialism, the moral of this terrible story is that the demon Silenus is correct *unless* an individual does something to prove Silenus wrong. Unless one *creates* something—and, for Nietzsche, creation itself is artistic—then it would be better that one had never been born. For Nietzsche, existence can only be redeemed artistically. "Only as an aesthetic product can the world be justified to all eternity" (Ibid., p. 42).

Having asserted the similarity between art and the world and the significance of this similarity for humans, Fallico then turns to the

**The World as
Not-Done-and-Having-to-Be-Attended-To**

difference between the world and art, which inheres in the fact that in its spontaneity, the world presents itself to us as "not-done-and-having-to-be-attended-to." The artwork, in contrast, presents itself as a totality, a completed unity, a fullness, and a completeness that is unavailable anywhere else in existence. The "still life" is the exemplar of all art. "In art," says Fallico, "everything *is*, nothing is becoming or has need to become." Only art conquers time. Like Faust, in Goethe's great drama of the same name, we cry out to time, "Stay!" But time does *not* stay. In art, time does stay. Art shows that "human existence is a lack rather

Art Reveals Our Homeless Condition

than a plenitude of being and meaning."[39] It is a testimony of "man's homeless condition and his lack of essence." So once again, according to Fallico, art shows us that we must *create*. "Art places on exhibit a way of validating existence."[40] Art shows us what value, in its pure possibility, is.

Another American author in the phenomenological-existential tradition is MAURICE NATANSON (1924–1996). The title of his book *The Journeying Self* also emphasizes our homeless nature. We are told by Natanson that the confrontation with art affords the individual the opportunity of passing from the typical to the symbolic or from the familiar to the transcendental. In artworks, we find represented the great "metaphysical constants of human existence, Birth, Aging, Intersubjectivity, and Death." Of course, in daily life, we continually run up against these great constants, too, but precisely because they are so enmeshed in our day-to-

day existence, we are unable to isolate these themes in terms of their true significance. In art, I confront birth, sociality, and death in a way that is "primordially unlike all my acquaintance with individual births and deaths." Here, "the naive attitude of daily life is forced to the edge of its limits" as "the symbolic cuts a gash in common sense and draws its hot blood."[41] The radical confrontation through art with the ultimate themes of birth, sociality, and death forces the individual to philosophize existentially as he or she struggles to construct the foundations of his or her own world. The existentialistic point might be best expressed by relating an anecdote told of the German poet Rainer Maria Rilke, who, after spending an afternoon contemplating the beauty of the statue of Apollo in an Athenian museum, returned to his hotel and made the following single entry in his journal: "You must change your life."[42] This anecdote demonstrates a major theme in existentialist theory. Art can and should provoke us into action and creativity.

Conclusion

Even if we accept the Wittgensteinian view about art—that it is a "radically open concept" and that art is always a part of the social fabric of any culture—we can still appreciate Plato's perplexity about art. We can recognize its seductive and manipulative features. (I am *not* speaking of sliced cows here.) Because art, as Plato and Freud point out, is extrarational and grounded in fantasy, it pulls us away from reality and "the reality principle." There is good news and bad news here.

The bad news: the pull is toward phoniness, frivolity, danger, and even madness. All art is, as Arnold Hauser has said, a version of Quixotism.[43] (You will recall that Don Quixote abandoned real life for the life of romantic novels and went mad in the process. And of course the delicious irony here is that Don Quixote himself is merely a character in a novel [and what a novel!]. *We readers* are the Don Quixotes who escape our real world for his. Art always offers an alternative reality, hence the possibility of madness or sometimes a substitute for the madness that is the everyday world [the title of Freud's book: *The Psychopathology of Everyday Life*].)

The good news: but art also pulls toward philosophy (as Aristotle and the existentialists have it) and toward joy and the celebration of life (as Nietzsche has it)—the large beside the small pleases!

Plato and all of ancient Greek culture called art a form of mimesis (imitation). The very term connoted for Plato a kind of simulacrum—a replacement for reality by something not as rich as what it replaced. This Platonic concept is too narrow (what do a painting by Jackson Pollock, a musical composition by John Cage, or James Joyce's *Finnegan's Wake* imitate?) but not so far off after all. Art does not imitate the world, but it *represents* the world. However, what it represents is neither Plato's icy, timeless Forms (though it does *formalize* and arrest what it represents and in that sense rescues it from time), nor does it represent mere "things." It represents the world in all its actual and possible aspects. And in doing so, it reveals itself as being a kind of infinite regress, as art represents itself representing itself. (Most paintings are influenced more by other paintings than by the natural world, and most books [including this one] are about other books.) The nature of art, then, is not so different from the nature of the mind, whose nature also is to represent the world and to represent itself to itself. So if art offers the possibility of madness and degradation, it also offers the possibility of insight, joy, progress, sophistication, and redemption. Once again, in this respect, it is like the human mind itself.

Topics for Consideration

1. Pick any painting (including one of your own, if you are an artist) and analyze it from the points of view of (a) the formalist, (b) the expressionist, and (c) the philosopher of "aesthetic experience." Which perspective, if any, do you find most convincing?
2. Consider the argument between Hyman and Gombrich made explicit in the titles of their respective books, *Art and Illusion* and *The Objective Eye*.

What role, if any, do you think the phenomenon of illusion plays in the experience of visual art?

3. If the umpire in a baseball game declares a runner to be "out," the runner is out. Who or what declares an artifact to be art, according to the early version of the "institutional theory of art," and how is this declaration authenticated?

4. Discuss what appears to be a contradiction between Marx's expressed disdain for "ideology" and his expressed enthusiasm for art.

5. Test the competing theories of Plato and Aristotle concerning the moral status of art by applying their views to television or movies, "art forms" that play a similar role in today's world to that of the theater in ancient Athens.

6. Freud is ambivalent about art as a form of sublimation. In some ways it seems successful. (It provides a substitutive satisfaction for both the artist and the audience.) But in other ways it seems too much like a neurotic symptom or even like a psychotic denial of reality and an escape into a self-created world of delusion. Discuss this thesis.

7. Why do you think that many existential philosophers (e.g., Sartre, de Beauvoir, Nietzsche, Unamuno) have also been artists, novelists, poets, and playwrights and that some novelists (e.g., Dostoyevsky, Kafka) have also been considered existential philosophers?

8. Pick a contemporary work of art that has puzzled or outraged some citizens (Damien Hirst's *Mother and Child Divided* [1995], Marcel Duchamp's *Fountain* [1917], Jake and Dinos Chapman's *Migraine* [2013], Mapplethorpe's "obscene" photos?) and discuss them from the Wittgensteinian/Weitzian perspective.

9. Just how "radically open, radically indefinable" is art? What could *not* count as art?

Suggestions for Further Reading: Paperback Editions

Lars Aagaard-Mogensen, ed., *Culture and Art* (Atlantic Highlands, NJ: Humanities Press, 1976). A good selection of philosophical essays on art, many from theorists influenced by Wittgenstein.

Aristotle, *The Poetics* in *Aristotle: On Poetry and Style,* trans. G. M. A. Grube (New York: Liberal Arts Press, 1958). Aristotle's classical treatise on art in general and poetry and drama in particular.

Peter de Bolla, *Art Matters* (Cambridge, MA: Harvard University Press, 2003). A sensitive book exploring four works of art—painting, sculpture, music, and poetry—trying to clarify the aesthetic experience as a confrontation with wonder, from which a new kind of knowledge emerges.

Noël Carroll, *Philosophy of Art: A Contemporary Introduction* (London and New York: Routledge, 1999). Using analytical philosophy of art, Carroll presents a very readable course on art theory, with balanced critiques of the various positions.

George Dickie, *Introduction to Aesthetics: An Analytic Approach* (New York and Oxford, England: Oxford University Press, 1997). A brief, up-to-date summary of the history of art theory, including the author's own views; competes well with Carroll's book above.

Sigmund Freud, *Leonardo da Vinci and a Memory of His Childhood,* trans. Alan Tyson (New York: Norton, 1964). A glimpse not only into Leonardo's mind but also into Freud's.

E. H. Gombrich, *Art and Illusion: A Study in the Psychology of Pictorial Representation* (Princeton, NJ: Princeton University Press, 1972). Not only one of the best books about philosophy, psychology, and art but also one of my favorite books of all time.

Arnold Hauser, *The Philosophy of Art History* (Cleveland, OH: Meridian Books, 1963). An excellent work touching on numerous topics discussed in this chapter.

John Hyman, *The Objective Eye: Color, Form, and Reality in the Theory of Art* (Chicago, IL and London: University of Chicago Press, 2006). Hyman is a razor-sharp philosopher of art, very sure of his defense of objectivism, usually with good reason.

Herbert Marcuse, *Eros and Civilization: A Philosophical Inquiry into Freud* (New York: Vintage Books, 1955). Marcuse's synthesis of Freud and Marx and his statement concerning the revolutionary status of art. Difficult and controversial but worthwhile.

Iris Murdoch, *The Fire and the Sun: Why Plato Banished the Artists* (New York: Oxford University Press, 1978). A short, excellent book written by a woman who was both a top-notch philosopher and a first-rate novelist.

Friedrich Nietzsche,*The Birth of Tragedy,* trans. Francis Golffing (Garden City, NY: Doubleday Anchor, 1990). A fantastic (in both senses of the word) account of the origins of art in ancient Greece.

Plato, "Republic," in *Great Dialogues of Plato,* eds. Eric H. Warmington and Philip G. Rouse, trans. W. H. D. Rouse (New York: New American Library, 1956). There are remarks about the relation between art and philosophy throughout the *Republic,* but Book Ten is dedicated to its discussion.

Adolfo Sánchez Vázquez, *Art and Society: Essays on Marxist Aesthetics,* trans. Maro Riofrancos (New York: Monthly Review Press, 1973). A fine collection of essays by a Mexican Marxist philosopher.

Notes

1. For example, George Dickie, *Introduction to Aesthetics: An Analytic Approach* (New York and Oxford, England: Oxford University Press, 1997); Noël Carroll, *Philosophy of Art: A Contemporary Introduction* (London and New York: Routledge, 1999). (Carroll writes, "In fact, the title of this book could be accurately expanded as *The Analytic Philosophy of Art,*" p. 2); John Hyman, *The Objective*

Eye: Color, Form, and Reality in the Theory of Art (Chicago, IL and London: University of Chicago Press, 2006). (Hyman writes, "This book is . . . a work of analytical philosophy, from beginning to end," p. xvi). Page numbers of future quotations from the books by Dickie, Carroll, and Hyman will be included in the text.

2. For example, George Dickie, p. 53.

3. A fine example of the attempt to explain the aesthetic experience as a form of wonder is found throughout Peter de Bolla's *Art Matters* (Cambridge, MA: Harvard University Press, 2003). De Bolla also treats the aesthetic experience as epistemic, that is, as producing a kind of knowledge.

4. E. H. Gombrich, *Art and Illusion: A Study in the Psychology of Pictorial Representation* (Princeton, NJ: Princeton University Press, 1972), p. 243. Page numbers of future quotations from this book will be included in the text.

5. Emphasis added.

6. Ludwig Wittgenstein, *Philosophical Investigations*, trans. G. E. M. Anscombe (New York: Macmillan, 1964), pp. 31–32. Page numbers of future quotations from this book will be included in the text.

7. Morris Weitz, "The Role of Theory in Aesthetics," in *Philosophy Looks at the Arts: Contemporary Readings in Aesthetics*, ed. Joseph Margolis (New York: Charles Scribner's Sons, 1962), p. 54.

8. Maurice Mandelbaum, "Family Resemblance and Generalization Concerning the Arts," *American Philosophical Quarterly* (1965), Vol. 2, pp. 219–228, 221.

9. Carroll, p. 222, 223, 225, 251.

10. I have borrowed the basics of this analysis from Renford Bambrough, "Universals and Family Resemblances," *Proceedings of the Aristotelian Society*, Vol. LXI (1960–1961), pp. 207–222. Reprinted in *Wittgenstein: The Philosophical Investigations—A Collection of Critical Essays*, ed. George Pitcher (Garden City, NY: Doubleday, 1966), pp. 186–204, 189.

11. Arthur Danto, "The Artworld," in *Culture and Art*, ed. Lars Aagaard-Mogensen (Atlantic Highlands, NJ: Humanities Press, 1976), p. 16.

12. George Dickie, "The Institutional Conception of Art," in *Language and Aesthetics*, ed. Benjamin R. Tilghman (Wichita, KS: University Press of Kansas, 1973), p. 23.

13. Ibid., p. 30.

14. More recently, Dickie has revised his institutional theory in the light of such criticism. He writes, "I have abandoned as too formal the notions of *status conferral* and *acting on behalf of* as well as those aspects of the earlier version that connected up with these notions. Being a work of art is a status all right, that is, it is the occupying of a position within the human activity of the artworld. Being a work of art does not, however, involve a status that is conferred but is rather a status that is achieved as the result of creating an artifact within or against the backdrop of the artworld" (p. 88). This move defuses the criticism but leaves us with a rather fuzzy answer to the main question—What justifies our decision to call a particular artifact a work of art?

15. Benjamin R. Tilghman, "Artistic Puzzlement," in Aagaard-Mogensen, *Culture and Art*, p. 80.

16. Ludwig Wittgenstein, *Lectures & Conversations on Aesthetics, Psychology and Religious Belief*, ed. Cyril Barrett (Berkeley and Los Angeles: University of California Press, 1972), p. 8.

17. Not long ago, a scientist named Alan Sokal managed to get an article published in the prestigious journal *Social Text*. The article was called "Transgressing the Boundaries: Towards a Transformative Hermeneutics of Quantum Gravity." The whole thing proved to be a joke on Sokal's part, full of intentional nonsense, mocking a certain **postmodern** school of social criticism. At least, when Sokal admitted his fraud, the editors of the journal were embarrassed. What would embarrass "the artworld" today? (The answer to this question is *not* "Donald Palmer's illustrations.")

18. Timothy Binkley, "Deciding about Art," in Aagaard-Mogensen, *Culture and Art,* p. 109.

19. George Dickie, whom we have already met in this chapter, is often thought to have given it a *coup de grace* to the idea of an aesthetic experience in his article, "The Myth of the Aesthetic Attitude" (*American Philosophical Quarterly* [1964], Vol. 1, pp. 56–66). Starr references this article in her bibliography, but, as far as I can determine, does not address it other than to say, "the beautiful as a category of experience or objects has been dismissed from and restored to the Western canon repeatedly" (p. xii).

20. G. Gabrielle Starr, *Feeling Beauty: The Neuroscience of Aesthetic Experience* (Cambridge, MA: The MIT Press, 2015), p. xi. Future references to this work will be included parenthetically in the body of the text.

21. We are informed that this network includes the posterior cingulate cortex and the anterior medial prefrontal cortex, among other brain sections (p. 61).

22. Plato, "Republic," in *Great Dialogues of Plato,* ed. Eric H. Warmington and Philip G. Rouse, trans. W. H. D. Rouse (New York: New American Library, 1956), pp. 369–370.

23. Arnold Hauser, *The Philosophy of Art History* (Cleveland, OH: Meridian Books, 1963), p. 56.

24. Aristotle, "Politics," in *Aristotle: On Poetry and Style,* trans. G. M. A. Grube (New York: Liberal Arts Press, 1958), pp. xv–xvi.

25. Ibid.

26. Quoted in Erich Fromm, ed., T. B. Bottomore, trans., *Marx's Concept of Man* (New York: Friedrich Unger, 1969), p. 38.

27. Karl Marx, "Alienated Labor," in Fromm, *Marx's Concept of Man,* p. 102.

28. Robert Tucker, *Philosophy and Myth in Karl Marx* (New York: Cambridge University Press, 1965), pp. 157–158.

29. Karl Marx, "Preface to a Contribution to the Critique of Political Economy," in Fromm, *Marx's Concept of Man,* pp. 217–218.

30. Karl Marx, "The German Ideology," in Fromm, *Marx's Concept of Man,* p. 212.

31. Karl Marx, "Theories of Surplus Value," quoted in Adolfo Sánchez Vázquez, *Art and Society: Essays in Marxist Aesthetics,* trans. Maro Riofrancos (New York: Monthly Review Press, 1973), p. 155.

32. Karl Marx and Friedrich Engels, "Manifesto of the Communist Party," in *Marx and Engels: Basic Writings on Politics and Philosophy,* ed. Lewis S. Feuer (Garden City, NY: Doubleday, 1959), p. 10.

33. Karl Marx, "Theories of Surplus Value," quoted in Sánchez Vázquez, *Art and Society,* pp. 200–201.

34. Karl Marx, "The German Ideology," quoted in Sánchez Vázquez, *Art and Society,* p. 282, 285, 286.

35. Friedrich Engels, "Letters on Historical Materialism," in Lewis S. Feuer, *Writings on Politics and Philosophy*, p. 396.

36. Jean-Paul Sartre, *Existentialism and Human Emotions* (New York: Philosophical Library, 1957), p. 15. Page numbers of future quotations from this book will be included in the text.

37. Arturo B. Fallico, *Art and Existentialism* (Englewood Cliffs, NJ: Prentice-Hall, 1962), p. 52.

38. Friedrich Nietzsche, *The Birth of Tragedy*, trans. Francis Golffing (Garden City, NY: Doubleday Anchor, 1956), p. 29.

39. Fallico, *Art and Existentialism*, pp. 74–75, 65.

40. Ibid., p. 66, 81.

41. Maurice Natanson, *The Journeying Self: A Study in Philosophy and Social Role* (Reading, Mass.: Addison-Wesley, 1970), p. 122.

42. Quoted in Arthur Danto, *Mysticism and Morality: Oriental Thought and Moral Philosophy* (New York: Harper & Row, 1972), p. 77.

43. Hauser, *The Philosophy of Art History*, p. 55.

Glossary

(Boldface type indicates terms that are cross-referenced within the glossary.)

a posteriori A belief, **proposition,** or argument is said to be a posteriori if its truth or falsity can be established only through observation. Classical **empiricism** was an attempt to show that all significant knowledge about the world is based on a posteriori truths.

a priori A belief, **proposition,** or argument is said to be a priori if its truth or falsity can be established independently of observation. Definitions, the propositions of arithmetic, and the principles of logic are usually held to be a priori. Classical **rationalism** was an attempt to show that all significant knowledge about the world is based on a priori truths, which most of the rationalists associated with **innate ideas.**

aesthetics Sometimes used interchangeably with the term **philosophy of art** (as is done in this book) and sometimes as a broader concept that comprises discussion both of art and of those natural phenomena that provoke appreciation of their beauty or grandeur. This field studies artistic concepts, such as art itself, representation, realism, and abstraction, and the nature of argument and judgment about goodness or badness in art.

agnosticism A view that holds open the possibility that God exists but that claims we do not know, or cannot know, whether in fact a deity exists.

aleatoric art Art in which unpredictability or chance is intentionally in its production.

analytic geometry The branch of mathematics created by René Descartes in which algebraic procedures are applied to geometry.

analytic philosophy The view that, in philosophy, logical analysis and analysis of meaning must be prior to the construction of philosophical theories about the world. Analytical philosophers believe that certain key concepts in ordinary language and in scientific, moral, religious, and **aesthetic** discourse are philosophically vague or misleading. Philosophical problems can be solved and pseudophilosophical problems can be dispelled through the clarification of these concepts. The theories that analytical philosophers do generate tend to be demonstrations of the logical relations among these different realms of discourse rather than grandiose **metaphysical** schemes. Although many of the pioneers of this school were continental Europeans, the movement has become primarily an Anglo-American one.

analytic proposition A **proposition** is analytic if its negation leads to a self-contradiction. For example, "squares have four sides" is analytic because its negation, "squares do not have four sides," is a self-contradiction. See also **tautology, conceptual truth,** and **a priori.**

anarchism The political doctrine according to which the state is both unnatural and unjustifiable, because it necessarily violates the rights or well-being of individuals.

animism The belief that some or all natural objects possess souls, spirits, or minds that can have benevolent or malevolent effects on human beings. In some versions, this belief is a form of religion.

anomie A sociological term, associated primarily with the French sociologist, Émile Durkheim (1858–1917), designating a condition in individuals or societies characterized by a loss of direction, meaning, values, and norms.

apocrypha Works, sayings, or acts misattributed to an important individual or an authoritative tradition when in fact they are inauthentic or fraudulent.

aretê A term in ancient Greek philosophy translated usually as "virtue," though sometimes as "excellence" or "quality."

atheism The view that there is no God.

atomism As an **ontological** theory, the view that the ultimate building blocks of reality are basic, irreducible particles of matter—atoms. (This view is a version of **materialism.**) As an **epistemological** theory, the view that the ultimate building blocks of knowledge are basic, irreducible, perceptual units—**sense data.** (This view, called "psychological atomism," is a version of **empiricism.**)

axiology The general term for the theory of values. It incorporates **aesthetics** and **ethics.**

bad faith A technical term in the philosophy of Jean-Paul Sartre naming a state of human inauthenticity, a flight from responsibility, **freedom,** and anguish. A kind of willful self-deception in which one tries to convince oneself that one is not the sole source of one's being and actions.

behaviorism The theory that only observable, objective features of human or animal activity need to be studied to provide an adequate scientific account of that activity. See also **hard behaviorism, soft behaviorism,** and **logical behaviorism.**

categorical imperative The name given by Immanuel Kant to a purported universal moral law: in one form, "So act that the maxim of your action could be willed as a universal law"; in another form, "So act as to treat humanity . . . always as an end, and never as merely a means."

category-mistake A key philosophical error noted by the British **ordinary language philosopher** Gilbert Ryle wherein a term that belongs to one logical category is mistakenly categorized as belonging to another. Then faulty questions are asked based on the miscategorization. An example would be (according to Ryle) Descartes's assuming that the mind is a *thing* in the same way that the body is a *thing* and then asking how these two "things" interact.

causal explanation A mechanical kind of explanation in which the object or event to be accounted for is rendered intelligible by demonstrating how that object or event follows necessarily from antecedent objects or events. Causal explanations are usually represented in terms of natural laws. Contrast with **teleology.**

cogito Latin for "I think." Descartes's foundation of knowledge, "I think, therefore I am" (*cogito ergo sum*). As a noun, the Cogito names the act of consciousness.

cognitive science An interdisciplinary study involving philosophy, psychology, linguistics, and computer science, stressing the computational model of the mind. See also **functionalism.**

coherence theory of truth The theory that a **proposition** is true if it coheres with the body of all the other propositions taken to be true; that is, if it follows logically from those propositions, or supports them and is supported by them, or at least does not contradict any of them. This theory, which contrasts with both the **correspondence theory of truth** and the **pragmatic theory of truth,** has been especially appealing to **rationalists.**

communism The political theory that advocates the abolition of private property and asserts that goods must be held in common and that the ideal social unit is the commune. See also **Marxism.**

compatibilism The view that **determinism** does not exclude **freedom** or responsibility; rather, all three can coexist simultaneously in the same system. Sometimes called **soft determinism.**

conceptual art A development in art during the last forty years of the twentieth century in which it is claimed that the technique, methods, and materials of production rather than the final artistic product are themselves the real work of art. Also, in some cases, the designation of concepts themselves rather than objects as works of art.

conceptual truth A **proposition** expresses a conceptual truth if that truth is based on a merely logical relationship rather than on an empirical fact. For example, "widows are female" is a conceptual truth. See also **analytic proposition, tautology,** and **a priori.**

conceptualism The epistemological view that concepts are generalized ideas existing only in the mind but that they are derived and abstracted by the mind from real similarities and distinctions in nature.

contingent (or **contingency**) A relation between two objects or ideas is contingent if one of the terms of the relationship could exist without the other. For example, Descartes says that the relation between the soul and the body is contingent, because the soul can exist without the body, and bodies can exist without souls.

contractualism The ethical theory according to which morally right behavior and obligation should be determined by a hypothetical contract in which parties agree to accept certain standards as reasonable.

conventionalism The claim that a certain body of facts has been established by human convention and not by nature, by social agreement and not by the way the world was prior to human intervention. For example, some people believe that gender roles are imposed by nature; others believe they are imposed by convention.

correspondence theory of truth The theory that a **proposition** is true if it corresponds with the facts. "Caesar crossed the Rubicon" is true if and only if there was in fact a man called Caesar, and he did in fact cross the Rubicon river; otherwise, the proposition is false. This theory, which contrasts with both the **coherence theory of truth** and the **pragmatic theory of truth,** has been especially appealing to **empiricists.**

cosmological argument An attempt to establish God's existence by deducing it from some observable facts in the world. For example, Thomas Aquinas's claim that from the observation of causal chains in the world we can deduce the necessity of a "first cause" or God.

creationism The view that Darwin's theory of **natural selection** is false and that the intricate complexity of the world indicates that the world was created by a higher power.

dada (or **dadaism**) From the French word for "hobbyhorse," a Continental art movement conceived as a protest against the mechanized slaughter of World War I. It manifested a **nihilistic** irrationality calculated to inform the public that all established moral and aesthetic values were meaningless after the horrors of the war.

deconstruction The intellectual creation of the late French philosopher Jacques Derrida; based on his eccentric but provocative reading of the linguistic theory of Ferdinand de Saussure, deconstruction is a theory of *texts* (philosophical, fictional, legal, scientific) according to which, because of the very nature of thought and language, almost all traditional texts can be shown to "deconstruct" themselves, to undermine and refute their own theses. Or, deconstruction is the activity of demonstrating that a particular text undermines and refutes itself.

deep ecology A development within the ecology movement decrying as "shallow" those currents within the movement that justify conservation as being in the interest of human beings. Deep ecologists (like Arne Naess, George Sessions, and Gary Snyder) find an intrinsic value in all living systems and condemn the human arrogance of anthropocentrism. They are committed to "ecocentric" political action such as the control of world population and abandonment of the goal of "increased standards of living" in areas where such an increase has already devastated nature.

definiens *X* is a definiens of *Y* if *X* defines *Y*. In such a case, *Y* is the "definiendum" of *X*.

determinism The view that every event occurs necessarily. Every event follows inevitably from the events that preceded it. There is no randomness in reality; rather, all is law governed. **Freedom** either does not exist (**hard determinism**) or exists in such a way as to be compatible with **necessity** (**soft determinism**).

distributive justice The form of justice that is achieved in a society when the opportunities and material goods of the society are fairly distributed in ways that recognize both the contributions and the needs of all members of the society.

dualism The **ontological** view that reality is composed of two kinds of beings, usually (as in Descartes) minds and bodies.

efficient cause A term from Aristotelian philosophy designating one of the four kinds of causes in the world—the physical force operating on the object undergoing change (e.g., the sculptor's chiseling of a piece of granite). (The other three Aristotelian causes are "the material cause" [the piece of granite], "the formal cause" [the idea of the statue in the mind of the sculptor], and "the final cause" [the ultimate purpose of the statue].)

ego In **psychoanalysis,** the name of the rational, most conscious, social aspect of the psyche, as contrasted with the **id** and **superego.**

egoism A theory of motivation according to which the motive behind all acts either *is* self-interest (**psychological egoism**) or *ought to be* self-interest (**moral egoism**). See also **hedonism.**

eliminative materialism A materialistic theory of mind according to which sentences that seem to refer to nonmaterial conscious states (such as "I have a headache") can be eliminated in favor of more accurate sentences referring to material states (such as "My C-fibers are firing").

eliminativism See **eliminative materialism.**

empiricism The epistemological view that true knowledge is derived primarily from sense experience (or, in "purer" strains of empiricism, *exclusively* from sense experience). For these philosophers, all significant knowledge is **a posteriori**, and **a priori** knowledge is either nonexistent or **tautological.** The "classical" empiricists were the seventeenth- and eighteenth-century Britons (Locke, Berkeley, and Hume), all of whom denied the existence of **innate ideas** and conceived of the human mind as a "blank slate" at birth.

Enlightenment, the A philosophical movement of the eighteenth century characterized by the belief in the power of reason to sweep away superstition, ignorance, and injustice.

entitlement This term has been used by philosophers in recent years to designate the good reasons by virtue of which a person can justify his or her beliefs and is therefore entitled to claim them as knowledge.

epistemology Theory of knowledge. The branch of philosophy that answers questions such as these: What is knowledge? What, if anything, can we know? What is the difference between opinion and knowledge?

eros The Greek word for sexual love; the name of the Greek god of love, which in **psychoanalytic** theory becomes the name of a purported "life instinct" and is opposed to Thanatos, the "death instinct."

ethics Moral philosophy. The branch of philosophy that answers questions such as these: Is there such a thing as the Good? What is "the good life"? Is there such a thing as absolute duty? Are valid moral arguments possible? Are moral judgments based only on preference?

ethnocentrism The biased belief that one's own ethnic, social, or cultural group holds values that are superior to those of other groups, leading to an attitude that blinds the believer to the values of other cultures or social systems.

eugenics The advocacy of controlled breeding in order to improve the human race.

ex nihilo From the Greek, "out of nothing." Used as an adverb designating the appearance of something that seems to have no material source. For example, "God created the world *ex nihilo.*"

existentialism A twentieth-century philosophy associated principally with Jean-Paul Sartre but also thought to have been anticipated by Søren Kierkegaard and Friedrich Nietzsche and to encompass the work of Karl Jaspers, Simone de Beauvoir, Martin Heidegger, Gabriel Marcel, Albert Camus, and Miguel de Unamuno, among others. More of a shared attitude than a school of thought, it can nevertheless be roughly defined by saying with Sartre that existentialists are those who believe that, in the case of humans, "existence precedes essence." This is the thesis that there is no human nature that precedes our presence in the world, and determines our actions. All humans individually create humanity at every moment through their free acts.

experience As a technical term in empiricistic **epistemology,** the term designating the data provided directly by the five senses. See also **sense data.**

experimental A theory or **proposition** is experimental if observable evidence is pertinent to its confirmation or falsification. See also **a posteriori, synthetic proposition,** and **principle of falsifiability.**

expressionism A theory of art according to which the function of art is to find release, to express and articulate a kind of emotional knowledge that is somehow deeper than knowledge of merely empirical or scientific facts.

false consciousness A term coined by Marx's colleague Friedrich Engels, designating the mentality formed by **ideology,** with the result that individuals in such a state of consciousness are motivated to think and act (and perhaps vote) in ways that are not in their best interest but rather are in the interest of their oppressors.

feminism The sociopolitical theory and practice defending women's dignity and rights against male chauvinism and male-dominated power structures that have denied legal and social equality to women and have demeaned, marginalized, and constricted women throughout history.

formalism A theory of art that distinguishes between form and content in art and claims that the **aesthetic** fact is found exclusively in formal features of art rather than, for example, in autobiographical, emotional, **epistemological,** historical, religious, or political features.

forms Usually associated with the philosophies of Plato or Aristotle. For Plato (in whose philosophy the word "Form" is capitalized in this text), everything that exists in the physical or conceptual world is in some way dependent upon Forms, which exist independently of the world but are the models (essences, universals, archetypes) of all reality. Forms are eternal, unchangeable, and the ultimate object of all true philosophizing. For Aristotle too, forms are the essences of things, but they exist *in* things and are not independent of them. For Aristotle, the form of an object and its function are ultimately related.

Frankfurt-type examples Imaginary cases named after the American philosopher who first conceived them, Harry Frankfurt. They are designed to refute the claim that freedom and responsibility presuppose genuine alternatives ("could have done otherwise") by hypothesizing cases in which freedom and responsibility for an act would normally be attributed to an agent who performed that act even though there were no genuine alternatives to the act. For example, not knowing that the door on the right is locked, the agent chooses to open the door on the left. Frankfurt would say that the agent in this case is free and responsible, even though unbeknownst to him or her the agent had no real alternative.

free will The ability to make choices that are uncoerced, undetermined, or uncaused; or, if caused, they are caused exclusively by the agent him- or herself.

freedom Freedom exists if there are such things as free acts and free agents, that is, if some acts are performed in such a way that the authors of those acts could legitimately be held responsible for them. Some philosophers (called **libertarians**) say that these acts *do* exist, that some acts are freely chosen from among genuine alternatives, and that therefore **determinism** is false. ("I did X, but under exactly the same circumstances, I could have done Y instead. Therefore X was a free act.") Other philosophers (called **soft determinists**) also say that free acts exist but define "free acts" not in terms of genuine alternative choices but in terms of voluntary acts. ("I wanted to do X, and

I did do X; therefore X was a free act.") Still other philosophers (called **hard determinists**), while agreeing with the definition of "free act" given by libertarians, deny that any such free acts or agents exist.

functionalism A currently popular theory in the **philosophy of mind** according to which minds are not "things"; rather, they are systems capable of interacting with their environment through computational activity. Any computational system capable of manipulating symbols to solve problems can be said to have mental states, according to functionalism, whether those systems be brains, computers, or extraterrestrials. In the case of humans, those mental states (desires, hopes, expectations, etc.) are real (i.e., are causally effective). They are realized in the brain but are not themselves brain states. The computations of computers are not themselves physical states but are realized in physical components of the computer hardware. Functionalists consider themselves to be **materialists,** but they oppose the **mind–brain identity theory** and **eliminative materialism.**

gestalt psychology The theory according to which perception does not occur as the summation of a number of perceptual parts; rather, these perceptual parts themselves are derived from the general perceptual field, which has properties that cannot be derived from any or all of the parts because they are the features of the field that contextualize the scene and allow certain recognizable features to be interpreted as "parts" of the field.

hard behaviorism The view that there are no minds and that therefore psychology can study only "behaviors"—an **ontological** view as opposed to the merely methodological view of **soft behaviorism.**

hard determinism The view that **determinism** is true and that therefore **freedom** and responsibility do not exist. Contrast with **soft determinism.**

hedonism A theory of motivation according to which the motive behind all acts either *is* pleasure (psychological hedonism) or *ought to be* pleasure (moral hedonism). See also **egoism.**

hypothetical imperative The name given by Immanuel Kant to the nonmoral use of the word "ought." This use of "ought" can always be stated in a hypothetical form (e.g., "You *ought* to be nice to people *if* you want them to like you").

id In **psychoanalysis,** the name given to one of the three aspects of the psyche. It is the mostly unconscious, antisocial, irrational but cunning "animal" self, containing the primitive sexual and aggressive drives, as contrasted with the **ego** (the rational, mostly conscious social self) and the **superego** (the irrational, authoritarian, mostly unconscious familial and social conscience).

idealism The **ontological** view that, ultimately, every existing thing can be shown to be spiritual or mental (hence, a version of **monism**), usually associated in Western philosophy with Berkeley and Hegel.

identity theory See **mind–brain identity theory.**

ideology As used in Marxism, a system of beliefs consciously held but unconsciously motivated by the interests of the ruling classes, justifying the domination of those classes over members of the oppressed classes, contaminating politics, religion, art, law, philosophy, and all other cultural products. See also **false consciousness**.

indefeasibility A **proposition** is indefeasible if no future event can prove it wrong. If future events might prove it wrong, then the proposition is defeasible.

indeterminism The view that there are such things as uncaused events and that therefore **determinism** is false.

infinite regress If proposition p is meant as an explanation of proposition or event x, but p is equally in need of an explanation p^1, which is equally in need of an explanation p^2, which is equally in need of an explanation p^3, and so on forever with no end; then, rather than explaining x, p has initiated an infinite regress; therefore, p is *not* an explanation of x.

innate idea An idea present at birth, hence, **a priori.**

intentionality As used in the **philosophy of mind,** the referential feature of mental phenomena—their "aboutness." Mental states refer to objects beyond themselves. One thinks *about* something, looks *at* something, alludes *to* something, is afraid *of* something. The term covers intentions in the nontechnical sense ("She intended to drop her philosophy class") and also desires, hopes, expectations, and fears. A major question in **materialist** theories in the **philosophy of mind** is this: How is it possible for certain material objects (brains or parts of brains) to have intentionality in this sense?

legal positivism The view that justice and legal legitimacy are defined exclusively by the established political powers.

liberalism The political view that advocates a democratic government and asserts that the state has a legitimate right and an obligation to set standards of living below which none of its citizens may be forced to live and to enforce laws providing equal opportunity and **distributive justice.**

libertarianism In this text, the view that **freedom** exists. Not closely related to the meaning of the word when it names the political party or mindset with the same name.

logic The branch of philosophy that studies the structure of valid inference; a purely *formal* discipline, interested in the structure and rules of argumentation rather than in its content.

logical behaviorism The **epistemological** and **ontological** view that all meaningful mentalistic terms can ultimately be traced back to some observable behavior and not back to some purely mental facts. For example, the term "intelligent" is ultimately related to certain observable capacities, not to a mental state called "intelligence."

logical construct A term from twentieth-century **empiricism** naming an entity that can be inferred from **sense data.** For example, the belief that a table exists independently of our perceptions is based on an inference drawn from our perceptions. In this view, only sense data can be known directly. Logical constructs can be known only by inference.

logical empiricism See **logical positivism.**

logical entailment A relation of logical **necessity** between two concepts or **propositions.** If concept or proposition X necessarily implies concept or proposition Y, then X logically entails Y. The assertion of X with the simultaneous denial of Y would constitute a self-contradiction; for example, the concept "brother" logically entails both the concept "sibling" and the concept "male."

logical positivism (or **logical empiricism**) A school of philosophy that flourished between the two world wars according to which the only cognitively meaningful utterances are those of science. All other utterances can be shown, under analysis, to be merely expressions of emotions or to be nonsense.

logical possibility Something is logically possible if its *idea* contains no self-contradiction (such as the idea of a one-million-sided figure). Conversely, something is logically impossible if its idea does contain a self-contradiction (such as the idea of a four-sided circle).

Logos (1) A Greek term meaning "word" or "study," from which is derived the English term "logic" and the "-logies" of "biology," "sociology," etc. (2) In Plato, a term designating the rational justification of beliefs. (3) As opposed to **Mythos,** Logos designates a scientific or philosophical account of the world.

Marxism A political or philosophical doctrine based on the writings of Karl Marx: politically a form of **communism,** philosophically a form of **materialism** known as **dialectical** materialism.

materialism The **ontological** view that all reality can be shown to be material in nature (e.g., that "minds" are really brains).

meme Molecular biologist Richard Dawkins coined this word in 1976 to designate ideas, images, or signs that become socially functional in the way that genes become bodily functional. Memes can become building blocks of cultures in the way that genes become building blocks of bodies. Memes are passed from generation to generation by communicative means rather than by sexual means, as in the case of genes. For example, "freedom" becomes an important meme in some cultures but not all.

Meno's paradox An **epistemological** paradox set forth by Meno in the Platonic dialogue of the same name: How is it possible to seek knowledge? If one does not know what one is looking for, one will not recognize it if one finds it. If one *does* recognize it, then one already knew it and did not need to seek it. Therefore, the pursuit of knowledge is either impossible or useless.

metaphysics The branch of philosophy that attempts to construct a general, speculative worldview: a complete, systematic account of all reality and experience, usually involving an **epistemology,** an **ontology,** an **ethics,** and an **aesthetics.** (The adjective "metaphysical" is often employed to stress the speculative, as opposed to the scientific or commonsensical, features of the theory or **proposition** it describes.)

methodological doubt (or **radical doubt**) The name of the philosophical method employed by Descartes to discover the absolutely certain foundations of all knowledge. Every belief that *can* be doubted *should* be doubted until one arrives at a belief that itself is indubitable.

mimesis Literally, "imitation" or "copy," but in **aesthetics,** the doctrine that art in its main function is imitative—of reality, ideality, or possibility.

mind–brain identity theory The **ontological** view that minds and brains are not two different kinds of things; rather, all references to minds and mental states are really references to brains and brain states.

minimal state The social ideal of certain theorists, such as Robert Nozick, according to which the only rights and obligations a government has are those of protecting the persons and property of its citizens, punishing offenses against those citizens, and taxing its citizens to finance these activities. The state has no other legitimate obligations or rights.

mode A property of an essential property. For example, for Descartes, "thought" is an essential property of "mind" and "understanding" is a property, or mode, of thought.

monism The **ontological** view that only one entity exists (e.g., as in Spinoza) or that only one *kind* of entity exists (e.g., as in Hobbes and Berkeley).

moral egoism See **egoism.**

moral realism The ethical view that there are moral facts that can be the basis of moral judgments. Therefore, moral judgments need not be merely subjective, or merely expressions of preference, or merely projections from the human mind.

mysticism The belief that a special mental or emotional experience can transcend ordinary rational procedures and provide a direct intuition of the presence of God or an extrarational insight into ultimate truth.

Mythos The whole body of myths, legends, and folktales that attempts to make sense of the world by placing it in a narrative context tracing things back to their supernatural origins. Sometimes contrasted with **Logos.**

naive realism The prephilosophical **epistemology** and **ontology** attributed to the person-in-the-street according to which the perceptual data in the mind accurately represent the external world as it actually is.

naturalism The **ontological** view that only natural objects, properties, and events are real; no supernatural objects, properties, or events exist. See also **atheism.**

natural selection The primary mechanism of Darwin's theory of evolution. Forms of life having natural characteristics that are better adapted to the environment into which those life forms were born will tend to survive longer and replicate those characteristics in future generations. The process is sometimes called "survival of the fittest."

necessary condition X is a necessary condition of Y if Y cannot exist in the absence of X. For example, oxygen is a necessary condition of fire. See also **sufficient condition.**

necessity In philosophical discussions of necessity, there are two key concepts that often appear: logical necessity and physical necessity. According to the first category, there is a relation of *logical necessity* (or **logical entailment**) between two propositions if the assertion of one of them, together with the denial of the other, results in a contradiction. For example, there is a relation of logical necessity between the propositions "Linda is my sister" and "Linda has at least one sibling" because the assertion of the one and the denial of the other results in a contradiction. According to the second category, there is a relation of *physical necessity* between two events X and Y if the occurrence of event X must be followed by the event Y. **Determinism** claims that every event is necessary, that is, every event follows necessarily from the events preceding it. Indeterminism claims that not all events are necessary.

nihilism As an **ontological** view, the theory that nothing exists; as a moral view, the theory that there are no values or that nothing deserves to exist.

occlusion shape An objective geometric shape of a physical figure that is relative to the line of vision between eye and object, producing such natural visual phenomena as the foreshortening of a prone body when seen feet first or the elliptical appearance of a coin when seen from certain angles. Originally suggested in *Optics,* by Euclid (300 B.C.E.), used today by J. Hyman to defend the idea of objectivism in art against subjectivists who call the phenomenon a form of illusion.

Ockham's razor (or **Occam's razor**) A principle of simplification derived from the medieval philosopher William of Ockham, according to which if there are two competing theories, both of which account for all the observable data, the simpler of the two is the preferable theory. "Do not multiply entities beyond necessity."

ontological argument An **a priori** attempt to prove God's existence by showing that, from the very concept of God, his existence can be deduced. This argument has been defended by a number of religious philosophers in the Platonic tradition. It was first formulated by St. Anselm and appears in one form or another in the work of Descartes, Spinoza, Leibniz, and Hegel. It had some able twentieth-century defenders (e.g., Charles Hartshorne and Norman Malcolm). But it has been rejected by some notables, too, including St. Thomas, Hume, Kant, and Kierkegaard.

ontology Theory of being. The branch of philosophy pursuing such questions as these: What is real? What is the difference between appearance and reality? What is the relation between minds and bodies? Are numbers and concepts real, or are only physical objects real? To ask about something's ontological conditions is to ask its status in reality.

operant conditioning A therapeutical practice used by **behavioral** psychologists to transform the behavior of a patient (replacing unwanted habits with new habits that are more socially acceptable) by structuring a format of repetition of the desired behavior encouraged by a program of positive reinforcement to the patient for each exhibition of the new behavior (in *positive* operant conditioning), or a program of punishment of the patient for each exhibition of the old, unwanted behavior (in *negative* operant conditioning).

ordinary language philosophy A strong movement in Anglo-American **analytic philosophy,** especially in the 1960s and 1970s, that saw philosophy's main task as the conceptual and logical analysis of ordinary language as it related to philosophical problems. This school rejected the attack on ordinary language that was engineered by earlier analytic philosophers such as Bertrand Russell and the logical positivists. Rather, ordinary language philosophers held that many philosophical errors were the result of disdain for ordinary language and a confusion about the nature of meaning. The confusion would be eliminated not through the construction of artificial mathematical languages but only by careful attention to the nuances of ordinary language. Major participants in this school included John Austin, Gilbert Ryle, and Ludwig Wittgenstein.

organicism The **ontological** view that reality is more like an organism than like a machine—that the whole is more real than any of the parts and that the parts are dependent on the whole for their reality.

pantheism The view that everything is divine, that God's "creation" is in fact identical with God: from the Greek *pan* (all) and *theos* (god).

paradigm shift A moment in intellectual history when the key conceptual apparatus of an age gives way to new ones, as when the essentially theological view of reality in the medieval world gave way to a more secular one involving new standards of judgment and criteria of evidence.

phenomenology A philosophical school created by Edmund Husserl, employing a method of analysis that purports to arrive at the pure data of consciousness and thereby provide the foundation for **epistemology** and **ontology.** The method involves "bracketing" certain features of experience, stripping them of all assumptions and presuppositions, and laying bare the essence of conscious experience.

philosophy of art The branch of philosophy that studies the **aesthetic** features of art and the judgments about those features.

philosophy of mind That branch of philosophy that deals with such **ontological** problems as the relation between minds and brains, minds and computers, and minds and behaviors.

pluralism The **ontological** view that reality is composed of a multiplicity of things or different kinds of things and that this multiplicity cannot be reduced to one or two categories.

political philosophy The branch of philosophy that explores questions concerning the justification of political entities and political relationships.

postmodernism A loosely applied term (1) designating an intellectual posture skeptical of **epistemologies, ontologies,** and institutions (governmental, academic, military, medical, religious) of the modern Western tradition; (2) challenging the basic tenets of liberalism, humanism, individualism, and capitalism; (3) designating a fascination with popular culture and the domination of technology over human endeavors; (4) dwelling on the contemporary **semiotic** strategies that privilege signs and images over substance and truth, reproduction over production, and representation over reality.

pragmatic theory of truth This theory asserts that to talk about the truth of a proposition is to talk about its power to "work," that is, its ability to put the individual who considers the proposition into a more satisfactory and effective relationship with the rest of the world. This theory employs the **correspondence theory of truth** and the **coherence theory of truth** not as criteria of truth but as two of several tests of efficacy. According to the pragmatic theory, the truth is relative and not absolute.

pragmatism An American philosophy that claims that the meaning of an idea can be established by determining what practical difference would be produced by believing the idea to be true and that the truth of an idea can be established by determining the idea's ability to "work."

primary qualities A term from seventeenth- and eighteenth-century **epistemology** and **ontology,** designating properties that inhere in material bodies independently of our perception of them (e.g., size, shape, location, and divisibility). Contrast with **secondary qualities.**

principle of falsifiability A criterion of scientific meaning set forth by Sir Karl Popper according to which a **proposition** or theory is scientific only if it is framed in such a way that it would be possible to state what kind of evidence would refute or falsify the theory, if such evidence existed.

property dualism While agreeing the **substance dualism** is false (i.e., there are not two kinds of *things:* minds and bodies), the brain does generate mental properties, such as thoughts and **qualia.**

proposition As employed in this text, a proposition is whatever is asserted by a sentence. The sentences "It's raining," *"Es regnet,"* and *"Llueve"* all assert the same proposition.

psychoanalysis The name given by Sigmund Freud to his method of psychotherapy, eventually becoming a theory of the mind, of selfhood, and of culture, in which psychological and social phenomena are traced to their origins in the unconscious mind.

psychological atomism The radical **empiricist epistemology** held by Locke, Berkeley, and Hume (though not named as such until the twentieth century, when it was also defended by the **logical positivists**) that all empirical knowledge is built up from simple, discrete mental data, such as the primitive sensory experiences of colors, sounds, and tastes. (See also **sense data.**)

psychological egoism See **egoism.**

qualia (singular: **quale**) A term in the **philosophy of mind** deriving from the Latin word for "quality," designating the qualitative (as opposed to quantitative) features of mental experience; the experience itself of softness, redness, pleasure, pain, and so on.

radical doubt See **methodological doubt.**

rationalism The **epistemological** view that true knowledge is derived primarily from reason (or *exclusively* from reason, in the purer strains of rationalism). Reason is conceived as the working of the mind on material provided by the mind itself. In most versions, this material takes the form of **innate ideas.** Therefore, for the rationalists, **a priori** knowledge is the most important kind of knowledge. In rationalistic **ontologies,** the mind and the world are seen to be in conformity—the real is the rational. The classical rationalists were the seventeenth- and eighteenth-century continental philosophers (Descartes, Spinoza, and Leibniz), but the concept is broad enough to include such philosophers as Plato and Hegel. Some contemporary philosophers also defend revised versions of rationalism, all of them deleting the notion of innate ideas.

representative realism An **empiricist epistemology,** usually associated with John Locke, according to which the data of perception *represent* the external world without literally duplicating it, very much the way a photo or a painting does.

secondary qualities A term from seventeenth- and eighteenth-century **epistemology** and **ontology,** designating perceived qualities (such as colors, tastes, odors) that appear to be real properties of material objects and in fact actually exist only in perception and are caused by the properties that do exist in material objects, viz., by **primary qualities.**

semiotics (Sometimes called semiology.) The study of the structure of the system of signs and of the signs therein. A "sign" is an arbitrary mark, sound, or image that has become imbued with meaning by virtue of its membership in a system of conventionality. Language is the most obvious case of such a system of signs, but behaviors, rituals, and institutions can also be studied semiotically.

sense data A sense datum is supposedly that which is perceived immediately by any one of the senses prior to interpretation by the mind. Sense data include the perceptions of colors, sounds, tastes, odors, tactile sensations, pleasures, and pains. Classical **empiricism** based itself on the supposed **epistemologically** foundational nature of sense data.

skepticism (or **scepticism**) A denial of the possibility of knowledge. General skepticism denies the possibility of *any* knowledge; however, one can be skeptical about fields of inquiry (e.g., **metaphysics**) or specific faculties (e.g., sense perception) without denying the possibility of knowledge in general.

social philosophy As used here, the study of the problem of justice, involving questions of the fair distribution of goods and services to members of a society. Related to **political philosophy.**

soft behaviorism The view that there is no need to include "minds" in the scientific study of humans, whether minds exist. The study of "behaviors" and their physical causes is sufficient for a complete psychology. Contrast with **hard behaviorism.**

soft determinism Also called **compatibilism.** The view that **determinism** is true but that **freedom** and responsibility can exist despite the truth of determinism. Contrast with **hard determinism.**

solipsism The view that the only true knowledge one can possess is knowledge of one's own consciousness. According to solipsism, there is no good reason to believe that anything exists other than oneself.

sophistry A form of argumentation more concerned with rhetorical success than with truth. The term derives from the "sophists" who taught in Greece in the fourth-century B.C.E., some of whom denied the possibility of knowledge or truth but—for a price—taught methods of achieving victory in public debate.

sublimation A term central to **psychoanalysis** that names the process whereby certain antisocial wishes and desires, many of which are unconscious, are directed away from their primary goal (the satisfaction of sexual or aggressive desires) and transformed into the production of socially valuable higher culture—art, religion, philosophy, law, science, and so on.

substance In philosophy, traditionally the term naming whatever is thought to be the most basic independent reality. Aristotle defined a substance as whatever can exist independently of other things, so a horse or a man (Aristotle's examples) can exist independently but the *color* of the horse or the *size* of the man cannot. The seventeenth- and eighteenth-century **rationalists** took the idea of substance as *independent being* so seriously that one of their members, Spinoza, claimed there could be only one substance in the world (i.e., only one *thing*), namely, God, because only God could exist independently. Under Berkeley's criticism of material substance and Hume's criticism of spiritual substance, the concept of substance was very much eroded. It turned up again in Kant but only as a "category" of knowledge, not as a basic reality itself.

substance dualism Minds and brains are different kinds of substances (things), and one kind cannot be explained in terms of the other. Essential in Descartes's view.

sufficient condition P is a sufficient condition of Q if the presence of P guarantees the presence of Q. For example, the presence of mammary glands in an animal is a sufficient condition for calling that animal a mammal. (It is also a **necessary condition** for doing so.)

superego In **psychoanalysis,** the component of the psyche that counteracts antisocial desires and impulses of the **id** by attaching conscious and unconscious feelings of guilt to them.

synthetic a priori Immanuel Kant's name for a new kind of proposition that he claimed to have discovered. Such a proposition is both **a priori** (not derived from sensorial data), yet referential to the observable world (without being **a posteriori**). The truth of such propositions is established by what Kant calls "the categories of understanding," which constitute a multiple cerebral gridwork that imposes contextuality on incoming sensorial data, producing **a posteriori** knowledge. Such categories are those of *space, time, substance* ("thingness"), *unity, plurality,* and *causality.* These categories are not natural characteristics of the ultimate world (which Kant calls "the-thing-in-itself") rather they are part of the structure of the mind that allows us to make sense of the world.

synthetic proposition A **proposition** is synthetic if its negation does not lead to a self-contradiction. For example, "Jupiter has a square moon" is synthetic (even though false, as it happens), because its negation, "Jupiter does not have a square moon," is not self-contradictory (usually associated with **a posteriori** propositions; the opposite of **analytic proposition**).

tabula rasa Latin for "blank slate." **Empiricism** from John Locke forward assumed that the mind is a *tabula rasa* at birth and that all knowledge must be inscribed on that blank slate by experience.

tautology A **proposition** is a tautology if it is in some way repetitive or redundant. For example, definitions are often tautological, because their predicates are equivalents of the term being defined. See also **analytic proposition.**

teleological argument An attempt to deduce God's existence from the fact that there is purposeful behavior in nature on the part of nonintelligent beings. (For example, the claim that the "purpose" of the sharp point on the bottom of an acorn is to break the surface of the ground when the acorn falls.)

teleology The study of the evidence for the existence of purpose, design, and intentionality in both human and nonhuman domains. A teleological explanation is an explanation in terms of goals, purposes, or intentions (from the Greek *telos* = goal). For example, "John closed the window because he didn't want his budgie to escape" and "An acorn has a sharp tip on its bottom in order to break the ground when it falls from the tree" are both teleological explanations, because they describe behavior in terms of intentions and goals. Contrast with **causal explanation.**

theism Belief in the existence of God or gods.

theoretical entity A term from twentieth-century **empiricism** naming entities that exist only as parts of theories, not as parts of reality. For example, "the average American housewife" is a theoretical entity.

transformational grammar A system of grammatical analysis that uses a set of algebraic formulas to express relations between elements in a sentence or between different forms or tenses of a phrase, such as active, passive, future, and present.

trompe l'œil French for "trick of the eye," designating a form of painting whose goal is to produce an illusion that appears to be reality so that the viewer does not realize that she is looking at an artwork.

utilitarianism The moral and social philosophy of Jeremy Bentham and John Stuart Mill according to which the value of any action or legislation can be derived from the principle of utility, which advocates "the greatest amount of happiness for the greatest number of people."

Index

Note: Page numbers in **bold** indicate glossary terms. Information in endnotes is indicated by *n*.

ethics in, 267–271
political philosophy in, 344–351
Homer, 9
Homo artisticus, 432
Homo faber, 373
Honderich, Ted, 232, 233–235, 239
Hospers, John, 226, 253
Hubbard, L. Ron, 184
Hume, David
cosmological argument and, 164–168
empiricism in, 90–95
ethics in, 304–306, 307, 333
in philosophy of religion, 160–161, 167–168,
171–175
teleological argument and, 172–173
Hursthouse, Rosalind, 297
Hyman, John, 400–403
hypothetical imperative, 279, 281–282, **457**

I

"I am," 62–63, 122
id, 226, 263, 424–426, **454, 457, 464**
idea(s)
complex, 78–79
innate, 39, 48–49, 65, 66, 70, 71, 72, 425
simple, 78–79
idealism, 85, 96, 114, 119, **457**
empiricism and, 85
identity, principle of, 18, 49
identity theory, 129
mind-brain, 119, 128–132
ideology, 180, **456, 457**
in Marx, 434–435, 437–438, 434–435, 437–438
Ignatius of Loyola, Saint, 200
ignorance, Socratic, 29–32
illusion, 58, 59, 180, 181, 187
artistic, 400–402, 422–423
images, in Plato, 43
imitation, 299, 393–394, 421, 445. *See also*
mimesis
immorality, 287, 288, 300, 307–308, 423. *See also*
ethics
incest taboo, 313, 425
incompatibilism, 233
indefeasibility, 108, **457**
indeterminism, 222, 228, 235–251, 254, **457**
individuals, in Marx, 371–372
inference, rules of, 16, 18–20
infinite regress, 230, **458**
innate ideas, 39, 48–49, 65, 66, 70, 71, 72, 76, 99,
425, **451, 458, 463**
Inquisition, the, 52, 203, 205–206
insanity. *See* madness
intentionality, 140, **458**
intersubjectivity, 86, 87, 444
intuition, 102, 279
moral, 287, 290, 292, 327
irony, Socratic, 30–31, 208
Isaac (Biblical figure), 207–209
Islam, 200. *See also* Muslims
is/ought problem, 315
"I think, therefore I am," 62, 244

J

Jaggar, Alison, 321
James, William, 194, 196–198, 205
Janet, Pierre-Marie, 245
Jaspers, Karl, 212
Jesus (of Nazareth), 199–200, 268, 286, 360, 422
Job (Biblical figure), 177–178
Johnson, Dr. Samuel, 85
Joyce, James, 35
Judaism, 200
Jung, C. G., 10
justice. *See also* ethics
as advantage of stronger, 259
distributive, 356, 359, 375
ethics and, 258–262
in Marx, 375, 378
in Rawls, 384

K

Kafka, Franz, 441
Kane, Robert, 241–242
Kant, Immanuel
ethics in, 281–292, 295, 303–305, 322–323,
326, 333
philosophy of religion and, 161–164, 167, 207
Sartre and, 303–304, 322, 323
Kepler, Johann, 77
Kierkegaard, Søren
existentialism of, 207–208, 210, 212, 246–248,
438, 440–441
in philosophy of freedom, 246–248
in philosophy of religion, 207–213, 214
Klein, Ezra, 189
Kluckhohn, Clyde, 313, 315
knowledge
belief and, 40–41
in Descartes, 55–56
in Plato, 49–50
a posteriori, 40
a priori, 40
use of term, 39
Kohlberg, Lawrence, 316–317, 318
Kripke, Saul, 147
Kroeber, Alfred, 313, 315

L

labor, division of, 339, 375
laissez-faire, 369
language
in Berkeley, 86–87
in Chomsky, 99–100
of logical positivism, 99–100
in Mandelbaum, 411
in Wittgenstein, 403, 404, 415
Laplace, Pierre-Simon, 221–222, 242
Lawrence, T. E. (of Arabia), 251
laws of nature, 187, 221, 238, 349
leap of faith, 192–193, 207
learning, in Plato, 47–48
legal positivism, 347, **458**